Sensible Selling Through Sensory Neuromarketing

Reena Malik
Chitkara Business School, Chitkara University, Punjab, India

Shivani Malhan
Chitkara University, Punjab, India

Manpreet Arora
Central University of Himachal Pradesh, India

A volume in the Advances
in Marketing, Customer
Relationship Management, and
E-Services (AMCRMES) Book
Series

Published in the United States of America by
    IGI Global
    Business Science Reference (an imprint of IGI Global)
    701 E. Chocolate Avenue
    Hershey PA, USA 17033
    Tel: 717-533-8845
    Fax: 717-533-8661
    E-mail: cust@igi-global.com
    Web site: http://www.igi-global.com

Library of Congress Cataloging-in-Publication Data

CIP Pending
ISBN: 979-8-3693-4236-7
EISBN: 979-8-3693-4237-4

British Cataloguing in Publication Data
A Cataloguing in Publication record for this book is available from the British Library.

All work contributed to this book is new, previously-unpublished material.
The views expressed in this book are those of the authors, but not necessarily of the publisher.

For electronic access to this publication, please contact: eresources@igi-global.com.

Advances in Marketing, Customer Relationship Management, and E-Services (AMCRMES) Book Series

Eldon Y. Li

National Chengchi University, Taiwan &
California Polytechnic State University,

MISSION

Business processes, services, and communications are important factors in the management of good customer relationship, which is the foundation of any well organized business. Technology continues to play a vital role in the organization and automation of business processes for marketing, sales, and customer service. These features aid in the attraction of new clients and maintaining existing relationships.

The **Advances in Marketing, Customer Relationship Management, and E-Services (AMCRMES) Book Series** addresses success factors for customer relationship management, marketing, and electronic services and its performance outcomes. This collection of reference source covers aspects of consumer behavior and marketing business strategies aiming towards researchers, scholars, and practitioners in the fields of marketing management.

Coverage

- Legal Considerations in E-Marketing
- CRM strategies
- Text Mining and Marketing
- Mobile Services
- Database marketing
- Relationship Marketing
- Data mining and marketing
- Cases on CRM Implementation
- Electronic Services
- Mobile CRM

IGI Global is currently accepting manuscripts for publication within this series. To submit a proposal for a volume in this series, please contact our Acquisition Editors at Acquisitions@igi-global.com or visit: http://www.igi-global.com/publish/.

Titles in this Series

For a list of additional titles in this series, please visit: www.igi-global.com/book-series

Ethical AI and Data Management Strategies in Marketing
Shefali Saluja (Chitkara Business School, Chitkara University, India) Varun Nayyar (Center for Distance and Online Education, Chitkara University, India) Kuldeep Rojhe (Center for Distance and Online Education, Chitkara University, India) and Sandhir Sharma (Chitkara Business School, Chitkara University, India)
Business Science Reference • copyright 2024 • 303pp • H/C (ISBN: 9798369366608) • US $215.00 (our price)

AI and Data Engineering Solutions for Effective Marketing
Lhoussaine Alla (Sidi Mohamed Ben Abdellah University, Morocco) Aziz Hmioui (Sidi Mohamed Ben Abdellah University, Morocco) and Badr Bentalha (National School of Business and Management, Sidi Mohammed Ben Abdellah University, Morocco)
Business Science Reference • copyright 2024 • 527pp • H/C (ISBN: 9798369331729) • US $395.00 (our price)

Improving Service Quality and Customer Engagement With Marketing Intelligence
Mudita Sinha (Christ University, India) Arabinda Bhandari (Presidency University, India) Samant Shant Priya (Lal Bahadur Shastri Institute of Management, India) and Sajal Kabiraj (Häme University of Applied Sciences, Finland)
Business Science Reference • copyright 2024 • 399pp • H/C (ISBN: 9798369368138) • US $255.00 (our price)

Compelling Storytelling Narratives for Sustainable Branding
Paula Rodrigues (Lusíada University Porto, Portugal & Research Centre in Organizations, Markets and Industrial Management (COMEGI), Porto, Portugal) Ana Pinto Borges (ISAG European Business School, Portugal) Elvira Vieira (ISAG European Business School, Portugal & Research Center in Business Sciences and Tourism (CICET-FCVC), Portugal) and Victor Tavares (ISAG – European Business School, Portugal & Research Center in Business Sciences and Tourism (CICET - FCVC), Porto, Portugal)

701 East Chocolate Avenue, Hershey, PA 17033, USA
Tel: 717-533-8845 x100 • Fax: 717-533-8661
E-Mail: cust@igi-global.com • www.igi-global.com

Table of Contents

Detailed Table of Contents

Aayushi Jain, SRM University, India
Pawan Kumar, SRM University, India

Today, marketing should evolve beyond focus groups and other classic marketing tactics. In the 19th century, businesses grabbed their customers' attention by using various traditional techniques like billboards, direct email, print ads, billboards, cold calling, radio advertising, broadcasting, etc. But traditional marketing techniques are not successful in today's era due to continuous change in the buying behavior of consumers. If a company wants to receive feedback, the chance of wrong feedback is greater. The need for a new concept has arisen, i.e., neuromarketing—the combination of neuroscience and marketing. It is the process of researching the brain pattern of consumers to reveal their responses to a particular advertisement and product before developing new advertisements, new campaigns. Neuromarketing makes the use of brain imaging techniques which aims is to serve guidance in designing marketing strategies like packaging, advertisement etc. by mapping customers mind and effect their buying decision.

Chapter 2

Namrata Prakash, Graphic Era Hill University, Dehradun, India
Priya Jindal, Chitkara Business School, Chitkara University, Punjab,
    India
Ansh Jindal, Chitkara Business School, Chitkara University, Punjab,
    India

The chapter captures the shift from conventional to cognitive analysis tools in the marketing landscape. It is clear that the promotional ecology has developed over time, and that it has shifted from using traditional methods to using cognitive analysis tools. In particular, it highlights how information from the study of neurology may be utilized to rethink marketing methods and construct cutting-edge technologies that probe deeper into the way people think to produce advertising efforts that are more correctly perceptive and successful. Among the many techniques that are used in the area of brain imaging, some examples include skin conductance, heart rate variability (HRV), eye tracking, and functional magnetic resonance imaging (fMRI). Whenever they embark on the examination of neural bases for consumer behavior to gain a fuller appreciation of the intricacies of customer behavior, these methods are used for studying consumer feedback as well as ethical issues that come up as a result of such investigation.

Chapter 3

Arpita Nayak, KIIT School of Management, KIIT University, India
Ipseeta Satpathy, KIIT School of Management, KIIT University, India

Sensory marketing is a growing field that examines how sensory inputs impact consumer perceptions, feelings, and actions. Marketers are increasingly using multi-sensory branding to create immersive brand experiences and increase customer engagement. The five senses are sight, hearing, smell, taste, and touch. Experiential marketing, music, and sound are key components of multimodal marketing. As digital information becomes more overwhelming, marketers must develop innovative strategies to engage consumers. Sonic branding, a key component of multimodal marketing, is becoming more popular. Vision, color, style, smell, and sound are essential components of multimodal marketing. These elements help create a lasting bond with customers, attracting new and repeat customers, and promoting brand loyalty. The study aims to add to the body of knowledge how sensory marketing theory helps in multisensory marketing.

Multi-Sensory experience explores the dynamic interplay of various sensory modalities in shaping human perception. The present work delves into the richness and complexity of multisensory integration, investigating how the brain synthesizes inputs from the five senses to construct a cohesive perceptual reality. It examines the role of multisensory experiences in enhancing cognitive processes, emotional responses, and behavioral outcomes. Understanding the mechanisms underlying multisensory perception is crucial for diverse fields, including neuroscience, psychology, design, marketing, and education. The present chapter underscores the significance of multisensory experiences in shaping human experiences and highlights avenues for further research and application in creating more engaging and impactful environments and interventions. By elucidating the basic building blocks of multisensory experience, the study contributes to a deeper comprehension of human perception, offering insights with far-reaching implications for fields ranging from neuroscience and psychology.

Marketing to the consumer senses is called sensory marketing. Notably, there has been a swell of interest in sensory marketing pertaining to (a) the role of senses in curating multisensory experiences for consumers, and (b) the recent sensory enabling technological advancements such as AR/VR and GenAI. The present chapter discusses the emergence, evolution, and emerging perspectives in the field. Specifically, the authors have found that the field of sensory marketing is derived from the hedonic consumption concept and emotional aspects of consumption. In addition, a sensory marketing mix has been constructed to delineate the working of senses in marketing. The study found that multisensory experiences form the core of buyer behavior in sensory marketing. Further, future research insights using sensory neuromarketing tools such as eye-tracking, EEG, GSR, and fMRI may be effective in growing the field. Lastly, the authors discuss the emerging perspectives and future directions for new marketing realities.

Neuromarketing seeks to utilize brain imaging to comprehend the neuronal connections and cognitive processes that play a role in customers' decision-making. This study aims to offer thorough examination of neuromarketing, including present utilization of neuroimaging physiological tools in the marketing mix. Additionally, it seeks to emphasize the neurological responses of consumer behavior that should be taken into account in the marketing mix. This study aims to examine the impact of recent neuromarketing techniques on marketing mix strategies. Managers can leverage these techniques to develop effective marketing strategies for specific target groups in various areas, including consumer buying behavior, pricing, advertising, the chapter explores potential use of neurological approaches in marketing management. The findings demonstrate the role of neuroscience in informing traditional marketing mix strategies and highlight the benefits of incorporating neuroscience in brand management.

Although neuromarketing presents marketers with great potential to gain insight into the neurological mechanisms that influence customer choices, it also brings up important ethical questions because it paves the way for unbridled manipulation of customers by providing unparalleled access to their mind. Thus, it is critical to discuss multi-facets of neuromarketing pertaining to its potential and limitations. This chapter delves into the challenges pertaining to policy implementation, limitations, and potential benefits of neuromarketing on individuals and society.

   Sneha Sindhuja, Christ University, India
   Reena Malik, Chitkara Business School, Chitkara University, Punjab,
      India

Neuromarketing is an interdisciplinary field consolidating neuroscience, psychology, and marketing, aiming to understand consumer behaviour at the subconscious level. However, as neuromarketing techniques become increasingly sophisticated, ethical issues and considerations have emerged as a focal point of debate and scrutiny. The paper critically evaluates foundational ethical principles, such as informed consent, beneficence and nonmaleficence, privacy and confidentiality, transparency, scientific or methodological rigor, predicting and influencing consumer choices, safeguarding the vulnerable population, and commitment to abiding and respecting the guidelines and codes of ethics. It also includes the emerging techniques and research, need for ethics and terms like neuroethics and brain privacy.

   Bhavna Taneja, Amity University, Ranchi, India
   Pooja Shukla, Amity University, Ranchi, India
   Manpreet Arora, Central University of Himachal Pradesh, India

Neuromarketing (a new field at the intersection of marketing and neurology) provides crucial information on how customers act and make decisions. This chapter examines neuromarketing laws and how they might be used to improve sales success. It discusses all five senses—sight, hearing, touch, smell, and taste—and how we can use each of them to create memorable marketing experiences. The chapter then discusses how neuromarketing might be applied to brand development, product packaging, and promotional strategies. The chapter also provides sales professionals with practical guidelines and case studies for incorporating sensory neuromarketing principles into their selling technique, with the ultimate goal of improving client engagement, satisfaction, and sales outcomes.

    Rita Devi, Central University of Himachal Pradesh, India
    Rachna Bhopal, Central University of Himachal Pradesh, India
    Varun Sharma, Central University of Himachal Pradesh, India

Investigating consumer perceptions concerning neuromarketing strategies employed by marketers and the resultant impact on brand equity constitutes the core of the study. This chapter investigates the various neuromarketing strategies to ascertain their importance in influencing brand equity with a specific focus on 162 consumers of the Kangra District of Himachal Pradesh using convenience sampling. By employing empirical analysis and conceptual framework, the study seeks to ascertain how the neuromarketing strategies—brand positioning, brand awareness, brand prestige, performance, feeling, judgment, branding, advertisement, purchase decision, product design, and innovation—influence the brand equity. The findings offer valuable insights that will enlighten businesses and consumers about the implications of neuromarketing on customer choices and brand perception through the development of more productive consumer enticement strategies.

    Surbhi Bhardwaj, National Institute of Technology, Kurukshetra, India
    Neeraj Kaushik, National Institute of Technology, Kurukshetra, India
    Manpreet Arora, Central University of Himachal Pradesh, India

In this competitive world, the human senses and their responsiveness play a vital role in influencing consumer behavior and purchase patterns. Brands are using neuromarketing to employ different sensory tactics to cover the maximum market share and connect with customers. Marketers use neurosciences techniques to connect with customers on emotional and behavioral aspects, known as the sensory branding approach. This trending approach of neuromarketing helps brands to create synergy in marketing with the creative use of psychology and neurosciences to make strategies for different customers at same time. The chapter aims to explore how brands use sensory emotional connections with customers to influence them to purchase. Using a conceptual approach for this chapter, it is explained what the sensory branding uses to create a powerful brand fit strategy for different customer profiles. The author observed that marketers faced challenges and used different kinds of techniques related to neuro sensory branding which help to understand consumer and make emotional bond.

    Anchal Luthra, Amity University, Noida, India
    Shivani Dixit, IMS Ghaziabad (University Courses Campus), India
    Anamica Singh, Amity University, Noida, India
    Seema Garg, Amity University, Noida, India
    Sharad Khattar, Amity University, Noida, India

This chapter delves into the field of sensory marketing, a rapidly growing discipline. It primarily focuses on the increasing use of multi-sensory experiences as a powerful tool in modern marketing. The chapter emphasizes the significant influence that the five primary senses-sight, hearing, smell, touch, and taste-have on consumer behaviour. It also provides a detailed exploration of each sense and how marketers can effectively use multiple sensory inputs to engage consumers emotionally and foster strong connections between their Brands and them. The chapter further examines various examples and current trends that deliberately incorporate points of contact with different sensory components, leading to enhanced brand differentiation in the dynamic landscape of contemporary marketing.

    Rishi Prakash Shukla, Jaipuria Institute of Management, Jaipur, India
    Sanjay Taneja, Graphic Era University, India
    Prashant S. Gundawar, Sasmira Group, India
    Ravi Kumar Jain, Sparsh Global Business School, India
    Priya Shukla, Independent Researcher, India

Neuromarketing integrates neuroscience, psychology, and marketing to explore consumers' subconscious and emotional reactions to marketing stimuli. This interdisciplinary approach utilizes advanced neuroimaging and psychophysiological techniques to provide deeper insights into consumer behavior. The research employs a comprehensive literature review and bibliometric analysis, revealing significant trends, gaps, and advancements in the field. The findings underscore the importance of integrating neuromarketing into advertising practices to create more compelling campaigns that resonate with consumers' subconscious motivations. The study also highlights the evolution of neuromarketing technologies and methodologies, emphasizing their practical applications in branding, pricing, advertising, packaging, and decision-making. By addressing research gaps and considering cultural and individual differences, this research contributes to both theoretical knowledge and practical marketing strategies, offering actionable insights for developing effective and engaging marketing campaigns.

The objective of this chapter is to gain an understanding of how the immersive quality of virtual reality (VR) affects customer perception, emotional engagement, and brand memory. Furthermore, the chapter investigates the physiological responses that are triggered by virtual reality advertising. This chapter investigates the neurological correlates that are linked with virtual reality (VR) experiences. These correlates include activation patterns in regions of the brain that are involved in attention, memory encoding, and emotional processing. Additionally, this chapter addresses the potential for virtual reality (VR) advertising to elicit stronger emotional responses and boost brand memorability in comparison to traditional advertising forms. The ethical considerations are addressed. This chapter, in its entirety, makes a contribution to our understanding of the neurological mechanisms that are responsible for consumer responses to virtual reality advertising and offers insights into the consequences that this phenomenon has for both consumers and marketers.

The retail sector is experiencing a significant transformation through the integration of augmented reality (AR) and virtual reality (VR) technologies. The convergence of AR and VR is driving a substantial change in the dynamic and ever-evolving retail business. This integration is ushering in a new era of immersive and personalized shopping experiences, fundamentally altering how consumers engage with products and environments. Through AR applications, customers can effortlessly use their smartphones to locate items, receive real-time promotions, and gain additional information about them. Augmented reality enables a virtual try-on experience, allowing buyers to visualize products in a virtual setting. This chapter explores the various applications, challenges and potential implications of AR and VR in the retail sector, highlighting the substantial transformations these technologies bring to the industry. Augmented reality is revolutionizing in-store navigation, providing consumers with an engaging and user-friendly navigational experience.

    Swati Sharma, University School of Business, Chandigarh University,
        Punjab, India
    Kavita Sharma, University School of Business, Chandigarh University,
        Punjab, India
    Anupal Mongia, Mody University of Science and Technology, India
    Reena Malik, Chitkara Business School, Chitkara University, Punjab,
        India

The well-being of individuals has taken precedence in the new era that Covid-19 has brought. Numerous viewpoints on medical care technology and the social sciences have been used to analyse the topic of wellbeing in digital communities. This chapter is a review of the literature that explains how understanding the comfort, happiness, and quality of life of members of virtual communities can help businesses develop their digital communication and marketing strategies.

    Rajneesh Ahlawat, Chaudhary Devi Lal University, India
    Pooja Swami, Chaudhary Devi Lal University, India

Neuromarketing is emerging as the next game-changing branch of marketing that applies the principles of neuroscience to better understand the customer's conscious and subconscious mind while deciding to purchase any product or service as well as during his choice-making processes. Color psychology is a key technique of neuromarketing that explores how people perceive different colors and how it affects their emotions and their purchasing decisions. By studying the subconscious associations and sensory responses to various colors, neuromarketers can develop a significant understanding of how color influences consumer choices and thereby, by leveraging color psychology and integrating it into each stage of their marketing process, they can boost their sales to the targeted segment. By reviewing the existing literature, this chapter aims to portray the interplay between neuromarketing, color psychology, and consumer behavior, and also highlights how the strategic use of colors can attract the right customer and enhance sales effectiveness.

Foreword

It is with great pleasure and appreciation that I introduce the book *Sensible Selling Through Sensory Neuromarketing*, edited by Reena Malik, Shivani Malhan, and Manpreet Arora. This remarkable compilation brings together diverse perspectives on neuromarketing, highlighting current trends and innovative approaches in modern marketing. As Vice -of Guru Ghasidas Vishwavidyalaya, Bilaspur, Chhattisgarh, I am honored to endorse this book, which reflects the dynamic nature of 21st-century marketing.

Neuromarketing, an interdisciplinary field combining neuroscience, psychology, and marketing, has emerged as a powerful tool in understanding consumer behavior. By delving into the subconscious mind, neuromarketing allows businesses to craft strategies that resonate deeply with their target audiences. This book provides comprehensive insights that are both academically enriching and practically applicable.

The editors, Reena Malik, Shivani Malhan, and Manpreet Arora, bring extensive expertise to this collection from institutions like Chitkara University and the Central University of Himachal Pradesh, enriching interdisciplinary research in consumer behavior and marketing strategies.

Each chapter explores unique aspects of neuromarketing, from theory to application, catering to students, researchers, and practitioners seeking a holistic understanding of the subject. The book emphasizes current trends, including advanced techniques such as eye-tracking and biometric analysis, which offer a glimpse into the future of marketing innovation.

Ethical considerations are also addressed, urging responsible use of neuromarketing's influence on consumer behavior. As we gain more power to influence consumer behavior, it is imperative that we use this knowledge responsibly. This ethical dimension, covered in this book should encourage readers to critically evaluate their marketing strategies.

In conclusion, the book *Sensible Selling Through Sensory Neuromarketing* breaks new ground in marketing theory and practice. It offers intellectually stimulating insights and practical tools essential for navigating today's rapidly evolving marketplace. This book will prove to be valuable for anyone interested in the future of marketing and the transformative role of neuroscience in understanding consumer behavior. I commend the editors for their exceptional work in bringing together such a diverse and insightful collection of chapters.

Alok Chakrawal

Guru Ghasidas Vishwavidyalaya Bilaspur, Chhattisgarh, India

Preface

Understanding consumer behavior in today's fiercely competitive marketplace is no longer just about demographics and surveys. It requires delving deeper into the intricate workings of the human mind, decoding its responses to stimuli, and leveraging these insights to craft effective marketing strategies. This is where the intersection of neuromarketing and sensory marketing becomes crucial.

The advent of neuromarketing has revolutionized how businesses understand and connect with their audiences. By tapping into neuroscience, marketers can unravel the subconscious triggers that influence consumer decisions. Similarly, sensory marketing explores how sensory experiences—sight, sound, touch, smell, and taste—can be harnessed to create impactful brand interactions that resonate with customers on a profound level.

Our edited volume, *Sensible Selling Through Sensory Neuromarketing*, aims to bridge the gap between theory and practice in this burgeoning field. Drawing on the expertise of esteemed contributors, we delve into the principles and applications of neuromarketing, offering practical insights and strategies that sales professionals can implement to enhance their effectiveness.

Throughout this book, readers will explore real-world case studies, actionable techniques, and innovative approaches that demonstrate the power of sensory neuromarketing in transforming customer engagement and driving business growth. Whether you're a researcher, academician, marketer, policymaker, or simply curious about the future of marketing, this volume serves as a comprehensive guide to navigating the evolving landscape of consumer neuroscience.

We hope this book inspires you to rethink traditional marketing paradigms and embrace the potential of sensory neuromarketing to create meaningful connections with your audience.

Chapter 1: From Traditional Marketing to Neuromarketing

Authored by Aayushi Jain and Pawan Kumar, this chapter traces the evolution from traditional marketing techniques to the advent of neuromarketing. It highlights the inadequacies of traditional methods in addressing contemporary consumer behavior shifts and introduces neuromarketing as a fusion of neuroscience and marketing. The chapter explores how brain imaging techniques are used to decipher consumer responses, guiding the development of effective marketing strategies.

Chapter 2: Neuro Marketing - Harnessing the Power of Cognitive Analysis

In this chapter by Namrata Prakash, Priya Jindal, and Ansh Jindal, the transition from traditional marketing to cognitive analysis tools is examined. It emphasizes the use of neuroscience in refining marketing methodologies, utilizing techniques such as skin conductance, heart rate variability, eye tracking, and fMRI to understand consumer behavior deeply. The chapter underscores the importance of cognitive analysis in creating perceptive and effective marketing campaigns.

Chapter 3: The Sensory Marketing Theory: A Journey into Multisensory Marketing

Written by Arpita Nayak and Ipseeta Satpathy, this chapter delves into sensory marketing and its impact on consumer perceptions and behaviors. It explores how marketers are leveraging sight, hearing, smell, taste, and touch to create immersive brand experiences. The chapter also discusses the role of experiential marketing and sonic branding in enhancing customer engagement and loyalty.

Chapter 4: Multi-Sensory Experience - The Basic Building Blocks

Authored by Anuj Kapoor, Raveena Gupta, and Harsh Verma, this chapter explores the integration of sensory modalities in shaping human perception. It investigates how multisensory experiences influence cognitive processes, emotional responses, and consumer behavior. The chapter emphasizes the foundational role of multisensory integration in various disciplines, including marketing and neuroscience.

Chapter 5: Senses Shall Sell: Origins, Emerging Concepts & Methods in Sensory Marketing

Shweta Kakhtan and Anuj Kapoor contribute to this chapter which investigates sensory marketing's evolution and contemporary perspectives. It discusses the role of sensory experiences in creating multisensory consumer interactions and examines recent technological advancements like AR/VR and GenAI in enhancing sensory marketing effectiveness. The chapter proposes future research directions to expand the field.

Chapter 6: Synchronizing Senses: Neuromarketing Techniques and the Marketing Mix

Roop Kamal and Shivani Malhan authored this chapter, focusing on neuromarketing's application in refining the marketing mix. It explores how neuroimaging tools are used to understand consumer neurological responses and optimize marketing strategies across various domains. The chapter highlights the integration of neuroscience in traditional marketing practices for enhanced consumer engagement and decision-making.

Chapter 7: Ethical and Unethical Considerations in the Realm of Neuromarketing

Raveena Gupta, Anuj Kapoor, and Harsh Sharma delve into the ethical dimensions of neuromarketing in this chapter. It examines the ethical implications of accessing and utilizing consumer neurological data, addressing concerns such as privacy, manipulation, and informed consent. The chapter discusses the ethical framework necessary for responsible neuromarketing practices.

Chapter 8: Exploring the Ethical Issues and Considerations in Neuromarketing

Written by Sneha Sindhuja and Reena Malik, this chapter critically evaluates ethical principles in neuromarketing. It reviews issues such as privacy, transparency, and the ethical use of neuroscientific techniques in consumer research. The chapter advocates for ethical guidelines and codes of conduct to ensure fair and responsible neuromarketing practices.

Chapter 9: Sensible Selling Through Sensory Neuromarketing - Enhancing Sales Effectiveness

Bhavna Taneja, Pooja Shukla, and Manpreet Arora contribute to this chapter, focusing on applying sensory neuromarketing principles to enhance sales effectiveness. It discusses leveraging all five senses to create compelling marketing experiences and improve customer engagement. Practical guidance and case studies are provided for sales professionals aiming to integrate sensory neuromarketing into their strategies.

Chapter 10: Decoding Neuromarketing Strategies - Unveiling its Role on Brand Equity

Rita Devi, Rachna Bhopal, and Varun Sharma explore neuromarketing strategies and their impact on brand equity in this chapter. They analyze how neuromarketing influences brand positioning, awareness, and consumer perceptions, using empirical analysis and consumer insights. The chapter offers valuable perspectives on enhancing brand strategies through neuromarketing approaches.

Chapter 11: Does Your Brain Have a Buy Button? - A Neuro Marketing Approach with Sensory Branding

Surbhi Bhardwaj, Neeraj Kaushik, and Manpreet Arora investigate sensory branding in this chapter, exploring how brands use neuroscientific techniques to create emotional connections with consumers. It examines the effectiveness of sensory branding in influencing purchase decisions and building brand loyalty across diverse customer segments.

Chapter 12: Sensory Storytelling - Crafting Brand Narratives through Sight, Sound, Smell, Touch, and Taste

Authored by Anchal Luthra, Shivani Dixit, Anamica Singh, Seema Garg, and Sharad Khattar, this chapter explores sensory marketing's role in crafting immersive brand narratives. It highlights the impact of multisensory experiences on consumer emotions and brand perception, using examples and current trends to illustrate effective sensory storytelling strategies.

Chapter 13: Behavior Examining Sensorimotor And Affective Responses To Marketing Stimuli Through Neuropsychology

Rishi Shukla, Sanjay Taneja, Prashant Gundawar, Ravi Jain, and Priya Shukla delve into neuropsychology's role in understanding consumer responses to marketing stimuli. This chapter employs neuroimaging and psychophysiological techniques to analyze subconscious and emotional reactions, offering insights for developing impactful marketing campaigns.

Chapter 14: Neurological Pathways to Impulse Buying in Virtual Reality

Roop Kamal, Yashmin Sofat, and Shipra examine the neurological responses to virtual reality (VR) advertising in this chapter. They explore how VR enhances emotional engagement and brand memorability through immersive experiences, addressing ethical considerations and implications for marketers and consumers alike.

Chapter 15: Modernizing Customers Experience through Augmented-Virtual Reality in Emerging Market: Sensible Selling towards Transforming Neuromarketing

Bhupinder Singh, Christian Kaunert, and Rishabha Malviya investigate the transformative impact of AR and VR technologies on retail experiences in this chapter. It explores how these technologies enhance consumer engagement and reshape retail strategies, offering insights into their applications, challenges, and future implications.

Chapter 16: Boosting Wellbeing Leveraging Virtual Communities Through Innovative Digital Marketing Strategies

Swati Sharma, Kavita Sharma, Anupal Mongia, and Reena Malik focus on digital communities and their impact on consumer wellbeing in this chapter. It reviews how understanding consumer comfort, happiness, and quality of life in virtual communities can inform digital marketing strategies, enhancing consumer engagement and satisfaction.

Chapter 17: The Right Color Attracts the Right Customer: The Art of Selling Smartly with Neuromarketing and Color Psychology

Rajneesh Ahlawat and Pooja Swami explore the interplay between neuromarketing, color psychology, and consumer behavior in this chapter. It examines how color influences consumer emotions and purchase decisions, offering insights into leveraging color psychology in marketing strategies to enhance sales effectiveness.

As editors of *Sensible Selling Through Sensory Neuromarketing*, we are delighted to present this comprehensive volume that explores the transformative intersection of neuromarketing and sensory marketing. In today's competitive marketplace, understanding consumer behavior demands more than traditional methods; it requires a nuanced understanding of how the human mind responds to stimuli, both consciously and subconsciously.

The chapters in this book collectively illuminate the evolution from traditional marketing practices to the sophisticated methodologies of neuromarketing. We begin by examining the foundational principles of neuromarketing, where contributors Aayushi Jain and Pawan Kumar delineate its emergence as a fusion of neuroscience and marketing research. From there, Namrata Prakash, Priya Jindal, and Ansh Jindal delve into cognitive analysis tools, emphasizing the role of neuroscientific techniques in refining marketing strategies.

Moving forward, Arpita Nayak and Ipseeta Satpathy explore sensory marketing theory, highlighting how marketers harness sight, sound, smell, taste, and touch to create immersive brand experiences. Anuj Kapoor, Raveena Gupta, and Harsh Verma then examine multisensory experiences, elucidating how these interactions shape consumer perceptions and behavior.

Throughout the subsequent chapters, authors such as Shweta Kakhtan, Anuj Kapoor, and Roop Kamal explore the integration of sensory and neuromarketing techniques into the marketing mix. They discuss ethical considerations raised by these methodologies, stressing the importance of responsible practices in accessing and utilizing consumer data.

Further contributions by Bhavna Taneja, Pooja Shukla, and Manpreet Arora provide practical insights into enhancing sales effectiveness through sensory neuromarketing strategies. Rita Devi, Rachna Bhopal, and Varun Sharma analyze the impact of neuromarketing on brand equity, underscoring its role in shaping consumer perceptions and purchasing decisions.

Moreover, Surbhi Bhardwaj, Neeraj Kaushik, and Manpreet Arora delve into sensory branding, demonstrating how emotional connections can drive consumer loyalty across diverse market segments. Anchal Luthra, Shivani Dixit, Anamica Singh, Seema Garg, and Sharad Khattar explore sensory storytelling as a powerful tool for crafting brand narratives that resonate deeply with consumers.

The application of neuroimaging and psychophysiological techniques in understanding consumer responses is examined by Rishi Shukla, Sanjay Taneja, Prashant Gundawar, Ravi Jain, and Priya Shukla. They highlight the profound insights offered by these methodologies in developing impactful marketing campaigns.

Additionally, chapters on virtual reality (VR), authored by Roop Kamal, Yashmin Sofat, Shipra, Prof. Bhupinder Singh, Prof. Christian Kaunert, and Rishabha Malviya, explore how AR and VR technologies enhance consumer engagement and reshape retail experiences. Swati Sharma, Kavita Sharma, Anupal Mongia, and Reena Malik then focus on digital communities and their implications for consumer well-being and digital marketing strategies.

Lastly, Rajneesh Ahlawat and Pooja Swami discuss the strategic use of color psychology in neuromarketing, illustrating how color influences consumer emotions and purchase decisions.

In conclusion, *Sensible Selling Through Sensory Neuromarketing* offers a comprehensive exploration of the cutting-edge techniques reshaping contemporary marketing practices. Whether you are a researcher, academician, marketer, or policymaker, this book provides invaluable insights and practical strategies for navigating the complex landscape of consumer neuroscience. We trust that this volume will inspire you to rethink traditional marketing paradigms and harness the transformative potential of sensory neuromarketing to forge deeper connections with your audience and drive business growth.

Warm regards,

Reena Malik
Chitkara Business School, Chitkara University, Punjab, India

Shivani Malhan
Chitkara University, India

Manpreet Arora
Central University of Himachal Pradesh, Dharamshala, India

Chapter 1
From Traditional Marketing to Neuromarketing

Aayushi Jain
SRM University, India

Pawan Kumar
https://orcid.org/0000-0003-2059-9818
SRM University, India

ABSTRACT

Today, marketing should evolve beyond focus groups and other classic marketing tactics. In the 19th century, businesses grabbed their customers' attention by using various traditional techniques like billboards, direct email, print ads, billboards, cold calling, radio advertising, broadcasting, etc. But traditional marketing techniques are not successful in today's era due to continuous change in the buying behavior of consumers. If a company wants to receive feedback, the chance of wrong feedback is greater. The need for a new concept has arisen, i.e., neuromarketing—the combination of neuroscience and marketing. It is the process of researching the brain pattern of consumers to reveal their responses to a particular advertisement and product before developing new advertisements, new campaigns. Neuromarketing makes the use of brain imaging techniques which aims is to serve guidance in designing marketing strategies like packaging, advertisement etc. by mapping customers mind and effect their buying decision.

DOI: 10.4018/979-8-3693-4236-7.ch001

INTRODUCTION

Business and trade have one most important aspect to engage with customers i.e. Marketing. Marketing is the process by which a company engages its target audience, develops strong relationships, and creates value to receive value in return. It is the process by which a firm profitably translates customer needs into revenue (Mark Burgess). Businesses have extended the traditional marketing mix's "4Ps"—Product, Prize, Place, and Promotion to "7Ps"—Product, Prize, Place, Promotion, People, Problem, and Proximity. It helps in better understanding that the market is changing quickly. In ancient times, the product was the most powerful P of marketing among all other marketing mixes. At that time there was a barter system; goods were exchanged with other goods. Products were exchanged through direct selling. Over some time, this barter system caused a competitive advantage due to which ancient marketing was turned into mass media marketing.

In the 19th century, companies were trying to grab consumer's attention through sales promotion, and advertising in newspapers, radio, and television. Companies started spending lots of money on commercialization. It started growing rapidly but eventually faded away because of the memory of consumers. Users use mass media platforms at their own pace and remember for a while. When Mass media was compared with digital marketing it exhibited that digital Marketing has more control over the content of advertisements and consumers recall it comfortably. With the increase in the use of the internet, digital marketing was shining like a star in the field of marketing and shows advertisement with the help of social media platforms like Facebook, Twitter, etc. It plays a vital role in influencing the consumer's choice *(Garcia, 2008; Leiva et al., 2019)*. However, consumers often wonder why we want something, and sometimes the reaction to this query is vague. People are not able to reveal their views regarding their behaviour and preferences about a certain product. They are more concerned about their mind than responses. Consumers can't decipher a lot of details they see and it becomes a typical task for companies to understand consumer's minds. The business addresses questions like: How do we develop clear and enduring customer preferences? How do we best accumulate coordination efforts to emphasize the efficiency of the message? *(Kahneman, 2011; Gakhal & Senio, 2008)*. This is because our preference for a certain good or a certain service is unconsciously realized. There are more questions than answers about our brains. We have no access to all processes happening there and we are not able to decode much of the information we can see. Martin Lindstrom is the man who decided to find out what lies behind the success or failure of brand experience nowadays. He rides on this Neuromarketing trend and promises to reveal the truths and lies of why we buy. For this purpose, he uses available knowledge about the human brain that identifies different areas responsible for different feelings, like love or fear. When those areas are stimulated, they lit up but there is no explanation of what kind of behaviour will follow or how the environment or part experiences stimulate the reaction of the scanned persons *(Lindstorm,2008; Hernández & Christiansen, 2014)*. To use that knowledge as an explanation is like "looking into people's windows from the street and trying to guess what they are talking about "Neuromarketing helps us to understand consumers' behaviour. Why do we choose Coca-Cola instead of Pepsi? Why do women do not prefer science-fiction movies? Why do men prefer sports cars? To make the consumers buy, the companies have to try to answer these kinds of questions and always find new ways of finding out how the consumers think. Neuroscience appeared when the Italian psychologist Angelo Mosso tried the following experiment: the analysed subject was lying on a balancing table which could be inclined only if the feet or the head became heavier. When the subject met an intellectual or emotional activity, the balance was inclined towards the head, as a result of the blood redistribution into the body *(Lindstorm, 2008;*Stasi et al., 2018*)*.

In an analysis of how the brain thinks and motivates human action by utilizing neuroscience. Moreover, the utilization of neuroscience in marketing is known as Neuromarketing. *"Neuromarketing is where science and marketing meet."* Neuroscience is the study of nervous system develops its structure. Neuroscience is to unlock the intellect and to dramatically alter the buying mechanism of each good or service by the combination of the findings of the market. Its ultimate goal is to consider the way the brain influences the actions of customers and to research the mechanism of selecting various products as well as to recognize the choice variable. It is not the modern method of commercialization. It is a new approach to analysing marketing. It serves as guidance in designing marketing strategies like branding, advertising effectiveness, product design, and packaging *(Kottier, 2014;Eser et al., 2011)*.

While we suppose a consumer buys a product for its features, its functions, or its price, the consumer's brain tells us something different. The neuroscience shows us that this developed organ develops preferences based on the intuitional relation with the product's brand and not based on the advertising message. The brain cannot make the distinction between the messages of the marketing department and the rest of the messages. Each experience related to the brand becomes part of our perception of this brand, and in the end, it determines the pro or against attitude regarding the brand. This explains why, for example, people buy "jeans" not for the way they look with them, but for the way this product matches their life. Therefore, nowadays, we buy products for the way these define us, and our brain has exactly this vision about products. Step by step, the product will not be taken into account in the same measure as the trademark or as the brand, as these contain the elements the individual identifies with *(Fisher, 2010; Pereira et al.;Yadava et al., 2017)*.

In a classical communication process, the marketers consider themselves to be the "emitter", and the customers, the "receptor". From the Neuromarketing point of view, the parts should be changed: the companies are the ones who need information regarding what products to commercialize, and the consumer has to make this information available, and not be informed about something that already exists. The companies should learn to build relationships *(Cruz et al., 2016;Ruanguttamanun, 2014)*. Given the fact that we are being daily "bombed" with commercial messages, there appear questions regarding the efficiency of the communication between the companies and the consumers. Expressions such as "better", "speedier", and "cheaper" do not make the public more sensitive, but a little, and have the disadvantage that they do not guarantee the consumer's trust. The deep understanding of what motivates us represents the future, and the companies have to focus on the consumer's impressiveness instead of producing commanding goods *(Bakardjieva & Kimmel, 2017;Marín & Alvarado, 2022)*.

Although a lot of research ways are in evolution, there remains the problem of the discrepancy between what the individual says and what he thinks or buys. It is known that 95% of his thinking is unconsciously realized. How do we expect then a focus group to solve a marketing problem? The neuroscience proposes to understand motivation from the sub-consciousness (positive or negative), motivation which impulses the individual to act or which stops the action, determining a preference, a purchase, or a behaviour *(Kumar et al., 2017)*.

If the companies understood the consumers and the way he is thinking, they could offer them what is necessary and would reconsider the way of communicating with the consumer. The neuroscience has the key as it opens the brain, and the combination of the results of this science and the business can significantly change the purchasing way of each product or service *(Costa,2016;Alvino et al., 2018)*.

The final purpose of the Neuromarketing is to understand the way the brain determines the consumers' behaviour and it supposes the study of the process of choosing different brands, as well as the identification of the factors determining the choice *(Costa,2016)*.

KEYS TO NEUROMARKETING

Another marketing specialist, Christophe Morin, co-author of *"Neuromarketing: Understanding the Buy Buttons in Your Customer's Brain"* emphasises some key points of Neuromarketing through which companies can improve their products, services, marketing strategies, and advertising. These aspects from Morin's argument are made subconsciously, in the nether regions of the mind he calls the primal brain, areas where "basic fight-or-flight instincts kick in. We buy, he says, "out of fear."

Therefore, some human features should be considered strong "buy buttons". These aspects help us to make the right decisions:

We're Self-Centered

To make decisions, egotism is an important landmark. "People are completely egocentric and all they want is something that will create a difference in their lives, eliminate pain, and possibly bring them more pleasure," Morin says.

We Crave Contrast

Sometimes our actions can be explained due to unedited things. Thus, the contrast is a significant way to captivate people. "The bottom line is, on any given day, we will receive about 10,000 ad messages, and only the ones that are huge contrasts will get any attention,"

We're Naturally Lazy

Simplicity is a substantial tool for advertising messages. About the message, it is recommended to keep it simple, but strong. "Most companies tend to create abstract messages and use too many words," Morin says. "Reading is much more a function of the "new brain". We recommend that, of course, companies use a lot of concrete visuals."

We Like Stories

Advertising and marketing with strong beginnings and ends create a catching reaction. That's why, Christophe Morin advises entrepreneurs to sum up and recap their strongest selling points at the end of any promotional material. He also underlines that people brain has a natural tendency to pay attention at the beginning and end of anything.

We're Visual

Visual memory can create a higher impact then a hearing one. Appealing video and graphic presentations can make the difference at cash registers where price and reason can't. Several times we make decisions visually, without being aware of them. Only later do we rationalize decisions we made.

Emotion Trumps Reason

"Give us the right emotion to ride on, and we'll buy what you're selling". "When we experience an emotion", Morin says, "it creates a chemical change in our brain, hormones flood our brain and change the speeds with which neurons connect, and it's through those connections we memorize. We don't remember anything if there isn't an emotion attached to that experience."

Where it Is Being Used

Neuromarketing is not a new kind of marketing — it's a new way to study marketing, so it's part of the field of market research. Here are six major areas where Neuromarketing is being used today:

- **Branding:** Brands are ideas in the mind that draw strength from the connections they make. Neuromarketing provides powerful techniques for measuring brand associations.
- **Product design and innovation:** Neuromarketing can measure consumer responses to product ideas and package designs that are largely automatic, emotional, and outside our conscious awareness.
- **Advertising effectiveness:** Much advertising impacts us through nonconscious means, even though we don't think it does. Neuromarketing explains how.
- **Shopper decision-making:** Neuromarketing shows how store environments directly influence how shoppers decide and buy, and it's not a logical process.
- **Online experiences:** The online world provides new challenges to our old brains. Brain science

Companies Using Neuromarketing

- **Cheetos:** The advertisement shown by Cheetos in which a woman did a prank on another person by putting orange snacks in a dryer full of white clothes. In the focus group method, participant disfavor the advertisement but by using EEG technique, company comes to know that participant actually liked the advertisement.
- **Hyundai:** Hyundai also used EEG technique while creating some exterior design of their car. Hyundai used EEG technique to known about the preferences of consumers and what encourage the customer for making purchase decision.

- **Paypal:** Through brain wave research, Paypal understand people are more attract towards the speedy services.
- **PepsiCo:** The biometric responses helped company why woman loved baked lays and enlighten that it was because of single serve packaging and ad campaign) etc..

Table 1. Neuromarketing vs. traditional marketing

Description	Traditional Marketing	Neuromarketing
Meaning	Traditional marketing has a one-way communication technique that leaves little possibility for participation or engagement.	Neuromarketing is the scientific study of how people's brains respond to advertisements and other brand-related communications using brainwave activity, eye tracking, and skin response.
Dependency	It depends on the self-report of the consumer.	It doesn't depend on the consumer's statement. it explores the deeper, unexpressed layers of consumer behaviour.
Consumer's Response	The participant has time to think to answer the research questions.	The participant faces the research question, his psychological responses are started to be collected simultaneously
Relationship	It has a moderate relation with other discipline other than marketing.	It has a close relation with other discipline other than marketing.
Acknowledgement	It acknowledges that consumer make their purchase decision after a certain rational process.	It acknowledges that consumer's makeup their minds about their preferences before they decide.
Biasness	Chances of Biasness is more	Chances of Biasness is less.
Methods	Traditional marketing uses focus groups, surveys etc.	Neuromarketing uses techniques like EEG, FMRI, PET and many more.
Accuracy	It doesn't have the potential to predict consumer with accuracy	It has the potential to predict consumer behaviour more accurately

Source: compiled by author

DIFFICULTIES OF TRADITIONAL MARKETING METHOD

In today's era, new product launches have a failure rate of approximately 80%. It is continuously increasing due to changes in buying behaviour of consumers. Traditional marketing techniques cannot interact with consumers and cannot understand the recent need of consumer. The traditional marketing is more expensive with less ROI. Companies invested large amount of money in traditional marketing but didn't get efficient ROI. It is difficult to target specific demographics effectively. It is difficult to describe the real emotions of consumer through surveys and other methods. Traditional methods lack real-time tracking and analytics. Traditional marketing didn't analyse the continuous change in purchasing behaviour of buyer. Modern consumers engage more with interactive and personalized content.

Consumers can attract through the customized advertisement which can attract the black box of the brain. Traditional marketing relies on self-reported data which can be influenced by personal and conscious biases. There is a lack of accurate data. Consumers cannot reveal their real emotions about a product. The impact of traditional marketing strategies is harder to measure than those of digital marketing strategies, where advertisers can track each click, view, or engagement. passed. Depending on the technique, traditional ads may offer marketers a constrained amount of time or area to convey their message.

TECHNIQUES USED IN TRADITIONAL MARKETING

Marketers employ freebies like brochures, flyers, or vouchers to promote a business, event, or deal. These flyers can be sent door-to-door, placed in the local newspaper, or displayed in public areas that the community uses often. Brochures help provide information about a firm, detail the features of a product and summarise services. The captivating imagery and textual content on billboards typically captivate onlookers as they drive past.

- **Creative billboard advertisements**: It may help you reach a large audience and make your target audience more aware of you. Marketers can reach a lot of individuals who take public transit with this helpful tool. These advertisements can be beneficial for more complex or lengthy messages that require more thinking because the visitor may have more time to read and process your content.
- **Direct Mail Printed:** Materials like letters, postcards, and flyers are sent to potential consumers' addresses in your target region via direct mail marketing. Direct mail can be sent to prospective clients or those who have expressed interest in your company depending on their zip code. If the materials provide a clear call to action, such a voucher or incentive that the receiver may use to fill out the form, they may be successful. Some product-based businesses utilise direct mail to give their audience seasonal catalogues that include purchase forms to streamline the buying process.

Figure 1. Techniques used in traditional marketing

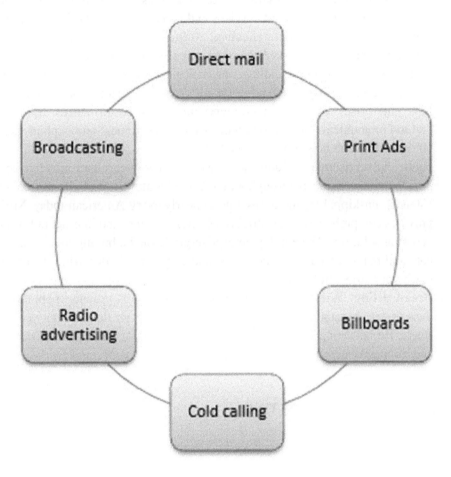

Source: Compiled by author

- **Print advertising:** It is a strategy used by marketers to reach a larger audience through publications like newspapers and magazines. An advertisement in the newspaper may help people discover more about your brand, services, or goods if you want to raise awareness in the community. One way to get referrals is to invite existing clients to inform others about the business and the advantages it provides. In return for discounts or other special incentives, several shops encourage their sales personnel to persuade consumers to recommend friends, relatives, or co -workers.

- **Cold Calling:** Cold calling is a traditional marketing tactic used in business-to-business (B2B) sales. These companies look out those who could benefit from their products or services and contact them to build a relationship and close a deal. And it's effective! 80% of buyers meet with salespeople who approached them first. According to a 2019 Forrester poll, 84% of respondents stated that cold calling was critical for their communication/sales strategy. Cold calling is effective for all types of organizations, including large enterprises, small businesses, and one-person performances. It allows you to communicate one-on-one with potential customers and explain what you're selling and how it would benefit them.
- **Radio Advertisement:** Radio advertising is a low-cost and effective approach to reach listeners throughout the United States. Best of all, it's free for listeners, unskippable, and accessible to nearly every American today. MPP provides comprehensive terrestrial (AM/FM), satellite, and internet radio advertising solutions. We employ enterprise-grade media buying tools to evaluate and purchase stations, schedules, and commercials that will effectively reach your target audience.
- **Broadcasting:** With Netflix and comparable channels growing popularity, there is less demand for television and radio. However, they are not yet obsolete. Broadcasting has been a key aspect of marketing strategy for decades, and it remains so today.

NEED OF NEUROMAREKTING

To comprehend how customer behaviour is evolving, Neuromarketing is crucial. It offers a straightforward route to understanding customers, which is the main objective of marketing. Analysing customer feelings and emotions towards a company's product, advertisements, logos, etc. is made easier by Neuromarketing. The Manufacturers design their products based on how customers perceive them. To design tactics that satisfy clients, Neuromarketing helps to resonate with their needs and desires. Neuromarketing provides a more in-depth look into human behaviour than traditional market research, which evaluates consumer behaviour at a higher-level using techniques like surveys and focus groups. Clients in a Neuromarketing environment are unable to mislead, making the data produced by these technologies more reliable. Just simply asking someone how they feel about something, one may change their emotional state. By avoiding this problem, Neuromarketing generates objective findings that aren't achievable with traditional consumer satisfaction surveys. Insights into the subconscious mind and succinct responses that are easily forgotten can be obtained using this strategy. Neuromarketing has the potential to increase the affordability and value of marketing research.

TOOLS AND TECHNIQUES OF NEUROMARKETING

(I)   With recording brain activity

Figure 2. With recording brain activity

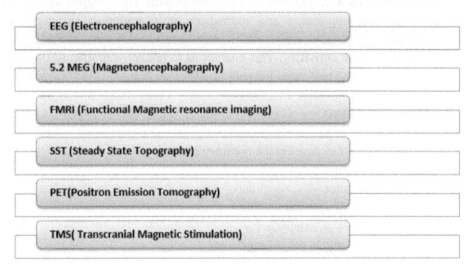

(I) With recording brain activity

- EEG (Electroencephalography)
- 5.2 MEG (Magnetoencephalography)
- FMRI (Functional Magnetic resonance imaging)
- SST (Steady State Topography)
- PET(Positron Emission Tomography)
- TMS(Transcranial Magnetic Stimulation)

Source: Compiled by author

1)   EEG (Electroencephalography)

Electroencephalography (EEG) is a neuro-research tool for detecting brain activity. It is a common technique in Neuromarketing research to monitor cognitive activities, such as calculations, in order to forecast consumer behavior. EEG analysed the brain electrical activity and registered by a headband or helmet that has small sensor which are placed on scalp. It detects the electrical currents of brain waves.

It Measures

- Attention
- Elation
- Sentimental values
- Cognitive process
- Memory consolidation

Uses

- **Measures brain activity:** This produces objective responses rather than conscious and reasonable verbal responses. This is significant since consumer behaviour is usually driven by unconscious responses rather than conscious ones.
- **Measurements are accurate to the millisecond:** This enables you to assess the first impression and immediate brain responses to marketing communications.
- **Assess cognitive activities:** This enables us to predict your clients' thinking and determine the best price for your goods or service.

It Is Operated When

- Evaluates as well as develop the commercial
- Evaluate fresh initiative
- Evaluate film trailer
- Testing website design and usability
- It is used for in-store experience
- Testing tagline what is the average cost?

Limitation

- **Data to be evaluated with caution:** This is due to EEG's lack of resolution in seeing activations unique to brain locations; it can only measure massive, synchronous brain activity across large brain regions.
- **Cannot predict every customer behavior:** While EEG has been verified for NeuroPricing, it is not suitable for analyzing complicated customer behavior. This is because EEG only detects activity in the cerebral cortex, not deeper locations.

- **Does not measure accurately:** It doesn't accurately measure the emotions such as fear, passion, value, or trust. This is because these emotions are processed in the brain's deeper areas.

2) MEG (Magnetoencephalography)

Magnetoencephalography is a non-invasive medical test that employs a super-conducting quantum interference device (SQUID) and a computer to detect neuro-magnetic activity in the brain.

MEG detects, records, and analyzes magnetic fields generated by electrical currents in the brain. The distribution of these magnetic fields is placed on an anatomical picture of the brain to assist in determining the source of activity.

A MEG research is a direct assessment of brain function and the most advanced way to record and evaluate the brain while it is working.

It Measures

- Perceptivity
- Attentiveness
- Remembrance

Uses

- **To identify the functional areas of brain**: It is used to mapping or identify the centers of sensory, motor, language and memory activities
- **To precise location of the source of epileptic seizures**: It is used to plan and precise the location. It uses magnetic potentials to brain activity at the scalp level.

It Is Operated When

- It evaluates new campaigns
- It is used for testing advertisement
- It is used for testing packaging design
- It is used for Identifying needs
- It is used for sensory testing

Limitations

- **Complex:** It is main disadvantage that MEG can only be used by professionals. Small business cannot hire professional for every testing. It is very complex to use.
- **Expensive:** It is very costly because for every testing there is need to hire practitioners and the machines used in this technique is also very expensive.

3) FMRI (Functional Magnetic resonance imaging)

Functional Magnetic Resonance Imaging (fMRI) is a neuro-research technology that allows us to monitor detailed activity throughout the brain. fMRI detects both conscious and unconscious emotions and responses deep within the brain in order to anticipate consumer behavior. It produces a signal that enables close examination of the structure of the brain by fusing magnetic fields with radio waves. It is expensive and using small sample size

It Measures

- Memory Consolidation
- Sensory perceptivity
- Reactivity of emotion
- Craving
- Reliance
- Brand allegiance
- Brand Choice
- Brand Recognition

Uses

- **Neuro Ad testing:** fMRI analyzes the unconscious emotions and behaviors triggered by your commercials. The measurements are compared to established benchmarks for effective advertising. This enables you to improve your ads and, if possible, lower ad spending by eliminating wasted advertising time.
- **Neuro Concept testing:** fMRI identifies the unconscious emotions and reactions triggered by your ad concept, enabling you to improve it for maximum ROI before going live.

- **NeuroBranding:** fMRI allows us to generate a Neuro Brand Signature: a pattern of neural associations in the consumer's brain that is unique to your brand. This can be utilized
- Evaluates New products: To assess the direct impact of your marketing communications on associations formed in your customers' brains. fMRI assesses the impact of your packaging on purchase intention.
- **Neuro Packaging:** fMRI assesses the impact of packaging on purchase intention.

It Is Operated When

- Evaluates New projects
- Testing and Developing ads or video content
- Testing packaging design
- Evaluates prices
- Repositioning the brand
- Predicting Consumer decision
- Determining Needs
- Sensory Evaluation

Limitation

- **Negative impact on test subject:** fMRI is performed in a laboratory setting, which may have a negative impact on test subjects.
- **Expensive:** fMRI is frequently assumed to be pricey because the MRI scanner costs millions of dollars.

    4) SST (Steady State Topography)

SST is used in cognitive neuroscience and Neuromarketing research for observing rapid changes and measuring human brain activity. It is used to monitor rapid changes and assess brain activity in studies on cognitive neuroscience and Neuromarketing.

It Measures

- Consumer Responses
- Video content effectiveness
- Long term memory consolidation
- Emotional acuity
- Consumer engagement

It Is Employed When

- Evaluates advertisement
- Evaluates new trailer
- Evaluates prints and images

5) **PET (Positron Emission Tomography):** Positron emission tomography (PET) assesses physiological function by examining blood flow, metabolism, neurotransmitters, and radiolabeled medicines. PET provides quantitative studies, allowing relative changes over time to be tracked as a disease progresses or in response to a specific stimulus. The approach is based on detecting radioactivity emitted after injecting a small amount of a radioactive tracer into a peripheral vein. The tracer is given as an intravenous injection, typically labeled with oxygen-15, fluorine-18, carbon-11, or nitrogen-13. The total radioactive dose is comparable to that used in computed tomography.

It Measures

- Sensory Perception
- Valence of emotions

It Is Operated When

- Testing New Products
- Testing advertisements
- Testing Packaging Design

6) **TMS (Transcranial Magnetic Stimulation):** Transcranial magnetic stimulation (TMS) is a therapy method that employs a magnetic field to impact brain function. It is noninvasive and can be useful when other treatment options are ineffective. It uses magnetic induction in order to modulate the activity of certain brain areas that are located 1-2 centimeter inside without reaching neocortex.

It Measures

- Attention
- Cognition

- Changes in behavior

It Is Operated When

- Testing new products
- Testing advertisement
- Testing packaging design
- Testing other marketing stimuli

(II) Without recording brain activity

Figure 3. Without recording brain activity

(II) Without recording brain activity

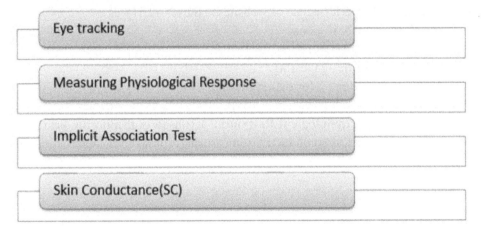

Source: Compiled by author

1) Eye Tracking
   - Eye tracking is where the subject's pupil dilation fluctuates as he stares at stimuli, depending on where he is looking, how long he is looking, and where he is looking in space. Eye-tracking technology employs sensors to track and record the movement of your eyes. This data can be utilized to determine what you are looking at, how you are looking at it, and your reaction to what you are seeing.

Eye-tracking technology is a technique for measuring and recording eye movements and gazes. It can track the eyes of one or more persons.

It Measures

- Concentration
- Explore
- Ocular movement
- Enthusiasm
- Concentration
- Pupil dilation

Uses

It is used when

- Evaluating the performance of websites and user interfaces
- Gauging customer response
- Testing video and commercial content
- Print and image design testing.
- Analysing consumer information filtering

2) **Measuring Physiological Response:** It is used in monitoring heart rate, blood pressure, skin conductivity, measuring arousal level, facial expression etc.

It Is Operated When

- Testing advertisement
- Testing movie trailer
- Testing website design
- Identify in-store reaction
- Identify consumer behaviour in its natural environment

3) IAT (Implicit Association Test)

It helps define product hierarchies and is used to measure individual behavior and experience.

It Measures

- Reaction Time
- Underlying attitude / evaluations

Uses

It is used when

- Celebrity Promotion (Choosing the right option)
- Market Segmentation
- Brand Differentiation

4) **Skin Conductance (SC):** It is based on analysis of subtle changes in galvanic skin response (GSR) when the autonomic nervous system (ANS) is activated. It also measures arousal and it is used while predicting market performance.

DISCUSSION

Nowadays, marketing should move forward from traditional marketing towards neuromarketing. If companies want to obtain any feedback on a product they must get inside consumers' heads. The information that is obtained during focus groups or other traditional techniques may not be accurate and the information is self-reported which can create biased report. Traditional marketing doesn't have the potential to predict consumer's preferences accurately. In today's visual pollution, knowing your audience and understanding their behavior also means to understands what simulates their attention to your advertising campaigns and explores the deeper, unexpressed layers of consumer behaviour (Owano, 2012).

Neuromarketing is where neuroscience and marketing meet. It is the process of researching the brain pattern of consumer to reveal their response to a particular advertisement and product before developing new advertisement campaigns (Williams, 2010). Its aim is to better understanding the consumer through his unconscious processes explaining consumer's preferences, motivation and expectations. Neuromarketing makes the use of brain imaging techniques (EEG, MEG, FMRI, SST, Eye Tracking and other technologies) as a key to unlock the secret of consumer behavior.

AI and big data enhance neuromarketing by providing deep insights into consumer behaviour and enabling precise, personalized marketing strategies. Post-COVID-19, entrepreneurs increasingly rely on these technologies to navigate market changes and drive data-driven decisions (Arora & Sharma, 2021). Artificial intelligence can optimize marketing strategies and streamline multi-business operations by providing data-driven insights and automating tasks (Arora & Sharma, 2023). In the metaverse era, post-truth marketing and communication can influence strategies by leveraging immersive, emotionally-driven experiences to shape consumer perceptions and behaviours (Arora, (2020); Arora, (2024). The metaverse can revolutionize branding, marketing, and entrepreneurship post-COVID-19 by creating immersive, interactive virtual environments for engaging consumers and fostering innovative business models (Dhiman & Arora, (2024); Kumar, Arora & Erkol Bayram, (Eds.). (2024). This shift enables brands to reach global audiences seamlessly and adapt to evolving digital trends. Neuromarketing can leverage the metaverse by using immersive experiences to tap into subconscious consumer responses, optimize marketing strategies and positively affect the way organisations communicate with stakeholders (Rathore & Arora, 2024).

Further, encapsulating persuasion and skill development in marketing communication is vital for brand building in this era, as it ensures compelling engagement and adaptability to evolving digital landscapes (Arora, 2023). Neuromarketing can play a significant role by utilizing insights into consumer behavior to create more persuasive and emotionally resonant marketing strategies. This helps brands effectively connect with their audiences and build stronger, more meaningful relationships.

CONCLUSION

Neuromarketing offers the perspectives of a quantitative method to test the effectiveness of ads, logos, and sounds before spending money on promotion. Given the existing overabundance number of ads, this new research tool is a vital instrument for those companies that want to better understand their targeted audience and to design better products for their clients. Thus, neuroscience is not something new; the new thing is its use in business in order to make business more intelligent. Neuroscience is opening the doors of knowledge in businesses. The innovations in neuroscience allow us to see and to measure what we feel and we think. If we are to synthesize the neuroscience importance and consequently of the neuromarketing importance for a company we would quote Joey Reiman: "NO BRAIN, NO GAIN".

CRITICISM AND IMPLICATIONS OF NEUROMARKETING

Many people think Neuromarketing should be a highly regulated field. Gary Ruskin of Commercial Alert, a non-profit organization that works toward regulation of advertising in the USA, has lobbied Congress and the American Psychological Association as well as threatened lawsuits against practitioners of the science. However, the government has chosen not to investigate the lawsuits and Congress and the APA have done nothing for his cause either. Most people feel that because it is still in such a preliminary phase and because most marketers don't even know how to apply the results, it is not a threat.

Considering this new form of marketing research was only really started in 2004, most opponents are worried about where the industry might be in a few more years. Scientists have already mapped the entirety of the brain and know exactly what parts light up when we make the decision to buy a product in certain industries.

Despite the general positive light in which Neuromarketing is seen, one cannot ignore the critics. Slate magazine's science writer Daniel Engber raised some serious doubts about the accuracy of the results obtained by brain mapping and its relevance for marketers. He writes, "Scanning one individual's brain and drawing shaky conclusions proves nothing. A few peer-reviewed studies correlating fMRI predictions of ad effectiveness with actual consumer purchases would mute the critics and do a lot more for industry credibility than any number of glossy articles that end up making Neuromarketing look like high-tech phrenology." There are other ethical and legal issues surrounding the area as well. As the researchers around the world are struggling to attain a go-ahead on issues like stem cell research and cloning etc, it is very tough that attaching brain mapping devices to someone's brain for a purely commercial purpose will find acceptance.

RESEARCH QUESTIONS OPEN FOR FUTURE RESEARCH

1. Is Neuromarketing vanishes traditional marketing technique?
2. Does neuromarketing create impulsive buying and affect consumer buying behavior?
3. Do consumers have two parallel circuits in their minds, one for thinking and one for doing?
4. Is the brain designed to avoid thinking by using shortcuts to make purchase decisions?
5. Is the marketer's challenge to shape the consumer's brand memory?

REFERENCES

Alvino, L., Constantinides, E., & Franco, M. (2018). Towards a better understanding of consumer behavior: Marginal utility as a parameter in neuromarketing research. *International Journal of Marketing Studies*, 10(1), 90–106. 10.5539/ijms.v10n1p90

Arora, M. (2020). Post-truth and marketing communication in technological age. In *Handbook of research on innovations in technology and marketing for the connected consumer* (pp. 94–108). IGI Global. 10.4018/978-1-7998-0131-3.ch005

Arora, M. (2023). Encapsulating Role of Persuasion and Skill Development in Marketing Communication for Brand Building: A Perspective. In *International Handbook of Skill, Education, Learning, and Research Development in Tourism and Hospitality* (pp. 1–17). Springer Nature Singapore.

Arora, M. (2024). Virtual Reality in Education: Analyzing the Literature and Bibliometric State of Knowledge. *Transforming Education with Virtual Reality*, 379-402. 10.1002/9781394200498.ch22

Arora, M., & Sharma, R. L. (2021). Repurposing the Role of Entrepreneurs in the Havoc of COVID-19. In *Entrepreneurship and Big Data* (pp. 229-250). CRC Press.

Arora, M., & Sharma, R. L. (2023). Artificial intelligence and big data: Ontological and communicative perspectives in multi-sectoral scenarios of modern businesses. *Foresight*, 25(1), 126–143. 10.1108/FS-10-2021-0216

Bakardjieva. E., & Kimmel. A (2017). Neuromarketing Research Practices: Attitudes, Ethics, and Behavioral Intentions. *Ethics and Behavior,*27(3), 179-200.

Costa, J., Freitas, C., & Paiva, T. (2016). Brain imaging during advertising: A neuromarketing study of sound and pictures. *The Marketing Review*, 15(4), 405–422. 10.1362/146934715X1450349053594

Cruz, C. M. L., Medeiros, J. F. D., Hermes, L. C. R., Marcon, A., & Marcon, É. (2016). Neuromarketing and the advances in the consumer behaviour studies: A systematic review of the literature. *International Journal of Business and Globalisation*, 17(3), 330–351. 10.1504/IJBG.2016.078842

Dhiman, V., & Arora, M. (2024). Current State of Metaverse in Entrepreneurial Ecosystem: A Retrospective Analysis of Its Evolving Landscape. In *Exploring the Use of Metaverse in Business and Education* (pp. 73-87). IGI Global. 10.4018/979-8-3693-5868-9.ch005

Eser, Z., Isin, F., & Tolon, M. (2011). Perceptions of marketing academics, neurologists, and marketing professionals about Neuromarketing. *Journal of Marketing Management, 27*(7- 8), 854-868.

Fisher, C. E., Chin, L., & Klitzman, R. (2010). Defining neuromarketing: Practices and professional challenges. *Harvard Review of Psychiatry*, 18(4), 230–237. 10.3 109/10673229.2010.49662320597593

Gakhal, B., & Senior, C. (2008). Examining the influence of fame in the presence of beauty: An electrodermal 'neuromarketing'study. *Journal of Consumer Behaviour*, 7(4-5), 331–341. 10.1002/cb.255

Garcia, J. R., & Saad, G. (2008). Evolutionary neuromarketing: Darwinizing the neuroimaging paradigm for consumer behavior. *Journal of Consumer Behaviour*, 7(4-5), 397–414. 10.1002/cb.259

Kahneman, D., & Egan, P. (2011). *Thinking, Fast and Slow*. Farrar, Straus and Giroux.

Kottier, W. G. (2014). *The added value of neuromarketing tools in the area of marketing research* (Bachelor's thesis, University of Twente).

Kumar, H., Mathur, N., & Jauhari, S. (2017). A Study of Consumer Satisfaction Towards Neuromarketing in India With Special Reference To Kano Model. *GE-International Journal of Management Research (GE-IJMR), 5.*

Kumar, J., Arora, M., & Erkol Bayram, G. (Eds.). (2024). *Exploring the Use of Metaverse in Business and Education.* IGI Global. 10.4018/979-8-3693-5868-9

Leiva, F., Méndez, J., & Carmona, D. (2019). Measuring advertising effectiveness in Travel 2.0 websites through eye-tracking technology. *Physiology & Behavior*, 200, 83–95, 200. 10.1016/j.physbeh.2018.03.00229522796

Lindstrom, M. (2008). *Buy-ology: Truth and Lies About Why We Buy.*

Marín, G., & Alvarado, M. (2022). Application of Sensory Marketing Techniques at Marengo, a Small Sustainable Men's Fashion Store in Spain: Based on the Hulten, Broweus and van Dijk Model. *Sustainability (Basel)*, 14(19), 12547. 10.3390/su141912547

Owano, N. (2012). *Consumer product giants' eye-trackers size up shoppers.* Physorg. https://phys.org/news/2012-07-consumer-product-giants-eye-trackers-size.html

Pereira, V., Fernández,V., & Freire, F. (2017). Neuroscience for Content Innovation on European Public Service Broadcasters. *Comunicar,25*(52), 09-18.

Rathore, S., & Arora, M. (2024). Sustainability Reporting in the Metaverse: A Multi-Sectoral Analysis. In *Exploring the Use of Metaverse in Business and Education* (pp. 147-165). IGI Global. 10.4018/979-8-3693-5868-9.ch009

Ruanguttamanun, C. (2014). Neuromarketing: I put myself into a fMRI scanner and realized that I love Louis Vuitton ads. *Procedia: Social and Behavioral Sciences*, 148, 211–218. 10.1016/j.sbspro.2014.07.036

Stasi, A., Songa, G., Mauri, M., Ciceri, A., Diotallevi, F., Nardone, G., & Russo, V. (2018). Neuromarketing empirical approaches and food choice: A systematic review. *Food Research International*, 108, 650–664. 10.1016/j.foodres.2017.11.04929735101

Vargas-Hernandez, J. G., & Christiansen, B. (2014). Neuromarketing as a business strategy. In *Handbook of Research on Effective Marketing in Contemporary Globalism* (pp. 146–155). IGI Global. 10.4018/978-1-4666-6220-9.ch009

Williams, J. (2010). *Campbell's Soup Neuromarketing Redux:• There's Chunks of Real Science in That Recipe*. FastCompany. https://www.fastcompany.com/article/rebuttal-pseudo-science-in-campbells-soup-not-so-fast

Yadava, M., Kumar, P., Saini, R., Roy, P. P., & Prosad Dogra, D. (2017). Analysis of EEG signals and its application to Neuromarketing. *Multimedia Tools and Applications*, 76(18), 19087–19111. 10.1007/s11042-017-4580-6

ADDITIONAL READINGS

Morin, C. (2011). *Neuromarketing and Ethics: Challenges Raised by the Possibility of Influencing Buy Buttons in Consumers Brains*. Academia. http://www.academia.edu/969187/Neuromarketing

Shayon, S. (2024). *Eye-tracking helping marketers boost shelf awareness*. Brandchannel. http://www.brandchannel.com/home/post/Eye-Tracking-CPG-071712.aspx

KEY TERMS AND DEFINITIONS

Branding: Branding is the process of establishing a distinct identity for a company in the minds of its target audience and the wider public.

Digital Marketing: Digital marketing, often known as online marketing, is the promotion of brands to potential clients using the Internet and other kinds of digital communication.

EEG: It is a common technique in neuromarketing research to monitor cognitive activities, such as calculations, in order to forecast consumer behavior.

fMRI: fMRI detects both conscious and unconscious emotions and responses deep within the brain in order to anticipate consumer behavior.

Marketing: Marketing is the science and art of exploring, creating and delivering value to satisfy the needs of a target market at a profit.

Neuromarketing: Neuromarketing is the scientific study of how people's brains respond to advertisements and other brand-related communications using brainwave activity, eye tracking, and skin response. These neuromarketing strategies are used to investigate the brain and anticipate customer decision-making behaviour.

Neuroscience: It is the study of the nervous system with primary focus on the brain.

Traditional Marketing: Traditional marketing is a promotional approach that addresses audiences using offline material.

Chapter 2
Neuro Marketing:
Harnessing the Power of Cognitive Analysis

Namrata Prakash
Graphic Era Hill University, Dehradun, India

Priya Jindal
Chitkara Business School, Chitkara University, Punjab, India

Ansh Jindal
Chitkara Business School, Chitkara University, Punjab, India

ABSTRACT

The chapter captures the shift from conventional to cognitive analysis tools in the marketing landscape. It is clear that the promotional ecology has developed over time, and that it has shifted from using traditional methods to using cognitive analysis tools. In particular, it highlights how information from the study of neurology may be utilized to rethink marketing methods and construct cutting-edge technologies that probe deeper into the way people think to produce advertising efforts that are more correctly perceptive and successful. Among the many techniques that are used in the area of brain imaging, some examples include skin conductance, heart rate variability (HRV), eye tracking, and functional magnetic resonance imaging (fMRI). Whenever they embark on the examination of neural bases for consumer behavior to gain a fuller appreciation of the intricacies of customer behavior, these methods are used for studying consumer feedback as well as ethical issues that come up as a result of such investigation.

DOI: 10.4018/979-8-3693-4236-7.ch002

INTRODUCTION

Neuromarketing is an area of marketing research that deals with consumer's physiological, cognitive and emotional responses to marketing stimuli. The term "neuromarketing" was first used in 2002. By using methods and approaches derived from neurology and psychology, firms, consultancies, and companies researching consumers and can understand and predict the actions of buyers. Consumer psychology may also be strongly associated with this. In layman's terms, buying behaviour is being translated here. The idea that it is not enough to know what the customer is doing but also needs to understand the reason behind this action has been at the core of this definition right from the beginning. This contrasts dramatically with conventional research approaches in marketing as a discipline.

The "black box" of a customer's brain has recently been investigated using the neuromarketing technique. It is based on the assumption that most decisions we make, either professional or personal ones are not rational rather they occur under the influence of our feelings or emotions. Many neurological and psychological studies have amassed evidence supporting this hypothesis over decades. Psychology and neurology methods are applied whenever consumers experience brands, which have an impact on them (Vences et al., 2020).

The chapter delves into the differences between traditional and modern marketing research approaches, as well as the many ways in which both may be applied to the modern world of online marketing. Companies require a strong grasp of customer behavior intricacies to thrive in today's hyper-connected market, where many products and services compete for consumers' attention. Although conventional advertising methods may shed light on the subject, they fall short of providing a comprehensive explanation of human behavior and the unseen factors that shape it. The neuroscience-based practice of neuromarketing helps businesses better understand their target audiences and overcome the usual obstacles to advertising (Spence, 2020). Through the advancements in cognitive analytics, marketers now have a far better grasp of what drives, influences, and preferences of their target audience. Executives gauge client sentiment through surveys and financial indicators. Both techniques have shed light on the impact of mental and natural factors on what customers choose, but more study is required. Understanding unintended neurological pathways may help explain how neuro-branding affects buyers. The science of biophysics neurological imaging, and visual perception research may help authorities understand consumer attitudes. Upon collecting this data, companies may generate customized ads to boost income. Neuromarketers use fMRI and electroencephalogram (EEG) to measure consumers' neuronal responses to advertising (Alsharif et al., 2022). Studies may reveal purchase habits by monitoring electromagnetic neural activity and blood flow. Companies may influence customers' brand opinions by appealing to their positive memories. Neuroimaging and eye tracking may reveal attention spans and understanding. Analyzing guests' eye habits while an ad or gift might reveal which items they prefer. Statistics may help businesses utilize their public relations expenditures. Consumer engagement and their feelings may be assessed by measuring the conductivity of their skin and heart rate variations. This helps to determine how emotionally involved the customer is. Marketers may discover that hormone reactions are beneficial in evaluating the subjective impact of their marketing and making improvements to their strategy. When it comes to promotion, emotional strategies have surpassed cerebral ones, which has resulted in a paradigm change. Because of this alteration, our understanding of the unconscious processes that drive consumer behavior has been expanded. In addition, this strategy has challenges (Bakardjieva et al., 2017). The importance of ethics, privacy, and making appropriate use of the results of neuroscientific research cannot be overstated if neuroscientists are to be a force for good in the world. In the book titled "Neurological" the marketing profession introduced "The Journey About Conventional to Cognitive Analysis Tools". The author also foreshadows a completely new era of advertising in which businesses will make use of neuroscience to gain a better understanding of the purchasing patterns of consumers and to develop media campaigns that are more successful and lucrative. Both of these goals will be accomplished through the application of neuroscience. The use of modern neuroscientific methodologies may make it simpler for marketers to comprehend the brain and establish a connection with their target audience. An atmosphere that is getting more competitive will, in the end, lead to a sense of fulfilment.

Origins of Neuromarketing

In the early 1990s, the word neurology was coined by neuropsychologist Roger Dooley in "Brainfluence: 100 Ways to Persuade and Convince Customers." Dooley believed that both neuroscience and psychology might help sales. This strategy is popular in promotion, manufacturing, & buyer studies. Neuromarketing is an emerging field that bridges the study of consumer behaviour with neuroscience. The most notable scientific advancements in the past 5-10 years have been in understanding emotion and non-conscious decision-making. These areas are changing marketing research fast. Many things especially impulsive purchases are influenced by emotion. The first choice is quick, and cheap and aims at being precise enough to draw immediate conclusions. Conventional methods in the market such as discussion groups and questionnaires do not give much thought to the subconscious decision-making of consumers. Oftentimes people have difficulty stating why they did, what they did or their reasons may just be rationalizations. Cognitive science has come a long way toward understanding these hidden processes with various research techniques

(De Marco et al., 2021). In marketing this knowledge can be used to gain a further understanding of what drives customers' decisions.

Transition From Conventional to Cognitive Analysis

Still, traditional advertising has used common sense, market research and theory. Neuromarketing uses real data from actual neurological responses. Also, learning how the brain handles information can help marketers make logical choices about pricing products, promoting them through marketing and the speed at which a brain processes information. Neuro-marketing predicts customer behaviour by using cognitive models (Shahriari et al., 2020). Through this method, marketers can grasp how individuals understand information and develop stronger messaging as a result. Original and persuasive ads may be created using this technique.

Benefits of Neuromarketing

Neuromarketing offers several advantages over conventional marketing techniques:

1. Scientific data shows that neuromarketing can scan neurons and provide marketers with objective information, bypassing human preferences and traditional surveys.
2. By personalizing, advertisers can create advertisements that are designed to reach a single customer's emotions and likes through neuro-marketing.
3. Using neuromarketing strategies enables organizations to improve their understanding of customers' thinking processes and engage them more effectively.
4. The needs of customers can be met in a better way by designers using neuro-marketing; thereby enhancing client loyalty and satisfaction in the process.

The use of neuromarketing in retail might lead to changes in shop design, signage, and product packaging that entice more customers to make a purchase.

Challenges With Traditional Marketing

There is a changing market that makes it tough for mailings, TV ads and print ads. These methods are faced with challenges.

Lack of Proper Addressing Accuracy: Standard advertising does not focus on demographics, making it less effective. This approach may fail in certain markets or not satisfy customers' needs.

Return on Investment (ROI) Calculation: Traditional advertising can prove difficult to evaluate in terms of return on investment (ROI). To know how much TV or print ads have contributed towards sales would require a long process with complicated calculations.

Little Interactivity and Engagement: Older marketing strategies were impersonal because mass media couldn't appeal to specific individuals. This led to less customer interaction as it took a general approach. Conventional media offer few advertisements and audienceship opportunities. Companies therefore have audience interaction problems, unlike digital platforms whose audiences experience quick dynamicity in terms of advertisements.

Expensive: Newspaper and television ads among other more traditional forms of promotion may be slightly expensive. It would not be easy for competitors to support start-ups with very low capital.

Inability to Reach Tech-Savvy Audiences: Advertising through conventional means is becoming irrelevant as internet channels take over targeting younger, more technologically advanced demographic groups. However great benefits could come from tailoring marketing campaigns towards identified consumer segments. On the other hand billboards or TV commercials have hard measurements since they lack many Key Performance Indicators (KPIs) offered by digital marketing platforms.

Slow Adaptation to Market Changes: The slow manufacturing and distribution processes typical of traditional marketing materials make it difficult for firms to respond quickly enough when there are changes in the market or feedback from customers.

Print & physical adverts aggravate environmental problems: Production, as well as disposal of conventional promotional items, causes environmental constraints that impair business sustainability efforts

Competition for Consumer Attention: In traditional marketing competition for clients' attention is high given the numerous channels and marketing messages being relayed through them thus making it even harder to make a mark in highly saturated markets.

Role of Neuroscience in Consumer Insights

The desire to know customer conduct was the force behind neuro branding. Advertising in a conventional way is based on numbers and questionnaires, which makes it hard to display complex decision-making processes. Companies must therefore look at their products' creative and imaginative abilities after understanding all the interpersonal as well as cognitive factors that lead to customer decisions (Makori, 2023). Through neuromarketing, they use neuroscience to understand how people act. Traditional methods are useful for describing the consumer mind but they lack some crucial information on consumer behaviour elements' interrelations' complexity. This change was brought about by finding out what caused it. For companies to survive in today's highly saturated markets, organizations must be able to identify why customers buy, what they feel and how they want things presented to them (consumer).

Rationale for Transition to Neuro Marketing

The two main reasons for the change to neuro-marketing are the necessity for more effective marketing strategies in a market that is becoming more and more competitive and the way that consumer behavior research is developing. These alterations are supported by these changes. Traditional marketing methods include focus groups, surveys, and demographic data to understand client preferences and motives. Since they rely on self-reported data and cannot account for subconscious influences on decision-making, these methods might provide inconsistent or inadequate findings. Further advancements in technology and digitalization have changed the whole trajectories of businesses in multi business scenarios (Arora & Sharma, 2023; Kumar, Arora & Erkol Bayram, 2024;Arora & Sharma, 2021). Neuro-marketing shifts paradigms by using consumer neuroscience. Thus, this improves our knowledge of marketing-induced reactions (Chattopadhyay, 2020). Neuro-marketers use cutting-edge EEG, eye-tracking, and fMRI to understand customer decisions' latent responses and emotional signals. Therefore, this illustrates the irrational demands and instincts of the customers. By linking their messaging and creative content to attention, emotion, and memory circuits companies can improve marketing campaigns as well as deepen customer relationships. In a world where there is information overload and resistance to adverts, the challenges to the marketers are manifold (Arora, 2020). The emerging concept of neuro-marketing is therefore a practical and effective way of cutting through the noise to attract customers' attention. Marketing materials for a company might unintentionally resonate with its target audience by employing neuroscience concepts which increases revenue, consumer loyalty and engagement (Jindal et al., 2023). More organizations will have access to neuro-marketing technology as it becomes cheaper. More individuals can now access complex consumer data that was hitherto confined to large corporations with huge research departments. Neuro-marketing can enable companies to create unique experiences that are emotionally charged and targeted towards more discerning consumers who desire authentic value or importance in their lives (Sung et al., 2020). However, transitioning into neuro-marketing has ethical implications. By ensuring consent, privacy and forcefulness marketers are expected to use neuroscientific approaches ethically, and transparently. Neuroscientists, marketers, ethicists and legislators designing collaboration models that foster the highest standards of professionalism in line with ethical principles aimed at safeguarding consumers from any misuse of such a rapidly expanding field are required by neuro-marketing (Royo-Vela & Varga, 2022). The alteration in the marketing plan resulted from neuro-marketing's capacity to facilitate consumer choice analysis; intensify marketing activities and enhance business-customer interactions. Therefore, neuromarketing techniques may give an organization a competitive advantage over others within a complicated industry by appealing to the subconscious beliefs of target audiences. Companies will find new avenues for growth, innovation, and customer satisfaction in an ever-changing business environment.

Limitations of Traditional Approaches

Marketing techniques such as questionnaires and market research are not enough to catch the hidden and implicit elements that affect customer behaviour.

The Need to Dig Deeper: Many people think that marketers must have a deep understanding of human psychology if they want to create more persuasive ads which are tailored to changing consumer preferences and stiff competition in the market.

Decrypting Subconscious Drives: Psychological studies in neuroscience indicate that neuromarketing is the only way of understanding what goes through customers' minds on an emotional level when making decisions.

Using New Techniques: Marketers can now better understand how their clients make choices by using these tools, including neuroimaging, eye tracker or finger-printing. This will enable them to know better what mental, or emotional factors affect consumers.

Neuromarketing's Strength in Personalization and Resonance: Complex audience emotions can be used by advertisers to target specific demographics.

Strategic Imperative in a Competitive Landscape: Companies should use neuromarketing to focus on customers located within specific regions if they want to maintain their competitive advantage over rivals.

Fine-Tuning Message Delivery and Product Placement: Neuroscientists can help marketing campaigns with advice on product placement strategies, customer communication methods, and engaging content development.

Developing Deep Relationships: The update emphasizes the importance of engaging loyal customers in strengthening our ties with our target audience.

Adapting to Changing Consumer Expectations: Any organization seeking effective advertising cannot continue using one approach because it has to understand that customer desires change constantly

Boosting Marketing Efficiency; Neuro marketing aims at making advertisements more effective by taking into account unidentified factors affecting customer behavior.

Some examples of successful neuromarketing campaigns include:

- Coca-Cola's "Share a Coke" campaign personalized the bottles of Coke with each person's name, evoking strong emotions.
- Googling employed EEG technology in its Micro-times Campaign to enhance consumer intent at key periods and brand loyalty.
- Apple emphasized the iPod's emotional appeal above its technical advantages at its launch.
- Microsoft's Edge browser's InPrivate feature was launched using neural marketing to capitalize on users' privacy and control concerns.
- Frito-Lay's Sensory Research: The corporation used EEG technology to investigate consumers' subconscious reactions to the crunch of their chips, enhancing the look of their products and packaging.
- PayPal's Emotional Messaging: Following a partnership with Neuro-Insight to assess viewers' emotions about their advertisements, PayPal evolved to an emotional storytelling approach.
- Hyundai's virtual showroom: By selecting car characteristics according to customer interest, Hyundai was able to enhance its marketing efforts via the use of virtual reality (VR) and eye-tracking technology.
- website optimization by Pradeo: Pradeo demonstrated how neuromarketing is used in practical digital marketing scenarios by using neuromarketing techniques to enhance the appearance and feel of their website.
- PepsiCo conducted taste tests of numerous kinds of Doritos using neuromarketing methods. The company found that naming flavors intentionally might elicit more positive responses from consumers.
- The Facebook "Like" button: In 2009, Facebook used neuromarketing to promote prolonged platform engagement by causing dopamine to be released in the brain.

Neuromarketing Techniques Used in Advertising

- **Eye tracking:** Tracking where customers glance may help designers of packaging, ads, and websites understand what grabs their attention.
- **Pupillometry**: is the measurement of pupil dilation to assess customer interest and provide suggestions for bettering product packaging, advertising, and online design.
- Using a technology called facial coding, advertisers may better captivate viewers by identifying emotional responses in their faces, such as happiness, fear, or satisfaction.

- **Biometrics:** Using skin respiration, conductance, and heart rate to measure the degree of contact and kind of response (positive or negative); supplying useful information for more effective advertising.
- **Sensory marketing** is the practice of persuading consumers without their awareness or agreement by using touch, sound, or fragrance.
- **EEG or Dynamic MRI:** An electroencephalogram (EEG) may reveal consumer preferences and mental processes in response to items and marketing.
- The psychology of coloring is utilizing color in adverts to persuade consumers to buy things based on their color preferences.
- Techniques for advertising may capitalize on people's fear of loss.
- **Framing:** Offering alternatives in a manner that drives purchases may improve ads.
- Anchored, which sets the tone for customer behavior and choices, may benefit marketing initiatives.

The aforementioned techniques may help marketers understand their target audience's subconscious ideas and actions, resulting in more successful ads.

Integration of Cognitive Analysis Tools

Behavioural analytic techniques are at the forefront of advertising, instruction, neurology, psychology, and biology. These tests can measure decision-making ability, problem-solving skills, motivation and memory. Different technological platforms and approaches are employed. The mind is increasingly realized by thinkers and professionals in this area using behavioural analytic methods (Alsharif et al., 2023). Additionally, to being useful for product design, marketing, educational intervention optimization and research on human behaviour these methods might also be useful to practitioners or researchers who are interested in understanding human behaviour as well. Examples of cognitive evaluation tools include mental health assessments together with brain scans. This paragraph attempts to cover all bases; numerous cognitive analytical techniques, how they usually function; ethical problems related to them. Cognitive abilities have been traditionally assessed in terms of intellectual competencies such as character qualities and emotional stability as part of conventional psychology. This innovative Cognitive Skills Assessment. Average scores derived from the test can help identify some levels like general cognition deficits, cognitive profile individual differences, and the effectiveness of intervention (Dangwal et al., 2023). The other problems may include cultural influences, honesty as well as trustworthiness. It requires fair evaluation procedures that must be accompanied by effective assessment technologies. Modern technological advancements have improved cognitive analysis, ML, and big data analytics providing valuable insights into large data sets. NLP systems will find out context, emotion, and language patterns from a given text. Thus, it could improve our knowledge about social interactions and communication's brain processes (Gupta et al., 2022). Moreover, machine learning algorithms can use changes in heart rate or electrical activity within electrodes to determine emotions and mind states thus revealing human emotions or social ties. Contextual analysis allows neurologists to monitor real-time brain activities combined with fMRI is a good method that describes how the brain perceives things, co-relates it with emotion then produces an action. fMRI localizes cognition-related areas while EEG tracks cell activity over time. Imaging advanced benefits brain disease study/therapy. The cognitive analysis would track student progress do we need to know about those who are growing and how can we improve teaching methods? Adaptive learning platforms provide personalized feedback, and grading assignments based on performance. Attendance, progress, and at-risk students can be identified through classroom analytics. 'Classroom biasing," Confidentiality and data protection are amplified. We suggest that these concerns be addressed with ethically appropriate open-ended instructional approaches. Understanding customer preferences, behaviour, and decision-making might be supported by employing citizen research and advertising with behaviour analytics. To reveal people's attentional biases, ads, product displays and packaging can be tracked eye-wise so that how much attention is given to them. To be able to create ads that generate wanted emotions, marketing specialists could employ facial expression analysis to evaluate the emotional reactions of individuals towards the marketing stimuli (Alsharif et al., 2021). Neuron correlates of customer preferences and purchasing decisions may be identified using neuromarketing techniques like functional magnetic resonance imaging (fMRI) and electroencephalography (EEG). However, cognitive analytics in marketing raises concerns about privacy preservation for clients as well as obtaining consent or manipulating consumers. Note the significance of ethics and government surveillance here. Cognitive statistical methods allow us to gain fresh insight into human cognition, behaviour, and experience. There are multiple implications for this discovery. Many different disciplines will be affected by cognitive analytics technologies' influence on research practice and policy making. These fields include consumer behaviours studies; marketing; healthcare services; and education among others. Both conventional psychological assessment strategies as well as state-of-the-art neuroimaging approaches are applied in this study. Due to the ethical dilemmas caused by privacy infringement via cognitive analytic methods such as transparency issues regarding privacy, fairness or even consent; ethical standards should go hand-in-hand with research guidelines monitoring regulations surrounding the responsible deployment of these tools. Cognitive analysis forms a key aspect of modern neuroscience and cognitive research today (Casado-Aranda et al., 2023). This type of examination aims to reveal very complicated processes taking place in our minds. Spatial or temporal features of brain activity can thus be captured using magnetoencephalography (MEG), electroencephalography (EEG) and functional magnetic resonance imaging (fMRI). Machine learning and statistical software programming languages like Python or MATLAB are often used by scientists when analysing big data sets because they are all complex. It is a complex dataset analysis. This integration enhances the interpretability of cognitive studies via pattern recognition and classification of cognitive states as well as predicting actions. Some examples of such integration outside the laboratory are real-time neurofeedback systems, cloud-based platforms for collaborative research and the embedding of cognitive analytic tools within diagnostic and treatment procedures. This interdisciplinary study brings together experts from computer science, neurology and other domains to explore cognition and mind.

Key Ethical Considerations in Neuromarketing

Brain marketing poses ethical issues due to its neurological and commercial underpinnings. Investigations must be exhaustive. Neuromarketing ideas have also been popularized at this time of rapid technological development when the commercial and governmental sectors are working together due to the intricacy of the problem. A few critical considerations are safety and the need for informed consent. Understanding the value of monitoring brain activity is challenging for neuromarketing researchers. Do it well and provide solid proof if you want proper approval. However, there are legitimate worries about the security and privacy of brain data preservation and collection (Clark, 2020). Researchers and practitioners must protect people's identities and private information from unwanted access to comply with legislation such as the General Data Protection Regulation (GDPR) and the California Consumer Privacy Act (CCPA). By targeting hyper-specific advertisements that speak to consumers' subconscious wants and needs, neuromarketing hopes to influence their purchase choices. As a result, when trying to persuade someone, it is crucial to suppress one's moral limits. Promoting health and uniqueness should exist side by side with enhancing the effectiveness of marketing initiatives via the use of neuroscience. Neuromarketers must remain committed to these ethical norms as the sector continues to expand. Essential values that must be upheld are openness, permission, confidentiality, and the reduction of damage.

Individuals must carefully consider the potential advantages and disadvantages before giving their informed permission for neuroscience research to go forward. It may be difficult to motivate agreement while also elucidating ideas. Its main objective is to use neurology and the study of brain activity to learn about preferences, emotions, and decision-making. The amount and technique of the data gathered by focus groups and polls are different. Study participants may have a hazy understanding of their role because of the studies' intricacy and the relative novelty of the neuroscience and research methods. All participants must be briefed about the research's data security protocols, any hazards, advantages, and goals. Being truthful but also honoring other people's freedom is essential for building trust. Neuromarketing collects personal data, raising privacy issues. In the industry, one must practice strong privacy to ensure the identification of participants and avoid data exploitation. Data must be managed properly, anonymized, encrypted, stored and disposed of properly. Those who wish to do so can retract their agreement for data retention if their beliefs change. The focus of neuromarketing should be on data security and privacy.

When it comes to manipulating persuasion and breaching the boundaries in neuro-marketing, ethical concerns arise from how certain tactics affect customer behavior. Misleading product designs and brain-stimulating advertising can influence customers' decisions through neuromarketing. Neuromarketers may use neuromarketing to sway their clients' emotions. Technological advancement within advertisement has resulted in manipulation as well as infringement of consumer freedom which raises ethical issues. Ethical decisions should be made by those always involved in the profession of neuromarketing. All interactions must be honest and ethical, aimed at building trust between both parties involved. Consumer behaviour does not always fit neuroscience explanations. Consumers are quietly manipulated daily by clever advertisers and product designers who are called neuromarketing. To affect consumers or understand what goes on within their mental faculties during the purchasing process? AI has marketing benefits, but its ethics raise questions related to whether it can harm consumers or infringe on autonomy. Adhering to ethics guidelines will help prevent taking part in aggressive or unethical behaviours among neuro marketers. For a company to succeed, it needs open communication that is genuine and has customers' interests at heart. At this point, two significant problems have emerged: (1) general ethical issues raised; and (2) unique psychological marketing challenges identified through this study. Discrimination could negatively impair an individual's cognitive abilities. It remains difficult however, to decode these findings about such types of brain-imaging tests as fMRI (functional magnetic resonance imaging) as well as EEGs (electroencephalograms), which may show responses in different brain regions. One should avoid cherry-picking or using a result to support their opinions. There is no room for any of these actions. Oversimplifications of neuromarketing have recently gained popularity with the increasing knowledge of neural bases underlying behavior regulation (Gupta & Bansal, 2023). On the other hand, there can be alternative outcomes as well. It's important for researchers to continually assess the reliability of findings and validate work through sound scientific practices. You will then realize that they are going out of their way to ensure that you are fully satisfied.

Unforeseen damage potential is another ethical problem within psychological marketing. Progress in advertising and customer services can bring negative results sometimes. If a firm uses misleading or intrusive ads, its customers may lose faith in it. Harassment of vulnerable populations and abuses of human rights are instances of immoral psychological techniques. Those involved in social neural advertising should regularly identify, evaluate, and solve any ethical dilemmas that may arise as one progresses within the field (Jayavardhan & Rajan, 2023) However, individual risk reduction efforts should coincide with increased societal benefits. Cerebral marketing entails many very important moral issues that require settling now. Given the sensitive nature of their work, those who specialize in social psychology but also engage in marketing would benefit from valuing transparency above all else. However, if this was an ideal world we would never risk data security, consent or lack of bias or manipulation (Mouammine & Azdimousa, 2023). Companies can choose to employ neuroscience in marketing while keeping honesty, privacy, and harm prevention intact; without flouting such principles or causing damages to them Ethical brain marketing demands not only compliance with laws and ethical standards but also building trust between customers and employees.

The Future of Marketing: Neuro Marketing Implications

Neuroscience-based marketing campaigns have the power to greatly influence popular culture. By employing subtle yet manipulative techniques, advertisers skilled in neuromarketing can sway consumer opinion (Karmarkar & Plassmann, 2019). This can only be accomplished if one has an intimate familiarity with the client's mental and emotional condition from the outset. Even when there is a chance to make money, there are ethical considerations when customers are taken advantage of and their autonomy is reduced in today's world. People working in neuromarketing should avoid being pushy or unethical and instead be kind, honest, and precise (Kalaganis et al., 2021). We must think about the ethical implications of neuro-marketing. The brain's processing of data and biases are intertwined. While fMRI and EEG can detect brain activity, it can still be difficult to comprehend. Professionals must not cherry-pick facts or manipulate results to align with their beliefs." The claims made by neuromarketing can be exaggerated considering the paucity of knowledge about brain function. Something may be wrong with it.

The emerging concepts like virtual reality and the metaverse revolutionize marketing by creating immersive, interactive brand experiences that deeply engage consumers, while also providing rich data insights into consumer behaviour and preferences (Arora, 2024). These technologies enable personalized, experiential marketing strategies that can significantly enhance brand loyalty and drive sales (Arora, 2023). Their interrelationship with the field of neuromarketing must be studied. The entrepreneurial ecosystem and the metaverse are transforming how stakeholders interact and collaborate by enabling virtual networking, investment opportunities, and market access (Dhiman & Arora, (2024). This digital shift fosters innovation, broadens reach, and facilitates real-time, immersive communication, thus accelerating business growth and ecosystem development (Rathore & Arora, (2024). Thus, the neuromarketers must consider these upcoming changes in the field of marketing.

Neuromarketing professionals who uphold ethical standards are required to follow strict scientific guidelines and carefully review their research methodology as well as conclusions. This is done to make sure the researcher is trustworthy and provides accurate findings. A portion of neuromarketing is one of the many legal issues in the sector that need attention. This is just one of the several difficulties. It is expected of neuromarketing who uphold moral principles that they would respond to situations with ethical dilemmas with candour and accountability. Respecting people's right to confidentiality and obtaining their informed consent is critical to prevent bias. Neuromarketing can enhance advertising effectiveness by utilizing psychology. It is possible to do this ethically by being transparent with clients, respecting their autonomy, and ensuring no harm is done (Kumar et al., 2020). Adhering to legal regulations and organizational protocols is essential in brain marketing, along with upholding moral values and having trust in clients. One of the legal issues facing the industry is brain marketing, which requires neuromarketers to act ethically and responsibly in the face of ethical dilemmas. It's crucial to respect individuals' privacy and obtain their consent to avoid discrimination. Neuromarketing can leverage psychology to improve advertising without harming clients or compromising their autonomy. Adhering to laws and industry best practices, as well as maintaining ethical standards, is essential in neuromarketing.

REFERENCES

Alsharif, A., Salleh, N. Z. M., Pilelienė, L., Abbas, A. F., & Ali, J. (2022). Current Trends in the Application of EEG in Neuromarketing: A Bibliometric Analysis. *Scientific Annals of Economics and Business*, 69(3), 393–415. 10.47743/saeb-2022-0020

Alsharif, A. H., Salleh, N. Z. M., Abdullah, M., Khraiwish, A., & Ashaari, A. (2023). Neuromarketing tools used in the marketing mix: A systematic literature and future research agenda. *SAGE Open*, 13(1), 21582440231156563. 10.1177/21582440231156563

Alsharif, A. H., Salleh, N. Z. M., & Baharun, R. (2021). Neuromarketing: Marketing research in the new millennium. *Neuroscience Research Notes*, 4(3), 27–35. 10.31117/neuroscirn.v4i3.79

Arora, M. (2020). Post-truth and marketing communication in technological age. In *Handbook of research on innovations in technology and marketing for the connected consumer* (pp. 94–108). IGI Global., 10.4018/978-1-7998-0131-3.ch005

Arora, M. (2023). Encapsulating Role of Persuasion and Skill Development in Marketing Communication for Brand Building: A Perspective. In *International Handbook of Skill, Education, Learning, and Research Development in Tourism and Hospitality* (pp. 1–17). Springer Nature Singapore.

Arora, M. (2024). Virtual Reality in Education: Analyzing the Literature and Bibliometric State of Knowledge. *Transforming Education with Virtual Reality*, (pp. 379-402). Wiley. 10.1002/9781394200498.ch22

Arora, M., & Sharma, R. L. (2023). Artificial intelligence and big data: Ontological and communicative perspectives in multi-sectoral scenarios of modern businesses. *Foresight*, 25(1), 126–143. 10.1108/FS-10-2021-0216

Bakardjieva, E., & Kimmel, A. J. (2017). Neuromarketing research practices: Attitudes, ethics, and behavioral intentions. *Ethics & Behavior*, 27(3), 179–200. 10.1080/10508422.2016.1162719

Casado-Aranda, L. A., Sánchez-Fernández, J., Bigne, E., & Smidts, A. (2023). The application of neuromarketing tools in communication research: A comprehensive review of trends. *Psychology and Marketing*, 40(9), 1737–1756. 10.1002/mar.21832

Chattopadhyay, R. (2020). Journey of neuroscience: Marketing management to organizational behavior. *Management Research Review*, 43(9), 1063–1079. 10.1108/MRR-09-2019-0387

Clark, K. R. (2020). A field with a view: Ethical considerations for the fields of consumer neuroscience and neuromarketing. In *Developments in neuroethics and bioethics* (Vol. 3, pp. 23–61). Academic Press.

Dangwal, A., Bathla, D., Kukreti, M., Mehta, M., Chauhan, P., & Sarangal, R. (2023). Neuromarketing science: A road to a commercial start-up. In *Applications of Neuromarketing in the Metaverse* (pp. 223–232). IGI Global. 10.4018/978-1-6684-8150-9.ch017

De Marco, M., Fantozzi, P., Fornaro, C., Laura, L., & Miloso, A. (2021). Cognitive analytics management of the customer lifetime value: An artificial neural network approach. *Journal of Enterprise Information Management, 34*(2), 679–696. 10.1108/JEIM-01-2020-0029

Dhiman, V., & Arora, M. (2024). Current State of Metaverse in Entrepreneurial Ecosystem: A Retrospective Analysis of Its Evolving Landscape. In *Exploring the Use of Metaverse in Business and Education* (pp. 73-87). IGI Global. 10.4018/979-8-3693-5868-9.ch005

Gupta, M., Sharma, S., & Bansal, S. (2022, April). Neuromarketing: An Emerging Domain in the Formal Education System. In *2022 3rd International Conference on Intelligent Engineering and Management (ICIEM)* (pp. 53-58). IEEE.

Gupta, T., & Bansal, S. (2023). Deciphering the Mind: Advancing Consumer Insights through Brain-Computer Interfaces in Neuromarketing for the Digital Age. *European Journal of Advances in Engineering and Technology, 10*(3), 25–35.

Jayavardhan, G. V., & Rajan, N. (2023). Recent Trends in Neuro marketing–A Review. *Journal of Coastal Life Medicine*, 11, 139–148.

Jindal, A., Jindal, P., & Chavan, L. (2023). Customer Engagement Through Emotional Branding. In *Promoting Consumer Engagement Through Emotional Branding and Sensory Marketing* (pp. 201–210). IGI Global.

Kalaganis, F. P., Georgiadis, K., Oikonomou, V. P., Laskaris, N. A., Nikolopoulos, S., & Kompatsiaris, I. (2021). Unlocking the subconscious consumer bias: A survey on the past, present, and future of hybrid EEG schemes in neuromarketing. *Frontiers in Neuroergonomics*, 2, 672982. 10.3389/fnrgo.2021.67298238235255

Karmarkar, U. R., & Plassmann, H. (2019). Consumer neuroscience: Past, present, and future. *Organizational Research Methods, 22*(1), 174–195. 10.1177/1094428117730598

Kumar, A., Gawande, A., & Brar, V. (2020). Neuro-Marketing: Opportunities and Challenges in India. *Vidyabharati International Interdisciplinary Research Journal*, 10(2), 214–217.

Kumar, J., Arora, M., & Erkol Bayram, G. (Eds.). (2024). *Exploring the Use of Metaverse in Business and Education*. IGI Global. 10.4018/979-8-3693-5868-9

Makori, R. (2023). The Influence of Neuro-Marketing Techniques on Consumer Decision-Making in Strategic Marketing Campaigns. *Journal of Strategic Marketing Practice*, 1(1), 21–29.

Mouammine, Y., & Azdimousa, H. (2023). An overview of ethical issues in neuromarketing: discussion and possible solutions. *Marketing Science & Inspirations, 18*(4).

Rathore, S., & Arora, M. (2024). Sustainability Reporting in the Metaverse: A Multi-Sectoral Analysis. In *Exploring the Use of Metaverse in Business and Education* (pp. 147-165). IGI Global. 10.4018/979-8-3693-5868-9.ch009

Royo-Vela, M., & Varga, Á. (2022). Unveiling neuromarketing and its research methodology. *Encyclopedia*, 2(2), 51. 10.3390/encyclopedia2020051

Shahriari, M., Feiz, D., Zarei, A., & Kashi, E. (2020). The meta-analysis of neuro-marketing studies: Past, present and future. *Neuroethics*, 13(3), 261–273. 10.1007/s12152-019-09400-z

Spence, C. (2020). On the ethics of neuromarketing and sensory marketing. *Organizational Neuroethics: Reflections on the Contributions of Neuroscience to Management Theories and Business Practices*, 9-29.

Sung, B., Wilson, N. J., Yun, J. H., & Lee, E. J. (2020). What can neuroscience offer marketing research? *Asia Pacific Journal of Marketing and Logistics*, 32(5), 1089–1111. 10.1108/APJML-04-2019-0227

Vences, N. A., Díaz-Campo, J., & Rosales, D. F. G. (2020). Neuromarketing as an emotional connection tool between organizations and audiences in social networks. A theoretical review. *Frontiers in psychology, 11*.

Chapter 3
The Sensory Marketing Theory:
A Journey Into Multisensory Marketing

Arpita Nayak
https://orcid.org/0000-0003-2911-0492
KIIT School of Management, KIIT University, India

Ipseeta Satpathy
KIIT School of Management, KIIT University, India

ABSTRACT

Sensory marketing is a growing field that examines how sensory inputs impact consumer perceptions, feelings, and actions. Marketers are increasingly using multi-sensory branding to create immersive brand experiences and increase customer engagement. The five senses are sight, hearing, smell, taste, and touch. Experiential marketing, music, and sound are key components of multimodal marketing. As digital information becomes more overwhelming, marketers must develop innovative strategies to engage consumers. Sonic branding, a key component of multimodal marketing, is becoming more popular. Vision, color, style, smell, and sound are essential components of multimodal marketing. These elements help create a lasting bond with customers, attracting new and repeat customers, and promoting brand loyalty. The study aims to add to the body of knowledge how sensory marketing theory helps in multisensory marketing.

DOI: 10.4018/979-8-3693-4236-7.ch003

INTRODUCTION

Sensory marketing, which plays on customers' senses to build an emotional bond with a brand, is a potent and frequently underutilized strategy. When implemented properly, multimodal marketing may raise consumer loyalty, raise brand exposure, and potentially improve revenues. Using all five senses, multisensory marketing is a novel idea in advertising. A marketing campaign may be more memorable and relatable to customers using several sensory components. Multimodal marketing makes use of many senses of communication, in this example, sight and sound. The goal of multisensory marketing is to advertise a brand by appealing to all senses. For them to return and time, you need to stay in their minds. To appeal to the audience, multisensory marketing integrates all five of the human senses. Using various senses for marketing objectives is known as multisensory markcting (Wiedmann et al.,2018). Multisensory marketing is the term for marketing that creates an experience for the consumer by utilizing many senses. Multisensory marketing is the term for marketing that creates a sensory experience for the consumer by utilizing many senses. Using many senses to communicate with the target audience is known as a multimodal marketing approach. It combines a variety of sensory elements to provide an overall impression on clients. An encounter that is multimodal, memorable, and significant is a marketing endeavor. This may be accomplished by utilizing a variety of senses to communicate a powerful message that appeals to the customer (Yoganathan et al.,2019). Using sensory marketing is a powerful strategy to increase brand appeal. By focusing on the senses, businesses can provide their customers with an immersive and unforgettable experience. When used effectively, sensory marketing may boost the profitability of your company. These four actions are necessary, according to marketing theory, to convince someone to purchase a product. This concept is used in marketing through sensory marketing, which appeals to the senses. The goal of this kind of marketing is to emotionally connect with the consumer by using recollected moments or experiences. When implemented effectively, sensory marketing may raise sales and improve brand appeal. Appealing to potential customers' senses and using them to form an emotional connection with the brand is the main objective of sensory marketing. This might include any aspect of a product, such as its feel, sound, or scent. Businesses may want to leave a lasting impression that will increase brand awareness and entice customers to come back by carefully designing an experience that appeals to the senses. One very effective technique for increasing brand appeal is sensory marketing. That makes your consumers' experience more enjoyable and memorable so they remember you long after they leave your store or business by appealing to their senses (Morrin & Tepper,2021). When done right, sensory marketing can be a powerful tool for premium goods. Brands may nudge people towards a purchase by delivering an engaging and memorable experience.

When executed well, this kind of marketing may increase brand appeal and increase sales. Through careful manipulation of the five senses as shown in Fig.1 —sight, hearing, touch, taste, and smell—brands can create unique and engaging experiences that captivate customers. Through influencing perception and memory, this multisensory interaction not only strengthens the perceived value of items but also helps them become more deeply ingrained in the minds of customers.

Figure 1. The five senses

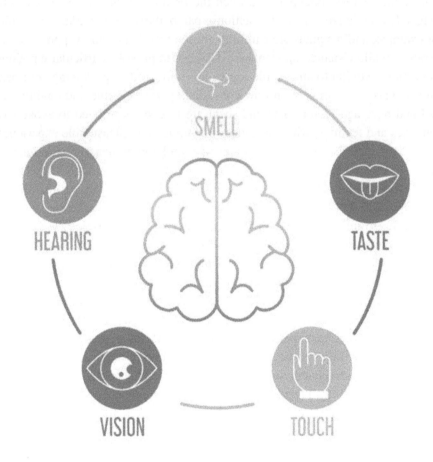

Source: iStock

By appealing to consumers' senses, sensory marketing goes beyond conventional marketing paradigms and affects their perception, behavior, and recall of a brand or product. Using their senses of taste, smell, touch, sound, and sight, this creative approach seeks to establish a deeper, more emotional bond with customers. Brands can increase the perceived value of their products, strengthen their emotional connection with customers, and ultimately influence loyalty and purchase choices by creating experiences that pique several senses. The foundation of sensory marketing is the knowledge that human experiences are multisensory and that using additional senses in brand interactions may increase their impact and memorability (Sagha et al., 2022). Every touchpoint between the brand and the customer is carefully designed to maximize sensory interaction as part of the sensory marketing technique. For example, audio signals are carefully chosen to enhance and support the brand narrative, while visual components are designed to provoke particular emotions or connections. Similar to this, tactile encounters with product packaging or in-person contacts have a big impact on how consumers perceive value and quality. In the food and beverage sector, taste and scent are frequently utilized to evoke strong memories and feelings, which enhances the unique and pleasurable experience of the product. Brands can create an immersive and comprehensive experience that captivates customers and makes a lasting impression by including these sensory aspects (Petit et al.,2019; Kumar, Arora & Erkol Bayram, 2024b; Arora, 2023; Kumar, Arora & Erkol Bayram, 2024a). The secret to sensory marketing's success is its capacity to influence consumers' decisions at the subconscious level. Studies have demonstrated that sensory signals can gently sway customers' opinions and behaviors without their conscious knowledge, which makes this tactic an effective tool for marketers. Brands can stand out in a competitive market, improve consumer happiness, and cultivate a devoted following by offering sensory-rich experiences. Sensory marketing is a means to satisfy customers' growing need for genuine and memorable brand experiences, giving businesses a competitive edge and changing the way that consumers interact with brands (Ranaweera et al.,2021). A business that effectively employs sensory marketing may capitalize on consumers' innate desire for interesting experiences. By concurrently engaging many senses—sight, hearing, smell, taste, and touch—marketers can create a complex brand experience that captivates consumers profoundly on an emotional level. Establishing an emotional bond with customers greatly raises the likelihood of fostering enduring brand loyalty. Our purchase behaviors are greatly influenced by visual signals. A product or store's colors, forms, and general aesthetics can arouse certain feelings and impressions among customers. For instance, bright and striking packaging might give the impression that a product is better-looking and more desirable. Attracting customers' attention may also be greatly aided by the strategic application of color psychology. Warm colors like red and orange might convey a sense of urgency and excitement, whilst cool colors like blue and green could suggest a sense of tranquility and dependability. Brands can successfully use visual signals to improve the entire shopping experience and influence purchase decisions by knowing how color affects customer behaviors (Haase et al.,2020). Aural cues can be just as important as visual ones in influencing consumer behavior and improving the entire shopping experience. A pleasant and upbeat ambiance may be created with well-chosen background music or sound effects, laying the groundwork for an enjoyable shopping experience. Imagine perusing a store as mellow, calming music permeates the space, fostering a sense of serenity and relaxation that encourages exploration and purchases. Certain noises can arouse perceptions of quality and freshness, which influences decisions to buy even more. Imagine the delightful crunch of a newly baked cookie or the crisp sound of an apple being chewed into. We are more inclined to select certain audio experiences over others because they not only pique our senses but also establish a link between the product and pleasant feelings. In the context of sensory marketing, the ability of sound to mold our perceptions and impact our purchasing decisions should not be undervalued (Spence,2021). Our memories and emotions are greatly shaped by our sense of smell, which frequently awakens long-forgotten connections that affect the things we choose to buy. Some smells have the power to take us back in time, bringing back happy memories and fostering a cozy, familiar feeling. A bakery, for instance, may quickly create a cozy and inviting atmosphere by infusing the air with the perfume of freshly made bread, bringing visitors in and tempting them to explore and savor the delectable products. In addition to improving the shopping experience, this sensory encounter builds a strong bond between the client and the brand, increasing the likelihood that they will make a purchase and come back for more in the future (Bhatia et al.,2021). Taste extends beyond food and drink to a wide range of other items, giving customers a more satisfying sensory experience overall. Samples and tastings are provided by brands, which not only let consumers experience the product directly but also build a powerful sensory bond that influences their decisions to buy. When a customer tastes a delectable sample, it creates a lasting impact on their palate, influencing their subsequent purchases and building brand loyalty. Taste-based sensory engagement is a potent tool that marketers can use to generate lasting impressions on their customers and foster enduring connections (Spence & Levitan,2021). Our views and purchase decisions are greatly influenced by the tactile sensation of handling a thing. A product's weight, texture, and general feel may elicit a variety of feelings and experiences, which might ultimately affect our desire to possess it. An instant feeling of luxury and satisfaction may be created by running your fingertips over a smooth, fluffy fabric; this will make the item seem like a wise purchase. The material's warmth and smoothness may make you feel sophisticated and at ease, making you see yourself looking put together and stylish when you wear it. A product's weight can also indicate its quality and robustness. You may be sure that a thing is well-made and long-lasting if it weighs a significant amount since this indicates durability and sturdiness. This tactile sensation may encourage you to assess the purchase favourably by fostering a sense of trust and dependability. Essentially, the tactile sensation of handling a thing involves more than just physical contact; it arouses feelings, modifies perceptions, and eventually directs our choice-making. Companies who are aware of the significance of tactile contacts may use this sensory cue to make their customer experiences more memorable and engaging, strengthening the bond between their goods and their customers (Liu et al.,2021). A fascinating path towards marketing techniques that use sensory inputs to produce meaningful experiences that pierce deeply into the psyche of their target audience is the integration of all senses in marketing. Incorporating carefully selected sensory elements such as eye-catching visuals, subdued background music, tactile experiences, sampling assortments, and captivating scents, marketers can create an engrossing narrative and impact consumers' perceptions that surpass the limitations of conventional advertising. Additionally useful for setting companies apart in the fiercely competitive industry is sensory marketing. Businesses may create highly recognizable brands and strong emotional connections with their target audience in this way.

HISTORY OF SENSORY MARKETING THEORY

The genesis of sensory marketing theory in India dates back to 2000, when corporations recognized the importance of sensory encounters in triggering feelings and ideas in consumers, hence influencing their decisions and behaviors. The sensory marketing notion is an outgrowth of the Western marketing paradigm that incorporates sensory, creative, emotional, and functional consumer encounters. Furthermore, it has been altered and evolved in India, impacted by cultural factors, customer preferences, and commercial pressures. Sensory marketing theory in India has grown tremendously as a result of the proliferation of retail outlets and shopping malls in major cities. Brands have employed visual displays, background music, and ambient fragrances to create an exceptional shopping experience, hence increasing consumer engagement. QSR businesses, such as Café Coffee Day and Amul, have employed flavors, scents, and texture as sensory aspects in their marketing campaigns. The hospitality sector has also helped to shape sensory marketing theory, with luxury hotels and resorts using multisensory branding tactics to correlate their visitor experiences with distinctiveness and creativity. These hotels create uplifting surroundings to elicit pleasant feelings and increase client satisfaction (Kumra & Arora,2022).

RESEARCH QUESTIONS

- How does the implementation of the sensory marketing theory in multisensory marketing help organizations attract customers?
- What part does multimodal marketing play in encouraging customers to engage with a company and make a purchase?

RESEARCH OBJECTIVES

- To understand the implementation of sensory marketing theory about multisensory marketing.
- To comprehend the practical implementation of multisensory marketing in organizations.
- To understand different aspects of sensory marketing theory about multisensory marketing.

THEORETICAL IMPLICATION

The introduction of stimuli into the customer's buying environment marks the start of the sensory marketing process. The buyer's five senses—visual, tactile, auditory, culinary, and atmospheric—then take in these inputs. Aradhna Krishna (2011) offered a theoretical structure for this procedure. The consumer's perception is constructed in part by the brain, which analyses the information received from the senses. However, emotional learning or cognitive processes may result from this perspective. Cognition is the mental process of learning and understanding through senses, experience, and thought process. The customer's attitudes, learning, behaviour, emotions, and memory are all impacted by emotional and cognitive learning, which also modifies the information stored there. A marketer's primary appeals are auditory and visual. Sight and sound are the main components of 99% of brand communication. However, when it comes to branding a product or company, sound and scent are frequently more powerful than sight. Additionally, when paired with a second sense, visual representations become much clearer. Using sensory branding mostly consists of appealing to the senses of the consumer. It is also used to increase market share and maintain it, increase profitability, ensure one-time and repeat sales, and understand the thoughts and emotions of consumers when they are drawn to, purchase, or use the product. Sensational branding uses taste, smell, touch, sound, and sight to create an experience that makes a customer want to spend money.

MARKETING THROUGH SENSES: SENSORY MODALITIES A MODERN MARKETING PRACTICE

Marketers from a range of sectors have been honing their skills in using the five senses to reach customers for the past 20 years. They have learned how to use cues that may amplify impressions of brands, including the sharp sting of mouthwash and the scratchy sound of a Sharpie pen. A recent study in Harvard Business Review states that the concept of "embodied cognition," which holds that our body experiences influence our judgments even when we are not conscious of it, is at the forefront of a lot of current research. For example, an experiment by Lawrence E. Williams of the University of Colorado at Boulder and John A. Bargh of Yale showed that participants were more likely to believe that a stranger was kind if they had momentarily touched a warm beverage than if they had held a cold one. Additionally, warm ambient temperatures made participants want to fit in with the group, according to a study performed by Sun Yat-sen University's Xun (Irene) Huang. Aradhna Krishna is regarded as the leading authority on the subject and is in charge of the University of Michigan's Sensory Marketing Laboratory. Many businesses, in her opinion, are just now becoming aware of how much our senses affect the back corners of our minds. Author Krishna became interested in the topic of why wine tastes better in a wine glass than it does in a water glass after reading Customer Sense: How the 5 Senses Influence Buying Behaviour in 2013. Why is it more visually attractive to place the fork to the right of the cake in an advertisement showing a piece of cake? Why does the scent of cinnamon appear to make a heating pad work better? Krishna found that the senses complement each other when there is some degree of consistency between them. Cinnamon gives a warming touch that enhances the appearance and functionality of a heating pad. The subtlety of these effects is precisely what gives them their potency (Krishna et al.,2016). Because they do not see advertising and other promotions as marketing communications, consumers do not react to them in the same manner. In many consumer industries, such as food, cosmetics, and lodging, taking sensory effects into account is standard procedure. Hershey's, for instance, has long known that people's experiences with regular chocolate may be elevated to a unique level by the tactile delight of unwrapping a Kiss. Another instance can be for years, automakers have been acutely aware of the senses. Their designers have worked hard to enhance the tactile feel of knobs, the satisfying sound of a door closing, and the unique scent of a freshly built vehicle. They have just started using cutting-edge technology. For example, BMW amplifies and records engine noises for its 2014 M5 model using the vehicle's speakers, even while the audio system is off. The goal is to make the automobile feel more athletic (Rathee & Rajain,2017). Many people are drawn to Glance by visual cues like color schemes and packaging design because they appeal to the sense of sight. As a result, people's emotions are triggered by auditory cues such as background music and jingles. Touch perceptions, which are a result of product textures and package features, provide a product a higher level of quality and make it more likable. Additionally, there are scent cues, like the aroma of a product or the surrounding air, which can evoke strong emotions and recollections. To put it briefly, adding flavor sensations, which are typically associated with food and soft drinks, to products helps them stand out from the competition and win over customers. Businesses can increase the immersion of their brand experiences and engage customers more deeply by implementing and carefully integrating these sensory modalities into their marketing strategies. This leads to stronger brand associations and the achievement of overall marketing objectives (Petit et al.,2019).

Vision

For us to survive, our eyesight is essential. Similarly, sight is considered the strongest sense and a highly successful marketing tool. In almost 80% of commercial and retail communications, visual sense is exploited. Creative teams must use all of their creative resources in order to produce visually appealing advertisements and messages that grab customers' attention. A kind of sensory marketing called visual marketing works to pique consumers' visual senses. Utilizing visual components like colors, forms, and pictures to provide customers with an eye-catching and captivating experience is known as visual marketing. Marketers may draw in customers, raise brand awareness, and change their opinion of a product or brand by using visual cues. According to research, visual signals may significantly influence customer behavior, including preferences for brands, purchasing decisions, and general satisfaction. Visually appealing marketing materials have the power to arouse pleasant emotions in customers and improve their whole experience, which increases brand loyalty and encourages repeat purchases. Through an awareness of the potential of visual marketing and the skillful application of visual stimuli, marketers may shape consumer behavior, leading to increased sales and a competitive edge in the marketplace (Hussain,2019). Colors, forms, and pictures are examples of visual stimuli that may arouse feelings in people and have a significant effect on how they perceive a brand. Packaging, logos, and ads that are visually appealing may draw in customers and improve brand identification. Consumers may establish connections and associations with a brand by using visual cues that communicate the personality, values, and positioning of the brand. Customers' experiences with brands may be improved by visual components, which help to make them more memorable and interesting. To strengthen brand identification and boost brand loyalty, marketers may establish a unified and consistent brand image across various touchpoints by utilizing visual senses (Bhatia et al.,2021; Savic et al.,202). Sight is the foundation of all branding and marketing. Businesses invest a great deal of time and resources into selecting and testing fonts, colors, images, photos, videos, and animations to discover how their target audience reacts to their work. This is because most individuals utilize sight as their primary sense of orientation in the environment. Any effective brand narrative in medical, digital, and social arenas must have strong, consistent, and cohesive images. For instance, everything from the color scheme to the lighting in their photos is identical to the visual experience you'll have in one of Mejuri's businesses when you engage with them online. Since our eyes provide us with 83% of the information we get, sight is the most developed sense. It is not only crucial for crucial retail moments, such as a customer's decision to enter a store, but it also conveys the brand's values and image. The store façade, the window display, and the inside, where the design, furnishings, lighting, and color selections all come together, all contribute to the customer's visual experience when they are in the store. With the help of our dynamic lightbox, Flowbox, marketers can create memorable and fascinating experiences for their customers by adding an active visual display element in-store (Oduguwa,2015). Customers' decision-making process is greatly influenced by sensory marketing, especially visual marketing, according to a Claro distributor's study. This conclusion is further supported by the study conducted on America cel Peru S.A.C., a telecom company distributor. It demonstrates that the visual components of sensory marketing—such as look, lighting, mood, and layout—have a favourable effect on how consumers make decisions. Consumers expressed great pleasure with visual marketing tactics, suggesting that these tactics had an impact on encouraging the purchase of goods or services (Salluca et al.,2022). One of the most sophisticated senses to employ in the advertising industry is sight. Brands that make full use of this marketing logic may readily engage customers. When it comes to encouraging a client to visit a store, for example, the sense of sight is crucial. It is also in charge of communicating the brand's image and values. Brands need to consider all that consumers will see while appealing to their visual sense. Recall to observe not just what they will see, but also how they will perceive it. An effective advertisement visual style can inspire people to create pictures. When incorporating sight into their sensory marketing initiatives, brands need to take two important factors into account. The goal is to achieve a favourable perception of the brand. When selecting images, consider their placement and orientation in space, their range of motion, and their content, which includes aspects like size, color, and form (Krishna et al.,2016).

Touch: Another component of sensory marketing is touch. It provides all the information needed to make an informed choice. Customers who use your product or service firsthand develop a deep affection for it. The strong sensation contributes to giving the customer a more engaged and connected experience. Given how much the digital world depends on images, almost 80% of marketing ignores touch, one of the most vital senses, and instead stops at sight.

One of our most vital senses is touch (Wiklik,2019). The embryo uses its touch capabilities to investigate its surroundings as early as eight weeks into a pregnancy. Touch comes before the other senses, thus all we know about the outside world and our immediate surroundings comes from our sense of touch. In addition to evoking feelings and creating enduring bonds with customers, providing them with tangible goods to handle, feel, and touch allows marketers to showcase their products' excellence and give consumers an indication of what to expect. (Marín et al.,2019). Temperature is a powerful sensory marketing tool that is applied in print as well as in physical retail settings. 'Rub and reveal' interactivity may be produced on marketing materials like magazine articles or promotional brochures by using thermochromic inks. When a consumer touches the heat-reactive ink, it transforms and reveals a secret marketing message below. We may discover more about an object's shape, size, texture, weight, and other attributes just by touching it. For this reason, a lot of luxury brands—from cosmetics to fragrances to Vogue magazine—use materials that exude luxury. We call it Mirri in our print-finishing world. Marketing materials may benefit from the magical touch of this globally recognized metallic substance, which enhances brand perception and emanates high value (Lluch et al.,2017). Using the sense of sensations through touch and skin is one of the distinctive features of sensory marketing; this tactic is known as tactile marketing. A tactile marketing strategy is allowing customers to become acquainted with a company's products by letting them handle, touch, or use the product in a way that allows them to experience it firsthand. The primary way that tactile sense is perceived is by stimulation of the skin. It is typically associated with sensations of pressure, texture, curvature, direction, temperature characteristics, vibration, and piercing (Nwachukwu,2022). In retail sales, the first guideline is to "get the customer to hold the product." Touch is a crucial component of sensory marketing since it improves how consumers connect with a company's merchandise. Products that are physically held might foster a sense of ownership that leads to "must-have" purchases. Studies in medicine have demonstrated that when pleasurable touch occurs, the brain releases oxytocin, sometimes known as the "love hormone," which promotes emotions of well-being and serenity. Tactile marketing cannot be done remotely, just like taste does. Direct consumer interaction with the brand is necessary, typically through in-store encounters. Because of this, a lot of merchants are now putting unboxed merchandise on open shelves as opposed to locked display cases. Well-known consumer electronics businesses, such as Best Buy and the Apple Store, have a reputation for pushing customers to handle expensive merchandise. According to studies cited by the Harvard Business Review, genuine human touch—a handshake or a quick pat on the shoulder—makes individuals feel safer and encourages them to spend more money. According to studies, waitresses who interact with the customers they are serving receive larger gratuities. For instance, Apple lets customers "experience" the brand to the fullest extent at its shops. Customers are welcome to view, touch, and learn about the complete Apple brand throughout these concept stores. The purpose of the shops is to persuade both current and potential Apple users that owning an innovative product is essential to living a "state of the art" lifestyle (Lluch et al.,2019).

Smell: "Smell has the best memory among the five senses," according to the quotation. We can hide our eyes, muffle our hearing, or refuse to taste, but the fragrance stays in the air and creates memories all around us. According to Kotler and Lindstrom (2005), as fragrance may evoke memories, it plays a significant role in successful brand communication, accounting for 45% of the experience. We may still recall the scents of our favorite foods from our early years, our grandparents, the rain bringing back happy memories, or the scent of flowers conjuring up melancholy images. Smell has a strong emotional connection and a big impact on our behavior. We stick to the same brand of perfume because it makes us feel and smell amazing—sometimes even revitalized. Similarly, scent influences judgments about what to buy and builds brand loyalty. We feel joyful, gratified, comfortable, and at ease when we smell. Customers can form either a short-term or long-term mental impression of a product through smell. Alluring fragrances leave a lasting impression on customers, who then plan to incorporate the brand into their daily lives. when we associate a certain fragrance with pleasant memories and emotional experiences. Additionally, this could be connected to either short-term or long-term marketing tactics (Dissabandara & Dissanayake,2019). According to researchers, scent is the sense most strongly associated with emotion, accounting for roughly 75% of our emotions. The modern fragrance business is becoming more and more concerned with creating scents that appeal to people's minds. At least 20 scent-marketing organizations globally, according to Harold Vogt, co-founder of the Scent Marketing Institute in Scarsdale, New York, are creating fragrances and odors for businesses to assist them in improving their marketing and reinforce their brand identification with clients. The consumer fragrance market is presently valued at billions of dollars. With the use of aromatherapy infusion technology, the fragrance business is expanding into the interior environment conditioning space. Both natural and artificial materials are emitted into the atmosphere to elevate moods and even boost productivity (Hensaw et al.,2016). These days, scent conditioning systems may be found in retail establishments, hotels, resorts, houses, and medical facilities. The aroma of freshly made chocolate chip cookies fills the Magic House in the Epcot Centre at Walt Disney World in Florida, making guests feel at ease and reassured. Coffee shops and bakeries with in-house bakeries, such as Mrs. Fields Cookies, Dunkin' Donuts, and Starbucks, know how important it is to have the aroma of freshly made coffee to draw customers. According to scent marketing analysts, although the scents of peppermint, thyme, and rosemary are energizing, those of lavender, basil, cinnamon, and citrus flavors are calming. Chocolate, licorice, ginger, cardamom, and rose are known to evoke love sentiments, while rose encourages optimism and happiness. Another recent study found that dental patients awaiting significant treatments reported feeling less anxious when they smelled oranges. Because of its fragrance, according to Stefan Floridian Waters, Singapore Airlines is deserving of a place in the hall of fame for sensory marketing. Presently a well-known brand airline, Stefan Floridian Waters is a component of the fragrance that flight attendants wear, along with the hotel towels provided prior to takeoff, and distributed throughout every Singapore Airlines aircraft cabin (Canniford et al.,2018). Dunkin' Donuts used sensory marketing in South Korea, playing their corporate jingle and filling the air with the aroma of coffee. If this sounds a little too extreme for your company, you may still appeal to your customers' sense of smell. Two smart options are to run scented adverts in reputable magazines or use a unique aroma in your place of business. Tests have demonstrated that pleasant fragrances may raise mood by forty percent, demonstrating the power of smell. Make a consistent effort to include fragrance in your brand (Barloso,2023). Smell is a sensation with the highest memory recall because it is linked to the limbic system, which controls emotions and memories. One company that excels with smell marketing is Rolls-Royce. Every time a customer brings their Rolls Royce to an authorised garage, the room is filled with the fragrances of leather and wood, creating the impression that the automobile is "brand new." This evokes recollections of the owner's first car purchase, creating an emotional brand connection. Disney theme parks provide yet another fantastic example of scent-based sensory marketing. The park's visitors experience more visceral experiences whether shopping or waiting in queue for an activity because of the Smellitzer, a patented fragrance generator that diffuses different aromas. (Campelo,2017). Fifteen percent of brand communication occurs through the sense of scent. Smell has a strong impact on human behavior and is closely related to both emotions and behavior. A lot of merchants think that smells may influence customers' behavior in a good way. Customers can evaluate stores more accurately when they employ scents to train them. A pleasant scent might help to recall things and support the additional value of products. They conclude that smell produces more fragrant memories over time and that scented objects are far more appealing than non-scented ones. Investigators that the smell significantly influences customer behavior in a retail center and directly impacts purchasers' perceptions. Furthermore, fragrance greatly affects how individuals view their environment and the calibre of goods. In a competitive setting, sellers have to think about strategically employing scent and pay more attention to how they do so (Shabgou & Daryani, 2014).

Hearing: It has long been known that sound plays a significant role in influencing mood, preferences, and consumer behavior. 41% of respondents had heard about brand building. The consumer's unconscious wants can be effectively communicated through sound. It influences the way we shop. The retail setting demonstrated that customers' pleasant feelings are evoked by music in stores and that a positive attitude towards the store is caused by a comprehension of music. Store music has been shown in other research to have a positive impact on purchase intentions and sales. Research on hearing discomfort among consumers, and how music is perceived positively affects the customer experience. Following the assessment of the store, the merchandise appears appealing, leading to a final increase in the amount of time and money spent there. The results verified that consumers' behavior may be influenced by appropriate music. Drawing from the preceding discourse, the third hypothesis posits that arousing auditory perception may impact customer conduct (Kato,2023). The diagnostic range for human ears is sixteen to twenty-eight thousand cycles per second. The majority of organizations are well aware that sound is regarded as a method for enhancing their overall brand and image. A corporation can have great chances to use sound to distinguish itself from its surroundings if it applies sound intentionally. If truth be told, sound affects behavior and purchasing habits, it also affects our opinions and remarks about the products and repairs that we tend to acquire (Singh et al.,2020). The feelings and emotions that result from noises activating the emotional part of the brain shape a person's mood. It is a continuous, subconscious activity that takes place all the time. According to Hultén et al., hearing is an active sense that is intrinsic and cannot be switched off. People and sound have a mutually beneficial relationship, and sound has a profound impact on each person's own life experiences. They are even able to permanently commit some sounds to memory, which they may then utilize to remember both the original sound and its related memories. Marketers have traditionally employed sound to increase the effect of joy at the point of sale. The whole experience of shopping revolves around sound, which can be heard in anything from the soothing sounds of running water in luxurious spas to the upbeat music of teenage stores. For example, when French music is playing at the store, customers are more likely to buy French wines. If there are any German tunes, customers choose German products without realizing that music affects their choice. A proper music selection within the establishment may help to create a more unified atmosphere and encourage a feeling of camaraderie among customers (Krishna,2016). The majority of marketing communication is, by definition, aural. The meaning may be conveyed by the sounds that comprise a word. Languages can be important in and of themselves. It has also been demonstrated that ambient music in stores affects customers' moods, how long they spend there, and how much they spend. Targeting clients' hearing sense, and auditory cues is essential to sensory marketing. They may have components like pace, music genres, slogans, and jingles. Auditory signals are employed to draw in customers and provide a lasting brand experience. They have the power to arouse feelings, generate favorable associations with a brand, and improve the whole consumer experience. Various age groups might respond differently to the music of different genres and tempos (Gupta et al.,2022). In a retail setting, auditory cues have been shown to affect customer behavior and subconscious decision-making. Research studies, including "The Influence of In-Store Music on Wine Selections," have demonstrated how customers' wine choices can be influenced by in-store music, with some musical genres being associated with higher sales of particular wines. This shows that auditory cues, like music, may set the tone or ambiance of a business, influencing the tastes and decisions of customers. In a retail context, the introduction of suitable audio stimuli can improve customer satisfaction and even boost sales (Kulkarni & Kolli,2022). A useful tactic in sensory marketing, which uses the purposeful application of sensory stimulation to boost consumption and brand ubiquity, is auditory marketing. By fostering an emotional bond between the customer and the product, it seeks to draw in clients, increase their duration of visit, and encourage purchases. In addition to affecting customer behavior, perceptions, and decisions, the use of aural stimuli in marketing can improve how effectively qualities like sound, smell, taste, color, or texture are perceived. Businesses may provide clients with a distinctive sensory experience by integrating aural components into their marketing strategy. This is especially appealing to younger generations who place a high value on sound and music when purchasing. This strategy highlights the necessity for persuasive audio marketing techniques that draw in and keep consumers, eventually boosting revenue and brand loyalty (Castro et al.,2015). A dynamic brain mechanism called auditory memory encodes and retains experience-related information. We might now question ourselves what is the basis for this sound information storage or why we sometimes entirely overlook certain noises while we can recall others. The listener's past emotional state, personality, and hobbies all play a role, but a lot of study has already been done to identify the section of the brain that is in charge of helping people memorize songs. Thus, the researchers suggested that individuals listen to a variety of songs, including Pink Panther's music and the Rolling Stones' "Satisfaction," as noted in a study using a sample of musical sound stimuli. It was shown that listening to instrumental music vs lyrical music changed the amount of brain activity and that songs like Satisfaction were remembered for extended periods (Marín et al.,2019).

Taste: The percentage of flavors associated with the entire structure is thirty-one. When there is intense rivalry among food product marketers, mishandling a natural expression of elegance is a useful tactic to sway consumer behavior. Colgate's toothpaste has an amazing design that is reminiscent of the Bang and Oleson gadget, Intel's digital sound, and Coca-Cola's white and red color scheme. Getting into the third of the five senses to brand is a common goal for all those completions (Wistoft & Qvortrup,2021). The five fundamental flavors are umami, sour, bitter, sweet, and salty. Tasting may be included in a sensory marketing strategy in a variety of ways. One common tactic is to encourage sampling and make the process pleasurable for consumers. If you own actual locations, you may arrange a pop-up event where consumers might try products for free. You may motivate consumers to become brand ambassadors and spread the word about your eCommerce website to their networks by carefully handing out free samples (Nenkov et al.,2019). Only five pure tastes are recognized by humans: umami, which means "delicious" and is derived from a Japanese food researcher, sweet, salty, sour, bitter, and umami. The additional elements that affect taste perception include how food feels, looks, smells, and sounds when consumed. Thus, a variety of elements, such as physical characteristics, brand name, and product information, influence how people perceive flavor. Although other sensory marketing strategies may be used in a variety of businesses, taste is one sense that is mostly used in the food and beverage industry. Similar to scent, taste elicits strong emotions, and businesses that have mastered a particular taste may capitalize on the strength of that bond. Certain businesses have managed to incorporate well-known and cherished childhood preferences into new forms. Consider the Dairy Queen Oreo Blizzard or the McDonald's Oreo McFlurry. Fast-food establishments collaborate with Oreo to provide their patrons with unique cookies and cream flavors because Oreo has such a distinctive flavor (Zha,2021). Taste is maybe the most difficult sense to employ in marketing since everyone has a different definition of what tastes nice. Given that they offer free tastings and samples, supermarkets are one of the few businesses that use taste marketing. However, a few businesses outside of the FMCG sector are looking at the possibility of creating a "taste" for their brand. Ikea is an example of a retail company that has effectively created a strong taste connection for its brand through its in-store cafés, with 30% of its customers visiting the store only for food. The eateries not only extend customer stays but also increase the chance to purchase additional Ikea merchandise in addition to meals (Haase et al.,2020). Giving up free samples is a popular way to give consumers more time to consider whether or not to purchase meals from a restaurant or food business. The product must first pass via the other senses listed under sensory marketing tactics, which act as filters, to reach this taste-based marketing. For example, letting clients try several kinds of ice cream rapidly would stimulate their taste receptors and increase sales. Additionally, sampling occurs during ground-activation initiatives run by FMCG companies. One instance of sensory marketing taste tests where consumers were allowed to try the brand is the blind taste test between Coca-Cola and Pepsi (Marín et al.,2019). Marketers may create unique sensory connections with their brands, improve the appeal of their products, and differentiate themselves in crowded marketplaces by employing taste stimuli. Taste also possesses the power to elicit connections and memories, which can impact customers' decision-making and promote brand loyalty. Through the use of multisensory packaging, flavor profiling, and product sample distribution, marketers can effectively engage consumers on a deeper level and create memorable brand experiences that resonate positively with their target audience by incorporating taste elements into their marketing strategies. Thus, understanding taste's place in sensory marketing theory enables marketers to create more compelling and memorable marketing campaigns that make use of taste's ability to influence and drive customer engagement.

CONSUMER PERCEPTION AND BEHAVIOR: EFFECT OF SENSORY MODALITIES

Sensational marketing has gained popularity in recent years as a way for businesses to set themselves apart from the competition in response to the constant need to create unique in-store experiences for customers. The following are the only sensory experiences that we can remember: A neuromarketing study from Rockefeller University indicates that we perceive 1% of what we touch, 2% of what we hear, 5% of what we see, 15% of what we taste, and 35% of what we smell. Managers and marketers are finding that understanding how customers define emotion and experience may be done more effectively with the use of sensory signals. A few examples of sensory cues that influence customer behavior are color, scent, and music. Consequently, managers should use these sensory and experimental cues to impact consumers' cognitive experiences. To provide a distinctive customer experience, Reese's, for example, promoted their peanut butter and chocolate cups as "two great tastes that taste great together". Retailers also frequently employ background music as a marketing strategy. Retailers and businesses are becoming more interested in focusing their marketing proposals on the senses that influence the consumer experience to capture customers' attention and provide a memorable experience. The majority of businesses that use sensory cues to give product fragrances, background music, graphical designs, and other things are stores and organizations. (Sagha et al.,2022). Through the integration of sight, sound, touch, taste, and smell, marketers may create enduring experiences that evoke strong emotions in their target audience. Bright colors and eye-catching artwork are examples of visual features that can arouse feelings and shape brand associations. For example, customers seeking refinement and innovation are drawn to Apple products because of their vivid colors and streamlined designs. In a similar vein, auditory signals that create a distinct identity, such as soothing music or appealing jingles, can improve brand recognition. Consider the enduring "I'm Lovin' It" jingle from McDonald's, which instantly evokes the upbeat vibe of the fast-food restaurant chain. Tactile experiences can also affect how people perceive the quality and appeal of a product (Furst et al.,2021). To communicate exclusivity and luxury and entice customers to engage in sensory pleasures, luxury brands frequently place premium-on-premium materials and textures. Think of the smoothness of high-end skincare products or the opulent feel of leather seats in a high-end vehicle. Moreover, scent and taste are strong inducers of brand loyalty and emotional ties. Food and beverage producers use these senses to develop distinctive scents and tastes that are memorable. For example, Starbucks creates a cozy and familiar atmosphere for its patrons by infusing its specialty drinks with the rich taste and fragrance of freshly brewed coffee (Joy et al.,2023). Technology has made it possible to use sensory marketing in ways that go beyond the five senses—taste, smell, touch, sound, and sight. The use of haptic feedback, augmented reality (AR), and virtual reality (VR) have completely changed how companies develop immersive experiences that blend the real and digital worlds and captivate customers in novel and fascinating ways (Arora, M. (2024) b; Arora (2024) a.; Chandel & Arora, (2024). Before making a purchase, for instance, customers can see things in their intended settings thanks to VR and AR applications. This lessens the possibility of consumer regret while simultaneously boosting their confidence. Apps that use augmented reality (AR) are used by furniture sellers such as IKEA to let clients virtually arrange furniture in their homes and get a realistic idea of how it would fit and look. This creates enthusiasm and anticipation in addition to making it easier to make well-informed decisions (Helmefalk,2019). Added to that, haptic feedback technology gives digital interactions a tactile element that enhances the sensory experience and increases user engagement. Gaming accessories that mimic physical sensations, such as force-feedback controllers, increase the fun and immersion of a game. Haptic feedback can be used in marketing to create memorable brand experiences, such as vibrating smartphone notifications or touchscreens that react to gestures by subtly vibrating. These exchanges strengthen the brand's message and create a feeling of kinship with the customer. Additionally, by evoking particular feelings and causing subconscious associations, multimodal branding techniques can affect consumer preferences and purchasing decisions. For example, the deliberate application of color psychology in packaging design can evoke a variety of emotions, from calmness to enthusiasm, influencing consumers' opinions about the value and quality of the product. The incorporation of ambient smells into retail spaces can arouse feelings of luxury or nostalgia, which might impact consumers' intent to buy and lengthen their stay. New opportunities in sensory marketing have been made possible by the convergence of technological breakthroughs and sensory modalities. Nowadays, brands have the chance to craft immersive experiences that enthrall customers and shape their attitudes and actions (Arora & Sharma, (2023).

SENSORY MARKETING TECHNIQUES USED BY DIFFERENT GLOBAL BRANDS AND INDIAN BRANDS

In today's cutthroat market, sensory marketing assists companies in evoking feelings and sustaining consumer interest. It helps businesses make customer interactions more engaging and significant by putting the customer experience front and center. To increase brand recognition, some of the biggest and most prosperous companies in the world employ sensory marketing. Marketers can shape brand impressions by utilizing multimodal experiences. The study on embodied cognition suggests that without conscious awareness, decisions are made based on physical judgments. Through sensory marketing, advertisers may take advantage of this well-studied area. It guarantees a stronger relationship with customers than standard print and broadcast marketing efforts and commercials. A marketing campaign's effectiveness is determined by the customer experience. Each of the five senses—taste, smell, hearing, touch, and sight—causes a distinct memory reaction. By stimulating your audience's senses, you may elicit the proper response and increase sales. This is known as sensory marketing. The global companies that use this technique are described below;

- McDonald's: McDonald's appeals to the five senses of its patrons through pictures. Every time a new menu item is announced, advertisements featuring incredibly close-up photos of the food preparation are released. Moreover, it enhances food sensations and makes use of autonomous sensory meridian response (ASMR) worthy noises. The movements of the models convey a sense of the texture and aroma of the dish. The advertisements form a perception in the minds of the viewers based on just one observation. They arouse appetites. The jingle from McDonald's, "Ba-da-ba-ba-ba - I'm lovin' it," is also among the most well-known in the modern era. The company has successfully, recognizable, and catchily used sound to its advantage in its marketing efforts with the help of the jingle.
- Visa: Visa created a sensory branding experience for its customers after each transaction because it understood that sound impacts purchasing decisions. A unique sound is played as part of the campaign when a Visa cardholder uses their card to make a transaction. The sound was meticulously polished by the firm. The intention was for customers to be able to identify with the sound and understand that it signifies a safe and successful transaction. Visa cardholders benefit from comfort and consistency from this sensory branding initiative. Customers are made to feel safe and trusting when they hear the Visa Checkout sound, and they associate that emotion with the brand.

- Apple: Apple uses a multisensory approach to its marketing. For example, every one of their storefronts is white, tidy, and simple. These design cues give buyers the impression that the firm is a slick, contemporary, high-end IT corporation. The packaging's appearance conveys the same idea. Additionally, the brand showcases every product in-store so that buyers can touch and feel it. Apple communicates with its consumers with sound in addition to sight and touch. For instance, iPhone owners would recognize and be able to recall the same sound that their devices produce when they attempt to lock their cellphones.

- Master Card: Establishing a new identity for credit card users—the sound identity—is the aim of Mastercard's sensory branding. Customers hear a sound once a transaction is complete, which represents the interplay of the red and yellow circles in the Mastercard logo. When utilizing voice search, in-store, or online shopping with their Mastercards, customers hear the sound. This type of sensory marketing appeals to the customer's auditory senses and evokes feelings of stability and security. With the familiar sound, customers may be sure that their transactions will be successful. Furthermore, the ad offers users an imaginative visual experience, with the sound representing the intersection of the circles in the Mastercard emblem.

- Rolls Royce: The goal of Rolls-Royce's Ghost Six Senses Concept was to arouse customers' senses in every way. Taste, smell, sound, sight, and touch are all intended to elicit a reaction from the new car's unique, custom attributes. The attention is drawn to the minute details, which activate the visual senses. The outside has unique wheels, while the interiors include plush leather. The stereo evokes the atmosphere of a Metallica or symphony concert, which appeals to the sense of sound. The brand effectively uses aroma to appeal to consumers' sense of smell; many vehicle aficionados find their cars to have a distinctive "new car" perfume.

- Starbucks: The robust aroma of freshly brewed coffee at Starbucks is relatable to most patrons. The reason for this is that every establishment grinds its special coffee beans, which causes the aroma to permeate the space and affect patrons as soon as they walk in. Starbucks maintains a powerful scent to stimulate the sense of smell. The corporation is aware that it will be more economical to ship packed and ground beans to various retailers. However, this will lessen the strong scent. The coffee business hopes to create a calming, enduring, and recognizable scent for its patrons and build a global brand for its shops.

- Titan Company Limited: Titan guarantees that clients get an engaging sensory experience while visiting Tanishq jeweler stores. The exquisite furnishings and well-designed lighting highlight the visual attractiveness of the jeweler

on show. Customers are invited to interact with the pieces by touching and trying them on to stimulate their sense of touch. Soft music fills the air, providing a relaxing mood, while pleasant smells enhance the entire ambiance, appealing to both the auditory and olfactory senses. These aspects combine to provide Tanishq clients with a distinctive and delightful buying experience.
- Café Coffee Day (CCD): Café Coffee Day (CCD) outlets are intentionally created to engage consumers and provide a welcoming environment.

The scent of freshly made coffee permeates the air, captivating consumers and enhancing their sense of smell. The interior décor, which includes comfortable seating arrangements and soft lighting, improves the visual appeal and provides a welcoming atmosphere. Customers may experience the flavor and texture of CCD's trademark coffee blends, which stimulates their sense of taste.

- Amul: Amul's ice cream parlors offer a sensory experience with a wide variety of flavors and textures. Customers are allowed to experience a variety of ice cream flavors, which will tantalize both their taste and scent. The vivid and creative design of Amul parlors enhances the experience, engaging the visual senses and creating a joyful and pleasurable environment for clients to indulge in.

CONCLUSION

Businesses and marketers are increasingly using sensory marketing. In a manner that other forms of marketing cannot, it may assist you in reaching your target market and clients. In addition to raising sales and income, you may increase customer loyalty and advocacy by appealing to one or more of their five senses. The field of multisensory marketing, which uses the power of sight, sound, touch, taste, and smell to create immersive brand experiences, is explored in a revolutionary way by the theory of sensory marketing. According to this theory, it's critical to interact with customers on a variety of sensory levels to elicit feelings, mold opinions, and affect behavior. Understanding how customer responses are influenced by sensory cues helps marketers create stories that captivate and compel their target audience to do desired actions and be loyal to their brand. Technology breakthroughs have also increased the potential for sensory marketing by bringing cutting-edge instruments like haptic feedback, augmented reality, and virtual reality to boost customer interaction even further.

REFERENCES

Abdolmohamad Sagha, M., Seyyedamiri, N., Foroudi, P., & Akbari, M. (2022). The one thing you need to change is emotions: The effect of multi-sensory marketing on consumer behavior. *Sustainability (Basel)*, 14(4), 2334. 10.3390/su14042334

Arora, M. (2023). Encapsulating Role of Persuasion and Skill Development in Marketing Communication for Brand Building: A Perspective. In *International Handbook of Skill, Education, Learning, and Research Development in Tourism and Hospitality* (pp. 1–17). Springer Nature Singapore.

Arora, M. (2024). Virtual Reality in Education: Analyzing the Literature and Bibliometric State of Knowledge. *Transforming Education with Virtual Reality*, 379-402. 10.1002/9781394200498.ch22

Arora, M. (2024). Metaverse Metamorphosis: Bridging the Gap Between Research Insights and Industry Applications. In *Research, Innovation, and Industry Impacts of the Metaverse* (pp. 275-286).

Arora, M., & Sharma, R. L. (2023). Artificial intelligence and big data: Ontological and communicative perspectives in multi-sectoral scenarios of modern businesses. *Foresight*, 25(1), 126–143. 10.1108/FS-10-2021-0216

Barloso, K. (2023, December 21). *How to use sensory marketing to boost brand appeal*. Thrive Internet Marketing Agency. https://thriveagency.com/news/sensory -marketing/

Bhatia, R., Garg, R., Chhikara, R., Kataria, A., & Talwar, V. (2021). Sensory marketing–a review and research agenda. *Academy of Marketing Studies Journal*, 25(4), 1–30.

Campelo, A. (2017). Smell it, taste it, hear it, touch it and see it to make sense of this place. In *Handbook on place branding and marketing* (pp. 124–144). Edward Elgar Publishing. 10.4337/9781784718602.00018

Canniford, R., Riach, K., & Hill, T. (2018). Nosenography: How smell constitutes meaning, identity and temporal experience in spatial assemblages. *Marketing Theory*, 18(2), 234–248. 10.1177/1470593117732462

Castro, W. R. A., Montes, L. S. P., & Vera, G. R. (2015). Auditory Stimuli in Neuro-marketing Practices; Case: Unicentro Shopping Mall in Cúcuta, Colombia. *Cuadernos de administración, 31*(53), 117-129.

Chandel, M., & Arora, M. (2024). Metaverse Perspectives: Unpacking Its Role in Shaping Sustainable Development Goals-A Qualitative Inquiry. In *Research, Innovation, and Industry Impacts of the Metaverse* (pp. 62-75). IGI Global.

Fürst, A., Pečornik, N., & Binder, C. (2021). All or nothing in sensory marketing: Must all or only some sensory attributes be congruent with a product's primary function? *Journal of Retailing*, 97(3), 439–458. 10.1016/j.jretai.2020.09.006

Gupta, S. D., Shah, M. M. A. D., Prasad, K. H., & Vishwaja, P. (2022). Effect of auditory signals in sensory marketing: Evidence from India. *International Journal of Business Excellence*, 28(1), 75–89. 10.1504/IJBEX.2022.125765

Haase, J., Wiedmann, K. P., & Bettels, J. (2020). Sensory imagery in advertising: How the senses affect perceived product design and consumer attitude. *Journal of Marketing Communications*, 26(5), 475–487. 10.1080/13527266.2018.1518257

Haase, J., Wiedmann, K. P., & Bettels, J. (2020). Sensory imagery in advertising: How the senses affect perceived product design and consumer attitude. *Journal of Marketing Communications*, 26(5), 475–487. 10.1080/13527266.2018.1518257

Helmefalk, M. (2019). Browsing behaviour as a mediator: The impact of multi-sensory cues on purchasing. *Journal of Consumer Marketing*, 36(2), 253–263. 10.1108/JCM-10-2017-2392

Henshaw, V., Medway, D., Warnaby, G., & Perkins, C. (2016). Marketing the 'city of smells'. *Marketing Theory*, 16(2), 153–170. 10.1177/1470593115619970

. Hussain, S. (2019). Sensory marketing strategies and consumer behavior: Sensible selling using all five senses. *IUP Journal of Business Strategy, 16*(3).

Jiménez-Marín, G., Bellido-Pérez, E., & López-Cortés, Á. (2019). Sensory Marketing: The Concept, Its Techniques And Its Application At The Point Of Sale. *Revista de Comunicación'Vivat Academia*, (148).

Joy, A., Wang, J. J., Orazi, D. C., Yoon, S., LaTour, K., & Peña, C. (2023). Co-creating affective atmospheres in retail experience. *Journal of Retailing*, 99(2), 297–317. 10.1016/j.jretai.2023.05.002

Koszembar-Wiklik, M. (2019). Sensory marketing–sensory communication and its social perception. *Communication Today*, 10(2), 146–156.

Krishna, A. (2012). An integrative review of sensory marketing: Engaging the senses to affect perception, judgment and behavior. *Journal of Consumer Psychology*, 22(3), 332–351. 10.1016/j.jcps.2011.08.003

Krishna, A., Cian, L., & Sokolova, T. (2016). The power of sensory marketing in advertising. *Current Opinion in Psychology*, 10, 142–147. 10.1016/j.copsyc.2016.01.007

Kulkarni, P., & Kolli, H. (2022). Sensory Marketing Theory: How Sensorial Stimuli Influence Consumer Behavior and Subconscious Decision-Making. *Journal of Student Research*, 11(3). Advance online publication. 10.47611/jsrhs.v11i3.3403

Kumar, J., Arora, M., & Erkol Bayram, G. (Eds.). (2024). *Research, Innovation, and Industry Impacts of the Metaverse*. IGI Global.

Kumar, J., Arora, M., & Erkol Bayram, G. (Eds.). (2024). *Exploring the Use of Metaverse in Business and Education*. IGI Global. 10.4018/979-8-3693-5868-9

Kumra, R., & Arora, S. (2022). Digital sensory marketing factors affecting customers' intentions to continue organic online purchases during COVID in India. *FIIB Business Review, 23197145221105674*.

Liu, Y. A., Shen, Y., Luo, C., & Chan, H. C. (2021). Reach out and touch: Eliciting the sense of touch through gesture-based interaction. *Journal of the Association for Information Systems*, 22(6), 1686–1714. 10.17705/1jais.00704

Lluch, D. L., & Artiaga, L. N. (2017). 6. The sense of touch. In *Sensory and aroma marketing* (pp. 127–146). Academic. 10.3920/978-90-8686-841-4_6

Morrin, M., & Tepper, B. J. (2021). Multisensory marketing: Effects of environmental aroma cues on perception, appetite, and consumption of foods and drinks. *Current Opinion in Food Science*, 40, 204–210. 10.1016/j.cofs.2021.04.008

Nenkov, G. Y., Morrin, M., Maille, V., Rank-Christman, T., & Lwin, M. O. (2019). Sense and sensibility: The impact of visual and auditory sensory input on marketplace morality. *Journal of Business Research*, 95, 428–441. 10.1016/j.jbusres.2018.07.047

Nwachukwu, D. (2022, October 22). *Engaging skeptic customers through Sensory Marketing Strategies Part 2: Using the sense of touch (tactile marketing) to appeal to customers emotion*. LinkedIn. https://www.linkedin.com/pulse/engaging-skeptic-customers-through-sensory-marketing-nwachukwu-ph-d-1f/

Oduguwa, E. (2015). *How Taste and Sight Impact Brand Loyalty in Sensory Marketing*.

Petit, O., Velasco, C., & Spence, C. (2019). Digital sensory marketing: Integrating new technologies into multisensory online experience. *Journal of Interactive Marketing*, 45(1), 42–61. 10.1016/j.intmar.2018.07.004

Petit, O., Velasco, C., & Spence, C. (2019). Digital sensory marketing: Integrating new technologies into multisensory online experience. *Journal of Interactive Marketing*, 45(1), 42–61. 10.1016/j.intmar.2018.07.004

Ranaweera, A. T., Martin, B. A., & Jin, H. S. (2021). What you touch, touches you: The influence of haptic attributes on consumer product impressions. *Psychology and Marketing*, 38(1), 183–195. 10.1002/mar.21433

Rathee, R., & Rajain, P. (2017). Sensory marketing-investigating the use of five senses. *International Journal of Research in Finance and Marketing*, 7(5), 124–133.

Salluca, M. Y., Valeriano, D. Y. A., Gutierrez, R. A., & Valeriano, H. A. (2022). Marketing sensorial y su incidencia en la toma de decisiones de los consumidores. *Revista Venezolana de Gerencia*, 27(8), 1263–1279. 10.52080/rvgluz.27.8.34

Shabgou, M., & Daryani, S. M. (2014). Towards the sensory marketing: Stimulating the five senses (sight, hearing, smell, touch and taste) and its impact on consumer behavior. *Indian Journal of Fundamental and Applied Life Sciences*, 4(1), 573–581.

Singh, S., Chandrakar, P., Jamsandekar, S., Ranjan, A., & Wanjari, S. (2020). A Review on The Impact of Sensory Marketing on Consumer Buying Behaviour. *Global Scientific Journals*, 8(6), 1308–1318.

Spence, C. (2021). Musical scents: On the surprising absence of scented musical/auditory events, entertainments, and experiences. *i-Perception, 12*(5), 20416695211038747.

Spence, C., & Levitan, C. A. (2021). Explaining crossmodal correspondences between colours and tastes. *i-Perception, 12*(3), 20416695211018223.

Wiedmann, K. P., Labenz, F., Haase, J., & Hennigs, N. (2018). The power of experiential marketing: Exploring the causal relationships among multisensory marketing, brand experience, customer perceived value and brand strength. *Journal of Brand Management*, 25(2), 101–118. 10.1057/s41262-017-0061-5

Wistoft, K., & Qvortrup, L. (2021). Seven dimensions of taste—taste in a sociological and educational perspective. In *Gastronomy and food science* (pp. 227–251). Academic Press. 10.1016/B978-0-12-820057-5.00012-1

Yoganathan, V., Osburg, V. S., & Akhtar, P. (2019). Sensory stimulation for sensible consumption: Multisensory marketing for e-tailing of ethical brands. *Journal of Business Research*, 96, 386–396. 10.1016/j.jbusres.2018.06.005

Zha, D. (2021). Gustative signatures as corporate brand identifiers: exploring the sensuality of taste as a marketing strategy. In *Corporate Brand Design* (pp. 251–263). Routledge. 10.4324/9781003054153-21

Chapter 4
Multi–Sensory Experience:
The Basic Building Blocks

Anuj Pal Kapoor
Indian Institute of Technology, Jodhpur, India

Raveena Gupta
Faculty of Management Studies, University of Delhi, India

Harsh Verma
Faculty of Management Studies, University of Delhi, India

ABSTRACT

Multi-Sensory experience explores the dynamic interplay of various sensory modalities in shaping human perception. The present work delves into the richness and complexity of multisensory integration, investigating how the brain synthesizes inputs from the five senses to construct a cohesive perceptual reality. It examines the role of multisensory experiences in enhancing cognitive processes, emotional responses, and behavioral outcomes. Understanding the mechanisms underlying multisensory perception is crucial for diverse fields, including neuroscience, psychology, design, marketing, and education. The present chapter underscores the significance of multisensory experiences in shaping human experiences and highlights avenues for further research and application in creating more engaging and impactful environments and interventions. By elucidating the basic building blocks of multisensory experience, the study contributes to a deeper comprehension of human perception, offering insights with far-reaching implications for fields ranging from neuroscience and psychology.

DOI: 10.4018/979-8-3693-4236-7.ch004

INTRODUCTION

In the intricate tapestry of human perception, the senses serve as the conduits through which we interact with and interpret the world. From the gentle caress of a breeze on the skin to the vibrant hues of a sunset painting the sky, our experiences are profoundly shaped by the myriad sensations that permeate our daily lives. At the heart of this sensory symphony lies the phenomenon of multisensory experience, a captivating interplay of sight, sound, touch, taste, and smell that converges to create a rich and multifaceted perception of reality.

The study of multisensory experience represents a fascinating intersection of neuroscience, psychology, and philosophy, offering profound insights into the fundamental mechanisms underlying human cognition and consciousness (Spence, 2004). By exploring how the brain integrates information from diverse sensory modalities, researchers seek to unravel the intricate workings of perception and unravel the mysteries of subjective experience (Calvert et al., 2004).

At its essence, multisensory experience is a testament to the remarkable versatility and adaptability of the human mind. From the moment we are born, we are immersed in a world teeming with sensory stimuli, each one vying for our attention and shaping our understanding of the environment. Through a process known as multisensory integration, the brain seamlessly combines inputs from different senses to form a unified perceptual representation of the world (Spence, 2004). This integration not only enhances the richness and depth of our experiences but also plays a crucial role in guiding our actions and decisions. One of the most remarkable aspects of multisensory experience is its ability to transcend the boundaries of individual sensory modalities, giving rise to novel perceptual phenomena that are greater than the sum of their parts. For example, the McGurk effect demonstrates how auditory and visual inputs can interact to create a perception of speech that differs from either modality alone. Similarly, the phenomenon of synesthesia blurs the lines between senses, leading individuals to perceive colors when hearing music or experiencing tastes in response to certain sounds.

Moreover, multisensory experiences are not confined to laboratory settings or controlled environments but are an integral part of everyday life. From the aroma of freshly brewed coffee awakening our senses in the morning to the comforting embrace of a loved one's hug, our daily experiences are imbued with a rich tapestry of sensory stimuli that shape our emotions, memories, and sense of identity. Understanding the intricacies of multisensory experience has far-reaching implications across a myriad of fields, ranging from healthcare and education to marketing and design. In healthcare, multisensory interventions have been shown to enhance patient well-being and facilitate recovery, while in education, they can foster more engaging and effective learning environments. In design and marketing, an understanding of multisensory perception can be leveraged to create products and experiences that captivate and resonate with consumers on a deeper level.

Through a multidisciplinary lens, we seek to shed light on the fundamental mechanisms of multisensory integration and explore the profound implications of these phenomena for science, society, and the human experience. In a world inundated with stimuli, where technology has advanced to unprecedented levels, the human experience is constantly evolving. In today's world, the design of multi-sensory experiences is increasingly recognized as a valuable tool across various domains. In marketing and advertising, for example, companies strive to create multi-sensory brand experiences that engage multiple senses, aiming to leave a stronger impression on consumers. Understanding the multi-sensory nature of human experience has profound implications for our interactions with the world and our ability to create meaningful, immersive, and engaging experiences. As we continue to explore the intricate interplay between our senses, we gain deeper insights into the richness and depth of human perception and cognition.

Understanding Multi-Sensory Experiences

At its core, a multi-sensory experience engages more than one of the human senses simultaneously. While traditional experiences often target one or two senses, such as sight or sound, multi-sensory experiences leverage a combination of sensory inputs to create a holistic and immersive encounter. The senses involved typically include sight, sound, touch, taste, and smell. By integrating these sensory modalities, multi-sensory experiences have the potential to captivate individuals on a deeper level, triggering a cascade of sensory responses that enhance engagement and leave a lasting impression.

Figure 1. Multi-Sensory framework

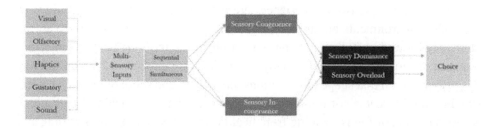

Literature Review

The theoretical foundation of multisensory experience is rooted in the understanding that human perception is inherently multimodal. Early research by psychologists like Ernst Weber and Gustav Fechner laid the groundwork for sensory integration, highlighting how different sensory inputs are combined to form coherent perceptions (Stein & Meredith, 1993). The concept of sensory integration posits that the brain processes information from various senses to create a unified representation of the environment (Calvert, Spence, & Stein, 2004). Neuroscientific research has advanced the understanding of the neural mechanisms underlying multisensory integration. Studies using functional magnetic resonance imaging (fMRI) and electroencephalography (EEG) have identified specific brain regions, such as the superior colliculus and the multisensory cortex, that are involved in processing multisensory information (Ghazanfar & Schroeder, 2006). These regions play a crucial role in enhancing perceptual accuracy and reaction times by integrating inputs from different senses. From a psychological perspective, multisensory experience significantly influences cognitive functions such as attention, memory, and learning. The dual coding theory, proposed by Paivio (1971), suggests that information is better retained when presented through multiple sensory channels. For instance, combining visual and auditory information can enhance memory recall and comprehension compared to using a single sensory modality (Mayer, 2001). In the field of marketing, multisensory experience is leveraged to create more engaging and memorable consumer experiences. Research has shown that sensory marketing, which involves appealing to multiple senses, can significantly influence consumer behaviour and brand perception (Krishna, 2012). For example, the use of scent in retail environments has been found to enhance the shopping experience and increase the time spent in stores (Spangenberg, Crowley, & Henderson, 1996). Educational settings also benefit from multisensory approaches, as they cater to diverse learning styles and improve information retention. Multisensory teaching strategies, which incorporate visual, auditory, and kinesthetic elements, have been shown to enhance student engagement and academic performance (Felder & Silverman, 1988). These methods are particularly effective for students with learning disabilities, as they provide multiple pathways for understanding and recalling information. Advancements in technology have further expanded the possibilities for multisensory experiences. Virtual reality (VR) and augmented reality (AR) platforms offer immersive environments that engage multiple senses simultaneously, creating more realistic and impactful experiences (Biocca & Delaney, (1995); (Arora, 2023). AI enhances VR and AR platforms by personalizing experiences, improving realism through advanced graphics and behavior modeling, and enabling real-time data processing for more interactive and engaging environments ((Arora & Sharma, 2023). These technologies are being used in various fields, including education, training, and entertainment, to enhance user engagement and effectiveness (Kumar, Arora & Erkol Bayram, (Eds.). (2024); (Rathore & Arora, (2024); (Dhiman & Arora, (2024); Arora, (2024).

The multisensory experience is a critical aspect of human perception and interaction with the environment. It enhances cognitive processing, memory, and emotional engagement across various domains, including psychology, neuroscience, marketing, and education. Continued research and technological advancements will likely uncover new applications and insights into the benefits of multisensory integration, further emphasizing its importance in enhancing human experiences.

Building Blocks

Multi-sensory experiences involve the integration of various sensory modalities to create a richer and more immersive perception. The building blocks of multi-sensory experiences typically include:

Sensory congruence/in-congruence refers to the alignment or harmony between different sensory modalities within an experience. When sensory stimuli across various modalities are consistent or complementary, it enhances the overall coherence and effectiveness of the experience. Elements defining sensory congruence are:

1. **Consistency**: Sensory stimuli are consistent when they convey the same message or theme across different modalities. For example, in a multi-sensory art installation depicting a forest scene, visual elements such as trees and foliage should be accompanied by auditory cues like rustling leaves and chirping birds to maintain consistency across sight and sound.
2. **Complementarity**: While consistency is important, sensory experiences can also benefit from complementarity, where different modalities enhance each other without necessarily replicating the same information. For instance, a visual presentation of a beach scene might be complemented by the sound of waves crashing and the scent of saltwater, creating a more immersive experience that stimulates multiple senses simultaneously.
3. **Integration**: Sensory congruence involves integrating various sensory inputs seamlessly to create a unified and immersive experience. This integration ensures that different modalities work together harmoniously rather than competing or conflicting with each other.
4. **Emotional Resonance**: When sensory stimuli are congruent, they are more likely to evoke consistent emotional responses across different individuals. For example, a multi-sensory dining experience that combines visually appealing presentation, aromatic scents, and flavorful tastes can evoke feelings of delight and satisfaction in diners, enhancing their overall enjoyment of the meal.

5. **Contextual Relevance**: Sensory congruence also depends on the context of the experience and the intended message or theme. For instance, in a virtual reality simulation of a space adventure, sensory congruence requires aligning visual, auditory, and tactile cues to create a convincing and immersive portrayal of outer space.

Overall, sensory congruence plays a vital role in creating engaging and immersive experiences across various domains, including art, entertainment, marketing, education, and therapy. By carefully aligning and integrating sensory stimuli, creators can enhance the impact and effectiveness of their multi-sensory experiences, fostering deeper engagement and emotional resonance with participants.

Sensory Dominance

Sensory dominance refers to the phenomenon where one sensory modality takes precedence over others in processing and perception (Stein et al., 1993). Humans rely on multiple sensory modalities, such as vision, hearing, touch, taste, and smell, to perceive and interact with the world. However, in certain situations, one sense may dominate over others, influencing perception, decision-making, and behavior. Elements defining sensory dominance are:

1. **Visual Dominance**: Vision is often considered the dominant sense in humans. Visual information typically receives more attention and processing resources than other sensory modalities. In many situations, people rely primarily on visual cues to gather information about their environment, recognize objects, and navigate their surroundings.
2. **Auditory Dominance**: While vision tends to dominate in many contexts, auditory dominance can occur in certain situations. For example, in a dark or visually cluttered environment, people may rely more on auditory cues to orient themselves and perceive their surroundings. Additionally, auditory stimuli such as alarms or loud noises can capture attention and override other sensory inputs.
3. **Tactile Dominance**: In some cases, touch or tactile sensations can dominate perception, especially when other sensory modalities are impaired or when tactile information is particularly salient. For instance, people may rely heavily on tactile feedback when exploring objects in a dark or visually obscured environment.
4. **Cross-Modal Interactions**: Sensory dominance can also be influenced by interactions between different sensory modalities. For example, the McGurk effect demonstrates how visual information can override auditory perception,

leading to the perception of different speech sounds when visual and auditory cues are incongruent.

5. **Individual Differences**: Sensory dominance can vary among individuals based on factors such as sensory acuity, prior experience, and cognitive processing styles. Some people may be more visually dominant, while others may rely more on auditory or tactile information in their perception and decision-making.

Understanding sensory dominance is essential for designing effective multi-sensory experiences and interfaces. By considering the relative dominance of different sensory modalities, designers can prioritize the presentation of information and stimuli to optimize user experience and engagement. Additionally, acknowledging sensory dominance can help researchers and practitioners develop strategies to address sensory biases and enhance accessibility for individuals with sensory impairments. Entrepreneurs in this era drive innovation and unlock new marketing opportunities by leveraging cutting-edge technologies and creative business models (Arora & Sharma,2021); Dhiman & Arora, 2024). Entrepreneurs are drivers of economic development and growth, significantly influencing consumer behaviour through innovative products and services (Arora, 2016). Big data and artificial intelligence help entrepreneurs by providing deep insights into market trends and consumer behavior, enabling more informed and strategic decision-making. Sensory marketing, like AI-enhanced VR/AR and big data analytics, creates personalized and immersive consumer experiences, driving deeper engagement and more effective marketing strategies.

Sensory Overload

Sensory overload occurs when an individual's sensory systems are overwhelmed by excessive or intense stimuli, leading to difficulties in processing and integrating sensory information (Deroy and Spence, 2013). This phenomenon can occur in various environments and situations, ranging from crowded public spaces to sensory-rich experiences such as concerts or theme parks.

1. **Multiple Stimuli**: Sensory overload often involves exposure to multiple sensory stimuli simultaneously, including visual, auditory, tactile, olfactory, and gustatory inputs. For example, being in a crowded and noisy environment where there are bright lights, loud music, and strong odors can overwhelm the senses.

2. **Overstimulation**: Excessive or intense sensory inputs can lead to overstimulation of the nervous system, causing heightened arousal and stress responses. Individuals may feel agitated, anxious, or irritable in response to sensory overload.

3. **Difficulty Concentrating**: Sensory overload can impair attention and concentration, making it challenging to focus on specific tasks or conversations. The abundance of sensory information competing for attention can disrupt cognitive processing and lead to mental fatigue.
4. **Physical Discomfort**: In addition to cognitive effects, sensory overload can cause physical discomfort, such as headaches, dizziness, or muscle tension. Prolonged exposure to overwhelming sensory stimuli may also contribute to sensory fatigue and exhaustion.
5. **Emotional Distress**: Sensory overload can elicit emotional responses such as frustration, overwhelm, or panic. Individuals may feel overwhelmed by the inability to filter or regulate sensory inputs, leading to feelings of helplessness or distress.
6. **Sensory Sensitivities**: Some individuals are more susceptible to sensory overload due to sensory sensitivities or sensory processing disorders, such as autism spectrum disorder or sensory processing disorder. In these cases, even moderate levels of sensory stimulation can trigger overwhelming reactions.
7. **Impact on Daily Functioning**: Severe or chronic sensory overload can significantly impact daily functioning and quality of life. It may interfere with social interactions, work performance, and participation in everyday activities, leading to increased stress and decreased well-being.

Managing sensory overload involves strategies to reduce sensory stimuli, regulate arousal levels, and provide support for individuals experiencing distress. This may include creating calm and quiet environments, using sensory tools like earplugs or noise-canceling headphones, practicing relaxation techniques, and implementing sensory accommodations for individuals with sensory sensitivities. By addressing sensory overload proactively, individuals can better cope with overwhelming sensory experiences and improve their overall comfort and well-being.

The Impact of Multi-Sensory Experiences in Marketing

In the realm of marketing, creating memorable brand experiences is paramount to success. Multi-sensory marketing strategies recognize the power of sensory stimuli in influencing consumer behavior and brand perception. For instance, consider the immersive retail environments crafted by leading brands like Apple and Nike. These stores are designed to engage customers on multiple sensory levels, from the sleek visual aesthetics to the tactile product displays and ambient music with a suitable aroma. By appealing to multiple senses, these brands foster emotional connections with consumers, leading to increased brand loyalty and purchase intent.

Moreover, research suggests that multi-sensory marketing can significantly impact consumer decision-making processes (Ernst et al., 2007). Studies have shown that sensory cues, such as the texture of packaging or the aroma of a product or store, can evoke strong emotional responses and influence purchase behavior. In a competitive market landscape, companies are increasingly leveraging multi-sensory strategies to differentiate their brands and create unique experiences that resonate with consumers on a visceral level.

The Role of Multi-Sensory Experiences in Decision Making

Human decision-making is a complex process influenced by various factors, including cognitive biases, emotions, and environmental stimuli (Velasco and Obrist, 2020). Among these stimuli, multi-sensory experiences play a significant role in shaping perceptions, preferences, and ultimately, the decisions we make. This essay explores the intersection of multi-sensory experiences and decision-making, examining how sensory inputs impact our choices in areas such as consumer behavior, product design, and environmental settings.

Multi-sensory decision making involves the integration of sensory information from multiple modalities, including sight, sound, touch, taste, and smell, to form judgments and make choices. Unlike unisensory experiences, which target a single sense, multi-sensory stimuli engage multiple sensory channels simultaneously, amplifying the overall sensory experience and influencing decision processes.

Research in cognitive psychology has demonstrated that sensory cues can exert a profound influence on decision-making processes, often operating at a subconscious level. For example, studies have shown that the color, texture, and shape of products can influence consumers' perceptions of quality and value, affecting their purchasing decisions. Similarly, environmental stimuli such as background music, lighting, and aroma can shape the ambiance of retail spaces and influence consumer behavior.

The Impact of Multi-Sensory Experiences on Consumer Behavior

In the realm of consumer behavior, multi-sensory experiences play a crucial role in shaping preferences, attitudes, and purchase decisions (Velasco and Obrist, 2020). Retailers and marketers leverage sensory cues to create immersive brand experiences that resonate with consumers on an emotional level, driving engagement and loyalty. For instance, consider the role of sensory branding in the food and beverage industry. Companies utilize packaging design, color psychology, and flavor profiles to evoke specific sensory associations and enhance brand recognition. Similarly, the ambiance of retail environments, including lighting, music, and scent, can influence consumers' perception of a brand's personality and value proposition.

Moreover, research suggests that sensory-rich experiences can lead to increased willingness to pay and higher levels of satisfaction among consumers. By engaging multiple senses, brands can create memorable moments that leave a lasting impression, fostering stronger connections with their target audience.

Product Design and Multi-Sensory Perception: In addition to consumer behavior, multi-sensory experiences influence the design and perception of products across various industries. Designers and engineers leverage sensory cues to enhance the functionality, aesthetics, and usability of products, catering to the sensory preferences of end-users. For example, in automotive design, manufacturers consider factors such as the tactile feel of materials, the sound of engine revving, and the visual aesthetics of interior and exterior features. By harmonizing these sensory elements, carmakers create vehicles that evoke positive emotional responses and enhance the overall driving experience.

Similarly, in product packaging, designers pay careful attention to sensory cues such as texture, color, and shape to create packaging that not only protects the product but also communicates its value and quality to consumers. Studies have shown that sensory-rich packaging can influence perceptions of taste and freshness, impacting consumers' willingness to purchase and repurchase products.

Environmental Design and Multi-Sensory Engagement

Beyond consumer products, multi-sensory experiences shape the design of built environments, including retail spaces, restaurants, and urban landscapes. Architects and urban planners recognize the importance of sensory cues in creating spaces that are both functional and aesthetically pleasing, fostering positive experiences for occupants and visitors. For instance, consider the design of shopping malls and commercial complexes. Architects incorporate elements such as natural light, spatial layout, and ambient music to create immersive environments that encourage exploration and social interaction. Similarly, in urban planning, considerations such as street furniture, landscaping, and public art contribute to the sensory richness of public spaces, enhancing the quality of life for residents and visitors alike.

Moreover, the concept of sensory urbanism emphasizes the importance of designing cities and neighborhoods that engage the senses and promote well-being. From sensory gardens and green spaces to interactive public installations, cities are increasingly embracing multi-sensory design principles to create vibrant and inclusive urban environments.

Education and Multi-Sensory Learning

In the field of education, multi-sensory approaches have long been recognized as effective tools for enhancing learning outcomes, particularly for individuals with diverse learning styles or sensory processing differences. Multi-sensory learning techniques engage students through a combination of visual, auditory, and kinaesthetic activities, catering to different modes of learning and reinforcing comprehension.

For example, educators often employ hands-on experiments, multimedia presentations, and interactive simulations to facilitate multi-sensory learning experiences. By incorporating tactile materials, audio-visual aids, and real-world examples, teachers can create dynamic learning environments that appeal to a broad range of learners. Research has shown that multi-sensory learning not only improves retention and understanding but also promotes active participation and critical thinking skills.

Challenges and Considerations

Despite the potential benefits of multi-sensory experiences in decision-making, there are challenges and considerations that must be addressed. One challenge is the potential for sensory overload or sensory mismatches, which can lead to cognitive fatigue or negative experiences. Designers and marketers must strike a balance between engaging multiple senses and ensuring a coherent and enjoyable experience for users. Furthermore, considerations of accessibility and inclusivity are essential in designing multi-sensory experiences that cater to diverse sensory needs and preferences. Ensuring that sensory-rich environments are welcoming and accommodating to individuals with sensory impairments or disabilities requires careful attention to design principles and guidelines. Furthermore, the rise of experiential entertainment venues, such as escape rooms and interactive museums, underscores the growing demand for multi-sensory experiences. These immersive attractions blur the line between reality and fiction, allowing participants to become active participants in the narrative. By engaging multiple senses, these experiences foster deeper levels of engagement and encourage social interaction among participants.

For instance, designing effective multi-sensory experiences requires careful attention to sensory balance and coherence. Overstimulation or mismatched sensory cues can detract from the overall experience and lead to sensory fatigue or discomfort. Furthermore, accessibility is a critical consideration in ensuring that multi-sensory experiences are inclusive and accommodating to individuals with sensory impairments or disabilities. Designing experiences that accommodate diverse sensory needs requires collaboration with experts in accessibility and inclusive design to ensure equal participation and enjoyment for all individuals.

Future Scope

The future of multi-sensory experiences holds immense potential for transforming the way we perceive and interact with the world around us. As technology continues to advance, we can expect to see the emergence of novel and innovative multi-sensory interfaces that seamlessly blend various sensory modalities, creating truly immersive and captivating experiences.

One area of significant promise is virtual and augmented reality (VR/AR) technologies. These platforms have already begun to incorporate multi-sensory elements, such as haptic feedback and spatial audio, alongside vivid visual displays. However, future iterations of VR/AR systems could take multi-sensory immersion to new heights by incorporating olfactory and gustatory stimuli, allowing users to experience realistic scents and tastes in virtual environments. This could revolutionize fields like education, training, and entertainment, enabling learners and audiences to engage with content in profoundly visceral and memorable ways.

The field of multi-sensory human-computer interaction (HCI) is also poised for significant advancements. As we move beyond traditional input methods like keyboards and mice, researchers are exploring innovative ways to leverage multi-sensory inputs for more intuitive and natural interactions with digital devices. Gesture recognition, voice control, and even brain-computer interfaces (BCIs) could be combined with haptic feedback, creating seamless multi-sensory interfaces that feel like natural extensions of our bodies and senses.

Moreover, the Internet of Things (IoT) and smart environments have the potential to create multi-sensory experiences that seamlessly integrate into our daily lives. Imagine homes and workplaces that can adapt lighting, temperature, ambient sounds, and even aromas based on our preferences and activities, creating tailored multi-sensory atmospheres that promote well-being, productivity, and overall satisfaction.

As our understanding of multi-sensory perception and cognition deepens, we may also witness groundbreaking applications in fields like healthcare and therapy. For instance, multi-sensory stimulation could be used to enhance rehabilitation processes for individuals with sensory impairments or to aid in the treatment of conditions like post-traumatic stress disorder (PTSD) or anxiety disorders.

The future scope of multi-sensory experiences is vast and exciting, promising to revolutionize the way we learn, work, play, and navigate the world around us. By harnessing the power of multiple sensory modalities, we can create richer, more engaging, and more meaningful experiences that tap into the full depth of human perception and cognition.

CONCLUSION

In conclusion, the exploration of multisensory experience unveils the remarkable complexity and richness of human perception. Through the intricate interplay of sight, sound, touch, taste, and smell, we navigate a world brimming with sensory stimuli, each contributing to our understanding of reality in unique and profound ways. The phenomenon of multisensory integration, whereby the brain synthesizes information from diverse sensory modalities to create a unified perceptual representation, underscores the remarkable adaptability and versatility of the human mind. Moreover, multisensory experiences transcend the boundaries of individual sensory modalities, giving rise to novel perceptual phenomena and enriching our understanding of the human experience. Beyond the realm of scientific inquiry, the study of multisensory experience holds profound implications for a wide range of fields, from healthcare and education to design and marketing. By leveraging an understanding of multisensory perception, researchers and practitioners can develop interventions and experiences that enhance well-being, facilitate learning, and create more engaging and impactful environments.

As we continue to unravel the mysteries of multisensory experience, it is clear that our perception of reality is far more nuanced and dynamic than previously imagined. Through ongoing research and exploration, we stand poised to unlock new insights into the fundamental mechanisms of perception and harness the power of multisensory integration to enrich lives and deepen our understanding of the human condition. In conclusion, multi-sensory experiences represent a powerful tool for enhancing human engagement, communication, and well-being across various domains. From marketing and entertainment to education and therapy, the integration of sensory stimuli offers opportunities for deeper connections and more meaningful interactions. By leveraging the innate power of the senses, creators and innovators can unlock new dimensions of human experience and shape the future of immersive storytelling and sensory design. As technology continues to advance, the potential for multi-sensory experiences to enrich our lives and expand our sensory horizons is virtually limitless.

REFERENCES

Arora, M. (2016). Creative dimensions of entrepreneurship: A key to business innovation. *Pacific Business Review International*, 1(1), 255–259.

Arora, M. (2023). Encapsulating Role of Persuasion and Skill Development in Marketing Communication for Brand Building: A Perspective. In *International Handbook of Skill, Education, Learning, and Research Development in Tourism and Hospitality* (pp. 1–17). Springer Nature Singapore.

Arora, M. (2024). Virtual Reality in Education: Analyzing the Literature and Bibliometric State of Knowledge. *Transforming Education with Virtual Reality*, 379-402. 10.1002/9781394200498.ch22

Arora, M., & Sharma, R. L. (2021). Repurposing the Role of Entrepreneurs in the Havoc of COVID-19. In *Entrepreneurship and Big Data* (pp. 229-250). CRC Press.

Arora, M., & Sharma, R. L. (2022). Coalescing skills of gig players and fervor of entrepreneurial leaders to provide resilience strategies during global economic crises. In *COVID-19's Impact on the Cryptocurrency Market and the Digital Economy* (pp. 118–140). IGI Global. 10.4018/978-1-7998-9117-8.ch008

Arora, M., & Sharma, R. L. (2023). Artificial intelligence and big data: Ontological and communicative perspectives in multi-sectoral scenarios of modern businesses. *Foresight*, 25(1), 126–143. 10.1108/FS-10-2021-0216

Auvray, M., & Spence, C. (2008). The multisensory perception of flavor. *Consciousness and Cognition*, 17(3), 1016–1031. 10.1016/j.concog.2007.06.00517689100

Biocca, F., & Delaney, B. (1995). Immersive virtual reality technology. In Biocca, F., & Levy, M. R. (Eds.), *Communication in the age of virtual reality* (pp. 57–124). Lawrence Erlbaum Associates.

Calvert, G. A., Spence, C., & Stein, B. E. (Eds.). (2004). *Handbook of multisensory processes*. MIT press. 10.7551/mitpress/3422.001.0001

Deroy, O., & Spence, C. (Eds.). (2013). *Multisensory flavor perception: From fundamental neuroscience through to the marketplace*. Frontiers Media SA.

Dhiman, V., & Arora, M. (2024). Current State of Metaverse in Entrepreneurial Ecosystem: A Retrospective Analysis of Its Evolving Landscape. In *Exploring the Use of Metaverse in Business and Education* (pp. 73-87). IGI Global. 10.4018/979-8-3693-5868-9.ch005

. Dhiman, V., & Arora, M. (2024). Exploring the linkage between business incuba-tion and entrepreneurship: understanding trends, themes and future research agenda. *LBS Journal of Management & Research.*

Ernst, M. O., Lange, C., & Newell, F. N. (2007). Multisensory recognition of actively explored objects. *Canadian Journal of Experimental Psychology*, 61(3), 242–253. 10.1037/cjep200702517974318

Felder, R. M., & Silverman, L. K. (1988). Learning and teaching styles in engineering education. *Engineering Education*, 78(7), 674–681.

Krishna, A. (2012). An integrative review of sensory marketing: Engaging the sens-es to affect perception, judgment and behavior. *Journal of Consumer Psychology*, 22(3), 332–351. 10.1016/j.jcps.2011.08.003

Kumar, J., Arora, M., & Erkol Bayram, G. (Eds.). (2024). *Exploring the Use of Metaverse in Business and Education*. IGI Global. 10.4018/979-8-3693-5868-9

Paivio, A. (1971). *Imagery and verbal processes*. Holt, Rinehart, and Winston.

Rathore, S., & Arora, M. (2024). Sustainability Reporting in the Metaverse: A Multi-Sectoral Analysis. In *Exploring the Use of Metaverse in Business and Edu-cation* (pp. 147-165). IGI Global. 10.4018/979-8-3693-5868-9.ch009

Spangenberg, E. R., Crowley, A. E., & Henderson, P. W. (1996). Improving the store environment: Do olfactory cues affect evaluations and behaviors? *Journal of Marketing*, 60(2), 67–80. 10.1177/002224299606000205

Spence, C. (2011). Crossmodal correspondences: A tutorial review. *Attention, Per-ception & Psychophysics*, 73(4), 971–995. 10.3758/s13414-010-0073-721264748

Stein, B. E., & Meredith, M. A. (1993). *The merging of the senses*. MIT press.

Velasco, C. (2020). Fundamentals of Multisensory Experiences. *Multisenso-ry Experiences: Where the senses meet technology*. Oxford Online. ,10.1093/oso/9780198849629.003.0002

Chapter 5
Senses Shall Sell:
Origins, Emerging Concepts, and Methods in Sensory Marketing

Shweta Kakhtan

Indian Institute of Technology, Jodhpur, India

Anuj Pal Kapoor

Indian Institute of Technology, Jodhpur, India

ABSTRACT

Marketing to the consumer senses is called sensory marketing. Notably, there has been a swell of interest in sensory marketing pertaining to (a) the role of senses in curating multisensory experiences for consumers, and (b) the recent sensory enabling technological advancements such as AR/VR and GenAI. The present chapter discusses the emergence, evolution, and emerging perspectives in the field. Specifically, the authors have found that the field of sensory marketing is derived from the hedonic consumption concept and emotional aspects of consumption. In addition, a sensory marketing mix has been constructed to delineate the working of senses in marketing. The study found that multisensory experiences form the core of buyer behavior in sensory marketing. Further, future research insights using sensory neuromarketing tools such as eye-tracking, EEG, GSR, and fMRI may be effective in growing the field. Lastly, the authors discuss the emerging perspectives and future directions for new marketing realities.

DOI: 10.4018/979-8-3693-4236-7.ch005

INTRODUCTION

In marketing, the extant understanding of consumer senses in influencing be-havior is constituted within the field of sensory marketing (Krishna & Schwarz, 2014). Sensory marketing is basically marketing that caters to consumers' senses. But why sensory marketing? Our senses are responsible for collecting information from the external environment, this sensory information leads to the construction of a sensory experience, which after being processed by the brain, may result in a behavior or decision. The stimuli present in the external environment are first received by our senses (sensation) and then interpreted by our brain (perception), which may be followed by a reaction (behavior) (Krishna, 2012). Marketers leverage this influence of sensory experiences and construct sensory elements to influence consumer behavior. Recall the experience of someone near you eating lays, can you remember the crunchy sound of them biting the chips and how you were instantly motivated to purchase a packet of lays? While visiting a store, do you observe the light, fragrance, or music that is playing and how instantly you might love to ex-plore the products and spend more time in the store. And how people love visiting Starbucks for a coffee, but not just for the coffee, the woody interiors, the aroma and the dim lighting that soothes one's soul. Similarly, can you remember a body wash smelling like coconuts, giving you the feel of Hawaiian beaches? These are a few instances of the involvement of senses in the marketing world.

Forbes (2022) report recognized the significance of multisensory experiences for brand building in the metaverse. The report stresses that perception is reality; more specifically what and how something is perceived and interpreted is the reality. The recent technological developments are rapidly imbibing sensations for consumers. It is possible to touch, smell and feel through multisensory experiences using aug-mented and virtual realities (AR and VR). In addition, there is a transformation in consumption habits of consumers due to the emerging GenAI and technological innovations. Various industrial reports point in the direction of sensory experiences as technological advancements unfold (BCG, 2024; McKinsey, 2023).

For over two decades now, marketing researchers have delved into understanding how colors, fragrances, pitch of music, aroma of food, and texture/temperature of a surface influence consumer attitude, choice, or perception. Contemporary marketing has moved far beyond merely identifying and meeting the needs of consumers. With the introduction of the hedonic consumption concept by Hirschman and Holbrook (1982), marketing researchers and practitioners shifted focus toward the emotion-al, fun, and multisensory aspects of consumption. Whereas prior, the main focus of marketers was on the utility aspect of consumption, there was a shift towards understanding the emotional behavior of consumers. This shift led to the paradigm shift in marketing research with the introduction of Experiential Economy (Pine &

Gilmore, 1998; Schmitt, 1999). According to the experiential economy perspective, consumers demand much more than just the product, they demand an experience that is memorable, pleasurable, and emotionally satisfying.

Schmitt (1999) classified customer experience into five dimensions, one of which was sensory experience. This became the primary onset of the exploration of senses in marketing. However, it was not until Krishna's (2012) integrative review on the role of senses in marketing that sensory marketing got the status of a separate field of research. The concept of sensory marketing has its roots in the theory of embodied cognition. According to the theory of embodied cognition, our bodily sensations can predict our feelings, behavior, and judgment without the conscious awareness of the mind (Barsalou, 1999; 2008). As stated in the beginning, the bodily sensations through the atmosphere we exist in are the backbone of further processing and action. The objective of this study is to provide a holistic understanding of senses in marketing, particularly the emergence, evolution, and emerging areas in the field.

THE SCOPE OF SENSORY MARKETING

For a successful implementation of sensory marketing, one must understand the origins of the field, the emergence of sensory marketing, what is marketed to the senses, and how it works. These aspects of sensory marketing are discussed below.

Emergence of Senses in Marketing

In marketing, the extant understanding of consumer senses in influencing behavior is constituted under the field of sensory marketing (Krishna & Schwarz, 2014). Krishna (2012) defines sensory marketing as marketing that engages consumer's senses to influence their judgment, perception, and behavior. The emergence of the five senses in marketing is attributable to the fact that human senses are the elemental gateways to information from the external environment. The stimuli from the environment impinge upon the human sense(s), causing a sensation in the human body. The human brain then processes and interprets these bodily sensations to form sensory perceptions (Krishna, 2012). The emergence of senses in marketing has been illustrated in *Figure 1*.

Figure 1. Emergence of senses in marketing

Store Atmospherics	Hedonic Consumption Concept	Experiential Economy	Embodied and Grounded Cognition
Early 1970s: Focus shifted towards store atmospherics to provide the consumers more than the tangible product i.e., a total product	*Early 1980s:* Introduction of the concept highlighted the multisensory, fun, fantasy, and other emotional aspects of consumption.	*Late 1990s:* Consumers demand more than just the product, a memorable experience. Thus, sensory experiences took birth in marketing	*Early 2010s:* Concepts from Psychology proposed notion of bodily states in cognition leading to importance of senses in understanding consumer behavior. Thus, 'Sensory marketing' was introduced as a separate field.

Store Atmospherics

Kotler (1974) first recognized the atmospherics as a marketing tool. The author defined the term atmospherics as "the conscious designing of space to create certain effects in buyers." More specifically, the atmospherics were attributed to the effort of constructing buying environments to produce emotional effects in buyers that may enhance their purchasing probabilities. The term atmospherics is derived from 'atmosphere.' The concept of atmosphere was used to describe the quality of the surroundings. The author noted that the early marketers were ignorant of considering atmospherics as a marketing tool, probably because 1) they were practical and rational thinkers and 2) did not understand that atmospherics are a silent language of communication. In addition, the author noted that the purchase decision-making of buyers was not merely limited to the tangible product but the total product. The total product constitutes services, warranties, packaging, pleasantries, advertising, images, and certain other features accompanying a product.

The notion of atmospherics as a marketing tool is linked with the human senses. The atmosphere is comprehended through the senses (Kotler, 1974). The main sensory channels describing the surrounding atmosphere are sight, sound, scent, and touch. More specifically, the visual channel absorbs the color, brightness, size, and shapes from the atmosphere. Similarly, the auditory channel is responsible for the volume and pitch of noise or music. The olfactory channel collects the scent and freshness of an atmosphere. Finally, the tactile channel assesses the texture and temperature of an atmosphere.

Thus, the birth of senses in marketing primarily lies in the notion of store atmospherics, wherein the marketers shifted their focus towards the aesthetics in the store atmosphere. Whereas earlier, the focus of marketers was merely on fulfilling the functional and practical needs of rational consumers, the focus had shifted towards providing the consumers with total products that were a sum of the tangible and intangible aspects constituting the product, services, aesthetics, pleasantries, advertising, and other related features. The emergence of sensory marketing as a field of research was further driven by the hedonic consumption concept which is elaborated in the following sub-head.

Hedonic Consumption Concept

The origins of sensory marketing mainly lie in the hedonic consumption concept. Hirshman & Holbrook (1982) first defined hedonic consumption as such facets of consumer behavior that may be related to multisensory, fantasy, and fun aspects of a product. The hedonic consumption marked a shift from the monotonous thinking of consumers as utility maximizers. However, consumers are rational beings focused on utilitarian consumption, but they can be rational only to a limited extent.

The introduction of the hedonic consumption concept marked a paradigm shift in consumer behavior research. Plato theorized that there are three faculties in the human mind- cognition (knowing), emotion (feeling), and conation (willing) (Scott, Osgood, & Peterson, 1979). These faculties have remained intact over the years and form the basis of consumer behavior research. Hirschman & Holbrook (1982) noted that the cognition (also known as the belief) component of mental activities had received considerable attention from consumer behavior researchers. According to the multi-attribute attitude framework (Holbrook, 1978), these three constructs are classified as belief, affect, and intention. The belief component was found to be considerably researched due to the traditional notion of marketing researchers that consumers are utility maximizers. The utility maximizers evaluated the utility of a product based on the tangible properties of products. However, products whose properties may be beyond tangible were not covered within the premises of the utilitarian consumption concept.

Additionally, the then information processing researchers focused merely on the processing of verbal information. It was found that information occurring in other sensory modalities, such as olfactory, visual, auditory, tactile, and gustative, was not covered by the past pattern of research. Thus, the hedonic consumption concept marked a paradigm shift in consumer behavior research by converging the extant research focusing on the multisensory, emotive, fantasy, and fun aspects of consumption (Hirschman & Holbrook, 1982). The hedonic consumer research oriented its focus toward exploring the sensory channels used by consumers to perceive and experience certain products. It cannot be denied that tangible or functional elements of products are extremely important. However, such a lens of research supplements the conventional viewpoint of researchers. Hence, the shift in focus towards hedonic consumption supplements verbal information processing with additional findings into nonverbal information processing or sensory impressions of products. The hedonic consumption paradigm led marketers to construct an experiential economy for the consumers, the conceptions in the experiential economy are elaborated in the following sub-head.

Experiential Economy

The paradigm shift brought by the hedonic consumption concept led to the birth of the Experiential Economy, which focused on providing the consumer with a holistic consumption experience. The traditional marketing approach was contrasted by a new approach called experiential marketing (Schmitt, 1999). The proponents of the Experiential Economy distinguished experience from services and products (Pine and Gilmore, 1998). The execution of an experience takes place when services are used as a stage with goods as props to engage customers and create memorable events. Traditionally, marketers defined consumers as rational thinkers or decision-makers who cared about functionality and utility. In contrast, in the novel experiential marketer's viewpoint, consumers were defined as rational and emotional individuals wanting to achieve pleasurable experiences. This new approach categorized experiences into five types of strategic experiential modules (SEMs). This highlighted sensory experiences as one of the pillars to provide the consumer with a pleasurable and memorable experience. The introduction of the experiential consumption concept in marketing led to the significant growth of research into senses in marketing.

Embodied and Grounded Cognition

The sensory experience dimension within the experiential economy caused a swell of interest in research on the role of sensory experiences in judgment and decision-making. This led to the formation of a separate field of sensory marketing. The field of sensory marketing explores the role of senses in consumer behavior (Krishna & Schwarz, 2014). Krishna (2012), in an integrative review of sensory marketing, defines sensory marketing as "marketing that engages consumer's senses and affects their perception, judgment, and behavior." She builds on the theory of embodied and grounded cognition and states that stimuli from the external environment impinge upon the sensory cells, thus creating sensations in the human body. These sensations are further processed and interpreted in the human brain to form sensory perceptions. The theory of embodied cognition denotes that our bodily states must be involved in cognition. The classical theories of cognition believed cognition to be amodal or independent of perception. However, there exists a contrasting school of thought with the belief that human bodily states, grounded action, and mental stimulations are all drivers of cognitive activity (Barsalou, 2008). Therefore, human bodily sensations are a source of information.

What is Marketed to the Senses?

Marketing to the senses is versatile. There are several domains where sensory marketing may be applied. The domains may be classified into goods, services, experiences, events, and online and offline store environments. These domains have been elucidated below.

Goods

Tangible goods cover a major proportion of the marketing efforts. These goods are sometimes a necessity and, at other times, a desire or a want. Goods are a lucrative option for marketers to leverage the benefits of sensory marketing. Marketers may construct pleasant sensory designs in product packaging by choosing the right shades of colors, packaging material, product fragrance, and dispensing mechanism. The goods provide a proper field for marketers to experiment with consumer's senses. However, this may not be easy as the goods are consumed over time and stay longer with them, which might influence the consumer's re-purchase decision.

Services

The services are the intangible offering by marketers. Emerging markets are increasingly offering services. They constitute hotels, lounges, airlines, consultancy, parlors, salons, etc. The consumer's senses are especially targeted by the service marketers. These services actively target the consumer's senses. For example, hotels target the visual senses with luxurious interiors such as soft linen and wooden flooring. Similarly, spas and parlors have a soothing odor. Lounges have soft couches that induce a feeling of comfort.

Experiences

Sensory marketing is the signature experience marketing technique. It is the right thing to market experiences. Tourism managers induce tourists in pre-visiting immersive experiences through AR/VR, that helps them get the multisensory feel of the actual experience. On the basis of such experiences consumers may make their final purchase decision.

Events

Marketing that involves celebrity performances, global sports events, trade shows, and other gatherings of crowd comes within event marketing. Events conducted into the metaverse where the participants have their own avatars involve immersive multisensory experiences. In addition, book reading events and exhibitions may also be sensory marketed to resemble the theme of the event.

In-Store Environment

The store environment includes the store lighting, temperature, textures, fragrance/odor, and the music/noise in the store. The store atmospherics are the key approach of sensory marketers (Spence et al., 2014). Marketers can design the store environment by keeping in mind their target consumers and whether they would like to maintain a premium or budget brand image.

Sensory Marketing Mix

The concept of marketing mix was first introduced by Neil H. Borden (Borden, 1964). The author called marketers a 'mixer of ingredients.' The marketing ingredients, when mixed together formed a marketing mix. These ingredients were popularized as the four Ps of marketing- *Product, Price, Promotion,* and *Place* (AMA, 2022). In this section, the four Ps of the marketing are customized into a sensory marketing mix with one added P for *Print* representing the sensory imprint on an individual's perception, memory, and cognition through the unique multisensory experiences. *Figure 2 & 3* represent the 5 elements of the sensory marketing mix and the sensory marketing mix respectively.

Figure 2. Elements of the sensory marketing mix

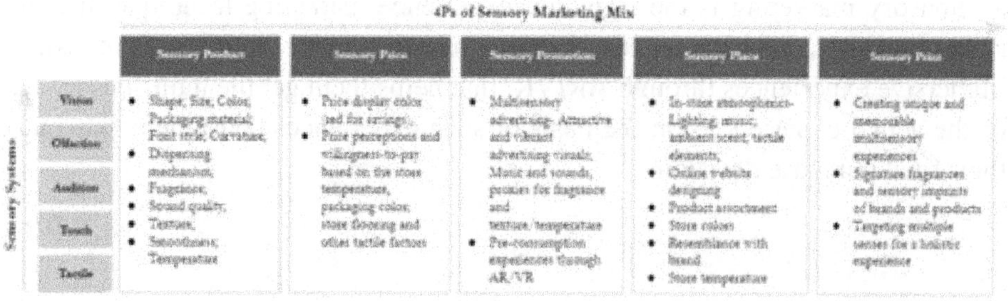

Figure 3. Sensory marketing mix

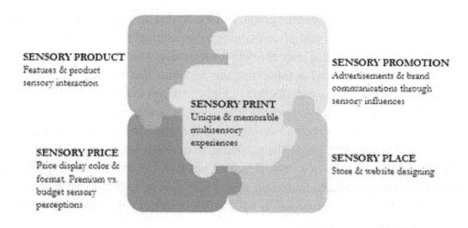

Sensory Product

The first P of the 4Ps of the marketing mix is the Product a marketer has to offer. The product may be either a good or service. Product planning constitutes the policies and procedures relating to product design and quality (Borden, 1964). The human senses play a significant role in product evaluation, perception, and choice (Biswas & Labrecque, 2021; Biswas & Szocs, 2019; Wiedmann et al., 2017). In the case of a product, the visual sense assesses the color, shape, size, packaging material, and label font, amongst several other visual factors. Similarly, the olfactory sense is responsible for assessing the intensity and quality of the fragrance/scent of the product. The tactile sense assesses the smoothness, roughness, and temperature of the product. In food products, the gustatory sense is responsible for assessing the liking and quality of food. Finally, the auditory sense evaluates the sound quality of products. For example, the Apple iPhone is a mix of excellent visuals such as the metallic body, unique color variants, and luxurious body. The iPhones have unique ringtones that may enable one to identify an iPhone by listening to the sounds. In addition, iPhones maintain a cold temperature with their metallic body and have vibrative features to signal call connections and unlocking. Marketers may design their product offer on the basis of the sensory systems they want to target.

Sensory Price

The second P is the Price of the product. Price defines the policies and procedures relating to the price level and price margins to be adopted by a marketer. Sensory marketing may be applied to price through the format in which the price is presented to the consumer. Research has found that the discounts that are shown in red color in promotional flyers induce the feeling of higher savings in a consumer (Ye, 2020). The findings based on an eye-tracking study proved that presenting only one price in red color lowers the perceived savings from the store. In addition, while the red color may be related to savings, the presentation of one price in red color, amongst others, may hurt the sales of a store. Research has also found that cold temperatures symbolize luxury products; as a result, consumers may be willing to pay a premium price when the store environment is cold. Also, cold store environments enhance consumer product evaluation.

Sensory Promotion

Sensory marketing plays a key role in the third P of the marketing mix, i.e., Promotion. Promotion constitutes advertising, broadcasting, and propagating the product. It involves the policies and procedures relating to special selling plans, consumer promotions, and trade promotions. Senses are especially targeted in promoting a product through advertising. For example, the food advertisements are made so luring with yummy-looking images, eating sounds or music, and the steaming smell of the food. Similarly, perfumes and soaps are advertised on television with vibrant visuals, proxies for scents, and lively music. In a marketing experiment, it was found that the taste perception of an advertised food was better when the advertisement text encompassed multiple senses compared to a single sense (Elder & Krishna, 2010). In another experimental study, it was found that scent advertising enhances the sense of proximity between a product and the consumer. However, the effect exists only when the advertised product is expected to have a scent and the scent is congruent with the product being advertised (Ruzeviciute et al., 2019).

Sensory Place

The fourth P of the marketing mix resembles the *Place*. Place encompasses policies and procedures related to channels of distribution such as wholesalers and retailers, and personal selling (Borden, 1964). Sensory marketing plays a highly significant role in designing the retail channel of distribution. Also, with the growing trend of online stores, sensory marketing is applied in website design. The store's atmospherics, such as lighting, music, ambient scent, and tactile finish, play a key role in increasing the time spent at the store by providing a pleasant experience to the consumer (Roggeveen et al., 2019; Spence et al., 2014). Marketers must design their place of distributing the product to the consumer keeping in mind their influence on the consumer's senses.

Sensory Print

The fifth P of sensory marketing mix is the sensory *Print*. Sensory print encompasses the impression or imprint created by multisensory stimulations related to a brand or product that curate memorable and unique experience for the consumers. Print encompasses the designing of multisensory experiences with unique aesthetics, pleasant scents, soothing music, quality haptics, and appetizing taste elements. The sensory print may create a unique image of a brand in the minds of consumers. For instance, the signature white tea fragrance of the Westin hotel chain, the apple iPhone ringtone, or the Singapore airline sensory experiences, all of these leave their marks in consumers' memory and perception. Sensory marketers must focus on imparting their imprint on consumers so the consumers come back and bring back to the brands.

MULTI-SENSORY EXPERIENCES: AN EMERGING MARKETING REALITY

Aristotle said that humans are born with senses (Krishna, 2012). In addition, vision is the most important sense, followed by touch. There are primarily five human sensory systems- visual, auditory, olfactory, tactile, and gustatory. These sensory systems work in unison. The understanding of sensory marketing is incomplete without understanding the multisensory experiences concept. All our senses are active all the time unless voluntarily shut down. The attempts to understand sensory marketing with regard to individual senses may not boost the understanding of the field to its total capacity (Spence, 2022).

Multisensory experiences are defined as "impressions formed by specific events whose sensory elements have been carefully crafted by someone" (Velasco and Obrist, 2020, p. 15). Hence multisensory experiences may be designed by marketers to derive intended consumer responses. Marketers and researchers in the past focused on the senses in isolation. For instance, the influence of visual elements such as colors on consumer choice or the influence of sound volume and pitch on consumer behavior. However, the human body collects sensations from the environment through the multiple sensory channels, which are then integrated into the brain, thus resulting in multisensory experiences. For marketers, it is considerably challenging to derive favorable results from sensory marketing implementation without understanding the multisensory experiences.

The human brain has designated chambers to process multisensory information (Krishna et al., 2010; Spence, 2020; Spence et al., 2014). In an attempt to comprehend multisensory experiences, one must understand cross-modal correspondences. Cross-modal correspondences represent the interaction between two sensory modalities. In general, it may be said that when sensory stimulation that is absorbed by one sensory modality creates a stimulation in another sensory modality too. For instance, if you are shown a drink that is purple in color, you may immediately associate it with blueberry or a blue lagoon. This happens due to the previous associations that you have formed with reference to that colored drink. In addition, suppose you are allowed to taste that drink and find that it tastes like a lemonade. How would you rate the drink? Most probably, you will give a lower rating. This happens because when the brain processes the collected sensory information, it checks for the fit or congruence of the information between multiple senses. Sensory congruence is defined as the degree of fit between sensory characteristics of a stimulus (Krishna et al., 2010). Hence, for marketers, it is crucial to maintain a balanced sensory congruence amongst their offerings to provide pleasant multi-sensory experiences.

HOW SENSORY MARKETING INFLUENCES BUYING BEHAVIOR

There is a rising swell of interest among marketers and researchers in understanding the influence of sensory stimulations and resultant sensory experiences on consumer buying behavior. It is evident that marketers understand the importance of targeting consumers' senses, from the fact that they spend effectively on designing their products and store experiences (Mood Media, 2018). More specifically, on the basis of research findings, marketers may influence consumer's buying behavior through consumer perception, consumer product evaluation, time spent in-store, customer satisfaction, consumer attention and emotional engagement, consumer choice, memory, willingness to pay, and recommendation behavior.

Multisensory experiences play a crucial role in the consumer decision-making process and the ultimate consumer choice. The stimulation of consumer's senses influences consumer approach intentions (Baek et al., 2018; Douc & Adams, 2020). According to Baek et al. (2018), a visually warm (vs. cold) store enhances store intimacy and approach intentions. Consumers with high relational needs are attracted to warm stores whereas this is not the case in luxury stores. Douc et al. (2020) state that adding a third sensory cue in a store might lead to high consumer arousal and decreased pleasantness, provided that the cue is processed by a higher sense.

Multisensory experiences with three high arousal (processed by the higher senses) cues cause sensory overload. Sensory overload may lead to reduced pleasantness which triggers an avoidance behavior and, as a result, negative store and product evaluations by the consumer. Consumer attitudes (Hasse et al., 2020), perceptions (Imschloss & Kuehnl, 2019; Klein, 2021), purchase intentions (Gvili et al., 2018; Mulcahy et al., 2022), willingness to pay (Heller et al., 2019) are also influenced by the multisensory approaches. Consumer well-being is a key focus of various authors in the multisensory experiences' domain. Multisensory experiences influence consumer well-being by making the consumer choose healthier food options through indulgent scents or inducing temptation avoidance through sour (vs. neutral) taste perception (Pomirleanu et al., 2020). Consumer choices are widely driven by multisensory experiences. For example, choice confidence coming from the direct touch (vs. traditional) interface leads to consumer choice in online shopping (Hattula et al., 2023). In advertising, audio-visual (vs. visual only) multisensory cues attract higher consumer attention (Simmonds et al., 2020). Customer satisfaction (Lee & Lee, 2019) and recommendation/WOM behavior (Mishra et al., 2020) are also associated with multisensory experiences.

Figure 4. Sensory marketing and the buyer behavior

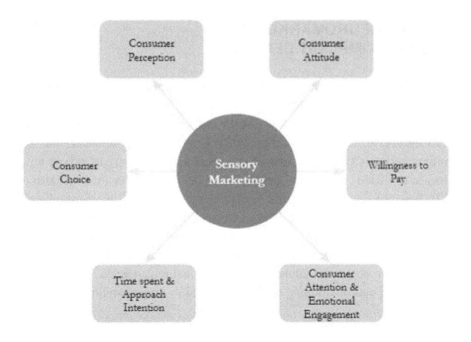

The sensory elements of products and stores are responsible for forming consumer's sensory perceptions. Sensory perceptions are the interpretations of certain information that is collected from the environment. North (1999), in an experiment, found that when French music is played in a wine store, consumers tend to buy more French wines. Whereas when Italian music is played, consumers choose Italian wines. This example proves the effect that music may have on taste perceptions and consumer choice. Similarly, it has been found that consumer choice and satisfaction are influenced by the nature of sensory stimulations they are exposed to. Biswas et al. (2019) found that the ambient scent influences consumers' choice in terms of the selection of a healthier option when the scent is indulgent compared to an indulgent smell.

(Lee & Lee, 2019) found that multisensory service innovations play a catalytic role in enhancing customer satisfaction and experience. In addition, when video advertisements are presented in audio-visual (vs. visual) format, the prompted recall is quicker, symbolizing greater memory storage (Simmonds et al., 2020). The sensory elements in a store also influence the willingness to pay and the perception of luxury. Whenever marketers design a store with cooler temperatures, the store is perceived as a luxury store, hence, increasing consumer willingness to pay a premium price (Park et al., 2019).

SENSORY- NEUROMARKETING: MEASURING IMPLICIT BEHAVIOR

The discussions on sensory marketing are incomplete without understanding the processing of the sensations in the human brain. Several researchers in the field have stated that sensory stimulation influences consumer behavior non-consciously (Bastiaansen et al., 2016; Gupta et al., 2023; Krishna, 2012; Shemesh et al., 2022). Neuromarketing is the application of neuroscientific tools to understand how the influence of various marketing approaches on consumer behavior (Shemesh et al., 2022). Some of the neuroscientific tools are eye-tracking, Electroencephalogram (EEG), Galvanic Skin Response (GSR), and functional Magnetic Resonance Imaging (fMRI). These neuroscientific tools provide neuro metrics that help understand an individual's psychological and physiological responses to a stimulus. These responses mainly measure consumer attention and emotional engagement, i.e., arousal and valence. When neuromarketing tools are applied to understanding the influences of sensory stimulations on consumer behavior, this leads to the construction of the sensory neuromarketing concept.

More specifically, eye-tracking measures pupil dilation diameter, fixation rates, blink rate, cognitive load, and Areas of Interest (AOIs). Eye trackers are usually attached to PCs; they track and record real-time eye responses. They come along with their data management software that can be accessed to derive valuable conclusions. This tool is helpful in evaluating the effectiveness of advertisements, packaging and labeling, brand campaigns, color combinations, and certain other visual elements (Neurons Inc., 2024).

; Ye et al., 2020). EEG measures the electrical signals in the brain through the surface of an individual's skull. This device comes in the form of a cap that has nodes/channels that are attached to the surface of respondents. These nodes collect brain signals from different parts of the brain. The data from the device is received in the form of electrical signals per millisecond. The specialty of EEG is that it may be used to study multisensory stimulations. GSR records the skin responses to measure the level of arousal and stress in response to a stimulus (Shemesh et al., 2022). fMRI is an advanced neuroscientific tool that measures the blood flow caused by brain activity (Kapoor et al., 2023). The data using this tool is highly reliable. However, it is very expensive. Lastly, the face recognition tool measures the respondents' facial reactions in response to what is presented to them.

The traditional data collection methods are not sufficient to understand sensory experiences holistically. Thus, it is crucial for marketers and researchers to quickly adapt to these measurement tools as they will complement and support the findings from traditional methods such as interviews and surveys.

SENSORY MARKETING TO THE NEW REALITIES

The field of sensory marketing is continuously evolving, pushing marketers to accept and learn working in the new realities. Recent technological advancements have necessitated marketers to understand consumer behavior from newer lenses. In this section, three areas have been highlighted that have raised the significance of sensory marketing.

GenAI and Sensory Marketing

GenAI refers to the Generation AI. This represents the generation that has grown up interacting with artificial intelligence, such as virtual assistants, recommendation algorithms, chatbots, smartphones, and smart speakers (Alexa). Such technological advancements may be understood better in intersection with sensory marketing. With the increasing demand for personalized experiences in consumers, AI algorithms may provide consumers with sensory preferences personalized to their choices. Customers' visual, aural, and auditory preferences may be identified through AI algorithms and hence provided to the consumer. GenAI may also bring multisensory engagement for customers, as customers respond more positively to multisensory immersive experiences that combine visual, tactile, olfactory, and auditory senses. This generation will also be an early adopter of Augmented and Virtual realities. Sensory marketers are advised to leverage this opportunity to create immersive experiences for consumers through VR and AR that allow consumers to interact with the products before an actual purchase. AI-powered marketing and sales reach new heights with generative AI- McKinsey & Co. (2023) state that artificial intelligence technology shall take marketing and sales to new heights as it has brought a creative disruption in the thinking of B2B and B2C players with regard to the creation of customer experience.

Digital Sensory Marketing

The rapid advancements in Sensory Enabling Technologies (SETs), such as AR/VR, and the shifting of consumption activities to digital platforms have led forward-thinking marketers to implement digital sensory marketing strategies (Petit et al., 2019). Such strategies are capable of providing the consumer with remote multisensory experiences. Whereas earlier consumers could only access visual or auditory information on digital platforms, now it may be possible to get the fragrance of the products remotely too. These advancements call for further research and conceptualization in the domain, especially in digital contexts.

Sensory Neuromarketing

The understanding of the senses is incomplete without understanding the interpretation of sensory information in the brain. Neuroscience tools may be applied to understand the workings of sensations in the brain. As stated by Krishna (2012), sensory marketing techniques influence consumer behavior non-consciously. Neuroscientific tools such as eye-tracking, fMRI, EEG, and GSR enable the measurement of implicit nonconscious responses in individuals (Gupta et al., 2023). Whenever an individual comes into contact with a sensory marketing stimulus or receives a multisensory experience, it may not always be recognized consciously by him/her. However, these do influence their perception and choices. The collection of such responses is not facilitated by conventional tools such as surveys and interviews. Surveys, interviews, and certain other data collection tools collect conscious responses from the consumers as the consumer is given time to process and respond. However, in purchase decision-making consumers do not always respond consciously. Thus, neuromarketing tools are the solution to measure such non-conscious purchase decisions. These tools help in collecting consumers' automatic and implicit responses toward given stimuli (Shemesh et al., 2022). Future marketers and researchers are advised to employ or outsource the findings using these tools to understand better and implement multisensory marketing strategies.

FUTURE SCOPE OF SENSIBLE SELLING THROUGH THE SENSES

Based on the discussions in the current chapter, there is a need to understand sensory marketing in greater depth by exploring the consumers' multisensory experiences. In addition, sensory multisensory interplay must be understood in recent trending contexts of the metaverse, AR/VR, and extended realities. The GenAI is increasingly generating the need to study how technological influences, novel algorithms, and AI influence consumer's multisensory experiences.

There are various concepts in the field that require in-depth understanding through future research. With the advent of Sensory Enabling Technologies, it has become crucial to understand the human senses in conjunction with these technologies. There is a vast scope for research in understanding the cross-modal correspondences between multiple senses. From a methodological and an interdisciplinary perspective, conclusions based on self-assessment reports may not suffice for research in the area. Hence, collecting psychological and physiological data using tools such as EEG, eye-tracking, and GSR is a valuable opportunity for future researchers.

The future of "Sensible Selling Through the Senses" holds immense promise as entrepreneurs, leveraging advancements in the metaverse, artificial intelligence (AI), and virtual reality (VR) education, are poised to redefine marketing paradigms (Arora & Sharma, 2023); (Kumar, Arora & Erkol Bayram, (Eds.). (2024)); Entrepreneurs are the drivers of economic growth and innovation (Arora & Sharma, 2021); Arora, (2016). Entrepreneurs can harness sensory marketing to create immersive brand experiences that transcend traditional boundaries, engaging consumers on a multisensory level (Arora, (2023). The metaverse offers a virtual environment where brands can establish interactive, persistent presences, fostering deeper connections with global audiences (Dhiman & Arora, (2024) a; Rathore & Arora, (2024). AI augments this experience by personalizing interactions based on extensive data analytics, ensuring each engagement is relevant and impactful. Furthermore, VR education empowers entrepreneurs to train teams remotely and immerse consumers in virtual product experiences, revolutionizing customer engagement and brand loyalty (Arora, (2024); Dhiman & Arora, (2024) b. Together, these innovations herald a future where sensory marketing not only enhances consumer experiences but also drives unprecedented growth and competitiveness in the global marketplace.

Marketers may design optimal multisensory experiences for consumers, thus reducing cognitive effort and enhancing customer satisfaction. Brands and store designers should remember that targeting multiple senses is beneficial. However, doing too much can cause a sensory overload and thus result in unfavorable outcomes. Additionally, marketers must target the consumers' senses in the pre-purchase stage itself and be at a competitive advantage. Targeting the senses during the purchase is obvious. However, it may be done in the need recognition and information stages too.

CONCLUSION

The discussions in the field mainly began in the 1970s when the focus of researchers and marketers shifted towards the emotional aspects of consumption. However, the field has evolved considerably since then. As marketers and consumers step into the extended realities, the expectations from marketing policymakers have evolved. In addition, with the advancing technology, forward-looking marketers are under the pressure of gaining a competitive edge. Sensory marketing is a boon for marketers to excel in their marketing strategies today. This chapter may be concluded by stating that sensory marketing is not a choice but a need for efficient and effective marketing. Various consumer behavior dimensions may be positively targeted by sensory marketing. Sensory marketing influences consumer perception, judgment, and choices. Marketing to the senses, gives marketers a competitive edge. Recently, there has been an increasing trend in understanding the depths of sensory marketing through the exploration of multisensory experiences (Helmefalk, 2019; Velasco & Obrist, 2021). Additionally, GenAI, AR/VR, and metaverse are fostering the need to study immersive multisensory experiences. Future researchers must explore sensory marketing and immersive multisensory experiences with chatbots, metaverse, Head Mounted Devices (HMDs), AR/VR, AI algorithms, and certain other digital contexts. Further, sensory experiences influence consumer decision-making unconsciously. Such unconscious influences may be recorded through implicit measurement tools. Sensory neuromarketing is an emerging area of research that involves the collection of consumers' emotional arousal, emotional engagement, and attention through measures such as pupil dilation, eye movements, fixation rates, blink rates, skin responses, and electrical signals in the brain. Future researchers are advised to apply neuromarketing tools to provide robust findings on how sensory marketing influences consumer decision-making.

ACKNOWLEDGEMENT

This research received no specific grant from any funding agency in the public, commercial, or not-for-profit sectors.

REFERENCES

American Marketing Association. (2022). *The Four Ps of Marketing*. AMA. https://www.ama.org/marketing-news/the-four-ps-of-marketing/

Arora, M. (2016). Creative dimensions of entrepreneurship: A key to business innovation. *Pacific Business Review International*, 1(1), 255–259.

Arora, M. (2023). Encapsulating Role of Persuasion and Skill Development in Marketing Communication for Brand Building: A Perspective. In *International Handbook of Skill, Education, Learning, and Research Development in Tourism and Hospitality* (pp. 1–17). Springer Nature Singapore.

Arora, M. (2024). Virtual Reality in Education: Analyzing the Literature and Bibliometric State of Knowledge. *Transforming Education with Virtual Reality*, (pp. 379-402). Wiley. 10.1002/9781394200498.ch22

Arora, M., & Sharma, R. L. (2021). Repurposing the Role of Entrepreneurs in the Havoc of COVID-19. In *Entrepreneurship and Big Data* (pp. 229-250). CRC Press.

Arora, M., & Sharma, R. L. (2023). Artificial intelligence and big data: Ontological and communicative perspectives in multi-sectoral scenarios of modern businesses. *Foresight*, 25(1), 126–143. 10.1108/FS-10-2021-0216

Baek, E., Jung, H., Hwan, S., & Lee, M. (2018). Using warmth as the visual design of a store : Intimacy, relational needs, and approach intentions. *Journal of Business Research*, 88(March), 91–101. 10.1016/j.jbusres.2018.03.013

Barsalou, L. W. (1999). *Perceptual symbol systems.*

Barsalou, L. W. (2008). Grounded Cognition. *Annual Review of Psychology, 59.*10.1146/annurev.psych.59.103006.093639

Bastiaansen, M., Straatman, S., Driessen, E., Mitas, O., Stekelenburg, J., & Wang, L. (2016). My destination in your brain : A novel neuromarketing approach for evaluating the effectiveness of destination marketing. *Journal of Destination Marketing & Management*. 10.1016/j.jdmm.2016.09.003

Biswas, D., Labrecque, L. I., & Lehmann, D. R. (2021). Effects of sequential sensory cues on food taste perception: Cross-modal interplay between visual and olfactory stimuli. *Journal of Consumer Psychology*, 31(4), 746–764. 10.1002/jcpy.1231

Biswas, D., & Szocs, C. (2019). The smell of healthy choices: Cross-modal sensory compensation effects of ambient scent on food purchases. *JMR, Journal of Marketing Research*, 56(1), 123–141. 10.1177/0022243718820585

Boston Consultancy Group. (2024). *Three Ways GenAI Will Transform Customer Experience*. Boston Consultancy Group. https://www.bcg.com/publications/2024/three-ways-genai-will-transform-customer-experience

Dhiman, V., & Arora, M. (2024). Exploring the linkage between business incubation and entrepreneurship: understanding trends, themes and future research agenda. *LBS Journal of Management & Research*.

Dhiman, V., & Arora, M. (2024)a. Current State of Metaverse in Entrepreneurial Ecosystem: A Retrospective Analysis of Its Evolving Landscape. In *Exploring the Use of Metaverse in Business and Education* (pp. 73-87). IGI Global. 10.4018/979-8-3693-5868-9.ch005

Doucé, L., & Adams, C. (2020). Sensory overload in a shopping environment: Not every sensory modality leads to too much stimulation. *Journal of Retailing and Consumer Services*, 57, 102154. 10.1016/j.jretconser.2020.102154

Elder, R. S., & Krishna, A. (2010). The effects of advertising copy on sensory thoughts and perceived taste. *The Journal of Consumer Research*, 36(5), 748–756. 10.1086/605327

Elder, R. S., & Krishna, A. (2022). A review of sensory imagery for consumer psychology. *Journal of Consumer Psychology*, 32(2), 293–315. 10.1002/jcpy.1242

Forbes. (2022). Are Multisensory Experiences The Next Frontier Of Building Brands In The Metaverse? *Forbes*.https://www.forbes.com/sites/forbescommunicatio nscouncil/2022/05/10/are-multisensory-experiences-the-next-frontier-of-building -brands-in-the-metaverse/?sh=abc199d28852

Franziska, K. W., Janina, L., & Nadine, H. (2017). The power of experiential marketing : Exploring the causal relationships among multisensory marketing, brand experience, customer perceived value and brand strength. *Journal of Brand Management*. 10.1057/s41262-017-0061-5

Gupta, R., Verma, H., & Kapoor, A. P. (2024). Neuromarketing in predicting voting behavior: A case of National elections in India. *Journal of Consumer Behaviour*, 23(2), 336–356. 10.1002/cb.2191

Gvili, Y., Levy, S., & Zwilling, M. (2018). The sweet smell of advertising: The essence of matching scents with other ad cues. *International Journal of Advertising*, 37(4), 568–590. 10.1080/02650487.2017.1339584

Hattula, J. D., Herzog, W., & Dhar, R. (2023). The impact of touchscreen devices on consumers' choice confidence and purchase likelihood. *Marketing Letters*, 34(1), 35–53. 10.1007/s11002-022-09623-w

Heller, J., Chylinski, M., de Ruyter, K., Mahr, D., & Keeling, D. I. (2019). Touching the untouchable: Exploring multi-sensory augmented reality in the context of online retailing. *Journal of Retailing*, 95(4), 219–234. 10.1016/j.jretai.2019.10.008

Helmefalk, M. (2019). Browsing behaviour as a mediator: The impact of multi-sensory cues on purchasing. *Journal of Consumer Marketing*, 36(2), 253–263. 10.1108/JCM-10-2017-2392

Imschloss, M., & Kuehnl, C. (2019). Feel the Music! Exploring the Cross-modal Correspondence between Music and Haptic Perceptions of Softness. *Journal of Retailing*, 95(4), 158–169. 10.1016/j.jretai.2019.10.004

Kapoor, A., Sahay, A., Singh, N. C., Pammi, V. C., & Banerjee, P. (2023). The neural correlates and the underlying processes of weak brand choices. *Journal of Business Research*, 154, 113230. 10.1016/j.jbusres.2022.07.056

Klein, K., Melnyk, V., & Voelckner, F. (2021). Effects of background music on evaluations of visual images. *Psychology and Marketing*, 38(12), 2240–2246. 10.1002/mar.21588

Krishna, A. (2012). An integrative review of sensory marketing : Engaging the senses to affect perception, judgment and behavior. *Journal of Consumer Psychology*, 22(3), 332–351. 10.1016/j.jcps.2011.08.003

Krishna, A., Elder, R. S., & Caldara, C. (2010). Feminine to smell but masculine to touch? Multisensory congruence and its effect on the aesthetic experience. *Journal of Consumer Psychology*, 20(4), 410–418. 10.1016/j.jcps.2010.06.010

Krishna, A., & Schwarz, N. (2014). ScienceDirect Sensory marketing, embodiment, and grounded cognition : A review and introduction. *Journal of Consumer Psychology*, 24(2), 159–168. Advance online publication. 10.1016/j.jcps.2013.12.006

Kumar, J., Arora, M., & Erkol Bayram, G. (Eds.). (2024). *Exploring the Use of Metaverse in Business and Education*. IGI Global., 10.4018/979-8-3693-5868-9

Lee, M., Lee, S., & Koh, Y. (2019). Multisensory experience for enhancing hotel guest experience: Empirical evidence from big data analytics. *International Journal of Contemporary Hospitality Management*, 31(11), 4313–4337. 10.1108/IJCHM-03-2018-0263

McKinsey & Co. (2022). *AI-powered marketing and sales reach new heights with generative AI*. McKinsey & Co. https://www.mckinsey.com/capabilities/growth-marketing-and-sales/our-insights/ai-powered-marketing-and-sales-reach-new-heights-with-generative-ai

Mishra, A., Shukla, A., Rana, N. P., & Dwivedi, Y. K. (2021). From "touch" to a "multisensory" experience: The impact of technology interface and product type on consumer responses. *Psychology and Marketing*, 38(3), 385–396. 10.1002/mar.21436

Mood Media. (2018). *Quantifying the impact of sensory marketing*. Mood Media. https://us.moodmedia.com/sensory-marketing/

Neurons Inc. (2024). *Why Brands Use Emotional Advertising & How to Effectively Measure Emotions*. Neurons Inc. https://www.neuronsinc.com/insights/emotional-advertising-effectively-measure-emotions

North, A. C., Hargreaves, D. J., & McKendrick, J. (1999). The influence of in-store music on wine selections. *The Journal of Applied Psychology*, 84(2), 271–276. 10.1037/0021-9010.84.2.271

Park, J., & Hadi, R. (2020). Shivering for status: When cold temperatures increase product evaluation. *Journal of Consumer Psychology*, 30(2), 314–328. 10.1002/jcpy.1133

Petit, O., Velasco, C., & Spence, C. (2019). Digital sensory marketing: Integrating new technologies into multisensory online experience. *Journal of Interactive Marketing*, 45(1), 42–61. 10.1016/j.intmar.2018.07.004

Pine, B. J., & Gilmore, J. H. (2011). *The experience economy*. Harvard Business Press.

Pomirleanu, N., Gustafson, B. M., & Bi, S. (2020). Ooh, that's sour: An investigation of the role of sour taste and color saturation in consumer temptation avoidance. *Psychology and Marketing*, 37(8), 1068–1081. 10.1002/mar.21363

Rathore, S., & Arora, M. (2024). Sustainability Reporting in the Metaverse: A Multi-Sectoral Analysis. In *Exploring the Use of Metaverse in Business and Education* (pp. 147-165). IGI Global. 10.4018/979-8-3693-5868-9.ch009

Roggeveen, A. L., Grewal, D., & Schweiger, E. B. (2019). The DAST Framework for Retail Atmospherics : The Impact of In- and Out-of-Store Retail Journey Touchpoints on the Customer Experience. *Journal of Retailing*. 10.1016/j.jretai.2019.11.002

Ruzeviciute, R., Kamleitner, B., & Biswas, D. (2020). Designed to s (m) ell: When scented advertising induces proximity and enhances appeal. *JMR, Journal of Marketing Research*, 57(2), 315–331. 10.1177/0022243719888474

Schmitt, B. (1999). Experiential marketing. *Journal of Marketing Management*, 15(1-3), 53–67. 10.1362/026725799784870496

Shemesh, A., Leisman, G., Bar, M., & Grobman, Y. J. (2022). The emotional influence of different geometries in virtual spaces: A neurocognitive examination. *Journal of Environmental Psychology*, 81, 101802. 10.1016/j.jenvp.2022.101802

Simmonds, L., Bogomolova, S., Kennedy, R., Nenycz-Thiel, M., & Bellman, S. (2020). A dual-process model of how incorporating audio-visual sensory cues in video advertising promotes active attention. *Psychology and Marketing*, 37(8), 1057–1067. 10.1002/mar.21357

Spence, C. (2022). *Experimental atmospherics : a multi-sensory perspective.* QMR. 10.1108/QMR-04-2022-0070

Spence, C., Puccinelli, N. M., Grewal, D., & Roggeveen, A. L. (2014). Store atmospherics: A multisensory perspective. *Psychology and Marketing*, 31(7), 472–488. 10.1002/mar.20709

Velasco, C., & Obrist, M. (2020). *Multisensory experiences: Where the senses meet technology.* Oxford University Press. 10.1093/oso/9780198849629.001.0001

Velasco, C., & Obrist, M. (2021). Multisensory experiences: A primer. *Frontiers of Computer Science*, 3, 614524. 10.3389/fcomp.2021.614524

Velasco, C., & Spence, C. (2019). The multisensory analysis of product packaging framework. *Multisensory packaging: Designing new product experiences*, 191-223.

Wörfel, P., Frentz, F., & Tautu, C. (2022). Marketing comes to its senses: A bibliometric review and integrated framework of sensory experience in marketing. *European Journal of Marketing*, 56(3), 704–737. 10.1108/EJM-07-2020-0510

Ye, H., Bhatt, S., Jeong, H., Zhang, J., & Suri, R. (2020). Red price? Red flag! Eye-tracking reveals how one red price can hurt a retailer. *Psychology and Marketing*, 37(7), 928–941. 10.1002/mar.21331

KEY TERMS AND DEFINITIONS

Cross-modal Correspondence: The effect that sensory stimulation in one modality has on another sensory modality is called cross-modal correspondence.

Electroencephalogram (EEG): An EEG cap is a neuroscientific tool that collects electrical signals in the brain through the surface of scalp.

Eye-tracking: The tool that tracks the eye movements of an individual in response to a stimulus.

Galvanic Skin Response (GSR) system: The device captures the skin responses and measures arousal and stress levels.

GenAI: GenAI stands for the generation that is growing using Artificial Intelligence (AI).

Neuromarketing: The application of neuroscientific tools to understand consumer responses to marketing approaches is called neuromarketing.

Sensory Congruence: The fit or compatibility between multiple sensory features of a product is called sensory congruence.

Sensory Marketing: Marketing that targets the consumer's senses to influence their choices, attitude, and behavior is sensory marketing.

SETs: Sensory Enabling Technologies are technologies that enable remote sensory experiences. These devices constitute AR and VR.

Chapter 6
Synchronizing Senses:
Neuromarketing Techniques and the Marketing Mix

Roop Kamal

Chandigarh University, India & RIMT University, India

Shivani Malhan

Chitkara University, India

ABSTRACT

Neuromarketing seeks to utilize brain imaging to comprehend the neuronal connections and cognitive processes that play a role in customers' decision-making. This study aims to offer thorough examination of neuromarketing, including present utilization of neuroimaging physiological tools in the marketing mix. Additionally, it seeks to emphasize the neurological responses of consumer behavior that should be taken into account in the marketing mix. This study aims to examine the impact of recent neuromarketing techniques on marketing mix strategies. Managers can leverage these techniques to develop effective marketing strategies for specific target groups in various areas, including consumer buying behavior, pricing, advertising, the chapter explores potential use of neurological approaches in marketing management. The findings demonstrate the role of neuroscience in informing traditional marketing mix strategies and highlight the benefits of incorporating neuroscience in brand management.

DOI: 10.4018/979-8-3693-4236-7.ch006

INTRODUCTION

With the idea of neuromarketing, the marketers can finally have a way to minimize the uncertainty and guesswork that often hinder their understanding of consumer behaviour. Neuromarketing, also referred to as consumer neuroscience, delves into the intricacies of the human brain to forecast and potentially influence consumer behaviour and decision making. In recent years, neuromarketing has gained credibility as a valuable tool for marketers, thanks to a series of groundbreaking studies (Alsharif et al., 2024). Understanding customers' motivations, preferences, and decisions through the measurement of physiological and neural signals is known as neuromarketing. This valuable insight can be used to enhance creative advertising, product development, pricing, and various other marketing strategies, where persuasion as well as skill development plays an important role (Arora, 2023). In the world of marketing, one has to also see the challenges lik   e misinformation and fake propaganda (Arora, 2020). But Methods of measurement commonly used include brain scanning, which measures neural activity, and physiological tracking, which measures eye movement and other proxies for that activity (Bhardwaj et al., 2023).

Neuromarketing is the fascinating intersection of brain science, technology, and marketing. It combines medical knowledge with cutting-edge techniques to enhance marketing strategies (González-Mena et al., 2022). Neuromarketing is an emerging area of marketing that focuses on understanding how consumers react to various marketing stimuli. Neuromarketing involves applying principles from neuroscience to the field of marketing. Neuromarketing involves utilizing brain imaging, scanning, or other brain activity measurement technology to gauge an individual's reaction to particular products, packaging, advertising, or other marketing components. There are instances where the brain responses measured by these techniques may go unnoticed by the subject, making this data more insightful than relying on self-reporting through surveys or focus groups (Grima et al., 2021).

Neuromarketing combines the fields of neuroscience and marketing to assist brands in assessing the emotional impact of their current and future campaigns. Teams utilize cutting-edge technology to monitor customers' neurochemical and physiological reactions during their consumption of marketing content (Alsharif et al., 2024). Marketers have the ability to test different ads to determine which ones generate the highest emotional engagement.

Neuromarketing is a relatively new tool in the hands of marketers; it has proven to help marketers gain insight into consumer behavior by prescribing to the marketer's basic understanding of the brain. Some of the most utilized conventional market research techniques cannot adequately solve this problem because the kind of data collected is self-reported, which might be skewed or false (Sood et al., 2023). Neuromarketing on the other hand applies more complex features from the neuroscience and psychology science and helps to reveal deeper motives that drive consumers, which are extremely helpful in furthering marketing efficacy.

This makes neuromarketing such a useful tool when it comes to understanding the customers' emotional/psychological reactions to marketing communication stimuli. Methods like fMRI and EEG record the brain's activity, enabling the marketers to identify which part of the brain responds to ads, products, or branding initiatives (Sangeeta, & Tandon, 2021). This information assists the marketers in determining what turns the clients' attention, stirs emotions and guides them to make purchases. Taken together, it enables the adjustment of the advertising message to better match the things to which consumers are most sensitively revealing themselves on a deeper level.

Neuromarketing also helps in product differentiation and innovation as it seeks to come up with ideas on the products shoppers and consumers need or would like to have in the market. Admirably, the study of psychological factors goes deeper trying to identify the consumers' wants and aspirations at a deeper, unconscious level; thus by doing so creates products that consumers will have a desire for. An illustration of where this occurs is in packaging, where packaging can be altered in a way to grab attention, hence having the likelihood to trigger positive feelings hence more sales (Alsharif et al., 2024). Furthermore, the neuromarketing concept can help establish new products with the help of the gaps within the market that appeals to people on an emotional level.

Neuromarketing also extends a great deal of value to branding activities. It is revealed that brands that create an emotional tie will conference higher loyalty and retain consumers more often (Cenizo, 2022). Neuromarketing assists in finding out the positive or negative feelings consumers have towards a certain brand and marketers can build on positive feelings and directly work on eradicating any negative feelings consumers might have towards the brand. It is useful to gain a deeper sense of customers' perception when it comes to branding; it paves the way to better branding and customer relationship.

THE HISTORY OF NEUROMARKETING

When neuroscience and marketing come together, it's like witnessing the convergence of two distinct areas of study. The concept of neuromarketing emerged naturally around 2002, without being attributed to any specific individual. Several U.S. companies, such as Bright house and Sales Brain, were pioneers in offering neuromarketing research and consulting services. They emphasized the importance of utilizing technology and knowledge derived from cognitive neuroscience (Bhardwaj et al., 2023). Neuromarketing can be seen as the marketing equivalent of neuropsychology in the field of psychology. Neuropsychology delves into the intricate connection between the brain and human cognitive and psychological functions, whereas neuromarketing emphasizes the importance of examining consumer behavior through a brain-focused lens.

Marketing research methods have long focused on understanding and forecasting the impact of advertising campaigns. Unfortunately, traditional methods have proven to be largely ineffective (Fortunato, et al., 2014). Understanding and modelling cognitive responses to selling messages has always been a methodological challenge, given the strong influence of emotions on how consumers process these messages. Researchers have traditionally relied on consumers' feedback to gauge their opinions on specific advertisements (Grima et al., 2021). This feedback is typically collected through methods like face-to-face interviews, surveys, or focus groups.

Regrettably, these methods come with significant limitations (Bhardwaj et al., 2023). First, it is assumed that individuals possess the ability to accurately articulate their cognitive process, disregarding the fact that this process is heavily influenced by subconscious factors. Incentives, time constraints, or peer pressure can all influence research participants to distort the reporting of their feelings (Alsharif et al., 2024).

Amidst this complex landscape, the advent of neuroimaging techniques has presented intriguing methodological options. Using these techniques, marketers can now delve into the minds of consumers to uncover valuable insights into the underlying processes that determine the success or failure of a message (González-Mena et al., 2022). By addressing the main challenge in traditional advertising research, this approach eliminates the need to rely on individuals' willingness and ability to accurately report their response to a particular advertisement (Lee et al., 2007).

Neuromarketing is gaining popularity in the marketing world. Today, it is fascinating to observe the remarkable growth of the term "neuromarketing" on Google, with a significant increase in hits from 2002 to 2010. Meanwhile, advertising agencies are increasingly recognizing the value of using brain-based tools like eye tracking, EEG, or fMRI to accurately predict the effectiveness of campaigns. Just like a marketing analyst, executives are under increasing pressure to accurately forecast and evaluate the ROI of their advertising campaigns in today's challenging economic climate (Sood et al., 2023). Considering all these factors, it is clear that there is a strong and timely demand for cutting-edge advertising research that incorporates the latest findings on the brain. If neuroscience is still in its early stages, then neuromarketing is even more nascent.

Many marketers are now realizing the potential of understanding the neural pathways that drive consumer behavior when it comes to product discovery, decision-making, and purchase. Numerous studies conducted by neuromarketers focus on commercial aspects and may not adhere to the rigorous standards and review process followed by academics. However, a significant amount of published evidence already exists to shed light on several fundamental neuro cognitive principles that come into play when consumers perceive advertising messages (Bhardwaj et al., 2023).

EXPLORING THE ADVANTAGES OF NEUROMARKETING

Neuromarketing offers a multitude of advantages, which include:

1. **Detailed understanding**. Neuromarketing offers a more detailed perspective on human behaviour compared to conventional market research methods like surveys and focus groups, allowing for a deeper understanding of consumer behaviour. Neuromarketing strategies carefully examine consumer behaviour, preferences, and tendencies (Kant & Yadete 2023). They utilise data that is typically difficult to quantify in order to assess a customer's emotions or potential reactions. Neuromarketing can offer real-time insights into customer behavior (Misra, 2023).
2. **Objective critique**. Since customers cannot deceive in a neuromarketing context, these methods produce more dependable data (Manpreet and Malhan, 2024). Merely inquiring about an individual's sentiments can have a profound impact on their emotional state. Neuromarketing offers a solution to this issue by providing objective results that go beyond what a traditional customer satisfaction survey can offer (Alsharif et al., 2024).
3. **Insights from the depths of the mind**. By adopting a marketing analyst's perspective, one can uncover valuable insights into the hidden workings of the human mind, including those fleeting responses that often escape our conscious memory (Fortunato, et al., 2014).
4. **Understanding Your Customers' Full Perspective:** Conventional market research analysis falls short in uncovering the entirety of consumer perceptions. There are various methods you can explore, including online surveys, reviews and testimonials, phone calls, and responses on social media (Cenizo, 2022).
5. **Efficient in terms of cost**. Utilising neuromarketing techniques can effectively optimise the cost and enhance the effectiveness of marketing research.
6. **Comprehensive approaches perceive your company**. However, one issue that arises is that customers may sometimes choose not to openly express their emotions as a matter of politeness. Understanding their subconscious response is crucial. Understanding the psychology of customers is essential for effective marketing (Manpreet et al., 2023). There's no need to depend solely on their word-of-mouth. It feels as if I'm conducting a survey with someone who can read minds. Gain insight into the genuine sentiments of your customers (Casado et al., 2023).

CRITICISMS OF NEUROMARKETING

1. **Calculating**. Opponents of marketing, like Gary Ruskin, who serves as the executive director of U.S. There are concerns that neuromarketing may exploit consumers' fears or manipulate their neural responses to stimuli, according to Right to Know. Many marketers argue that achieving such precise manipulation is neither feasible nor desirable (Alsharif et al., 2024). As per BrightHouse, a consulting firm based in Atlanta, neuromarketers strive to gain insights into the factors that drive customers to form connections with products, brands, and companies.
2. **Questionable methodology.** Neuromarketing is frequently associated with pseudoscience and exaggerated claims, lacking support from credible neuroscientific evidence (Cenizo, 2022). Some critics, such as University of Pennsylvania professor Joseph Turow, have dismissed it as a gimmicky method for marketers to gain insight into consumer opinion (Fortunato, et al.,2014).

NEUROMARKETING VS. TRADITIONAL MARKETING

Neuromarketing and traditional marketing can be seen as the two opposite views on customers' behavior regulation. The conventional marketing methods that have dominated the markets for many years are what is referred to as the traditional marketing techniques, some of which include survey, focus groups, and market segmentation (Sood et al., 2023). These tools collect survey data and basic demographics, which give a general insight into customers' tendencies. This is especially the case of surveys and questionnaires in that they are able to cover a vast population and enable the determination of consumers' perceptions and attitudes. Compared to personal interviews, discussions in focus groups present the subtleties of people's attitude and thoughts to the products or advertisements. Market segmentation enables the marketer to target the marketing communication at specific segments that can be classified by demographic characteristics or psychographic or behavioral variables. However, these methods have some drawbacks, such as, the data is self-reported, which can be affected by the subjects' desire to respond favorably or the difficulty to recall the events happened in the past. Also, conventional marketing communication usually provides insights at the explicit level which decreases the understanding of consumers' latent motives and desires (González-Mena et al., 2022).

While neuromarketing, focuses on the neuroscience and psychological methodology to look into the subliminal level. Located at a neurological foundation, neuromarketing employs \

POrogressive technologies such as functional Magnetic Resonance Imaging (fMRI) and Ele0ctroencephalography (EEG), which translate the brain's output that we, as the consumers, d0o not even fully perceive into reliable data that shows how we exactly react to particular stimuli (Ha et al., 2022). The two most likely chosen methods for monitoring eye movements are related to visual attention and interest, or to attention and interest towards the object of observation The second probable method, which connected with subject's emotions, is Galvanic Skin Response (GSR), in which the changes in skin conductivity indicate the level of emotional arousal. Facial coding looks at changes in facial features to define reactions. These tools allow for the collection of factual evidence, handing the key to the consumers' truthful feelings and thought patterns. Neuromarketing provides profound understanding of what attracts consumers' attention, what stimuli bring emotional response, and as a result, more successful selling strategies (Arora, 2024).

However, it is not free of its pitfalls or as what has been referred to as the dark side of neuromarketing. Neuromarketing research can be expensive because the equipment used is modern and requires specialists in their field (Casado et al., 2023). Further, neuromarketing data itself is quite diverse, and requires certain professional input for its interpretation. Ethical issues are also an issue, most importantly the privacy issue and coercive persuasion which needs to be well handled to avoid a consumer backlash.

Both variables of neuromarketing and traditional marketing can be beneficial when incorporated together to have extensive understanding on consumers. Traditional techniques provide wide, inexpensive information and demographical classification, whereas neuromarketing dominates individuals' emotions and preposterous behavior. Together it allows marketers to develop the ideas that are effective in masses and at the same time work like emotions nearby to the hearts of the people (Sangeeta, & Tandon, 2021). Through the combined application of systems marketing and nature marketing, there is a stronger foundation to build awareness to consumers hence a better and effect way of performing the tasks of marketing.

Traditional marketing research typically involves gathering self-reported responses from test subjects, which may be influenced by biases that can impact the accuracy of your customer's feedback (Casado et al., 2023). Neuroscience helps mitigate the influence of biases on your research and data collection. Traditional marketing research can be influenced by three main biases:

1. **Response bias** occurs when a customer's test response is influenced by various factors, such as their interaction with the interviewer, the research environment, or their inclination to be a cooperative test subject (Yüksel, 2023).

2. **Self-assessment bias** refers to a situation where a customer feels uncertain about their own response or emotional state during a test, which can impact the accuracy of their recorded response (González-Mena et al., 2022). It's important to note that a customer's response to a product may not always be as straightforward as what can be determined through a brain scan or physiological response.
3. **Researcher bias** can significantly impact the way data is reported in marketing tests. When proctoring a focus group, researchers may unintentionally bring their own subjective biases into the equation. Neuromarketing eliminates the impact of a potentially biassed researcher (Mittal et al., 2022).

NEUROMARKETING TECHNIQUES

Figure 1. Techniques of neuromarketing

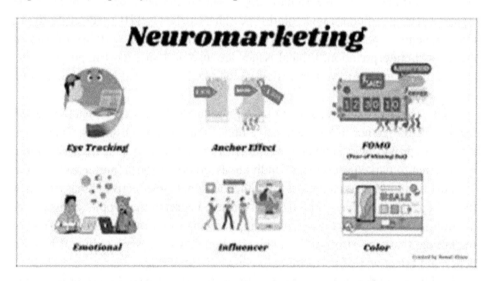

Researchers employ various neurological and physiological research methods and techniques to gauge customer responses. These methods encompass:

1. **Functional Magnetic Resonance Imaging (fMRI)** is a brain imaging technique that utilises magnetic fields to monitor blood flow in the brain (Sangeeta, & Tandon, 2021). It is possible to monitor a customer's intricate neural reactions, memory recall, and level of involvement using an fMRI.

2. **Electroencephalography (EEG)** is a brain imaging technique that involves the placement of electrodes on the scalp to measure neural activity (González et al., 2022). Tracking customer engagement and brain activity can be done rapidly, within a matter of seconds, using an EEG.

3. **Eye tracking** is a valuable tool for understanding customer behaviour. By analysing the eye's fixation points and measuring pupil dilation, we can gain insights into attention and arousal levels (Ha et al., 2022). It is possible to measure engagement and attention using this.

4. **Understanding facial expressions**: By closely monitoring subtle shifts in facial expressions, valuable information can be gained about how customers are feeling (Arora, 2023).

5. **Monitoring heart rate**: An uptick in heart rate indicates heightened excitement in your customer.

NEUROMARKETING: A RISING PHENOMENON IN THE WORLD OF MARKETING

Figure 2. The companies that have embraced the power of neuromarketing

1. Coca-Cola

Coca-Cola has a firm belief in the power of neuromarketing, so much so that they have built their own in-house lab. They have the ability to analyse brain activity in volunteer subjects in order to determine which advertisements are most likely to yield optimal results. By utilising neural activity, you can obtain impartial results, making this approach highly effective for devising marketing strategies (Alsharif et al., 2024). When a company seeks feedback from consumers about an advertisement, there is a chance that the customer may not provide an honest response. Maybe they wouldn't want to risk upsetting the company by expressing their positive opinion about a commercial, even if they don't genuinely like it (Casado et al., 2023). However, when examining brain activity, marketers can consistently obtain accurate results.

2. Hyundai

The car manufacturing industry is also influenced by the impacts of neuromarketing. Hyundai conducted a study involving 30 participants, consisting of an equal number of men and women, who were asked to examine various components of their vehicle models (Kajla et al., 2024). Through a thorough analysis of neural activity, the company gained valuable insights into the aspects of the product that resonated with consumers. Given the high costs associated with designing and launching a new car model, this approach could prove to be a cost-effective strategy for companies embarking on future projects (Cenizo, 2022).

3. Campbell's

Companies understand the impact of their packaging on sales and are skilled at leveraging neuromarketing techniques to drive results. Eye-catching designs have the power to attract a larger customer base, appealing to those who value both aesthetics and the quality of the product (Sangeeta, & Tandon, 2021). Brain activity can be measured when consumers respond to factors like touch and images found on the packaging. Colours play a significant role in influencing consumer behavior (Casado et al., 2023). Using neuromarketing techniques, Campbell's successfully revamped the labels on their soup packaging. They enhanced the consumer appeal by leveraging neural responses to specific elements.

4. Yahoo

When launching a $100 million branding campaign, the search engine giant utilised neuromarketing techniques. As part of their strategy, they featured a commercial showcasing joyful individuals dancing across different locations around the globe (Kajla et al., 2024). Prior to launching the advertisement, the company conducted a thorough analysis of consumers' brain activity using an electroencephalogram (EEG). With the ability to observe the responses in the test subject's brains, they could have greater confidence in the success of their campaign.

5. Facebook

Although consumers may not always be forthcoming with a company that has previously annoyed them, their intentions are not always to deliberately withhold the truth. Many individuals may be unaware of their subconscious responses to various stimuli (Siddique et al., 2023). Facebook conducted a comprehensive analysis of how its advertising system impacted the perceptions and emotions of the test subjects, revealing previously unknown insights. By adopting the mindset of a marketing analyst, you can gain valuable insights into what strategies will yield positive results for your business and which ones will fall flat.

EXAMINING THE REGIONAL ASPECTS OF NEUROMARKETING

Figure 3. Regional analysis of neuromarketing

The Neuromarketing Technology Market is projected to experience a significant growth rate of 9.12% throughout the forecast period. The projected value of the Global Neuromarketing Technology Market is estimated to be US$ 2.37 Billion by 2029.

The report reflects the revenue impact of the COVID-19 pandemic on the sales revenue of market leaders, market followers, and market disrupters (Casado et al., 2023). The report study thoroughly examined this impact.

UNDERSTANDING THE DYNAMICS OF THE NEUROMARKETING TECHNOLOGY MARKET

The growing popularity of neuromarketing technology among market researchers worldwide, as a means to analyse and comprehend customer perceptions, is a significant catalyst for market growth (Aslan and Özbeyaz 2022). With this technology, marketing companies and market research firms can gain valuable insights into customer expectations, enabling them to adapt and enhance their services accordingly (Kamal, 2024). The market is expected to experience significant growth during the forecast period due to the increasing technological advancements in consumer neuroscience technology, the wide-scale adoption of neuromarketing technology by various organisations to boost their business, and the rising adoption of medical insights and techniques to better understand customer decision-making processes (Du & MacDonald, 2014). Neuromarketing technology offers several advantages, including gaining new perspectives on the market, measuring the impact of priming, and revealing customers' subconscious and emotional responses. These factors are driving the market's growth (Kamal et al., 2024).

Nevertheless, the market growth may face obstacles due to the significant expenses related to neuromarketing research, ethical considerations, and the costly equipment required for neuromarketing technology (Manpreet et al., 2023).

INTERSECTION OF NEUROMARKETING AND METAVERSE

The integration of metaverse, specifically, and neuromarketing in particular have a significant, revolutionary character in the marketing approach. Facebook's metaverse is regarded as an extensive virtual world that simulates regular environments and individuals with live activity share some experiences (Jeetesh et al., 2024). Thus, it is quite possible that neuromarketing, which explores consumer behavior in the subliminal level, could make use of the metaverse to gather more helpful and satisfactory data as well as to create better and more efficient marketing strategies.

The metaverse gives marketers an opportunity to reach their audience in a virtual world that can as well mimic reality to a greater extent. For example, virtual stores can imitate the shopping centers where the consumer is able to look at items, communicate with salespersons and even 'wear' the products with a help of avatars. The tools of neuromarketing, including eye tracking and facial coding, can be incorporated into these virtual, environments to measure the consumers' reactions in real-time (Arora, 2024). This is factual since it allows marketers to receive instant results on what grabs the client's attention, generates positive feelings, and compels them to interact, so they can adjust the approach accordingly.

Also, it is necessary to notice that the metaverse provides neuromarketing research with an extensive data perspective. Using biometrics and other features people reveal in virtual environments, marketers can gain more profound understanding of consumers' tendencies. For instance, understanding the ways that users interact with virtual environments, which features of a space and/or interface they tend to gravitate towards, and their affective responses to various stimuli can be applied to designing better virtual experiences (Chandel and Arora, 2024).

The combination of the metaverse and neuromarketing also helps with more ethical and better regulated studies. Compared to actual neuromarketing approaches, virtual neuromarketing allows marketers to experiment with various situations and collect information nonintrusively and with a minimal impact on people's privacy (Arora and Sharma, 2023). This may result in increased number of greater and more consumer relevance strategies in marketing.

In other words, it is critical to understand that the application of neuromarketing to the metaverse shall yield promising results in the formation of enthralling, differentiated, and evidenced-based marketing initiatives. Since the concept of the metaverse is still growing, it will for sure become a priority focus area for marketers interested in the effective implementation of tools for analyzing consumers' behavior patterns. Creating immersive and interactive virtual environments for the purpose of engaging customers and encouraging novel business models is one of the ways in which the metaverse has the potential to revolutionise branding, marketing, and entrepreneurship after COVID-19 (Dhiman & Arora, (2024); Kumar, Arora & Erkol Bayram, (Eds.). (2024). With this transformation, brands are able to easily reach consumers all over the world and adapt to the ever-changing trends in digital technology. Through the utilisation of immersive experiences, neuromarketing has the potential to utilise the metaverse in order to tap into the subconscious responses of consumers, optimise marketing tactics, and favourably influence the manner in which companies connect with stakeholders (Rathore & Arora, 2024).

ANALYSIS OF MARKET SEGMENTS IN NEUROMARKETING TECHNOLOGY

The technology of functional magnetic resonance imaging (FMRI) dominated the market in 2022 and is projected to experience steady growth at a CAGR of xx% throughout the forecast period. FMRI measures brain activity by detecting alterations associated with blood flow (Du & MacDonald, 2014). The market is experiencing growth as more and more people are adopting FMRI technology. This technology has the unique ability to capture images of deep brain structures, allowing for more accurate results, especially when it comes to capturing emotional responses (Parkash et al., 2023).

On the other hand, the Eye-tracking segment is expected to experience rapid growth at a CAGR of xx% throughout the forecast period (Aslan and Özbeyaz 2022). Eye-tracking technology allows businesses to gain valuable insights into consumer behaviour, visual attention, and memorability by capturing data on eye pupil and eye gaze movements (Kim & Kim 2024). The market is projected to experience significant growth during the forecast period, thanks to the increasing adoption of eye-tracking technology in virtual reality headsets (Kant & Yadete, 2023). The Weather Channel, PepsiCo, Ebay, and Daimler are among the leading brands utilising neuromarketing technology for market research purposes. Furthermore, large enterprises such as LinkedIn, Tata Group, Vodafone-Idea, Kimberly Clark, and Mars have embraced neuromarketing technology to enhance their advertising, packaging, and marketing strategies (Cenizo, 2022).. Research shows that a significant number of companies, around 80%, are embracing neuromarketing research technology as they gear up to compete primarily or entirely on customer experience

REGIONAL ANALYSIS OF THE NEUROMARKETING TECHNOLOGY MARKET

In 2022, the market was dominated by North America and is projected to maintain its dominance throughout the forecast period with a CAGR of xx%. The market in the region experiences significant growth due to the contributions of the US and Canada. The growth can be attributed to the rising investment in neuroscience technology. The market is experiencing significant growth due to the strong presence of several top neuromarketing solution providers in the region.

Our report aims to provide a thorough analysis of the Global Neuromarketing Technology Market, covering all industry stakeholders (Aslan and Özbeyaz 2022). The report provides an overview of the industry's historical and current state, along with projected market size and trends. It breaks down complex data into easy-to-understand language. The report provides a comprehensive analysis of the industry, focusing on key players such as market leaders, followers, and new entrants. The report includes a presentation of the PORTER, SVOR, PESTEL analysis, along with an assessment of the potential impact of micro-economic factors on the market. Thorough analysis has been conducted on both external and internal factors that can impact the business, providing decision-makers with a clear understanding of the industry's future outlook (Sood et al., 2023).

This report provides valuable insights into the dynamics and structure of the Global Neuromarketing Technology Market by analysing its market segments and projecting its future. The report provides a comprehensive analysis of key players in the Global Neuromarketing Technology Market, including their application, price, financial position, product portfolio, growth strategies, and regional presence (Du & MacDonald, 2014). This detailed information serves as a valuable resource for investors.

THE INCREASING POPULARITY OF NEUROMARKETING

Figure 4. The level of usefulness that consumers in India perceive in neuromarketing

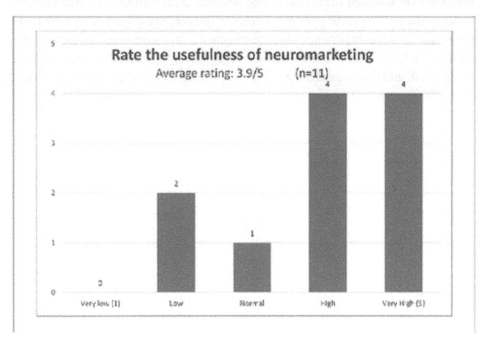

In today's market, customers have a wide range of products to choose from, whether they prefer shopping in-store or online. Just about every product or brand has its own unique selling points, packaging, colour combinations, and other marketing tactics that they employ to stand out to customers in a distinctive way. It's becoming more and more difficult for brands to capture the attention of consumers, whose attention spans are shrinking rapidly (Aslan and Özbeyaz 2022). Given the abundance of options, consumers often make purchasing decisions without much consideration, which can be exploited by marketers who create a sense of urgency when it may not be necessary (Ha et al., 2022).

Neuro-marketing encompasses a wide range of disciplines, such as psychology, marketing, neuroscience, and market research, to provide a comprehensive understanding of consumer behavior. Understanding the importance of selecting the right area of focus is essential for students pursuing a degree in neuro-marketing, given the wide range of programme choices available. For individuals interested in exploring the realm of consumers, there are various programmes designed for marketers, researchers, and other enthusiasts to pursue a career in this field.

Working for a neuro-marketing consultancy firm is a popular career choice, but there are also opportunities in brand marketing intelligence departments or traditional market research firms (Arora and Sharma, 2023). However, three domains in neuro-marketing can be pursued: careers in science, marketing, or data. With the right education and experience, one can pursue a wide range of lucrative careers in these fields, including those of marketing research analyst, research and development coordinator, and neuro-marketing researcher, among many others (González-Mena et al., 2022).

REFERENCES

Al Sharif, A. H., Salleh, N. Z. M., Baharun, R. O., & Yusoff, M. E. (2021). Consumer behaviour through neuromarketing approach. *Journal of Contemporary Issues in Business and Government*, 27(3), 344–354.

Alsharif, A. H., Salleh, N. Z. M., Alrawad, M., & Lutfi, A. (2024). Exploring global trends and future directions in advertising research: A focus on consumer behavior. *Current Psychology (New Brunswick, N.J.)*, 43(7), 6193–6216. 10.1007/s12144-023-04812-w37359681

Alsharif, A. H., Salleh, N. Z. M., Hashem, E. A. R., Khraiwish, A., Putit, L., & Arif, L. S. M. (2023). Exploring factors influencing neuromarketing implementation in malaysian universities: Barriers and enablers. *Sustainability (Basel)*, 15(5), 4603. 10.3390/su15054603

Arora, M. (2020). Post-truth and marketing communication in technological age. In *Handbook of research on innovations in technology and marketing for the connected consumer* (pp. 94–108). IGI Global. 10.4018/978-1-7998-0131-3.ch005

Arora, M. (2023). Encapsulating Role of Persuasion and Skill Development in Marketing Communication for Brand Building: A Perspective. In *International Handbook of Skill, Education, Learning, and Research Development in Tourism and Hospitality* (pp. 1–17). Springer Nature Singapore.

Arora, M. (2024). Metaverse Metamorphosis: Bridging the Gap Between Research Insights and Industry Applications. In *Research, Innovation, and Industry Impacts of the Metaverse* (pp. 275-286). Research Gate.

Arora, M., & Sharma, R. L. (2023). Artificial intelligence and big data: Ontological and communicative perspectives in multi-sectoral scenarios of modern businesses. *Foresight*, 25(1), 126–143. 10.1108/FS-10-2021-0216

Aslan, R., & Özbeyaz, A. (2022). Analysis of brand visibility on smartphone images with three-stage model using eye-tracking and EEG: A decision-making study in neuromarketing. *Middle East Journal of Management*, 9(4), 417–434. 10.1504/MEJM.2022.123727

Bhardwaj, S., Rana, G. A., Behl, A., & de Caceres, S. J. G. (2023). Exploring the boundaries of Neuromarketing through systematic investigation. *Journal of Business Research*, 154, 113371. 10.1016/j.jbusres.2022.113371

Casado-Aranda, L. A., Sánchez-Fernández, J., Bigne, E., & Smidts, A. (2023). The application of neuromarketing tools in communication research: A comprehensive review of trends. *Psychology and Marketing*, 40(9), 1737–1756. 10.1002/mar.21832

Cenizo, C. (2022). Neuromarketing: Concept, historical evolution and challenges. *Journal ICONO*, 14(20), 1.

Chandel, M., & Arora, M. (2024). Metaverse Perspectives: Unpacking Its Role in Shaping Sustainable Development Goals-A Qualitative Inquiry. In *Research, Innovation, and Industry Impacts of the Metaverse* (pp. 62-75). IGI Global.

Dhiman, V., & Arora, M. (2024). Current State of Metaverse in Entrepreneurial Ecosystem: A Retrospective Analysis of Its Evolving Landscape. In *Exploring the Use of Metaverse in Business and Education* (pp. 73-87). IGI Global. 10.4018/979-8-3693-5868-9.ch005

Du, P., & MacDonald, E. F. (2014). Eye-tracking data predict importance of product features and saliency of size change. *Journal of Mechanical Design*, 136(8), 081005. 10.1115/1.4027387

Fisher, C. E., Chin, L., & Klitzman, R. (2010). Defining neuromarketing: Practices and professional challenges. *Harvard Review of Psychiatry*, 18(4), 230–237. 10.3109/10673229.2010.49662320597593

Fortunato, V. C. R., Giraldi, J. D. M. E., & de Oliveira, J. H. C. (2014). A review of studies on neuromarketing: Practical results, techniques, contributions and limitations. *Journal of Management Research*, 6(2), 201. 10.5296/jmr.v6i2.5446

González-Mena, G., Del-Valle-Soto, C., Corona, V., & Rodríguez, J. (2022). Neuromarketing in the digital age: The direct relation between facial expressions and website design. *Applied Sciences (Basel, Switzerland)*, 12(16), 8186. 10.3390/app12168186

Grima, S., Kizilkaya, M., Sood, K., & ErdemDelice, M. (2021). The perceived effectiveness of blockchain for digital operational risk resilience in the European Union insurance market sector. *Journal of Risk and Financial Management*, 14(8), 363. 10.3390/jrfm14080363

Ha, J., Choi, K. M., & Im, C. H. (2022). Feasibility of using electrooculography-based eye-trackers for neuromarketing applications. *IEEE Transactions on Instrumentation and Measurement*, 71, 1–10. 10.1109/TIM.2022.3217849

Kajla, T., Raj, S., Kansra, P., Gupta, S. L., & Singh, N. (2024). Neuromarketing and consumer behavior: A bibliometric analysis. *Journal of Consumer Behaviour*, 23(2), 959–975. 10.1002/cb.2256

Kamal, R. (2024). Exploring the Synergy: Venture Capital's Impact on the Startup Ecosystem. In *Fostering Innovation in Venture Capital and Startup Ecosystems* (pp. 242-264). IGI Global.

Kamal, R. (2024). *Artificial Intelligence-Powered Political Advertising: Harnessing Data-Driven Insights for Campaign Strategies.* IGI Global. 10.4018/979-8-3693-2964-1.ch006

Kant, S., & Yadete, F. D. (2023). Neuro-marketing in understanding consumer behavior: Systematic literature review. *RADINKA JOURNAL OF SCIENCE AND SYSTEMATIC LITERATURE REVIEW*, 1(1), 1–13. 10.56778/rjslr.v1i1.86

Kaur, M., Kaur, J., & Kaur, R. (2023). *Adapting to Technological Disruption: Challenges and Opportunities for Employment.* IEEE. .10.1109/ICCCIS60361.2023.10425266

Kaur, M., & Malhan, S. (2024). The Role of the Manufacturing Sector in Driving India's Long-Term Growth. Kumar, N., Sood, K., Özen, E. and Grima, S. (Ed.) *The Framework for Resilient Industry: A Holistic Approach for Developing Economies (Emerald Studies in Finance, Insurance, and Risk Management).* Emerald Publishing Limited, Leeds. 10.1108/978-1-83753-734-120241021

Kim, J. Y., & Kim, M. J. (2024). Identifying customer preferences through the eye-tracking in travel websites focusing on neuromarketing. *Journal of Asian Architecture and Building Engineering*, 23(2), 515–527. 10.1080/13467581.2023.2244566

Kumar, J., Arora, M., & Erkol Bayram, G. (Eds.). (2024). *Exploring the Use of Metaverse in Business and Education.* IGI Global. 10.4018/979-8-3693-5868-9

Lee, N., Broderick, A. J., & Chamberlain, L. (2007). What is 'neuromarketing'? A discussion and agenda for future research. *International Journal of Psychophysiology*, 63(2), 199–204. 10.1016/j.ijpsycho.2006.03.00716769143

Misra, L. (2023). Neuromarketing insights into consumer behavior. *IUJ Journal of Management*, 11(1), 143–163.

Misra, L. (2023). Neuromarketing insights into consumer behavior. *IUJ Journal of Management*, 11(1), 143–163.

Mittal, A., Mantri, A., Tandon, U., & Dwivedi, Y. K. (2022). A unified perspective on the adoption of online teaching in higher education during the COVID-19 pandemic. *Information Discovery and Delivery*, 50(2), 117–132. 10.1108/IDD-09-2020-0114

Mordor Intelligence Research & Advisory. (2023, September). *Neuromarketing Market Size & Share Analysis - Growth Trends & Forecasts (2024 - 2029).* Mordor Intelligence. https://www.mordorintelligence.com/industry-reports/neuromarketing-market

Rathore, S., & Arora, M. (2024). Sustainability Reporting in the Metaverse: A Multi-Sectoral Analysis. In *Exploring the Use of Metaverse in Business and Education* (pp. 147-165). IGI Global. 10.4018/979-8-3693-5868-9.ch009

Razbadauskaitė-Venskė, I. (2024). Neuromarketing: a tool to understand consumer behaviour. *Regional formation and development studies*, (1), 101-109.

Robaina-Calderín, L., & Martín-Santana, J. D. (2021). A review of research on neuromarketing using content analysis: Key approaches and new avenues. *Cognitive Neurodynamics*, 15(6), 923–938. 10.1007/s11571-021-09693-y34790262

Sangeeta, & Tandon, U. (2021). Factors influencing adoption of online teaching by school teachers: A study during COVID-19 pandemic. *Journal of Public Affairs, 21*(4), e2503.

Siddique, J., Shamim, A., Nawaz, M., & Abid, M. F. (2023). The hope and hype of neuromarketing: A bibliometric analysis. *Journal of Contemporary Marketing Science*, 6(1), 1–21. 10.1108/JCMARS-07-2022-0018

Singh, P., Alhassan, I., & Khoshaim, L. (2023). What Do You Need to Know? A Systematic Review and Research Agenda on Neuromarketing Discipline. *Journal of Theoretical and Applied Electronic Commerce Research*, 18(4), 2007–2032. 10.3390/jtaer18040101

Sood, K., Kaur, B., & Grima, S. (2022). Revamping Indian non-life insurance industry with a trusted network: Blockchain technology. In *Big Data: A game changer for insurance industry* (pp. 213–228). Emerald Publishing Limited. 10.1108/978-1-80262-605-620221014

Yadete, F. D., & Kant, S. (2023). Neuro-Marketing in Understanding Consumer Behavior: Systematic Literature Review. *Partners Universal International Innovation Journal*, 1(2), 105–116.

Yüksel, D. (2023). Investigation of Web-Based Eye-Tracking System Performance under Different Lighting Conditions for Neuromarketing. *Journal of Theoretical and Applied Electronic Commerce Research*, 18(4), 2092–2106. 10.3390/jtaer18040105

Chapter 7
Ethical and Un–Ethical Consideration(s) in the Realm of Neuromarketing

Raveena Gupta
Faculty of Management Studies, University of Delhi, India

Anuj Pal Kapoor
Indian Institute of Technology, Jodhpur, India

Harsh Vardhan Sharma
Faculty of Management Studies, University of Delhi, India

ABSTRACT

Although neuromarketing presents marketers with great potential to gain insight into the neurological mechanisms that influence customer choices, it also brings up important ethical questions because it paves the way for unbridled manipulation of customers by providing unparalleled access to their mind. Thus, it is critical to discuss multi-facets of neuromarketing pertaining to its potential and limitations. This chapter delves into the challenges pertaining to policy implementation, limitations, and potential benefits of neuromarketing on individuals and society.

INTRODUCTION

Amidst ongoing technological advancements that reshape the domains of commerce and communication, the incorporation of neuroscience principles into marketing strategies has surfaced as a potent instrument for comprehending consumer behaviour. Neuromarketing, a burgeoning field at the intersection of neuroscience and

DOI: 10.4018/979-8-3693-4236-7.ch007

marketing, offers insights into the subconscious drivers of consumer decision-making, promising unparalleled precision in crafting persuasive communication messages, packaging, and products. However, with this promise comes a host of ethical considerations that demand careful examination.

The ethical dimensions of neuromarketing are multifaceted and complex, touching upon fundamental principles of autonomy, privacy, and transparency. As marketers delve into the realm of the human mind to decode its mysteries, questions arise regarding the boundaries of permissible persuasion, the sanctity of personal privacy, and the potential for manipulation. Can the insights gleaned from neural data collection be harnessed responsibly, or do they pose a threat to individual autonomy and free will? How should marketers navigate the delicate balance between innovation and consumer protection in this rapidly evolving landscape?

As we embark on this exploration, it is imperative to recognize the significance of addressing ethical considerations in neuromarketing. Beyond mere compliance with regulations, ethical conduct in neuromarketing holds the key to fostering trust, credibility, and long-term sustainability in the marketing industry. By engaging in critical dialogue and collaborative efforts, we can strive to unlock the full potential of neuromarketing while safeguarding the rights and well-being of consumers. This chapter aims to explore these pressing ethical concerns surrounding the practice of neuromarketing. By delving into the nuances of privacy, consent, manipulation, and transparency, we seek to shed light on the ethical challenges and objections inherent in leveraging neuroscience techniques for commercial gain.

While neuroscience has undoubtedly made great steps forward in recent years (Ariely & Berns, 2010), the intersection with business and the issues that dominate large corporations remains a complex challenge (Spence, 2019). It faces challenges in four areas since stages of inception, namely, small samples and big data, inferences, costs and ethics. Also, to find and develop common language or lexicon pertaining to neuromarketing is a challenge. Neuromarketing terminology tends to lean heavily on scientific and abstract language, while marketing, particularly in the realm of consumer insights, emphasizes narratives, storytelling, and diverse methods of conceptualizing and interpreting data. Thus, to comprehend the neuroscience lexicon becomes a challenge.

The commendable and essential aspect of marketing lies in its willingness to embrace concepts and methodologies from a wide array of fields. However, a serious problem arises when the foundational principles and methodological rigour developed in the originating discipline are not carried over with precision.(Baron, Zaltman and Olson, 2017). This emerging field suffers from many inconsistencies. A lack of systematic validation of metrics derived from neuroscience, conceptual inconsistencies, methodological differences, and dubious business practices are all indications of a discipline that requires further development and rigour. Notwithstanding significant scientific and commercial advancements, the field continues to confront numerous challenges, such as ambiguity surrounding the methodologies and metrics employed, scepticism regarding the interpretation of results, and an enduring lack of confidence from the business community in the provided methods and metrics (Ramsøy, 2019). It involves difficult data analysis, an artificial environment, and high cost. Furthermore, during the design of a neuro-study and data collection, there are no established criteria for confounding variables, baseline measurement, or synchronisation. Furthermore, these methods are often costly and require expert knowledge.

LITERATURE REVIEW

Neuromarketing, a field that combines neuroscience and marketing, aims to understand how consumers' brains respond to marketing stimuli. This understanding can help create more effective advertising and product designs. However, the application of neuroscientific methods to marketing raises significant ethical concerns. This essay explores these ethical issues, drawing on relevant literature. Neuromarketing employs techniques such as functional magnetic resonance imaging (fMRI), electroencephalography (EEG), and eye-tracking to gather data on consumer behaviour. While these methods can provide valuable insights, they also pose risks related to privacy, manipulation, and informed consent.

One of the primary ethical concerns in neuromarketing is the potential invasion of privacy. Researchers collect and analyse data on consumers' brain activity, which can reveal highly sensitive information about their thoughts, preferences, and vulnerabilities. This type of data collection can be seen as a form of surveillance, raising questions about how much information marketers should have about individuals. As Ariely and Berns (2010) note, "The capacity to peer into the consumer's brain raises the spectre of an Orwellian future where advertisers can manipulate purchasing behaviour without the individual's conscious awareness." The potential for manipulation is another significant ethical issue in neuromarketing. By understanding the neural mechanisms that drive consumer behaviour, marketers can design campaigns that exploit these mechanisms to influence purchasing decisions. This raises concerns about consumer autonomy and the possibility of coercive marketing practices. According to Stanton, Sinnott-Armstrong, and Huettel (2017), "Neuromarketing techniques can be used to craft messages that are not just persuasive, but irresistible, thereby undermining the consumer's ability to make free and informed choices." Informed consent is a cornerstone of ethical research, ensuring that participants understand what they are agreeing to and the potential risks involved. In neuromarketing, obtaining truly informed consent can be challenging. Consumers may not fully grasp how their brain data will be used or the implications of such data collection. Farah (2012) emphasizes the complexity of this issue, stating, "The challenge of obtaining informed consent in neuromarketing is exacerbated by the novelty and complexity of the techniques used, which are often poorly understood by the general public." The security and use of the data collected in neuromarketing studies also pose ethical challenges. There is a risk that sensitive brain data could be misused or fall into the wrong hands, leading to potential harm to individuals. Ensuring robust data protection measures and clear policies on data use is crucial. As Murphy, Illes, and Reiner (2008) argue, "Neuromarketing researchers and companies must implement stringent data security protocols and be transparent about how they intend to use the data they collect." To address these ethical concerns, there is a need for regulatory frameworks and ethical guidelines specific to neuromarketing. Professional organizations and regulatory bodies must develop standards that protect consumers while allowing for the advancement of neuromarketing research. Harris, Ciorciari, and Gountas (2018) suggest that "Developing comprehensive ethical guidelines for neuromarketing can help balance the benefits of these techniques with the need to protect consumer rights and welfare."

In conclusion, while neuromarketing holds significant promise for enhancing our understanding of consumer behaviour, it also raises important ethical issues. Privacy, manipulation, informed consent, data security, and the need for regulatory guidelines are critical areas that must be addressed to ensure that neuromarketing practices are ethical and respectful of consumer rights. As the field continues to evolve, ongoing ethical scrutiny and dialogue will be essential to navigate these complex challenges.

Ethical Considerations and Objections

Apart from inconsistencies, this field is under the lens for its ethical concerns pertaining to rights of consumers and right to information. Due to its capacity to penetrate the underlying motivations of consumer behaviour, neuromarketing raises a multitude of ethical concerns that intersect with the principles of fairness, privacy, and autonomy. This section explores significant ethical considerations that are intrinsic to the field of neuromarketing, recognising the intricate relationship between commercial interests, scientific progress, and individual rights. Below are the objections which has often come across in the field of neuromarketing:

Informed Consent: A key ethical consideration in neuromarketing research revolves around informed consent. Participants in neuroimaging studies might lack a complete understanding of the ramifications of their involvement or how their data could be utilized for marketing objectives. Without informed consent, individuals may unknowingly contribute to studies that reveal intimate insights into their preferences, emotions, and decision-making processes Hence, in the pursuit of ethical neuromarketing practices, it is critical to establish robust mechanisms that secure informed consent and uphold the autonomy of individuals over their personal data.

Privacy and Data Security: Neuromarketing study entails gathering intimate data about people's neurological reactions and emotional states. Unlike traditional marketing research methods, which often rely on self-reported data, neuromarketing techniques involve accessing individuals' neural activity without their explicit awareness. This raises significant concerns regarding privacy invasion and the erosion of personal autonomy. Ensuring the privacy and confidentiality of participants' data is critical for upholding the integrity and trustworthiness of business operations and research. To mitigate the risk of data breaches and unauthorised access, neuromarketers are required to comply with rigorous data protection protocols, which encompass encryption, anonymization, and secure storage methods. By prioritizing data security and confidentiality, marketers can uphold ethical standards and demonstrate a commitment to respecting consumer privacy rights.

Manipulation: Neuromarketing has frequently faced allegations of divulging consumers' "buy" buttons; consequently, ethical considerations emerge concerning the manipulation of consumer decisions or the exploitation of susceptibilities for commercial gain. It holds the potential to influence consumer behavior at a subconscious level, raising ethical questions about the boundaries of permissible persuasion. Through the utilisation of knowledge derived from neural data, marketers are able to customise messages and stimuli in a manner that circumvents logical reasoning, which may compromise the autonomy and free will of persons. Moreover, the use of persuasive techniques based on neural insights may exploit vulnerabilities in consumers, leading to decisions that are not in their best interests. Ethical neuromarketing necessitates a delicate balance between leveraging scientific insights for effective communication and respecting individuals' right to make autonomous decisions free from undue influence.

Transparency and Accountability: At the core of ethical neuromarketing lies the fundamental tenet of communication transparency. Consumers have a right to know when their neural data is being collected and how it will be used to inform marketing practices. Consequently, marketers are ethically obligated to provide full disclosure regarding the utilisation of neuromarketing techniques in consumer research, advertising, and product development. Effective and open communication cultivates confidence and enables people to make well-informed decisions regarding their engagement. Moreover, it enables consumers to exercise greater control over their personal data and reinforces the ethical responsibility of marketers to prioritize consumer welfare over commercial interests. While it is the responsibility of marketers and researcher to mitigate these concerns and increase the trust. They should be transparent about the use of neuromarketing techniques in advertising and promotional campaigns, providing clear disclosures about the nature of the research and its implications for consumer privacy and autonomy. Furthermore, establishing mechanisms for accountability and oversight can help mitigate the risks of unethical conduct and ensure compliance with ethical standards and regulations.

Vulnerability and Targeting: The ethical ramifications of neuromarketing's targeting of vulnerable populations—including infants, the elderly, and individuals with cognitive disabilities—are a subject of concern. While these groups may be more susceptible to persuasive techniques, their limited capacity to understand and critically evaluate marketing messages makes them particularly susceptible to exploitation. Ethical neuromarketing practices require careful consideration of the potential impact on vulnerable populations and a commitment to avoiding harm or exploitation. Marketers must exercise caution in targeting strategies and refrain from exploiting vulnerabilities for commercial gain, prioritizing the well-being and dignity of all consumers.

Neuromarketing Ethical or Unethical?

There are two perspectives to consider. On one hand, some may argue that neuromarketing renders marketers excessively effective. They have too much influence on the unconscious side of the consumer choice and they can trick people into being consumer zombies. To that defense, it has always been that way, the marketers know a lot about their customers and their behavior. With neuromarketing, they have gotten better tools to be efficient. Furthermore, it can be unethical towards shareholders not to pursue these techniques from the business perspective. If the intent is not to distort the economic behavior of consumers, it can serve as a competitive advantage as it helps to build products that are more attractive and useful to consumers.

Neuromarketing has been misunderstood in sofar as they are intended only to predict consumers' behavior and not to compel them to purchase products (Sung et al., 2020) and predictions are probabilistic rather than deterministic. It focuses on 'more likely to buy' rather than pressing a 'buy button. The act of predicting behavior is distinct from compelling customers to act against their will, therefore, prediction does not necessarily negate or weaken the rationality or the dignity of individuals whose behavior is being predicted (Stanton, Sinnott-Armstrong and Huettel, 2017). Moreover, regarding the matter of privacy, it should be noted that an individual customer is not directly targeted in a privacy infringement. Instead, results are derived by extrapolating from a limited experimental group to the broader audience, as is done in current marketing research (as well as biological and behavioral research).

The other thing is whether it is conducted correctly - a question about validity and reliability of the methods and providing true insights, which is a genuine concern. Other important and genuine concerns of neuromarketing can be attributed to increasing prices of the product or service since employing neuromarketing can increase the cost thus, increasing prices of the product and services. It might fuel consumerism. Advertisements can amplify consumer desires to an extent that may not be beneficial, as consumers may be compelled to pay a significantly higher price for a product that provides few benefits. The fundamental apprehension can be associated with enhancing the potency of advertisements, perhaps leading to the emergence of new desires or the reinforcement of current desires in manners that are harmful to consumers' well-being. These anxieties may also stem from the successful application of conventional marketing research methods. Industry -related ethical violations are an even greater concern, as is the possibility that neuromarketing or marketing could exacerbate irrational decision making or increase the probability that consumers will purchase products that do not provide any benefit to them. But these issues are not pertaining to neuromarketing only, these are the challenges of marketing as a whole (Stanton, Sinnott-Armstrong and Huettel, 2017).

Shouldering Responsibility: Researchers, Marketers and Firms in Ethical Neuromarketing

As neuromarketing continues advancing and diffusing into wider corporate adoption, the practitioners in this emerging field bear a profound responsibility in shaping its ethical trajectory. While navigating the ethical complexities of neuro-marketing, it is imperative for researchers, marketers, and companies to adopt a principled approach that prioritizes respect for individual autonomy, transparency in communication, and the protection of consumer welfare. By adhering to ethical guidelines and fostering dialogue between stakeholders, the marketing industry can harness the potential of neuromarketing while upholding ethical standards that promote trust, integrity, and social responsibility.

In addition, neuromarketing firms should be ethically bound to abstain from disseminating false assertions or exaggerating the efficacy of their methodologies. It is imperative that they refrain from overpromising results beyond the realistic capabilities of neuromarketing techniques. Such practices not only erode trust within the industry but also deceive clients and consumers, potentially leading to misguided expectations and disillusionment. Upholding integrity and transparency in all communications is essential for maintaining credibility and fostering sustain-able relationships with stakeholders. Instead, neuromarketing firms should focus on accurately communicating the strengths and limitations of their approaches, ensuring that clients have realistic expectations and making informed decisions based on reliable information.

Adhering to ethical standards, prioritizing consumer welfare, and safeguarding the integrity of the discipline are essential practices that contribute to the holistic advancement of the field. By upholding these principles, practitioners not only foster trust and credibility within the industry but also ensure the well-being of consumers and maintain the integrity of neuromarketing as a discipline. This commitment to ethical conduct not only benefits individual practitioners and firms but also strengthens the reputation and sustainability of the entire field, ultimately leading to its continued growth and evolution in a responsible and ethical manner.

Initiatives in Formulating Ethical Standards for Neuromarketing

As the ethical conundrums around neuromarketing have gained more public awareness in recent years, various organizations and thought leaders have put forth proposals for guidelines and best practices to mitigate potential risks while allowing research to proceed responsibly.

One of the earliest efforts came in 2004 when the NeuroMarketing Science & Business Association (NMSBA), a professional association for the neuromarketing industry, published a "Code of Ethics" covering principles like respecting human dignity, prohibiting deception, protecting data privacy and confidentiality, avoiding exploitation of vulnerable groups, and upholding scientific integrity. It marks the first step towards setting universal standards for utilizing neuroscientific methods to assess the effectiveness of:

- advertising campaigns
- packaging and product design
- communication initiatives by non-profit organizations and government bodies.

The Code of Ethics within the neuromarketing sector tackles three critical concerns:

- reinstating public trust in the credibility and honesty of neuromarketing practitioners
- safeguarding the privacy of research participants
- ensuring the protection of consumers availing neuromarketing services.

The "Neurotechnology Industry Body Reform Trust" released a report in 2012 called "Solution for Regulating Neuromarketing." According to this report, any type of neuromarketing technique used on the general public must receive prior approval from regulatory authorities. Additionally, organisations that use neuromarketing internally should appoint responsible officers to ensure ethical practices are followed.

The following year, consumer rights groups like Consumer Watchdog in the United States and Citizens' Representative Council of Japan began calling for regulations prohibiting neuromarketing practices targeted towards children under 16 years old due to their heightened neurological vulnerabilities. They argued even consenting parents could not fully comprehend the mental privacy implications of neuromarketing on child brain development. In 2014, the European Society for Opinion and Marketing Research (ESOMAR) published guidelines for neuromarketing research member companies. Key tenets included obtaining informed consent, restricting data only for legitimate market research purposes, transparency regarding neuromarketing methodologies, and specific ethical review for research involving vulnerable groups or relating to potentially manipulative product categories.

Alongside industry groups, ethicists and academic institutions have proposed neuromarketing frameworks as well. A 2012 article from neuroscientists at the University of Pennsylvania laid out an "Open Neuroethics" model built on informed public discourse, education, and multi-stakeholder collaboration to uphold moral reasoning as neuroscience and neurotechnology rapidly advance.

Murphy et al.'s (2008) "Neuroethics of Neuromarketing" guidelines remain among the most comprehensive proposals covering principles like:

- Informed Purchaser Freedom of Choice for consumers seeing neuromarketing-influenced materials
- Transparency about data collection and methodology
- Respect for autonomy through strict consent protocols
- Protection of consumer privacy and data confidentiality
- Upholding distributive justice and preventing exploitation of vulnerabilities
- Commitment to beneficence (doing good) and non-malfeasance (not inflicting harm)
- Regulatory oversight and enforcement mechanisms

Other notable ethical proposals have emerged from the Magna Neuromarketing Ethics Project, Stanford University's Human Sciences and Technologies Advanced Research Institute, the Interdisciplinary Center for Neuromarketing Studies at Copenhagen Business School, and the NeuroThics & NeuroMarketing Research Group at Erasmus University. Similarly, the Advertising Research Foundation (ARF) and the American Marketing Association (AMA) have developed ethical principles that address the responsible use of neuroscience techniques in advertising and consumer research. Concerns emerged about inconsistent methodologies and difficulties evaluating neuroscience data quality from neuromarketing providers. To address this, the Advertising Research Foundation launched NeuroStandards in 2011. NeuroStandards aims to establish methodological best practices and auditing processes for neuroscience-based market research. It brings together neuroscientists, researchers, marketers, and neuromarketing firms to develop standards around aspects like experimental design, data acquisition, statistical analysis, ethics protocols, and auditing frameworks. The goal is to raise scientific rigor and client confidence in commercial neuroscience applications through these vetted standards. As of 2023, over 30 companies have received NeuroStandards certification. However, critics argue process standards alone cannot address ethical concerns around neural marketing's potential for manipulation. They contend external regulation is still needed beyond self-governance.

While specific implementation details vary, most proposals emphasize multi-stakeholder collaboration among academia, the private sector, regulators, and civil society organizations to instantiate appropriate governance and enforcement mechanisms. The development of ethical guidelines for neuromarketing necessitates a comprehensive and collaborative endeavour involving professionals, researchers, policymakers, and other stakeholders. These guidelines should encompass the entirety of ethical considerations in neuromarketing, including the ethics of research (such as avoiding overclaiming, ensuring proper research conduct through informed consent and protection of vulnerable participants, and maintaining ethical data practices including research design, scientific validity, confidentiality, and addressing potential dual use of research), the ethics of neuromarketing technologies (ensuring no harm, protecting privacy, and addressing incidental findings), and the ethics of neuromarketing applications (addressing manipulative and deceptive marketing practices and the potential exacerbation of emotional factors).

While challenges remain in implementing and enforcing the guidelines, continued efforts to uphold ethical standards would foster trust, credibility, and social responsibility in the field of neuromarketing.

Unveiling the Social Benefits of Neuromarketing

Beyond its role in consumer behaviour and brand management, neuromarketing holds significant potential to generate social benefits and can contribute to addressing societal challenges, enhancing public health initiatives, and promoting social welfare. It has got huge potential in bringing people from thought bubble to action, in addressing problems of loneliness, addiction, mental health, digital addiction, responsible consumption, fair work place and most importantly Climate change behaviour. By understanding the neural mechanisms underlying societal-related decision-making, policymakers and behavioural advocates can design interventions that resonate with target audiences on a deeper level. Below are the few ways, neuromarketing can benefit the society and individual:

Public Health Campaigns: Neuromarketing techniques can be applied to enhance the effectiveness of public health campaigns aimed at promoting healthy behaviours and preventing disease. By understanding the neural mechanisms underlying health-related decision-making, policymakers and health advocates can design interventions that resonate with target audiences on a deeper level. For example, neuromarketing research can inform the development of anti-smoking campaigns by identifying the most compelling messaging, imagery, and emotional appeals to discourage smoking initiation and encourage cessation. Similarly, in nutrition education initiatives, neuromarketing insights can help design interventions that encourage healthier food choices and combat obesity.

Behavioural Economics and Nudging: Behavioural economics, which explores how psychological factors influence economic decision-making, intersects with neuromarketing to create interventions known as "nudges." Nudges are subtle changes in the environment or presentation of options that steer individuals towards making more desirable choices without restricting their freedom. Neuromarketing research can inform the design of nudges that promote socially beneficial behaviours, such as conservation, recycling, and charitable giving. For instance, by leveraging principles of behavioural economics and neuroscience, policymakers can design interventions that encourage energy conservation by framing messages in ways that appeal to individuals' intrinsic motivations and emotional responses.

Social Marketing Campaigns: Social marketing campaigns aim to promote behaviours that benefit individuals and society as a whole, such as environmental conservation, community engagement, and public safety. Neuromarketing insights can enhance the effectiveness of social marketing initiatives by identifying persuasive messaging strategies and communication channels that resonate with target audiences. For example, in campaigns to promote seat belt use or discourage driving under the influence of alcohol, neuromarketing research can inform the design of messages that evoke strong emotional responses and emphasize social norms and personal safety. By tailoring interventions to individuals' cognitive biases and emotional triggers, social marketers can maximize the impact of their campaigns and drive positive behaviour change.

Political Communication and Civic Engagement: Neuromarketing techniques can also be applied to political communication and civic engagement initiatives, facilitating more effective voter outreach, persuasion, and mobilization efforts. By understanding the neural mechanisms underlying political attitudes and decision-making, campaigners and policymakers can craft messages that resonate with voters and drive civic participation. For instance, neuromarketing research can inform political campaigns about the most persuasive framing of policy issues, the optimal timing and frequency of communication, and the selection of imagery and slogans that evoke desired emotional responses. By leveraging insights from neuroscience, political actors can engage voters in meaningful dialogue, foster informed decision-making, and promote democratic values.

Discussion and Future Scope

Marketing in the digital era is crucial as it enables businesses to reach a global audience with personalized, data-driven strategies, enhancing customer engagement and loyalty. Digital platforms provide cost-effective, measurable marketing solutions that drive growth and competitive advantage in a fast-paced market. VR and emerging concepts like the metaverse are transforming digital marketing by creating immersive, interactive experiences that engage consumers on a deeper level. These technologies enable brands to offer unique virtual environments and personalized interactions, enhancing customer engagement and driving innovative marketing strategies in the digital landscape (Arora, (2024) a, Rathore & Arora, (2024)).

The metaverse can bring significant opportunities to entrepreneurs and marketers by providing a new frontier for innovation and customer engagement (Kumar, Arora, Erkol Bayram, Eds, 2024b; Arora,2023). Entrepreneurs can create and monetize virtual products, services, and experiences, while marketers can leverage immersive environments to develop highly interactive and personalized marketing campaigns (Dhiman & Arora 2024a; Dhiman & Arora, 2024b) . This opens up new revenue streams, enhances brand visibility, and offers unique ways to connect with global audiences. The entrepreneurial ecosystem shapes new innovations and promotes newer concepts of digitalization and the metaverse by fostering a culture of creativity, risk-taking, and collaboration (Arora & Sharma,2021; Arora 2016; Arora & Sharma,2022). This ecosystem includes support networks, funding opportunities, and access to cutting-edge technologies, enabling entrepreneurs to experiment with and develop pioneering digital solutions (Chandel & Arora 2024; Arora 2024b). In relation to marketing, this environment encourages the adoption of advanced digital tools and platforms, such as AI, VR, and AR, allowing marketers to create more engaging, personalized, and immersive experiences. As entrepreneurs push the boundaries of what's possible, they drive the evolution of marketing strategies, ensuring businesses can effectively connect with and captivate their audiences in a rapidly changing digital landscape (Kumar, Arora & Erkol Bayram, Eds.,2024a). Neuromarketers are intricately related to the entrepreneurial ecosystem, digitalization, and the metaverse as they apply neuroscience principles to understand consumer behavior and optimize marketing strategies. In the entrepreneurial ecosystem, neuromarketers provide insights that drive innovative product and service development, ensuring that new offerings resonate deeply with consumers. Through digitalization, they leverage big data and AI to analyze consumer responses and tailor personalized marketing campaigns (Arora & Sharma,2023). In the metaverse, neuromarketers create immersive experiences that engage multiple senses, enhancing emotional connections and brand loyalty. Their expertise helps businesses navigate these advanced technologies, ultimately leading to more effective and impactful marketing efforts. The integration of neuromarketing, digitalization, and the metaverse into entrepreneurial and marketing strategies raises several ethical dilemmas. Privacy concerns are paramount, as the collection and analysis of vast amounts of personal, biometric, and neurological data can lead to significant privacy issues. Consumers may not be fully aware of how their data is being used or have adequate control over it. Moreover, neuromarketing techniques have the potential to manipulate consumer behavior on a subconscious level, raising questions about the fairness and transparency of marketing practices. Ensuring that consumers give informed consent for their data to be collected and used is particularly challenging in immersive environments like the metaverse, where the extent of data collection may not be immediately apparent.

Additionally, the digital divide poses a significant ethical concern as digitalization and the metaverse become more prevalent. Those with access to advanced technology stand to benefit, potentially leaving others behind. The immersive nature of VR and the metaverse can also have psychological effects, such as addiction and altered perceptions of reality, which marketers and entrepreneurs must consider responsibly. Transparency in how neuromarketing data and techniques are used is essential to ensure consumer trust. Balancing the innovative potential of these technologies with the need to safeguard consumer rights and well-being is crucial for ethical and responsible marketing practices

The concept of ethics in neuromarketing will increasingly involve addressing emerging challenges and opportunities as the field evolves. With advancements in technology and deeper integration of neuroscientific methods into marketing strategies, ethical considerations will become more complex and multifaceted. As neuromarketing techniques become more sophisticated, protecting consumer privacy will remain a critical ethical concern. Future developments may include more robust privacy protections and guidelines to ensure that sensitive brain data is collected, stored, and used ethically. Innovations such as anonymization techniques and secure data storage solutions will be essential to prevent misuse and unauthorized access to consumer information. Additionally, there may be a push for greater transparency in how neuromarketing data is used, with companies required to disclose their data practices more clearly to consumers. The concept of informed consent will also evolve as neuromarketing becomes more prevalent. Ensuring that consumers fully understand what they are consenting to when participating in neuromarketing studies will be crucial. Future standards may involve more detailed and comprehensible consent forms, as well as continuous consent processes that keep participants informed about how their data is being used over time. This approach will help address the complexity and novelty of neuromarketing techniques, ensuring that consumers are adequately informed and can make autonomous decisions about their participation. The establishment of comprehensive regulatory frameworks will be essential for addressing the ethical challenges in neuromarketing. Future regulations may involve collaborations between governments, professional organizations, and industry stakeholders to create standards that protect consumer rights while allowing for the advancement of neuromarketing research. These frameworks could include certification programs for neuromarketing practitioners, ethical review boards to oversee research practices, and legal protections for consumers against unethical uses of their data. the future scope of ethics in neuromarketing will involve addressing increasingly complex challenges related to privacy, informed consent, manipulation, data security, and regulatory frameworks. As the field continues to evolve, ongoing ethical scrutiny, transparent practices, and robust regulatory measures will be essential to ensure that neuromarketing advances in ways that respect and protect consumer rights.

CONCLUSION

In conclusion, neuromarketing presents a thought-provoking dilemma between scientific progress, corporate interests, and consumer autonomy. While the potential for neuromarketing to generate positive effects on society and consumers is widely acknowledged, the ethical implications of this developing technology warrant significant public discourse. Neuromarketing exhibits significant potential in elucidating the intricacies of consumer behaviour and providing valuable insights for marketing strategies. However, it also poses ethical challenges that must be resolved in order to ensure that neuroscientific techniques are utilised responsibly and ethically in marketing research and practice. In order to cultivate trust and integrity in their engagements with consumers and society as a whole, marketers can effectively navigate the ethical intricacies of neuromarketing by adhering to the following principles: transparency, accountability, informed consent, and privacy protection.

REFERENCES

Ariely, D., & Berns, G. S. (2010). Neuromarketing: The hope and hype of neuroimaging in business. *Nature Reviews. Neuroscience*, 11(4), 284–292. 10.1038/nrn279520197790

Arora, M. (2016). Creative dimensions of entrepreneurship: A key to business innovation. *Pacific Business Review International*, 1(1), 255–259.

Arora, M. (2023). Encapsulating Role of Persuasion and Skill Development in Marketing Communication for Brand Building: A Perspective. In *International Handbook of Skill, Education, Learning, and Research Development in Tourism and Hospitality* (pp. 1–17). Springer Nature Singapore.

Arora, M. (2024). Virtual Reality in Education: Analyzing the Literature and Bibliometric State of Knowledge. *Transforming Education with Virtual Reality*, (pp. 379-402). Wiley. 10.1002/9781394200498.ch22

Arora, M. (2024). Metaverse Metamorphosis: Bridging the Gap Between Research Insights and Industry Applications. In *Research, Innovation, and Industry Impacts of the Metaverse* (pp. 275-286). Research Gate.

Arora, M., & Sharma, R. L. (2021). Repurposing the Role of Entrepreneurs in the Havoc of COVID-19. In *Entrepreneurship and Big Data* (pp. 229-250). CRC Press.

Arora, M., & Sharma, R. L. (2022). Coalescing skills of gig players and fervor of entrepreneurial leaders to provide resilience strategies during global economic crises. In *COVID-19's Impact on the Cryptocurrency Market and the Digital Economy* (pp. 118–140). IGI Global. 10.4018/978-1-7998-9117-8.ch008

Arora, M., & Sharma, R. L. (2023). Artificial intelligence and big data: Ontological and communicative perspectives in multi-sectoral scenarios of modern businesses. *Foresight*, 25(1), 126–143. 10.1108/FS-10-2021-0216

Baron, A. S., Zaltman, G., & Olson, J. (2017). Barriers to advancing the science and practice of marketing. *Journal of Marketing Management*, 33(11-12), 893–908. 10.1080/0267257X.2017.1323839

Chandel, M., & Arora, M. (2024). Metaverse Perspectives: Unpacking Its Role in Shaping Sustainable Development Goals-A Qualitative Inquiry. In *Research, Innovation, and Industry Impacts of the Metaverse* (pp. 62-75). IGI Global.

. Dhiman, V., & Arora, M. (2024)b. Exploring the linkage between business incubation and entrepreneurship: understanding trends, themes and future research agenda. *LBS Journal of Management & Research*.

Dhiman, V., & Arora, M. (2024)a. Current State of Metaverse in Entrepreneurial Ecosystem: A Retrospective Analysis of Its Evolving Landscape. In *Exploring the Use of Metaverse in Business and Education* (pp. 73-87). IGI Global. 10.4018/979-8-3693-5868-9.ch005

Ducu, C. (2017). *Topoi in neuromarketing ethics. Ethics and Neuromarketing: Implications for Market Research and Business Practice*, (pp. 31-64). Research Gate.

Farah, M. J. (2012). Neuroethics: The ethical, legal, and societal impact of neuroscience. *Annual Review of Psychology*, 63(1), 571–591. 10.1146/annurev.psych.093008.10043819575613

Harris, J. M., Ciorciari, J., & Gountas, J. (2018). Consumer neuroscience and digital/social media health applications: Ethical considerations. *Journal of Consumer Behaviour*, 17(1), 179–189.

Kumar, J., Arora, M., & Erkol Bayram, G. (2024). *Research, Innovation, and Industry Impacts of the Metaverse*. IGI Global.

Kumar, J., Arora, M., & Erkol Bayram, G. (2024). *Exploring the Use of Metaverse in Business and Education*. IGI Global. 10.4018/979-8-3693-5868-9

Murphy, E. R., Illes, J., & Reiner, P. B. (2008). Neuroethics of neuromarketing. *Journal of Consumer Behaviour*, 7(4-5), 293–302. 10.1002/cb.252

NMSBA Code of Ethics - NMSBA. (n.d.). *NMSBA Code of Ethics*. NMSBA. https://www.nmsba.com/neuromarketing-companies/code-of-ethics

Ramsøy, T. Z. (2019). Building a foundation for neuromarketing and consumer neuroscience research: How researchers can apply academic rigor to the neuroscientific study of advertising effects. *Journal of Advertising Research*, 59(3), 281–294. 10.2501/JAR-2019-034

Rathore, S., & Arora, M. (2024). Sustainability Reporting in the Metaverse: A Multi-Sectoral Analysis. In *Exploring the Use of Metaverse in Business and Education* (pp. 147-165). IGI Global. 10.4018/979-8-3693-5868-9.ch009

Spence, E. H. (2015). Ethics of neuromarketing: Introduction. In *Handbook of neuroethics* (pp. 1621–1625). Springer Netherlands. 10.1007/978-94-007-4707-4_101

Stanton, S. J., Sinnott-Armstrong, W., & Huettel, S. A. (2017). Neuromarketing: Ethical implications of its use and potential misuse. *Journal of Business Ethics*, 144(4), 799–811. 10.1007/s10551-016-3059-0

Sung, B., Wilson, N. J., Yun, J. H., & Lee, E. J. (2020). What can neuroscience offer marketing research? *Asia Pacific Journal of Marketing and Logistics*, 32(5), 1089–1111. 10.1108/APJML-04-2019-0227

Chapter 8
Exploring the Ethical Issues and Considerations in Neuromarketing

Sneha Sindhuja
https://orcid.org/0009-0008-5809-2231
Christ University, India

Reena Malik
Chitkara Business School, Chitkara University, Punjab, India

ABSTRACT

Neuromarketing is an interdisciplinary field consolidating neuroscience, psychology, and marketing, aiming to understand consumer behaviour at the subconscious level. However, as neuromarketing techniques become increasingly sophisticated, ethical issues and considerations have emerged as a focal point of debate and scrutiny. The paper critically evaluates foundational ethical principles, such as informed consent, beneficence and nonmaleficence, privacy and confidentiality, transparency, scientific or methodological rigor, predicting and influencing consumer choices, safeguarding the vulnerable population, and commitment to abiding and respecting the guidelines and codes of ethics. It also includes the emerging techniques and research, need for ethics and terms like neuroethics and brain privacy.

DOI: 10.4018/979-8-3693-4236-7.ch008

INTRODUCTION

Technological breakthroughs and interdisciplinary collaboration have been driving forces behind advancements in consumer behaviour research. With the use of contemporary instruments like artificial intelligence, big data analytics, and neuroimaging methods, researchers can better comprehend the preferences, decision-making processes, and buying habits of their target audience (Arora & Sharma, 2023). Furthermore, a comprehensive understanding of consumer behaviour is offered by interdisciplinary approaches that incorporate sociology, psychology, economics, and neuroscience. Thanks to these developments, marketers can now more precisely anticipate trends, better customize their approach, and give customers individualized experiences. All things considered, consumer behaviour research is still evolving and revolutionizing how companies interact with their target market in the fast-paced industry of today.

Neuromarketing has garnered a global area of interest in the recent times, due to its fastening advancements and collaboration between neuroscience and marketing. The preferment of the neuroimaging techniques that maps the physiological measures to understand various variables in consumer behaviour has led to the use of neuromarketing profusely in the market research. Neuromarketing employs various non-invasive brain signal recording methods to directly gauge a customer's brain reaction to marketing stimuli, surpassing conventional survey techniques. Functional Magnetic Resonance Imaging (fMRI), Electroencephalography (EEG), Magnetoencephalography (MEG), Transcranial Magnetic Stimulation (TMS), facial encoding, Steady State Topography (SST), Positron Emission Tomography (PET), functional Near-Infrared Spectroscopy (fNIRS), among other techniques, represent neural recording devices utilized in Neuromarketing investigations (Rawnaque et al., 2020).

Neuromarketing can help uncover various insights related to consumer behaviour, preferences, and decision-making processes. Emotional responses of consumers towards the marketing stimuli, level of attention and engagement towards the advertisements, memory encoding and brand perception, subconscious conception to product design and packaging, as well as consumer decision making processes are researched and cast light upon using the emerging neuromarketing techniques.

LITERATURE REVIEW

Ülman et al., (2014) conducted a study on the ethical issues in neuromarketing. The paper elaborates on the interdisciplinary field of neuromarketing that has emerged recently, bridging the conventional divides between marketing research, neuroeconomics, and neuroscience. There has been a growing public distaste and outcry against this emerging field because its main goals are to boost sales and improve marketing methods. The recent responses seen at Baylor School of Medicine and Emory University in the United States serve as examples of these protests. It is also noteworthy that there has been a recent effort in France to discontinue the neuromarketing research. The associated ethical concerns have been receiving a lot of attention lately, particularly since there are now more than 300 neuromarketing companies worldwide. The paper provides a quick overview of neurotechnology and outlining its current uses as well as its drawbacks. It also concentrates on the moral dilemmas that surrounds the neuromarketing research.

Dierichsweiler (2014) examined the ethical issues in neuromarketing, so as to define the moral criticism and find a way to efficiently resolve them. According to the study's findings, neuromarketing has a lot of potential for consumer research. It may be used to effectively gather fresh and more accurate data as well as novel insights into human behaviour than was before feasible. In the field of neuromarketing, the rules and guidelines cryptic and deficient. The ethical questions in this situation are unclear. The two primary issues commonly found and must be dealt seriously are the invasion of privacy and consumer autonomy. Reevaluating the autonomy claims and significantly lowering privacy concerns are possible with the implementation of global standards in neuromarketing. Consumer protection as well as privacy rights should be given the utmost importance.

Gonçalves et al. (2024) explored the ethical and privacy concerns associated with the use of AI and ML in neuromarketing. It evaluates how these technologies affect consumer privacy and human rights by combining bibliometric analysis, empirical data from expert interviews conducted in the US and Spain, and a study of the literature. The study highlighted the conflicts that exist between the necessity to safeguard consumer privacy and the effectiveness of neuromarketing strategies, especially in relation to the GDPR's (General Data Protection Regulation) impact on international practices. By comparing and contrasting US and EU policy, it highlights the necessity for globally standardized ethical norms and consumer data protections. The results of the study also help in recommending the idea of policy generation to help reduce the ethical dangers and encourage the ethical advancement of neuromarketing.

Hensel et al. (2017) conducted a study on practitioners' perspectives on neuromarketing ethics. The primary goal of the study was to determine whether there is an agreement with the responses given by neuromarketing practitioners regarding the validity of additional ethical aspects that have been developed in addition to the NMSBA (Neuromarketing Science & Business Association) code of ethics and included in the EGNM (Ethical Guideline in Neuromarketing) guideline. The second goal was to improve the ethical guideline by adding details that are pertinent to practitioners. The study incorporated a qualitative approach and interviewed 10 professionals about their experiences and views regarding the ethical issues and considerations in the context of neuromarketing.

Pop et al. (2014) conducted a study on the ethical responsibility of neuromarketing companies in harnessing the market research. The study so addresses various controversial issues in the context of ethics in neuromarketing. The analysis of the conventional persuasion model that incorporates elements of the neuromarketing study was investigated. The study also discusses the advantages and disadvantages that participants in neuromarketing research may experience, and carefully examining the Neuromarketing Science and Business Association's (NMSBA) Ethical Code of Conduct. The authors tested a few hypotheses about the ethical dilemmas that neuromarketing organizations face through an exploratory online study. 67 global members of the NMSBA that specialize in neuromarketing were the subjects of the study.

Background

History of Neuromarketing

Hugo Münsterberg, regarded as the founding figure in organizational psychology, demonstrated early interest in the field as far back as 1913. However, it wasn't until the 1990s that advancements in biomedical imaging technology enabled researchers to gain profound insights from human brain activity (Chi, 2022). Although the term "neuromarketing" is credited to Dutch marketing professor Ale Smidts in 2002, significant research and experimentation in the field had already begun in the 1990s. Professor Gerald Zaltman, a marketing expert from the United States, was among the pioneers, having filed a patent four years prior to the term's coinage (Sindhuja, 2023). Zaltman's patent centered on the Zaltman metaphor elicitation technique (ZMET), a marketing research tool designed to delve into both conscious and subconscious thoughts of individuals. By employing carefully selected image sets, ZMET aimed to evoke positive emotional responses, thereby potentially influencing purchasing behaviour (Chi, 2022). ZMET rapidly gained traction among numerous leading corporations, with clients ranging from Coca-Cola and General Motors to Nestle and Procter & Gamble. Zaltman and his team were commissioned by these companies to analyse brain scans and monitor the neural responses of consumers. In 1999, Zaltman pioneered the use of functional magnetic resonance imaging (fMRI) to establish connections between consumer brain activity and marketing stimuli.

This innovative approach allowed for a deeper understanding of how marketing efforts influence neurological processes (Kelley, 2002).

Several U.S. companies such as Brighthouse and SalesBrain emerged as pioneers in providing neuromarketing research and consultancy services. They promoted the utilization of technology and insights derived from cognitive neuroscience in their offerings (Morin, 2011b). The first research into neuromarketing was done by a scientist named Read Montague in 2003. He asked people to drink either Pepsi or Coca-Cola while their brains were scanned in a special machine. The study found that when people knew they were drinking Coca-Cola, the frontal lobe, responsible for executive functions such as attention, short-term memory, and planning seemed to be engaged or active. But when they did not know which soda they were drinking, with activity in the limbic system, the brain structure associated with emotional and instinctual responses were being activated. This study did not fully convince everyone that neuroscience could help understand why we make certain choices, but it did make people realize that our brains play a big role in the decisions as consumers.

Emerging techniques and research

In the ever-evolving scenario of marketing, understanding consumer behaviour is of paramount importance. Technological advancements also lead to various opportunities to deepen our understand of the human brain. The emerging techniques and research in neuromarketing assist in getting into the consumer "black box" and gravely study the processes undergoing, to help design effective marketing strategies for businesses.

Neuroimaging techniques such as functional magnetic resonance imaging (fMRI), electroencephalography (EEG), and magnetoencephalography (MEG) are the cutting-edge measurement devices in the neuromarketing research. These techniques allow researchers to observe the brain activity in real-time as participants engage with the various marketing stimuli, thus providing invaluable insights into the neural mechanisms underlying the cognitive processes within the consumer brain. By correlating the neural responses with behavioural outcomes, researchers can identify neural markers such as attention, emotion, and memory, helping businesses in optimizing their advertising campaigns, product designs, as well as the branding strategies.

Biometric measurements, includes galvanic skin response (GSR), heart rate variability (HRV), and eye tracking measures, and it offer additional insight into consumer responses. These physiological measures provide objective indicators of emotional arousal, cognitive load, and visual attention, allowing marketers to gauge the effectiveness of their marketing materials and identify areas for improvement.

Implicit association tests (IAT) are psychological assessments that measure subconscious biases and preferences. In neuromarketing, IATs are used to uncover implicit attitudes towards brands, products, and advertising messages. Implicit attitudes are the judgement that transpire unconsciously. By measuring the time of response to the stimuli presented on a screen, researchers can infer underlying attitudes and associations that may not be consciously accessible to consumers. Understanding these implicit biases can help marketers tailor their messaging and branding to resonate more deeply with consumers on a subconscious level. Russell Fazio has dedicated his research in understanding how attitudes shape human behaviour, where he introduced a model that delineates attitudes into two components: the explicit, overtly stated opinion, typically assessed through surveys, and the implicit accessibility, representing the strength of the attitude, gauged by the time taken to respond—a reflection of respondents' confidence (Matukin & Ohme, 2016). Fazio's studies have demonstrated that individuals with swift reaction times (indicating high certainty) when expressing their opinions exhibit stronger correlations between attitudes and behaviour. This suggests that highly accessible attitudes wield a more potent influence on consumer behaviour.

Machine learning algorithms and data analytics techniques are exceedingly being applied to neuromarketing research. These computational tools allow the researchers to analyse large datasets of neuroimaging, biometric, and behavioural data, uncovering patterns and relationships that traditional statistical methods may ignore or overlook. By identifying predictive models of consumer preferences and decision-making processes, machine learning enables marketers to develop more targeted and personalized marketing strategies, leading to higher engagement and conversion rates.

Collaboration between neuroscientists, psychologists, marketers, and other professionals is essential for advancing the field of neuromarketing. By combining expertise from diverse disciplines, researchers can develop innovative methodologies and approaches that address complex questions about consumer behaviour. Cross-disciplinary collaboration always promotes creativity and innovation, driving forward the development of new techniques and technologies in the neuromarketing research. Further, immersive customer engagement opportunities in the field of marketing have been also playing a critical role in multi-business scenarios (Kumar, Arora & Erkol Bayram, Eds., 2024). They are emerging as important concepts for brand building (Arora, 2023). The concepts like virtual reality, augmented reality, blockchain technology and metaverse are reshaping the world of business as well as education (Arora, 2024; Arora & Sharma, 2021). The metaverse offers businesses new revenue streams and immersive customer engagement opportunities, revolutionizing digital interaction and commerce. It also facilitates innovative marketing strategies and remote collaboration, enhancing productivity and brand presence (Dhiman & Arora, 2024). The metaverse provides entrepreneurs with a vast, dynamic platform for innovation, enabling unique business models and virtual marketplaces. It also offers new avenues for networking and funding, fostering a more connected and resource-rich entrepreneurial ecosystem by communicating to various stakeholders in the immersive world (Rathore & Arora, 2024). But again, the ethical dilemmas and issues in the virtual world are posing challenges for the marketers. In this post-truth era, the marketing communication has been affected by fake news, propaganda, misinformation as well as disinformation (Arora, 2020).

Need for ethics

Neuromarketing has garnered both curiosity and careful surveillance due to its clever potential to decode consumer brain at the subconscious level. Therefore, ethical consideration becomes very pivotal in conducting the research even if it involves non-invasive neuroimaging techniques. At its essence, ethics in neuromarketing familiarly involves the principles of respect for autonomy, privacy, fairness, and transparency. Levy (2011) discusses on the Neuromarketing Science and Business Association (NMSBA) Code of Ethics. The terms neuroethics as well as the stealth marketing are currently trending in the emerging domain of consumer neuroscience. Roy and Chattopadhyay (2010) describe stealth marketing as a marketing strategy that is hidden, covert or is undercover, and the consumers are unaware that they are being targeted for the purpose of product persuasion. It is sometimes interchangeably referred to as undercover marketing wherein the consumers are unsuspecting that the marketers are subtly advertising and promoting their products and services.

Informed consent emerges as a primary principle in conducting not only neuromarketing research, but any kind of research in general. Participants should be willingly engaging in the studies utilizing brain imaging techniques such as functional Magnetic Resonance Imaging (fMRI) or Electroencephalography (EEG) with a clear understanding of the research's purpose, procedures, as well as the potential risks. Any kind of delinquency in obtaining informed consent from the participants compromises the integrity of the research conducted, and also increases the likelihood of exploiting participants' vulnerability or manipulating their responses, raising serious ethical concerns.

Privacy concerns, in case of neuromarketing research, the term "Brain Privacy" can be used, is another noted ethical issue which needs to be seriously discussed and taken care of. Safeguarding the privacy of individuals' "neurological" data becomes crucial to prevent any unauthorized access, misuse, or breaches of the participant's personal privacy. Strong ethical standards are necessary in neuromarketing because they reduce the possibility of intrusive marketing tactics or data abuse.

Another relevant issue in ethical discussions within neuromarketing lies the differentiation between persuasion and manipulation. While persuasive marketing aims to impact consumer behaviour through logical arguments and open communication, manipulation resorts to deceitful methods or takes advantage of cognitive biases to compel individuals into choices contrary to their likes and well-being. Hence, the ethical assessment focuses on guaranteeing that neuromarketing strategies adhere to values such as honesty, sincerity, and acknowledgment of individuals' independence, avoiding manipulative tactics that corrupt the trust and risk and threaten consumer welfare.

The involvement of certain demographic groups further complicates the ethical considerations in neuromarketing. Children, the elderly, or individuals with cognitive impairments may demonstrate increased vulnerability to neuromarketing tactics, highlighting the necessity for heightened ethical awareness. Protecting these vulnerable populations from exploitation or harm requires the establishment of critical ethical frameworks that prioritize their welfare and minimize the potential dangers that might occur due to the complex procedures of the research.

Not to ignore and forget the lasting impact of neuromarketing interventions on societal norms, values, and public health becomes apparent. Ethical reflections encompass evaluating the enduring consequences of marketing strategies on individual behaviours, societal interactions, and cultural narratives. Through examining the broader societal implications of neuromarketing, ethical frameworks aim to cultivate conscientious marketing approaches that prioritize societal welfare and cultivate a culture of ethical consciousness and responsibility.

Furthermore, adherence to ethical guidelines in neuromarketing is instrumental in ensuring regulatory compliance and industry integrity. By aligning with existing regulations and industry standards, companies can mitigate legal risks and bolster consumer trust, thereby nurturing a conducive ecosystem for ethical innovation and responsible marketing practices.

Neuroethics and Brain Privacy

The term neuroethics was first used by William Safire in 2002, at the Neuroethics Conference: Mapping the Field, organised by the Dana Foundation (Sebastian, 2014). He defined neuroethics as "the examination of what is right and wrong, good and bad about the treatment of, perfection of, or unwelcome invasion of and worrisome manipulation of the human brain." Neuroethics addresses the moral dilemmas in the pursuit of brain manipulation and knowledge, and it is well-positioned to provide direction for the beneficial and non-destructive application of neuromarketing strategies (Olteanu, 2015). In simple terms, neuroethics deals with the ethical, legal, and social consequences of neuroscience, as well as ethical issues within neuroscience research (Illes & Bird, 2006). It is a contemporary field bridging bioethics and neuroscience and discusses the ethical issues related to mind and behaviour.

Neuroethics holds considerable importance in neuromarketing techniques due to its focus on the ethical, legal, and societal implications of neuroscience applications, including concerns about consent, privacy, manipulation, and effects on vulnerable groups. A primary goal of neuroethics in neuromarketing involves creating established guidelines for safeguarding subjects that are on par with the stringent protections mandated in academic and medical research institutions (Murphy et al., 2008).

Neuroprivacy, or "brain privacy," refers to the rights of people with regard to the gathering, use, and interpretation of neurological data that is extracted from their brains. This idea is strongly related to fields like neuroethics, neurosecurity, and neurolaw, and it has become more and more popular as a variety of neuroimaging technologies advance. One aspect of neuroethics is neuroprivacy, which is centered on the use of neurological data in court cases, neuromarketing campaigns, surveillance projects, and other external uses, as well as the moral and societal implications that accompany these uses.

Moore (2016) states that personal rights and control over personal information are two broad ethical considerations surrounding neuroprivacy. It is feasible that in the future, gathering neurodata without permission or awareness will be simpler or more frequent as technology advances. One argument is that since gathering neurodata entails both scanning the body and analyzing mind, it violates both intellectual property rights and personal property rights. A primary ethical dispute surrounding neuroprivacy pertains to the dilemma of mind-body duality and the question of free will. The extent to which neurodata can predict thoughts and actions is an area of potential worry because it is unknown how much or how completely brain activity drives thoughts and behaviours (Reyna, 2014).

Ethical issues and considerations in neuromarketing

With the ever-refining techniques and research in neuromarketing comes the need to monitor the moral thinking and rationale of the procedures. It has raised a series of ethical issues which has been the centre of heated discussion over years. The examination of ethics in marketing overall, and particularly in marketing research, holds immense importance for advancing marketing theories and enhancing their practical implementation (Mouammine & Azdimousa, 2023). There are various issues associated with instigating neuroscience into marketing. Understanding them is crucial, as above all, the well-being of the human subjects is to be prioritized.

Informed Consent

One of the most important ethics in any domain is the informed consent. Informed consent holds paramount importance in the field of neuromarketing due to its ethical implications and the unique nature of the research involved. Neuromarketing, as we know, explores the subconscious responses of individuals to marketing stimuli using techniques such as fMRI and EEG, requires a strong need to have an ethical framework involving the appropriate measures when it comes to taking the informed consent of the participants of the research. Firstly, the informed consent ensures that the participants are fully and mindfully aware of the purpose, procedures, and potential risks associated with the study they are taking part in, allowing them to make autonomous decisions about their contribution by participating in it. Given the potential sensitivity of the data collected in neuromarketing studies, including individuals' neural responses to advertisements or products, obtaining informed consent is essential to respect participants' right to "brain" privacy and take charge of their very personal information.

Moreover, informed consent serves to mitigate the risk of threat or manipulation inherent in research involving the subconscious influences. By providing participants with transparent information about the study's objectives and methodologies, researchers can foster trust and transparency, thereby reducing the likelihood of unnecessary influence or exploitation. This is particularly important in neuromarketing, where the goal is to understand the various processes in consumer behaviour. Informed consent acts as a safeguard against unethical practices and ensures that participants' autonomy and well-being are prioritized throughout the research process.

Additionally, informed consent in neuromarketing helps to uphold the integrity and credibility of research findings. By ensuring that participants understand the study's parameters and voluntarily agree to participate, researchers can minimize the risk of bias or invalid results stemming from compelled or uninformed participation. Ethical research practices, including obtaining informed consent, are essential for maintaining the scientific rigor and validity of the neuromarketing studies, thereby enhancing the field's credibility and contributing to its evolution and furtherance.

Furthermore, informed consent in neuromarketing is essential for regulatory compliance and adherence to ethical guidelines. Many countries and institutions have specific regulations governing research involving human participants, requiring researchers to obtain informed consent as a fundamental ethical principle. By complying with these regulations and ethical standards, researchers in neuromarketing can ensure that their studies are conducted ethically and legally, thereby avoiding potential legal consequences, and safeguarding the rights and welfare of participants.

Beneficence and nonmaleficence

In the domain of neuromarketing ethics, the principles of beneficence and non-maleficence play a crucial role in guiding ethical conduct and decision-making. Beneficence entails the obligation to promote the well-being of individuals and society, while nonmaleficence emphasizes the compulsion to avoid causing any harm (Ülman et al., 2014). The principle of beneficence suggests that marketers and researchers should strive to use their findings and insights to enhance consumer welfare and societal well-being. This could involve developing products and marketing strategies that genuinely meet consumers' needs and preferences, thereby improving their overall satisfaction and quality of life. For example, neuromarketing research can be used to create more effective health campaigns that encourage healthier behaviours or to design products that enhance users' experiences without exploiting cognitive vulnerabilities.

Conversely, the principle of nonmaleficence emphasizes the importance of avoiding harm to consumers or society through neuromarketing practices. This includes refraining from using neuromarketing techniques in ways that manipulate or deceive consumers, leading to adverse consequences such as uninformed purchasing decisions or negative psychological effects. For instance, marketers should avoid exploiting cognitive biases or subconscious cues to force or manipulate individuals into buying products they do not need or cannot afford.

Privacy and Confidentiality

Privacy and confidentiality are fundamental ethical considerations in neuro-marketing, reflecting the need to protect individuals' rights and autonomy in the collection, analysis, and usage of their neurodata (Laureckis & Miralpeix, 2016). In neuromarketing, the privacy pertains to individuals' control over their neural responses, preferences, and decision-making processes. It encompasses the safeguarding of personal "neurological" data obtained through the neuroscientific techniques, which reveal complex insights into the subconscious thoughts and behaviours of the consumers.

On the other hand, confidentiality focuses on preserving the anonymity and privacy of individuals whose neurodata is collected for the purpose of the study. This involves ensuring that sensitive information about participants' neural responses and identities remains confidential and is not disclosed to unauthorized parties. Neuromarketers must employ anonymization techniques, securely store data, and restrict access to authorized personnel to protect the confidentiality of neurodata. Participants should have confidence and faith that their neurodata will be used solely for the intended purposes that were conveyed to them prior to the study or marketing campaign, and will not be shared or disclosed without their explicit consent. Ultimately, by prioritizing privacy and confidentiality in neuromarketing ethics, practitioners can uphold individuals' rights, manage the trust between researchers or marketers and participants or consumers, and protect the integrity of the neuromarketing research and marketing practices.

Transparency

Transparency in neuromarketing ethics ensures the commitment to openness, honesty, and accountability in all aspects of neuromarketing research and marketing practices (Trettel et al., 2016). It involves providing clear and comprehensive information to consumers tuned participants, as well as the stakeholders about the purpose, methods, and implications of research being conducted.

When it comes to data collection, transparency demands that neuromarketers communicate openly with the participants about the neuroimaging technologies being used, the type of the data being collected from them, and how this data will be harnessed for the purpose of the proposed study. This also includes providing layman explanations of complex neuroscience concepts and ensuring that participants fully comprehend the implications of their involvement in the neuromarketing studies. Additionally, transparency also incorporates informing the participants about their rights regarding data privacy, confidentiality, and the option to withdraw from the study at any point time without having to give any explanations regarding their decision to withdraw from the research study.

Furthermore, marketers have a responsibility to disclose the use of neuromarketing techniques in advertising and branding campaigns, ensuring that consumers are aware of the strategies being employed to influence the purchasing decisions of the targeted consumer audience, thus catering to consumer trust, promote informed decision-making, and pacify any potential concerns about the manipulation or exploitation of any consumer behaviour processes.

Transparency in neuromarketing ethics also involves the disclosure of potential risks, limitations, and ethical considerations associated with neuroscientific research and marketing practices. There is an obligation to communicate openly about the uncertainties and ethical dilemmas that comes with using neuroimaging techniques to study consumer behaviour. Despite the potential advantages, it is unlikely and doubtful that neuromarketing companies will choose transparency in the process (Stanton et al., 2016).

Scientific or methodological rigor

Scientific rigor refers to the implementation of the highest standards and the finest approaches in the scientific research conducted to ensure the credibility and validity of the study. The best practices also help to ensure an unbiased scientific experiment that would lead to significant results and uncovering the truth.

Scientific rigor in neuromarketing ethics involves adhering to finest research methodologies, transparent reporting practices, and ethical guidelines to ensure the reliability, validity, and ethical integrity of the research findings. This includes employing vigorous experimental designs, transparent data collection processes, and appropriate statistical analyses, while prioritizing the ethical principles such as informed consent, brain privacy, and fairness. Peer review and collaboration further enhance the scientific rigor by providing opportunities for critical evaluation, accountability, and interdisciplinary exchange of ideas. By authentically conducting scientific rigor in ethical neuromarketing practices, researchers can promote trust, credibility, and the responsible use of neuromarketing techniques while adding to the body of knowledge.

But the case in reality is a bit different. The neuromarketing firms often employ poor research methods, including personnels with insufficient and quality training, and conduct the experiment on insufficient sample that may lead to a false or below par results (Stanton et al., 2016).

Predicting and influencing consumer choices

Another frequently perceived ethical concern is consumers' apprehension that neuromarketing may extend beyond prediction to actively influencing consumer decisions (Stanton et al., 2016). Predicting and influencing consumer choices raise significant ethical considerations in neuromarketing, once again touching upon issues of autonomy, transparency, and manipulation. Although neuroscience holds promise in enhancing predictions of consumer behaviour, there is currently no evidence supporting the existence of a definitive "buy button" in the brain. Critics may argue that while neuromarketing may not compel consumers to purchase specific products outright, it still possesses the capability to influence buying decisions, raising ethical concerns when such influence operates beneath the threshold of consciousness. The neuromarketing measures enables consumer choices to maintain their freedom, even when they are substantially influenced by physiological factors beyond consumers' control.

Furthermore, the capacity to predict and influence consumer behaviour via physiology is not unique to neuromarketing, as behavioural studies also uncover methods to influence consumer choices outside of the consumer's conscious awareness. In both scenarios, consumers may be unaware of the factors influencing their decisions, yet they still exercise their free choice.

Safeguarding the vulnerable population

A vulnerable consumer is one who, due to sociodemographic/behavioural traits, personal circumstances, or the market environment, is more likely to encounter unfavourable outcomes in the marketplace, has limited capacity to maximize his or her well-being, finds it difficult to obtain or process information, finds it more difficult to purchase, select, or obtain appropriate products, or is more susceptible to specific marketing tactics (Javor et al., 2022).

Ethical considerations regarding children, older adults, and individuals with disabilities in neuromarketing are supreme due to their potential vulnerability and the need to safeguard their rights and well-being. When targeting these demographic groups, neuromarketers must adhere to strict ethical standards to ensure that their research practices are fair, respectful, and lacks any kind of exploitation (Hensel et al., 2016).

When conducting neuromarketing research involving children, special care must be taken to obtain informed consent from both the children themselves and their parents or guardians (Trettel et al., 2016). Children may have limited understanding of the implications of participating in such studies, making it essential to provide age-appropriate information and ensure that their participation is voluntary. It must be ensured that the research is conducted in a manner that minimizes any potential harm or distress to the children, both during the study and in the dissemination of findings.

Similarly, when targeting older adults, neuromarketers must recognize the potential cognitive and physical limitations that may affect their ability to provide informed consent or comprehend complex marketing messages. It is important to adapt research methodologies and communication strategies to cater to the needs of older adults, ensuring that they are fully informed as well as sound enough to make their decisions regarding their participation in the neuromarketing studies.

Ethical considerations in neuromarketing further extends to the individuals with disabilities, who may face unique challenges in understanding and responding during the entire process, from informed consent to the dissemination of the end results. The research methodologies and marketing strategies should be of inclusive and accessible to the individuals with disabilities, accommodating diverse needs and communication preferences.

No matter how desperate the researchers are to conduct the research and gain the ground breaking findings, if the physiological and psychological well-being of the vulnerable participants are compromised, then the ethos and morality of the entire purpose of the study is liable to questioning.

Commitment to abiding and respecting the guidelines and codes of ethics

Commitment to abiding by and respecting the guidelines and codes of ethics in neuromarketing is perhaps the most essential for confirming the integrity of the field, protecting consumer rights, and fostering trust among the stakeholders. Adhering to ethical guidelines ensures that neuromarketing practices are conducted responsibly, transparently, and with respect for individuals' autonomy and well-being. One key aspect of this commitment involves aligning with established ethical frameworks and guidelines, such as those set forth by professional organizations like the Neuromarketing Science & Business Association (NMSBA) or the American Marketing Association (AMA). These guidelines typically emphasize principles such as transparency, informed consent, privacy protection, and avoidance of manipulation in neuromarketing research and practice. By following these guidelines, practitioners demonstrate their commitment to ethical conduct and contribute to the advancement of responsible neuromarketing practices.

Moreover, commitment to ethical guidelines in neuromarketing involves ongoing education, training, and professional development to be aware of the emerging ethical issues and best practices in the field. This includes cultivating a culture of ethical awareness and accountability within neuromarketing organizations and research institutions, where practitioners are encouraged to engage in ethical discussions, seek guidance from the experts, and actively reflect on the ethical implications of their works being done. By fostering a commitment to continuous learning and improvement, neuromarketers can enhance their ethical decision-making skills, identify potential ethical dilemmas proactively, and mitigate risks of harm to consumers and society.

Besides, commitment to ethical guidelines entails accountability mechanisms to address violations of ethical standards and ensure that ethical lapses are promptly identified, investigated, and remedied. By holding themselves and their peers accountable for ethical conduct, neuromarketers can uphold the trust and credibility of the field and demonstrate their dedication to promoting ethical values and principles in neuromarketing research and practice.

Discussion and Conclusion

Concerns about neuromarketing ethics are growing due to the complexity and moral dilemmas that might arise from using cutting-edge neuroscientific methods to analyse the consumer cognitive and behaviour processes. An acceptable number of significant ethical concerns have surfaced as neuromarketing continues to gain popularity not only in business and marketing, but also in academia, and thus should be carefully considered and closely evaluated.

If ethical issues are neglected in neuromarketing, it could lead to potential harm. It has also come to light that the importance of the brain health of the consumers should also be focused on while conducting not only neuromarketing research, but also marketing research of different kinds. The preservation of adequate brain integrity and mental and cognitive processes, along with the absence of neurological and psychiatric illnesses, is referred to as "brain health" Wang et al. (2020). The brain health of consumers participating in marketing and neuromarketing research is often neglected (Javor et al., 2022). This, no doubt is a topic of discussion in ethics of neuromarketing. Therefore, it becomes necessary to heed on the relevance of the topics being discussed in this chapter.

The ethical issues and considerations in neuromarketing are indeed very complex and require careful attention to ensure responsible and transparent practices. From concerns surrounding brain privacy, informed consent, and manipulation to the ethical implications of targeting vulnerable populations, the ethical domain of neuromarketing is elaborate and evolving. However, by adhering to ethical guidelines, promoting transparency, and prioritizing consumer welfare, practitioners can navigate these challenges mindfully and responsibly while harnessing the potential of neuroscientific insights to inform marketing strategies ethically. Ultimately, a commitment to ethical principles not only safeguards consumer rights and trust but also contributes to the credibility and sustainability of neuromarketing as a valuable tool for understanding consumer behaviour in an increasingly complex marketplace.

The subject of ethics in neuromarketing, no doubtedly has further future research and implications, especially in terms of the legal frameworks adhering to the global standards. Critics debate that the current ethical structure is feeble and unconvincing. Therefore, the strengthening of the legal pursuits will surely not only help diminish the moral dilemmas that the researchers and marketers currently face, but also abate the violation of the rules and reduce the risk of harming the consumers/participants of the neuromarketing research.

REFERENCES

Arora, M. (2020). Post-truth and marketing communication in technological age. In *Handbook of research on innovations in technology and marketing for the connected consumer* (pp. 94–108). IGI Global., 10.4018/978-1-7998-0131-3.ch005

Arora, M. (2023). Encapsulating Role of Persuasion and Skill Development in Marketing Communication for Brand Building: A Perspective. In *International Handbook of Skill, Education, Learning, and Research Development in Tourism and Hospitality* (pp. 1–17). Springer Nature Singapore.

Arora, M. (2024). Virtual Reality in Education: Analyzing the Literature and Bibliometric State of Knowledge. *Transforming Education with Virtual Reality*, 379-402. https://doi.org/10.1002/9781394200498.ch22

Arora, M., & Sharma, R. L. (2021). Repurposing the Role of Entrepreneurs in the Havoc of COVID-19. In Entrepreneurship and Big Data (pp. 229-250). CRC Press.

Arora, M., & Sharma, R. L. (2023). Artificial intelligence and big data: Ontological and communicative perspectives in multi-sectoral scenarios of modern businesses. *Foresight*, 25(1), 126–143. 10.1108/FS-10-2021-0216

Braeutigam, S., & Kenning, P. (2022). Ethics of Consumer Neuroscience. In *Oxford University Press eBooks* (pp. 211–220). 10.1093/oso/9780198789932.003.0012

Chi, A. (2022, June 5). *A brief history of neuromarketing*. Boonmind. https://www.boonmind.com/a-brief-history-of-neuromarketing/

Dhiman, V., & Arora, M. (2024). Current State of Metaverse in Entrepreneurial Ecosystem: A Retrospective Analysis of Its Evolving Landscape. In *Exploring the Use of Metaverse in Business and Education* (pp. 73-87). IGI Global. https://doi.org/10.4018/979-8-3693-5868-9.ch005

Dierichsweiler, K. (2014). *Ethical issues in neuromarketing*. https://essay.utwente.nl/65384/

Gonçalves, M., Hu, Y., Aliagas, I., & Suárez, L. M. C. (2024). Neuromarketing algorithms' consumer privacy and ethical considerations: Challenges and opportunities. *Cogent Business & Management*, 11(1), 2333063. Advance online publication. 10.1080/23311975.2024.2333063

Hensel, D., Iorga, A. M., Wolter, L., & Znanewitz, J. (2017). Conducting neuromarketing studies ethically-practitioner perspectives. *Cogent Psychology*, 4(1), 1320858. 10.1080/23311908.2017.1320858

Hensel, D., Wolter, L., & Znanewitz, J. (2016). A Guideline for Ethical aspects in conducting Neuromarketing studies. In *Springer eBooks* (pp. 65–87). 10.1007/978-3-319-45609-6_4

Illes, J., & Bird, S. J. (2006). Neuroethics: A modern context for ethics in neuroscience. *Trends in Neurosciences*, 29(9), 511–517. 10.1016/j.tins.2006.07.00216859760

Isa, S. M., Mansor, A. A., & Razali, K. (2019). *Ethics in Neuromarketing and its Implications on Business to Stay Vigilant*. KnE Social Sciences., 10.18502/kss.v3i22.5082

Javor, A., Koller, M., Lee, N., & Breiter, H. C. (2022). Vulnerable consumers: Marketing research needs to pay more attention to the brain health of consumers. *Marketing Letters*, 34(2), 337–342. 10.1007/s11002-022-09654-336345295

Kelly, M. (2002). The Science of Shopping. Commercial Alert., Retrieved March 30, 2016, from.

Kumar, J., Arora, M., & Erkol Bayram, G. (Eds.). (2024). *Exploring the Use of Metaverse in Business and Education*. IGI Global., 10.4018/979-8-3693-5868-9

Laureckis, E., & Miralpeix, À. M. (2016). Ethical and legal considerations in research subject and data protection. In *Springer eBooks* (pp. 89–100). 10.1007/978-3-319-45609-6_5

Moore, A. D. (2016). Privacy, Neuroscience, and Neuro-Surveillance. *Res Publica (Liverpool, England)*, 23(2), 159–177. 10.1007/s11158-016-9341-2

Morin, C. (2011b). Neuromarketing: The new science of consumer behavior. *Society*, 48(2), 131–135. 10.1007/s12115-010-9408-1

Mouammine, Y., & Azdimousa, H. (2023). An overview of ethical issues in neuromarketing: Discussion and possible solutions. *Marketing Science and Inspirations*, 18(4), 29–47. 10.46286/msi.2023.18.4.3

Muñoz, J. M. (2023, October 5). neuroethics. Encyclopedia Britannica. https://www.britannica.com/topic/neuroethics

Murphy, E. R., Illes, J., & Reiner, P. B. (2008). Neuroethics of neuromarketing. *Journal of Consumer Behaviour*, 7(4–5), 293–302. 10.1002/cb.252

Olteanu, M. D. B. (2015). Neuroethics and responsibility in conducting neuromarketing research. *Neuroethics*, 8(2), 191–202. 10.1007/s12152-014-9227-y

Pop, N. A., Dabija, D., & Iorga, A. M. (2014). Ethical responsibility of neuromarketing companies in harnessing the market Research – a global exploratory approach. *DOAJ (DOAJ: Directory of Open Access Journals).* https://doaj.org/article/71 73bd2fbdaf4986982b6008a624633d

Rathore, S., & Arora, M. (2024). Sustainability Reporting in the Metaverse: A Multi-Sectoral Analysis. In *Exploring the Use of Metaverse in Business and Education* (pp. 147-165). IGI Global. https://doi.org/10.4018/979-8-3693-5868-9.ch009

Rawnaque, F. S., Rahman, K. M., Anwar, S. F., Vaidyanathan, R., Chau, T., Sarker, F., & Mamun, K. A. (2020). Technological advancements and opportunities in Neuromarketing: A systematic review. *Brain Informatics*, 7(1), 10. Advance online publication. 10.1186/s40708-020-00109-x32955675

Reyna, S. P. (2014). Free will, agency, and the cultural, reflexive brain. In *Springer eBooks* (pp. 323–342). 10.1007/978-94-007-4707-4_138

Roy, A., & Chattopadhyay, S. P. (2010). Stealth marketing as a strategy. *Business Horizons*, 53(1), 69–79. 10.1016/j.bushor.2009.09.004

Sebastian, V. (2014). Neuromarketing and Neuroethics. *Procedia: Social and Behavioral Sciences*, 127, 763–768. 10.1016/j.sbspro.2014.03.351

Sindhuja, S. (2023). A Review on the Potential Growth of Neuromarketing and Consumer Behaviour Research in India. *International Journal of Indian Psychology*, 11(4).

Stanton, S. J., Sinnott-Armstrong, W., & Huettel, S. A. (2016). Neuromarketing: Ethical Implications of its Use and Potential Misuse. *Journal of Business Ethics*, 144(4), 799–811. 10.1007/s10551-016-3059-0

Trettel, A., Cherubino, P., Cartocci, G., Rossi, D., Modica, E., Maglione, A. G., Di Flumeri, G., & Babiloni, F. (2016). Transparency and reliability in neuromarketing research. In *Springer eBooks* (pp. 101–111). 10.1007/978-3-319-45609-6_6

Ülman, Y. I., Çakar, T., & Yıldız, G. D. (2014). Ethical Issues in Neuromarketing: "I Consume, Therefore I am!". *Science and Engineering Ethics*, 21(5), 1271–1284. 10.1007/s11948-014-9581-525150848

Wang, Y., Pan, Y., & Li, H. (2020). What is brain health and why is it important? *BMJ (Clinical Research Ed.)*, m3683, m3683. 10.1136/bmj.m368333037002

KEY TERMS AND DEFINITIONS

Brain Privacy: Brain privacy refers to ensuring the confidentiality and integrity of individuals' neural data, assuring it is not accessed, utilised, or shared without consent. It involves ethical considerations to protect sensitive neurological information obtained through neuroimaging techniques.

Consumer Behaviour: Consumer behaviour refers to the study of people, groups, or organizations as well as all the actions related to buying, using, and disposing the goods or products. It studies the way that a consumer's feelings, attitudes, and preferences influence their purchasing decisions. In short, it is the study of people as consumers.

Ethics: Ethics refers to the set of principles, values, and moral guidelines that govern what is right or wrong within a given context. It involves considerations of fairness, honesty, integrity, respect, and responsibility in interactions with the society.

Neuroethics: Neuroethics is the branch of ethics concerned with the moral implications in the field of neuroscience research and technology. It examines the ethical questions surrounding issues like brain privacy, cognitive enhancement, and the use of neurotechnology in various fields.

Neuromarketing: Neuromarketing is a multidisciplinary field that applies principles from neuroscience, psychology, and marketing to understand consumer behaviour at the subconscious level. It involves using neuroscientific techniques, such as brain imaging and biometrics, to measure physiological and neural responses to marketing stimuli, with the aim of optimizing marketing strategies and understanding the consumers thoroughly.

Neuroscience: Neuroscience is the scientific study of the brain and the nervous system. It deals with the of its complex structure and various function.

Subconscious: The subconscious refers to the part of the mind that functions below the level of conscious awareness. It encompasses thoughts, feelings, desires, as well as memories that influence behaviour but are not readily accessible to conscious awareness.

Chapter 9
Sensible Selling Through Sensory Neuromarketing:
Enhancing Sales Effectiveness

Bhavna Taneja
https://orcid.org/0000-0002-5447-7758
Amity University, Ranchi, India

Pooja Shukla
Amity University, Ranchi, India

Manpreet Arora
https://orcid.org/0000-0002-4939-1992
Central University of Himachal Pradesh, India

ABSTRACT

Neuromarketing (a new field at the intersection of marketing and neurology) provides crucial information on how customers act and make decisions. This chapter examines neuromarketing laws and how they might be used to improve sales success. It discusses all five senses—sight, hearing, touch, smell, and taste—and how we can use each of them to create memorable marketing experiences. The chapter then discusses how neuromarketing might be applied to brand development, product packaging, and promotional strategies. The chapter also provides sales professionals with practical guidelines and case studies for incorporating sensory neuromarketing principles into their selling technique, with the ultimate goal of improving client engagement, satisfaction, and sales outcomes.

DOI: 10.4018/979-8-3693-4236-7.ch009

INTRODUCTION

Neuromarketing is a growing field that combines new technologies and neuro-science to gain insight into how consumers behave, and it provides groundbreaking information on the way we understand decision making. It represents a paradigm shift in how marketers understand and influence consumer choices, moving beyond traditional market research methods to tap into the subconscious mind directly. Neuromarketing decodes neural processes that influence consumer behavior, to extract the hidden drivers of why people act in a certain way when it comes to buying products.

Next-generation business companies cannot compete without knowing how their customers buy. While traditional market-research methods offer insight into customer attitudes and behaviors, they fail to capture the emotions, memories, sensory expe-riences and economic context within which decisions are made. Neuromarketing is a more direct and nuanced way bypassing the conscious mind to access deeper, subconscious insights.

At its core, neuromarketing seeks to answer fundamental questions about con-sumer behavior: Why do people buy certain products? What drives brand loyalty? How can marketing messages be tailored to resonate more effectively with target audiences? By studying brain activity using techniques such as functional magnetic resonance imaging (fMRI) and electroencephalography (EEG), neuromarketing can uncover the neural correlates of consumer behavior, providing a more comprehensive understanding of how marketing stimuli are processed and interpreted in the brain.

One of the key strengths of neuromarketing lies in its ability to reveal insights that consumers may not be consciously aware of. For example, a consumer may express a preference for a particular brand based on rational criteria such as price or features, but neuroimaging studies may reveal that their decision is influenced by subconscious factors such as brand associations or emotional responses triggered by marketing stimuli. By tapping into these hidden drivers of behavior, marketers can craft more persuasive and impactful campaigns that resonate with consumers on a deeper level.

Furthermore, neuromarketing has the potential to inform a wide range of marketing strategies, from product design and packaging to advertising and pricing. By under-standing how different sensory stimuli affect brain activity, marketers can optimize the sensory elements of their campaigns to create more engaging and memorable experiences for consumers. For example, research has shown that certain colors can evoke specific emotions, while certain sounds can trigger powerful memories. By incorporating these insights into their marketing strategies, businesses can create more compelling brand experiences.

Neuromarketing represents a powerful tool for understanding and influencing consumer behavior. By combining the insights of neuroscience with the principles of marketing, neuromarketing can unlock new ways to connect with consumers and drive sales. However, ethical considerations must be carefully considered to ensure that neuromarketing is used responsibly and transparently.

OBJECTIVE AND METHODOLOGY

Neuromarketing, (a new area at the crossroads between marketing and neuro-science) delivers important information about how consumers behave and make decisions. This paper examines the laws of neuromarketing and details how they can be used in improving sales performance. It covers all five senses, sight, sound, touch smell and taste and how we can use each of these to design memorable marketing experience. Then the paper talks about how Neuromarketing can be used to build Brand, Product Packaging and Promotional Strategies. It furthers elaborates Repurchase Intentions, Neuro Sensory Marketing and Digital Marketing

The paper also offers practical guidance, and case studies for sales professionals to integrate sensory neuromarketing principles into their selling approach, ultimately aiming to improve customer engagement, satisfaction, and sales outcomes.

BACKGROUND

From Traditional Marketing to Neuromarketing

For businesses, traditional marketing has always been the keystone from which they communicate with their customers. But in recent years, consumers have changed, and their behaviours are so complex (Cohen et al., 2018) that the traditional paradigms of marketing do not fully capture nor influence many areas of consumer decision making. This section elaborates on how marketing techniques have evolved from traditional methods to neuromarketing and the benefits of using them over others in perceiving consumer behaviour.

Erickson (2017) explains that marketers wanting to gain an insight into their target market continuedly use the traditional marketing tools such as surveys, focus groups and demographic analysis. Even though these methods report insightful information into customer's tastes and actions, at the same time they are often limited by their reliance on conscious responses from consumers says Zoëga et al., (2019). Surveys and focus groups, for instance, could miss the subconscious elements that affect judgment, like feelings, memories, and sensory perceptions.

Contrarily, neuromarketing provides a clearer and more perceptive means of comprehending customer behavior (Misra, 2023). Neuromarketing uses tools like fMRI and EEG to analyze brain activity, and reveals the neural processes that underpin consumer decision-making. According to Golnar-Nik et al., (2021), this gives marketers access to deeper, subconscious insights into customer preferences and motives, resulting in a more thorough grasp of why consumers make the decisions they do.

Finding insights that consumers might not be aware of is one of the main benefits of neuromarketing (Gurgu et al., 2020).). A customer might, for instance, state that they prefer a specific product over another based on features or price, which are reasonable criteria. However, neuromarketing research may show that subconscious elements like brand connections or feelings sparked by marketing stimuli have an impact on their choice. According to Smith & Hanover (2016), marketers may create more engaging and persuasive ads that resonate with customers on a deeper level by leveraging these underlying determinants of behavior.

Overall, neuromarketing is a major development in marketing theory and application. Using non-traditional techniques and the subconscious mind, neuromarketing provides marketers with an effective instrument for comprehending and moulding consumer behavior. Through the application of neuroscience findings, marketers may develop more compelling and successful campaigns that increase revenue.

MAIN FOCUS OF THE CHAPTER

Neuromarketing/Sensory Marketing Tools and Marketing Mix

The conventional marketing mix is changing because of the introduction of cutting-edge techniques and technologies by neuromarketing and sensory marketing. This section examines various instruments and how they fit into the marketing mix, emphasizing how they affect customer behavior and the efficacy of marketing.

Neuromarketing Tools

Functional Magnetic Resonance Imaging (fMRI)

This technique identifies regions of the brain that light up in reaction to marketing stimuli by monitoring changes in blood flow. (Hsu 2018; Hsu & Cheng 2018). This tool offers insightful information about how customers interpret and react to marketing messages.

Electroencephalography (EEG)

EEG provides real-time information on brain wave patterns by measuring electrical activity in the brain. This technique is especially helpful for analysing customer engagement and attention levels, assisting marketers in determining which elements of their campaigns are most successful, according to Bazzani et al. (2020); Cherubino et al. (2019).

Eye tracking: This technology tracks the location and duration of a consumer's gaze on different components of a marketing stimulus, like an advertisement or product packaging. This tool assists marketers in creating materials that are more visually appealing and captivating (Huddleston et al., 2018; Duerrschmid & Danner, 2018).

Facial Expression Analysis: This technique uses cameras to record and examine people's expressions to gain insight into how they are feeling in response to marketing materials. Using this technique, marketers can better craft their messaging to elicit the desired feelings from their target audience (Pham & Wang, 2017; Kessler et al., 2020).

Integration in the Marketing Mix

To increase efficacy, neuromarketing and sensory marketing techniques can be included into every facet of the marketing mix:

Product: By discovering attributes that appeal to customers' subliminal feelings, neuromarketing can assist in improving the design of products. Studies have demonstrated, for instance, that colors can elicit feelings, which can be used to the advantage of product packaging and branding. (Nilazzi et al., 2020; Bhatia, 2014).

Price: By studying how consumers perceive value, neuromarketing can assist decide the most effective pricing methods, according to Gill & Singh (2022); Gurgu et al. (2020). Studies have revealed, for instance, that the way prices are displayed (e.g., $19.99 vs. $20.00) can influence purchasing decisions.

Place: To produce a more interesting and enjoyable shopping experience, neuromarketing can influence store layout and design. For instance, Avendaño et al. (2021); Gonchigjav (2020); say that Scent marketing can affect the mood and behavior of consumers.

Promotion: By determining the most successful messaging and creative components, neuromarketing may maximize advertising and promotional initiatives says Zito et al. (2021). For instance, Micu et al. (2021) states that marketers can use neuroimaging techniques to identify which advertising campaigns evoke the highest emotional responses.

Strong insights into customer behavior are provided by neuromarketing and sensory marketing technologies, which can be used to develop more compelling and successful marketing campaigns. Marketers can obtain a competitive advantage by incorporating these techniques into their marketing mix and gaining a deeper insight of their target audience.

APPLICATION OF SENSORY AND NEURO MARKETING TO SUSTAIN IN EMERGING MARKETS

For marketers, emerging countries provide special opportunities and problems. Using sensory and neuromarketing strategies can help them navigate these dynamics especially well. In this section examines the application of sensory and neuromarketing to sustain and grow in emerging markets.

Recognizing Cultural Nuances: The varied customs and cultures found in emerging nations can have an impact on customer behavior. Marketers can adapt their techniques to appeal to local sensibilities by using sensory marketing. For example, using scents that are familiar and appealing to local consumers can enhance the effectiveness of marketing campaigns Sheth, et al., (2016).

Developing Emotional Bonds: In developing countries, consumer behavior is driven by emotions, which is something that neuromarketing may assist marketers understand. Through the identification and utilization of these drivers, marketers may craft campaigns that have a profound impact, resonate deeply with consumers, building strong emotional connections to brands (Makori, 2023; Cherubino et al., 2019).

Adapting to restricted Resources: Different customers purchase differently because of limited resources and priorities, in emerging markets. Sensory marketing can help marketers create products and packaging that are perceived as valuable, even if they are priced higher than competing products (Tyagi & Tyagi, 2022).

Leveraging Technology: Emerging markets frequently see rapid adoption of new technologies, opening new avenues for creative marketing approaches. By understanding how consumers use technology, marketers can better target their ads with neuromarketing to make them more engaging and effective (Makori, 2023; Srivastava & Bag, 2024).

Overcoming Infrastructure Obstacles: Lack of infrastructure in emerging markets can affect product distribution and accessibility. According to Sinha & Sheth (2018), sensory marketing can assist advertisers in creating packaging that is aesthetically pleasing and long-lasting, guaranteeing that goods reach customers in good condition.

Establishing Trust: In developing countries, where customers could be dubious of new brands or products, trust is crucial. According to Meijer et al., (2021), by fostering favourable sensory experiences that are connected to the brand, sensory marketing can aid in the development of trust.

In emerging regions, the use of sensory and neuromarketing strategies can be quite successful in building and maintaining brand recognition. Campaigns that connect with customers and lead to long-term success can be developed by marketers by comprehending and utilizing the distinctive qualities of these markets.

EMERGENCE OF FIVE SENSES IN MARKETING WORLD

The way businesses interact with customers has completely changed with the rise of sensory marketing, which uses the five senses—taste, smell, touch, sound, and sight—to create memorable and engaging brand experiences. This part examines the ways in which each sense is being is being strategically employed in the marketing world.

Visual (Sight): Since visual stimuli frequently serve as a consumer's initial point of contact with a brand, they are extremely important in marketing. Marketers produce eye-catching images that grab attention and communicate brand messages by utilizing colors, font, imagery, and visual storytelling. Ads that employ striking colors and eye-catching imagery, for instance, have the power to elicit powerful emotional reactions and leave a lasting impact on viewers.

Auditory (Sound): Sound is a great instrument in marketing since it may elicit strong feelings and memories. To improve the entire brand experience and establish brand associations, marketers employ sound effects, jingles, and music. A memorable jingle, for instance, can aid customers in remembering a company and its message even after they have heard or seen an advertisement.

Olfactory (Smell): Due of its strong associations with memory and emotion, smell is a powerful marketing tool. Scent marketing is a tool used by marketers to encourage favourable connections with their businesses. For instance, the aroma of freshly made cookies in a shop setting might entice customers to stay and make a purchase by creating a warm and inviting environment.

Tactile (Touch): How a product or brand is perceived by customers can be greatly influenced by their sense of touch. Marketers create an impression of quality and elegance by utilizing tactile factors like textures, packaging materials, and product ergonomics. For example, the smooth, sleek surface of a smartphone can convey a sense of sophistication and modernity.

Gustatory (Taste): Although it is not as frequently employed in marketing, taste can still have an impact. The sense of taste can contribute to the development of brand experiences even though it is not as frequently exploited in marketing. Taste is a tool used by food and beverage firms to set their products and give customers memorable experiences. A food tasting event, for instance, might provide customers a chance to sample a brand's offerings, fostering a favourable impression and promoting repeat business.

With the rise of sensory marketing, there are now more opportunities for marketers to interact emotionally and more deeply with customers. Marketers can build immersive brand experiences that connect with consumers and encourage brand loyalty by utilizing the five senses.

SENSORY MARKETING AND ITS INFLUENCE ON BUYING BEHAVIOR

Through the creation of distinctive and memorable brand experiences that connect with customers subconsciously, sensory marketing plays a critical role in influencing consumer purchasing behavior. This section examines how sensory marketing affects consumer behavior and how businesses may use this information to increase sales.

Impact on Emotions: Consumer perceptions and purchase decisions can be significantly impacted by sensory marketing that arouses strong emotions in them. For instance, using nice smells in retail establishments can make the space feel inviting and enhance the chance that customers would stay and make a purchase.

Brand Differentiation: In highly competitive markets, brands can stand out from the competition with the use of sensory marketing. Brands may differentiate themselves from competition and establish powerful emotional bonds with customers by producing unique sensory experiences. For instance, luxury companies frequently employ premium materials and elegant packaging to create a sense of exclusivity and luxury.

Memory and Recall: A sensory cue may bring up associations and memories that affect a person's purchasing decisions. For instance, a decision to buy a perfume might be influenced by the scent, which could bring back memories of a memorable event. With this information, marketers may develop sensory cues that strengthen favourable brand connections and improve brand recall.

In-Store Experiences: Because brick-and-mortar stores allow customers to engage with things and get a hands-on experience, sensory marketing works especially well there. Interactive exhibits and product demos, for instance, can stimulate a variety of senses and produce lasting impressions that encourage buy intent.

Online and Digital Channels: Online and digital marketing are also significant domains for sensory marketing. Digital marketers may build captivating experiences by incorporating both visual and audio clues into their website design and digital marketing. For example, Video advertisements that feature captivating images and music, for instance, have the power to evoke powerful emotions and increase brand engagement.

Cross-Modal Effects: When stimuli in one sensory modality affect perceptions in another, sensory marketing can also have an impact on consumer behavior. For instance, a product's texture may affect how people perceive its taste, resulting in a more positive assessment of the item.

One effective strategy for influencing customer purchasing behavior is sensory marketing. In competitive markets, marketers can enhance sales, foster brand loyalty, and set themselves apart from competitors by crafting captivating and unforgettable sensory experiences.

BUILDING BRAND DIFFERENTIATION AND LOYALTY

Businesses need to develop brand loyalty and distinction to succeed in cutthroat markets. The use of sensory marketing to produce distinctive brand experiences that connect with customers and encourage loyalty is examined in this section.

Crafting Authentic Brand Experiences: Through sensory marketing, companies may set themselves apart from rivals by crafting enduring and distinctive experiences. Using all five senses—taste, smell, touch, sound, and vision—brands can create immersive experiences that stick with customers. For instance, premium firms differentiate themselves from mass-market brands by creating an opulent and exclusive atmosphere in their stores using fine materials, exquisite packaging, and calming music.

Emotional Connection: Consumers who are exposed to sensory marketing are more likely to feel strongly about the brand. Customers are more inclined to stick with brands that make them feel a particular way, therefore emotions play a big part in creating brand loyalty. A company can build a deep emotional connection with its audience and encourage loyalty by using nostalgic imagery or music in its advertising.

Consistent Brand Experience: Developing brand loyalty requires consistency. Across all touchpoints, a consistent brand experience may be achieved with the use of sensory marketing. For instance, a company can establish a recurring olfactory experience that strengthens customer loyalty and maintains brand identity by using a distinctive aroma in its retail locations.

Personalization: Individual customers' brand experiences can also be made more tailored for with the use of sensory marketing. Brands may customize their marketing campaigns to create individualized experiences that connect with customers on a personal level by learning about the preferences and sensory triggers of their target audience. A company can foster a sense of exclusivity and loyalty by providing tailored product recommendations based on a customer's past purchases, for instance.

Establishing Trust: By fostering gratifying sensory connections between the brand and its audience, sensory marketing can assist in establishing trust with consumers. Customers are more inclined to stick with brands they trust, therefore establishing trust is crucial to increasing brand loyalty. Customers that respect natural components, for instance, may develop trust in a business that employs natural, organic fragrances in its goods.

Using sensory marketing to establish a brand is an effective strategy. Brands may encourage consumer loyalty and stand out in crowded marketplaces by developing distinctive brand experiences, arousing emotions, maintaining consistency, customizing the brand experience, and establishing trust.

THE IMPACT OF PRODUCT PACKAGING AND PROMOTIONAL STRATEGIES ON CONSUMER PURCHASE BEHAVIOR

The way that products are packaged and promoted is a major factor in how customers behave while making purchases. This section looks at how promotional tactics and product packaging can be improved with sensory marketing to influence consumer choices.

Visual Impact: Product packaging and promotional materials' visual components have a big impact on consumers' purchasing decisions. Designs, colors, and images that strike the eye of customers can provide a good first impression. Bold fonts and vivid colors, for instance, can raise a product's perceived worth and help it stand out on the shelves.

Tactile Experience: Consumer purchasing decisions may also be influenced by the tactile feel of product packaging. Packaging can influence consumers' impressions of a product by projecting an air of quality and luxury through its texture, weight, and feel. Embossed logos and soft-touch finishes, for instance, can provide a high-end vibe that draws in customers looking for luxury goods.

Sensory Branding -Using sensory inputs to create a unique brand experience is known as "sensory branding." A memorable brand experience can be created, for instance, by the sound of a Coke can being opened or the sensation of leather seats in a high-end vehicle. By adding tactile components to product packaging and promotional materials, brands can create a unique and memorable brand identity that resonates with consumers.

Emotional Appeal: Consumer purchasing decisions can be influenced by the emotions that product packaging and marketing tactics arouse in them. For instance, touching commercials or nostalgic package designs can foster a sense of community and brand loyalty among customers. Brands may establish a strong connection with their target audience and increase buy intent by appealing to consumers' emotions.

Promotional Techniques: Using techniques like discounts, exclusive deals, and time-limited promotions, one can also affect consumer behavior. Brands can persuade customers to buy by establishing a sense of urgency or exclusivity. Limited-edition packaging or promotional bundles, for instance, can instil a sense of scarcity in customers, encouraging them to purchase.

Promotional tactics and product packaging are important factors that affect consumers' purchasing decisions. Brands may improve the feel and visual appeal of their products, forge emotional bonds with customers, and influence purchase decisions by utilizing sensory marketing strategies. Through an awareness of how sensory stimuli influence customer behavior, brands can design packaging and promotional materials that effectively connect with their target market and increase sales.

NEXUS AMONG NEURO SENSORY MARKETING AND REPURCHASE INTENTIONS

The integration of sensory marketing strategies with neuroscience in neuro-sensory marketing has the potential to greatly influence client loyalty and repurchase intentions. The relationship between neuro-sensory marketing and repurchase behavior is examined in this section, emphasizing the ways in which brands might use sensory cues to promote repeat business.

Building Good Connections: Neuro-sensory marketing can assist in fostering favourable connections between brand features and sensory cues. For instance, a company might establish a pleasant and memorable shopping experience that customers will identify with the brand by using a certain aroma across its locations. The brand becomes more appealing and memorable as a result of these favourable associations, which can raise repurchase intentions.

Emotional Engagement: Customers repurchase intentions may be impacted by neuro-sensory marketing's ability to elicit significant emotional reactions in them. A company can enhance customer loyalty and encourage repeat business by, for instance, using emotive storytelling in its advertising to establish a deep emotional connection with viewers.

Brand Loyalty: As brand loyalty and repurchase behavior are closely related, sensory marketing can also help develop brand loyalty. Brands may establish a powerful emotional bond with customers and promote repeat business by crafting a distinctive sensory experience that appeals to them. Customers may become accustomed to and loyal to a brand by using a distinctive sound or emblem, for instance.

Trust and Consistency: Fostering trust and promoting repurchase behavior in sensory branding requires consistency. Through the constant use of sensory cues, like colors, sounds, and scents, brands can establish consumer trust and strengthen their brand identity across all touchpoints. Because they feel surer about their brand decision, consumers may be more inclined to repurchase because of this trust.

Sensory Packaging: Packaging has a significant impact on repurchase behavior and is essential to sensory marketing. A product that has luxurious packaging that stimulates the senses, for instance, might provide the impression that it is of greater quality, which increases the likelihood that customers will repurchase it.

There is a high correlation between neuro-sensory marketing and repurchase behavior, as sensory cues have a major impact on how consumers perceive and behave. Through the utilization of sensory marketing tactics, brands may foster enduring relationships with their clientele and promote repeat purchases by establishing good associations, emotional engagement, brand loyalty, consistency, and trust.

NEURO SENSORY MARKETING AND DIGITAL MARKETING

In the context of digital marketing, where companies are looking for novel methods to interact with customers online, neuro-sensory marketing is becoming more and more significant. This section looks at ways to incorporate neuro-sensory marketing into digital marketing tactics to make campaigns more interesting and successful.

Visual Content: Neuro-sensory marketing can assist in optimizing visual aspects to draw in customers and elicit strong feelings. Visual content is essential to digital marketing. For instance, employing visually appealing and immersive high-quality photographs, videos, and graphics can result in a more memorable and engaging marketing experience.

Audio-Visual Integration: Another crucial area of digital marketing that neuro-sensory marketing may be used in is audio-visual integration. Through the integration of fascinating visuals with captivating soundtracks, marketers can craft a message that is both impactful and memorable and that resonates with consumers on a deeper level.

Personalization: In digital marketing, personalization is crucial, and neuro-sensory marketing can assist in adjusting messages to suit unique tastes and behavioural patterns. Brands may develop customized ads that appeal to consumers' sensory preferences and boost engagement and conversion rates by utilizing data analytics and consumer insights.

User Experience (UX) Design: Neuro-sensory marketing can assist in optimizing the user experience to maximize engagement. UX design is essential to digital marketing. Users can have a more pleasurable and engaging experience, for instance, by utilizing interactive components, responsive design, and intuitive navigation. This can enhance brand loyalty and repurchase intentions.

Virtual and Augmented Reality (VR/AR): These emerging technologies present brands with intriguing chances to use digital marketing to create immersive sensory experiences. Through the utilization of these technologies, brands may provide more realistic and captivating interactions between consumers and products, hence increasing brand engagement and sales.

Social Media Marketing: Brands can use neuro-sensory marketing to stand out in the crowded social media space. Social media is a great tool for digital marketing. Brands can grab consumers' attention, encourage participation and sharing, and create visually spectacular and emotionally compelling content.

Exciting opportunities exist for organizations seeking to improve their digital marketing strategies through neuro-sensory marketing. Through the utilization of many sensory stimuli, including graphics, music, personalization, UX design, VR/AR, and social media, marketers can craft more impactful and successful campaigns that foster consumer loyalty.

SOLUTIONS AND RECOMMENDATIONS

Ethical Issues and Considerations

Neuro-sensory marketing is rife with ethical issues, particularly considering its ability to subtly alter consumer behavior. Some of the most important ethical questions and factors that marketers should think about while utilizing neuro-sensory marketing strategies are covered in this section.

Transparency: In neuro-sensory marketing, transparency is one of the most important ethical factors. Marketers ought to be open and honest about how and why they employ sensory stimuli. Customers need to know how their sensory data is gathered, processed, and applied to change their behavior.

Consumer Informed Consent: Before utilizing neuro-sensory marketing strategies, marketers should get the informed consent of their target audience. Customers must be informed about the type of sensory stimuli being employed, the way their data will be gathered and examined, and the possible consequences.

Privacy: Since neuro-sensory marketing collects and analyses sensitive data about people's sensory responses, privacy is a big concern. Marketers should follow data protection laws and anonymize consumer data to safeguard their privacy.

Manipulation: By appealing to consumers' irrational feelings and desires, neurosensory marketing can influence their behavior. Marketers ought to employ these strategies sensibly and morally, abstaining from any kind of compulsion or manipulation.

Targeting Vulnerable Groups: When using neuro-sensory marketing tactics to target vulnerable groups, such as children or those with mental health concerns, marketers should exercise caution. It is important to use extra caution to prevent the exploitation or manipulation of these groups by means of sensory inputs.

Cross-Cultural Sensitivity: Cultural variations in sensory perceptions and responses should be considered in neurosensory marketing. Something that works well or is appealing in one culture could not be seen the same way in another. Marketers must be aware of these variations and adjust their approaches accordingly.

Long-Term Effects: Marketers must take into account how neuro-sensory marketing may affect customers' behavior and general well-being in the long run. Although these methods might produce immediate benefits, they might have unforeseen long-term effects on people's decision-making and mental health.

Neuro-sensory marketing must take ethics into account to guarantee that customers are treated fairly and that their rights are upheld. Marketers can employ neuro-sensory marketing tactics ethically by being open and honest, getting informed consent, respecting privacy, avoiding deception, taking cultural differences into account, and thinking about long-term impacts.

Case Studies

Case studies and real-world examples can offer insightful information about how neuro-sensory marketing strategies are used in the real world. The case studies and real-world examples in this section demonstrate how neuro-sensory marketing can effectively change consumer behavior.

Case Study One: Donut Shop

To draw customers, Dunkin' Donuts ran a campaign in South Korea in 2018 that featured the aroma of its coffee. The business put in coffee-scented billboards near bus stations, which, when the advertisements were shown, produced the perfume of freshly made coffee. Foot traffic to Dunkin' Donuts locations close to bus stops has significantly increased, demonstrating the effectiveness of this sensory marketing strategy.

Case Study Two: Coca-Cola

Coca-Cola has long been at the forefront of sensory marketing, utilizing smell, sound, and visual cues to generate unforgettable brand experiences. A well-known instance is the "Hilltop" advertising campaign, which included the well-known tune "I'd Like to Buy the World a Coke." Increased sales and brand loyalty were the results of the campaign's use of music and imagery to arouse good feelings and foster a feeling of community.

Case Study Three: KitKat

KitKat gave its consumers a distinctive and unforgettable brand experience by using sensory marketing. The business started a promotion where they turned large "KitKat Chunky" bars into bus shelters in the UK. The shelters had a lever that, when pulled, released a free KitKat, and were covered in KitKat logo.

Case Study Four: Lush

Lush is a cosmetics business that attracts customers with its sensory-rich boutiques that appeal to their touch, smell, and sight. Vibrant displays, alluring aromas, and engaging product demos abound in the stores. Customers are drawn in and encouraged to investigate and buy things by this sensory experience.

Case Study Five: Spotify

Spotify displayed their tailored music recommendations with an ingenious neuro-sensory marketing strategy. The business developed a tool called "Taste Rewind," which produced playlists according on users' nostalgic tastes. Spotify was able to improve user retention and deeper user engagement by leveraging the emotional power of music and memories.

Case Study Six: Heineken

During the UEFA Champions League final, Heineken used neuro-sensory marketing to launch "The Dream Island," an immersive virtual reality experience. To have a Heineken drink and watch the game, participants were flown to a tropical island. Heineken stood out from the competition and gave customers a memorable brand experience because to this creative sensory experience.

Case Study Seven: Amazon

On its website, Amazon employs neuro-sensory marketing to improve the customer experience. Customers' evaluations, an intuitive UI, and individualized product recommendations all work together to create a sensory-rich experience that entices customers to explore and buy. Amazon has become a dominant player in e-commerce because to this strategy.

Case Study Eight: Disney

Disney is an expert in neuro-sensory marketing, enchanting visitors to its theme parks with sights, sounds, and even scents. Disney connects customers emotionally through the employment of iconic characters, themed attractions, and immersive narrative, resulting in the creation of enduring memories and a strong sense of brand loyalty.

Case Study Nine: Starbucks

Starbucks is renowned for creating a sensory-rich atmosphere in its stores, complete with the smell of freshly brewed coffee, the sound of heating milk, and the feel of a warm cup in your hand. Customers are encouraged to stay and return by these sensory aspects, which provide a warm and engaging experience. The business's use of sensory marketing has proven crucial in increasing sales and fostering customer loyalty.

These case studies show how neuro-sensory marketing can effectively change consumer behavior. By leveraging sensory stimuli such as scent, sound, and touch, brands can create unique and memorable experiences that resonate with consumers and drive brand loyalty and sales.

CONCLUSION AND FUTURE RESEARCH DIRECTIONS

With the help of neuro-sensory marketing, brands can craft memorable and engaging experiences that appeal to consumers' subliminal senses. The five senses—sight, hearing, touch, smell, and taste, allow brands to craft distinctive brand experiences that set them apart from rivals, foster strong emotional bonds with customers, and increase sales and brand loyalty.

Neuro-sensory marketing has been successfully applied in several industries, including retail, food and beverage, entertainment, and internet marketing, as demonstrated by the case studies. Brands that have adopted neuro-sensory marketing have been able to develop creative advertising campaigns that captures customers attention, arouse powerful emotions, and eventually affect their purchasing decisions.

Marketers must handle neuro-sensory marketing sensibly and ethically. When using sensory stimuli to affect consumer behavior, transparency, informed permission, privacy protection, and avoiding manipulation are important factors to consider.

There are countless opportunities for neuro-sensory marketing as long as technology keeps developing. The landscape of sensory marketing will be further enhanced by interactive technologies, personalised experiences, and virtual and augmented reality, which will give brands new and interesting methods to communicate with customers.

Neuro-sensory marketing signifies a major change in the way companies are moving from conventional techniques and toward more immersive and experiential tactics. In a market that is getting more and more competitive, brands may succeed by recognizing and utilizing the power of sensory stimulation to build meaningful connections with customers.

REFRENCES

Alsharif, A. H., Salleh, N. Z. M., Baharun, R., Hashem, E. A. R., Mansor, A. A., Ali, J., & Abbas, A. F. (2021). Neuroimaging techniques in advertising research: Main applications, development, and brain regions and processes. *Sustainability (Basel)*, 13(11), 6488. 10.3390/su13116488

Bazzani, A., Ravaioli, S., Trieste, L., Faraguna, U., & Turchetti, G. (2020). Is EEG suitable for marketing research? A systematic review. *Frontiers in Neuroscience*, 14, 594566. 10.3389/fnins.2020.59456633408608

Bhatia, K. (2014). Neuromarketing: Towards a better understanding of consumer behavior. *Optimization*, 6(1), 52–62.

Cherubino, P., Martinez-Levy, A. C., Caratù, M., Cartocci, G., Di Flumeri, G., Modica, E., Rossi, D., Mancini, M., & Trettel, A. (2019). Consumer behaviour through the eyes of neurophysiological measures: State-of-the-art and future trends. *Computational Intelligence and Neuroscience*, 2019(1), 1976847. 10.1155/2019/197684731641346

Cherubino, P., Martinez-Levy, A. C., Caratù, M., Cartocci, G., Di Flumeri, G., Modica, E., Rossi, D., Mancini, M., & Trettel, A. (2019). Consumer behaviour through the eyes of neurophysiological measures: State-of-the-art and future trends. *Computational Intelligence and Neuroscience*, 2019(1), 1976847. 10.1155/2019/197684731641346

Cohen, J. B., Pham, M. T., & Andrade, E. B. (2018). The nature and role of affect in consumer behavior. In *Handbook of consumer psychology* (pp. 306-357). Routledge., Duerrschmid, K., & Danner, L. (2018). Eye tracking in consumer research. In *Methods in Consumer Research,* (pp. 279-318). Woodhead Publishing.

Erickson, G. S. (2017). *New methods of market research and analysis*. Edward Elgar Publishing. 10.4337/9781786432698

Gurgu, E., Ioana-Andreea, G., & Rocsana, B. (2020). Neuromarketing for a better understanding of consumer needs and emotions. *Independent Journal of Management & Production, 11.* 10.1016/j.matpr.2020.08.730

Golnar-Nik, P., Farashi, S., & Safari, M. S. (2019). The application of EEG power for the prediction and interpretation of consumer decision-making: A neuromarketing study. *Physiology & Behavior*, 207, 90–98. 10.1016/j.physbeh.2019.04.02531047949

Gonchigjav, B. (2020). Results of neuromarketing study of visual attention and emotions of buyers in retail store environment. *Proceedings of the Mongolian Academy of Sciences*, 52-64. Research Gate.10.5564/pmas.v60i1.1337

Gurgu, E., Gurgu, I. A., & Tonis, R. B. M. (2020). Neuromarketing for a better understanding of consumer needs and emotions. *Independent Journal of Management & Production*, 11(1), 208–235. 10.14807/ijmp.v11i1.993

Hsu, M. Y. T. (2018). *Cognitive systems research for neuromarketing assessment on evaluating consumer learning theory with fMRI*. Science Direct.

Hsu, M. Y. T., & Cheng, J. M. S. (2018). fMRI neuromarketing and consumer learning theory: Word-of-mouth effectiveness after product harm crisis. *European Journal of Marketing*, 52(1/2), 199–223. 10.1108/EJM-12-2016-0866

Huddleston, P. T., Behe, B. K., Driesener, C., & Minahan, S. (2018). Inside-outside: Using eye-tracking to investigate search-choice processes in the retail environment. *Journal of Retailing and Consumer Services*, 43, 85–93. 10.1016/j.jretconser.2018.03.006

Kessler, S. J., Jiang, F., & Hurley, R. A. (2020). The state of automated facial expression analysis (AFEA) in evaluating consumer packaged beverages. *Beverages*, 6(2), 27. 10.3390/beverages6020027

Makori, R. (2023). The Influence of Neuro-Marketing Techniques on Consumer Decision-Making in Strategic Marketing Campaigns. *Journal of Strategic Marketing Practice*, 1(1), 21–29.

Meijer, G. W., Lähteenmäki, L., Stadler, R. H., & Weiss, J. (2021). Issues surrounding consumer trust and acceptance of existing and emerging food processing technologies. *Critical Reviews in Food Science and Nutrition*, 61(1), 97–115. 10.1 080/10408398.2020.171859732003225

Micu, A., Capatina, A., Micu, A. E., Geru, M., Aivaz, K. A., & Muntean, M. C. (2021). A NEW CHALLENGE IN DIGITAL ECONOMY: NEUROMARKETING APPLIED TO SOCIAL MEDIA. *Economic Computation and Economic Cybernetics Studies and Research*, 55(4).

Misra, L. (2023). Neuromarketing insights into consumer behavior. *IUJ Journal of Management*, 11(1), 143–163.

Nilashi, M., Yadegaridehkordi, E., Samad, S., Mardani, A., Ahani, A., Aljojo, N., Razali, N. S., & Tajuddin, T. (2020). Decision to adopt neuromarketing techniques for sustainable product marketing: A fuzzy decision-making approach. *Symmetry*, 12(2), 305. 10.3390/sym12020305

Pham, P., & Wang, J. (2017, March). Understanding emotional responses to mobile video advertisements via physiological signal sensing and facial expression analysis. In *Proceedings of the 22nd International Conference on intelligent user interfaces* (pp. 67-78). ACM. 10.1145/3025171.3025186

Sheth, J. N., Sinha, M., & Shah, R. (2016). *Breakout strategies for emerging markets: Business and marketing tactics for achieving growth.* FT Press.

Sinha, M., & Sheth, J. (2018). Growing the pie in emerging markets: Marketing strategies for increasing the ratio of non-users to users. *Journal of Business Research*, 86, 217–224. 10.1016/j.jbusres.2017.05.007

Smith, K., & Hanover, D. (2016). *Experiential marketing: Secrets, strategies, and success stories from the World's greatest brands.* John Wiley & Sons. 10.1002/9781119176688

Srivastava, G., & Bag, S. (2024). Modern-day marketing concepts based on face recognition and neuro-marketing: A review and future research directions. *Benchmarking*, 31(2), 410–438. 10.1108/BIJ-09-2022-0588

Tyagi, P. K., & Tyagi, P. (2022). Customer perception and brand image through sensory marketing. In *Disruptive Innovation and Emerging Technologies for Business Excellence in the Service Sector* (pp. 41–68). IGI Global. 10.4018/978-1-7998-9194-9.ch003

Zito, M., Fici, A., Bilucaglia, M., Ambrogetti, F. S., & Russo, V. (2021). Assessing the emotional response in social communication: The role of neuromarketing. *Frontiers in Psychology*, 12, 625570. 10.3389/fpsyg.2021.62557034149513

Zoëga Ramsøy, T., Michael, N., & Michael, I. (2019). A consumer neuroscience study of conscious and subconscious destination preference. *Scientific Reports*, 9(1), 15102. 10.1038/s41598-019-51567-131641234

Chapter 10
Decoding Neuromarketing Strategies:
Unveiling Its Role on Brand Equity

Rita Devi
https://orcid.org/0000-0002-9874-8679
Central University of Himachal Pradesh, India

Rachna Bhopal
https://orcid.org/0000-0003-2954-7838
Central University of Himachal Pradesh, India

Varun Sharma
Central University of Himachal Pradesh, India

ABSTRACT

Investigating consumer perceptions concerning neuromarketing strategies employed by marketers and the resultant impact on brand equity constitutes the core of the study. This chapter investigates the various neuromarketing strategies to ascertain their importance in influencing brand equity with a specific focus on 162 consumers of the Kangra District of Himachal Pradesh using convenience sampling. By employing empirical analysis and conceptual framework, the study seeks to ascertain how the neuromarketing strategies—brand positioning, brand awareness, brand prestige, performance, feeling, judgment, branding, advertisement, purchase decision, product design, and innovation—influence the brand equity. The findings offer valuable insights that will enlighten businesses and consumers about the implications of neuromarketing on customer choices and brand perception through the development of more productive consumer enticement strategies.

DOI: 10.4018/979-8-3693-4236-7.ch010

INTRODUCTION

In a perfect world, consumers weigh a wide range of factors, such as product attributes, cost, availability, and flexibility, before selecting between various goods and services. However, when the products and services of numerous companies are astonishingly equivalent, the choice is ultimately determined by the reputation of the particular brands. In essence, a brand is a product with unique qualities that distinguish it from competing goods made to meet the same demands. In today's age of internet and technology driven marketing, businesses are increasingly adopting a range of programmers to increase consumer affinities for their brands. Theodore Levitt (1986), a Harvard professor, asserted that " the new competition is not between what business entities produce in their factories, but rather between what they add to their manufacturing output in the form of the packaging, services, advertisements, consumer advice, delivery structures, financing, storage, and other things that the people value." Kotler and Armstrong (2001), delineated "brand as a name, term, sign, symbol, or design, or a combination of these, that identifies the maker or seller of a product or service." We live in a culture where mass customization has replaced mass manufacturing as the dominant economic model, where branding is significant, well-liked, and information wealthy (Neumeier, 2005). Customers choose brands for practical and emotional reasons (Doyle & Stern, 2006) and brand loyalty (Casey, 2004). The strategic advancements pursued by any company largely hinge on the marketing tactics of its products or services (Arora, 2020).

Utilizing a unified conceptual framework, brand equity interprets the possible outcomes of diverse brand strategies. The concept essentially emphasizes the significance of brands' roles in marketing strategies. Marketing experts believe that brands possessing greater equity inspire consumer pride in ownership, inspire greater trust, and offer pertinent and unique commitments. Arora (2024) highlighted the importance of AR and VR in making experiences more engaging, immersive, and entertaining, thereby enhancing learning outcomes. Businesses are enabled by the metaverse to use innovative technology for e-commerce, branding, and marketing (Kumar et al., 2024), where neuromarketing optimise the user experience in metaverse (Nilashi & Abumalloh, 2023). Neuromarketing techniques have enabled firms to understand and influence consumer behavior on a deeper, subconscious level, outperforming traditional marketing strategies. This improved understanding has resulted in more targeted and successful policies, boosting economic growth and transforming customer experiences (Lim, 2020). Artificial intelligence-powered strategies known as neuro-marketing and facial recognition marketing offer cognitive understanding of human behavior (Srivastava & Bag, 2024).

Technological advancements propel towards a more integrated and interconnected digital future (Dhiman & Arora, 2024). By leveraging ontological and communicative perspectives, businesses can effectively navigate market complexities, strengthen consumer trust and loyalty (Arora & Sharma, 2023), and create innovative environments with metaverse products (Rathore & Arora, 2024).

Neuromarketing

Every day, people encounter over 3,000 advertisements across various platforms including the Internet, social media, billboards, radio, and television. Within milliseconds, our brains form initial impressions of products, selectively retaining certain ads over others. Characteristics such as target demographics, age groups, occupations, and gender influence the effectiveness of advertisements. The utilization of neuroscientific methods to better our understanding of human behavior is referred to as neuromarketing, a logical step in promoting research. Customer behaviors and the neurology of customer's behavior are combined in neuromarketing. Neuromarketing methods evaluate every aspect of the brand and propagate it to every single retail customer who has already received a wealth of knowledge about it via advertisement. Collaboration between modern marketers and retail customers remains a continual driving force in reaching marketing objectives by establishing a relatable rapport (Mariampolski, 2006).

The goal of marketing in the twenty-first century is to build a positive sales connection by meeting the needs of retail customers, though the way the entrepreneurs or managers now adopt the marketing techniques are much affected by Covid 19 pandemic (Arora & Sharma, 2021). Adapting to changing consumer needs improves retail customer happiness because current marketers use specialized talents to understand unique consumer preferences (Wang & Ji, 2010). In this process persuasion skills play an important role (Arora, 2023). Understanding retail customers' wishes allows marketers to promote corporate growth, in contrast to previous practices in which sales were frequently made without regard for consumer preferences. Modern marketers' recent attempts strive to successfully distribute information to a wide range of retail buyers by employing a variety of marketing tactics (Paquette, 2013).

The importance of neuromarketing is to comprehend a buyer's psychology through understanding their way of thinking, emotions, ideas, or preferred values. Its purpose is to obtain a better knowledge of the clients' needs, motivations, and values. Essentially, neuromarketing seeks to predict customer behavior and reactions to different stimuli. The breakthrough result of neuromarketing research states emotions heavily influence the consumers' decision-making processes (Stoll et al., 2008). Particularly neuroscience clarifies how important internal emotional reactions of customers are to their decision-making (Solnais et al., 2013). Neuroscience seeks to comprehend the basis of complex ideas including reasoning, decision-making, object representation, emotion, memory, and customer responses to marketing. The goal of neuroscience is to comprehend the underlying principles of complex ideas like emotion, memory, object representation, reasoning, decision-making, and consumer response to marketing (Perrachione & Perrachione, 2008). Furthermore, neuroscience offers understanding of how people generate, retain, remember, and interact with information—including brands—in their everyday lives (Asmadi & Hailat, 2021). Results of neuromarketing research provide a comprehension of the consumer mentality that is not possible with conventional marketing techniques. By augmenting conventional research methods, Neuromarketing is helping marketers to understand customer preferences more deeply (Mashrur, 2022).

Neuromarketing Strategies

The concept of marketing development known as "neuromarketing" has recently emerged with a notable impact on the selling of products or services to end customers. The term "neuromarketing" pertains to a branch of commercial marketing communication that investigates the cognitive responses of consumers to marketing stimuli while integrating retail consumer neuropsychology into marketing research (Zurawicki, 2010). To be effective in the marketing environment, neuromarketing seeks to comprehend the ethics of retail consumers making purchasing decisions as well as the feedback on marketing stimuli.

Neuromarketing methods are a crucial component of a person's mentality while considering a purchase (Suomala et al., 2012). Modern marketers choose a variety of ways to entice retail customers by anticipating their purchasing patterns (Fisher et al., 2010). To build a relationship with retail consumers, modern marketers engage in a specific engagement. To capture the attention of every retail customer, modern marketers mostly use advertising. The identified needs of the retail consumer serve as the foundation for the purchasing process. When a retail consumer's habitual demands increase, the need can be determined using the stimuli (Wood & Neal, 2009). Retail consumers obtain the most comprehensive information about a product from advertisements developed by modern marketing. The commercial media usually help the retail customer become aware of and knowledgeable about the brands that are accessible in the market.

Modern marketer need to develop neuromarketing techniques to enable brand recognition and expertise (Ismajli et al., 2022). Outstanding product usability and design are another approach to increase retail consumer power. Product usability and design show how a brand is represented externally. Outstanding design attracts attention so that the brand can function properly. To please retail customers, neuromarketing in advertising heavily anticipates psychological image (Parchure et al.,

2020). Retail customers instinctively get eager to acquire when items are in short supply out of concern that they might sell out. Retail customers feel a connection that they don't want to miss. The dynamic of scarcity is a popular neuromarketing strategy for many contemporary marketers. As a result, current marketers construct neuromarketing tactics by paying less attention to product qualities and scientific requirements—almost to the point where retail shoppers benefit from branded products. The traditional criticism of contemporary marketers is that they use neuromarketing techniques to make brands more approachable to retail customers. Instead of considering the brand's mission, retail customers base a large portion of their purchasing decisions on their mental associations with it. With their retail customers, Band equity cultivates an emotional bond that will guarantee enduring brand loyalty. Branding fosters emotional ties to products and builds consumer trust. Markets are influenced by this attachment to make a choice. The market wants a powerful brand change that choose the ownership experience and affects the purchasing decision. Modern marketers need to focus on generating a quick return on their investments. (Loureiro et al., 2012). The value proposition inspires contemporary marketers to comprehend the needs of retail customers who have an emotional connection to the brand.

Techniques of Neuromarketing

Modern neuroscience makes it simple to become perplexed by the variety of neuromarketing strategies available as it aids in the development of strategies to mitigate its impact on both physical and mental health (Sohal & Sharma, 2024). It's important to comprehend the differences and workings of the many methodologies employed in the industry, even if almost all of them might be useful in understanding consumer buying behaviour. Neuromarketing approaches commonly used include eye tracking, brain imaging (EEG and fMRI), face encoding, sensory marketing, and psychological methodology. These techniques are applied to determine how well they work and to discover the specific situations in which they are most effective (Parchure et al., 2020).

- **Eye Tracking**

Eye tracking involves tracking individuals' eye movements, as the name would imply. It's a tool that enables you to view your company, location, or advertisement from the perspective of your target market. Modern eye tracking technology allows for the creation of real-time situations and the recording of users' natural eye gaze since it is so lightweight and portable. In conclusion, eye tracking provides a fantastic approach to learn things that are hard to learn via conventional marketing research. Eye tracking is a technology that can measure customer eye movements online in addition to in-store, used to find out if putting a product in TV shows actually draws in more customers. Eye tracking tools have the potential to track customers' eyes, which can measure attention and fixation point of an eye, as well as arousal (pupil dilation), facial expression coding (reading the minute movement of muscles in a face), heart rate, emotional response, respiratory rate, and skin conductivity. According to basic research conducted in neuroscience, according to a report, brand-driven changes in product flavour were linked to greater activation via an automatic associative chain reaction including memories. One example is the Hallo effect, which is frequent with well-known companies. A consumer is more likely to think that an established brand's product is better than one from a new or untrustworthy company. Additionally, the customer's early emotional product evaluation is related to choice and significantly affects conscious decision-making. It is expected to develop extensive knowledge in the field to effectively compete through the implementation of appropriate strategies (Devi & Bhopal, 2023).

- **A look within the Consumer's Brain: FMRI**

There are additional methods we may employ if we want to learn a little more about what individuals believe as opposed to what they see. You may be familiar with MRI and EEG equipment as examples of technologies that may read brain activity in a medical setting. Neuromarketers employ brain scanning technologies to examine the brain activity of individuals, with the goal of developing persuasive commercials, websites, and packaging that stimulate clients' buying instincts.

- **Facial Coding**

In 1872, Charles Darwin postulated that human facial expressions might contain the potential to reveal meaning. Subsequently, it has thoroughly investigated how this information can be optimized for marketing purposes. Sensors capable of tracking subtle muscle movements can be affixed to the face, functioning similarly to apparatus that evaluate cerebral activity and eye fixation. Diverse emotions, including surprise and wrath, are conveyed through the use of distinct muscle groups, as is the case with smiling. Although a faint smile or slight expression may not invariably signify pleasure, facial coding technology has the capability to discern subtle, frequently unconscious reactions to stimuli that unveil our genuine emotions. Moreover, it possesses the capability to forecast the actions that ensue from specific expressions.

- **Touch, Smell, See and Hear: Sensory Marketing**

There are more practical kinds of neuromarketing that encourage customers in the proper path as opposed to research-oriented techniques like those we've covered above. To increase the efficacy of marketing, we may draw on already-established results and ideas. Sensory marketing is an excellent illustration of this in the retail industry. In internet commerce, neuromarketing technologies offer perceptions into gauging the influence that advertisements have on consumers (Singh, 2020). Organizations must ensure meticulous selection of tools and technologies, effective execution of change management, and the development of a digital workplace strategy to fully embrace the impact of digitalization (Bhopal & Devi, 2022).

Brand Equity

Brand equity is the financial value that a brand adds to a product (Aakcr, 1992). The accumulation of resources associated with a brand either increases or diminishes its value to customers and enterprises (Farquhar, 1989). Regarding a market with differentiated brands versus one without brand differentiation, brand equity signifies the inherent evaluation made by consumers regarding the brand. (Swait et al., 1993). This additional growth is caused by each individual customer's increased likelihood of choosing the brand over competing options, without making any steps to establish the brand or likelihood of choosing the product (Srinivasan et al., 2005). Various networks of relationships or exchanges between the brand, its channel partners, and the parent company, confer upon the brand the ability to generate more revenue or maintain higher profit margins than it might in the absence of its brand identity. In response to changing consumer preferences, the hotel industry needs to enhance and innovate its services while increasing brand equity via differentiation, customer satisfaction, and loyalty.

From a behavioral perspective, brand equity is a multifaceted concept crucial for establishing points of distinction that result in a competitive advantage through non-price competition. (Aaker, 1992). Along with other proprietary brand assets, it comprises of brand associations, perceived quality, perceived brand loyalty, and brand awareness. While Keller (1993) presented brand knowledge, which includes brand awareness and brand image, and (Shocker & Weitz, 1988) proposed brand loyalty and brand associations. Brand equity was conceptualized by Farquhar (1989) as having three benefits:

- **Financial:** This way of thinking about brand equity is focused on figuring out how much more expensive a name-brand product is than a generic one. When utilizing this methodology for quantifying brand equity, expenditures such as promotional costs are likewise accounted.

- **Consumer-based:** A strong brand influences consumers' attitudes more strongly towards the connected product. Of course, user encounters with a product have an impact on how strong an attitude is. Consequently, stronger attitudes imply that trial samples may be more effective than advertising when a new brand is introduced. Consumer awareness and associations eventually result in perceived quality, implied qualities, and loyalty for a brand.
- **Brand extensions:** A strong brand can serve as a springboard for the introduction of related items. This aids in maximizing the already-present brand recognition, cutting down on advertising costs and lowering risk from the consumers' point of view. But it is more challenging to quantify this process.

Metrics about brand equity generally conform to one of the three classifications delineated by Keller and Lehmann (2003). The primary emphasis is on results pertaining to the product market. In this particular category, the metric that is most frequently applied is the amount consumers pay for a brand compared to a fundamental (unbranded) product (Holbrook b & Batra 1987; Srinivasan et.al., 2005). Price premium can also be measured using related concepts of brand susceptibility and clout, as defined by the brand's own and cross-price elasticity (Kamakura & Russell, 1989). Additional measures of this type are the residual in the hedonic regression (Hjorth-Andersen, 1984) that assesses market inefficiency, and constant (Srinivasan, 1979). The drawback of this brand equity measurement strategy is that it ignores interactions between the many constraints of the marketing mix, such as price and advertising or price promotion and advertising, among others being addressed in the works of (Jedidi et al., 1999) and (Erdem et al., 2003).

The second set of metrics is focused on consumer mindset, which comprises the attitudes, opinions, affiliations, and emotional ties that consumers have with the company (Ambler & Barwise, 1998). The financial measures serve as the foundation for the final measuring category. These evaluate a brand's value specifically in terms of financial assets. These measurements encompass aspects such as the acquisition price during brand transactions (Mahajan et al., 1994), as well as the discounted cash flow elements associated with royalties and licensing. Brand equity is quantified by the additional financial flow produced by the sale of branded products in comparison to unbranded products, excluding other sources of business value (Simon et al., 1993). The majority of brand equity research has examined this problem from either a firm's standpoint or from a customer perspective. Usually entails the gathering and use of information from surveys or experiments that examine brand equity in terms of customer thinking. Strong brand equity has grown to be a crucial element influencing consumer brand behavior. Successful brand management requires a thorough grasp of brand equity and effective management of it to produce specific characteristics that will impact customers' decisions. Brand equity grows consumers' willingness to pay premium prices, the potential for brand licensing, the effectiveness of marketing communication, the stores' willingness to work together and offer support, consumers' receptivity to price reductions, and their insensitivity to high prices (Barwise, 1993; Simon & Sullivan, 1993).

Brand equity is a group of assets and liabilities associated to a brand that, in the eyes of the customer, either increase or decrease the value of a good or service (Aaker, 1991). This value is evident in consumers' thoughts, actions, and feelings towards the brand, shaped by their perceptions of marketing efforts. For a business, brand equity is an essential intangible asset with both financial and psychological value determining the worth of brand with customer's purchasing decision (Singh & Islam, 2017). Fig1 elucidates the Aaker model of brand equity where these five factors of brand equity (brand loyalty, brand awareness, perceived quality, brand associations, other proprietary brand assets) provide value to customers and value to firms. It provides value to customers by enhancing customers interpretation/ processing of information, and confidence in the purchase decision. Efficiency and effectiveness of marketing programs, brand loyalty, prices/margins, brand extensions, trade leverage, and competitive advantage provides value to firm.

LITERATURE REVIEW

Literature Review on Neuromarketing

Neuroscience research is examining how signals from marketing and advertising impact the human brain from deep inside the skull. Research reveals a lot of the subtle, typically unconscious, psychological processes that either build or burst the effectiveness of marketing strategy (Parchure et al., 2020).

The ability to peek into customers' minds has given businesses the chance to better understand consumer behavior, which underpins an individual's decision-making process. Commercial organizations have benefited from the use of neuromarketing approaches to identify and target the true requirements, aspirations, and wants of consumers (Cherubino et al., 2019). Researchers investigated a range of subjects including heart rate and galvanic skin response, eye tracking, reaction time testing, and facial expressions. These investigations are crucial for understanding how products impact customers' decision-making process. By recognizing the cognitive relationship between brand and retail consumers, a competent marketer prepares to give direction and concentration to the brand product or manufacturer (Hsu & Chen, 2018). The strategies navigate the challenging choices and demonstrate flexibility in adapting to shifting business goals (Bhopal & Devi, 2023). Marketers use specific strategies known as neuromarketing tactics to comprehend the relationship.

Marketing strategies are carried out by quickly gauging retail consumers' attitudes towards a product or brand. Since then, government agencies have developed marketing methods like increasing retail consumer knowledge of available items (Cronin et al., 2011). Neuromarketing strategies such as branding, product design & innovation, advertisement, entertainment, online marketing, and purchase decisions need to prioritize sustainable development (Nazma et al., 2023). Companies like Sales Brain and Bright House commercially debuted neuromarketing as a marketing profession in 2002. These businesses began providing marketing and consulting services based on neuroscience methodologies (Morin & Renvoisé, 2018). McClure utilized fMRI data in the first neuromarketing research to identify the brain correlates of participants' preferences between Coke and Pepsi (Morin & Renvoisé, 2018). Alsharif et al., (2023) provided a comprehensive overview of neuromarketing tools used in the marketing mix and highlighted neural responses to consumer behavior, using the PRISMA framework to uncover key brain areas linked to marketing elements like advertising and brand. The brain regions are activated during the purchase decisions and are found to be highly relevant to neuromarketing applications (Khondakar et al., 2024). The marketers utilize gamification and neuromarketing to comprehend online consumer engagement, proposing a theoretical framework for self-determination theory in digital marketing strategies, revealing marketers' interest in neuromarketing due to its potential to save costs, enhance marketing plans, and provide accurate insights through advanced techniques like brain imaging (Behl et al., 2024)

Literature Review on "Brand Equity"

Lhotáková and Olšanová (2013) examined that brands play an increasingly important role in consumers' decision-making due to increased market competition on both the domestic and international levels. Consumers can choose from a variety of brands to find goods that meet their wants, appeal to their emotions, and support them in expressing who they are as members of society. The unique value of the brand from the perspective of customers and cultural norms who work for the same company, on the relevance and acceptability of globally renowned scientific models that are regarded as credible, as well as the fundamentals of modal addition (Nemati et al., 2013). Jamal Abad and Hossein (2013) conceptualized client-based brand equity in the financial-related services sector and determined it effects on brand perception. Discovered that brand equity's influential criteria for perceived quality, brand loyalty, brand awareness, and brand association increased brand perception in the financial services sector. Brand association appeared to have more of an impact on brand equity than the other three of the four aspects discussed.

Pouromid and Iranzadeh (2012) looked at how brand equity affected brand choice and purchase intentions One of the capitals that maintains a company's worth and inspires client loyalty is brand equity. The more brand equity a corporation has in its customers' minds, the more profits it may generate. While there are disagreements over the opposing roles of some marketing mix elements, Ghorban (2012) explained how marketing mix components have a vital influence in building brand equity and its dimensions. Alsharif and Salleh (2021) in the study found that the human brain regulates all feelings and sensations and takes into account all that is taken in while perceiving something or identifying oneself with an occasion or experience where neuroimaging is used to explain every aspect of human behavior in terms of brain activity. Nam (2011) explicated the correlation among brand loyalty, customer satisfaction, and customer-based brand equity within the hotel and restaurant industry. Green bonds issuance has also been correlated with the positive brand reputation as it attracts the attention of people (Jangid & Bhardwaj, 2024).

With particular reference to the Indian auto sector, (Thiripurasundari & Natarajan, 2011) examined an empirical result of the factors of brand equity. Brands are now said to as "cultural accessories and personal philosophies" due to their growing significance as economic and cultural drivers (Chattopadhyay, 2010). The brand choice model created by (Erdem & Swait, 2001) was integrated and expanded with the brand equity development model created by (Yoo et al., 2000). Data gathered by neuroimaging would produce more accurate information about customer preferences than marketing pattern studies and would be devoid of biases that are present in conventional research (Ariely & Berns, 2010). This occurs because conventional market research techniques are unable to access the customers' subconscious thought processes. Instead, they aim to assess customer sentiments towards the brands, which might not translate into real consumer behaviour at the point of purchase (Agarwal & Dutta, 2001). Liyin (2009) developed a study framework for assessing website brand equity from the viewpoint of web content. In circumstances when there are doubts regarding brand qualities, the association is not present between components that are not directly connected to the marketing strategy and brand equity (Chattopadhyay et al., 2009). Kayaman and Arsali, (2007) identified that the four elements of brand equity—brand awareness, brand loyalty, perceived quality, and brand image are responsible for improving customer-based hotel brand equity where services are processed by considering relationships between client-based brand equity components. The association between emotions and customer brand loyalty was investigated using neuromarketing to reveal subconscious processes, emotional triggers using neuroimaging methods and found that neural mechanisms underlie emotional responses to brands (Shukla et al., 2024). Neuromarketing delves into subconscious minds to understand behavior, while AI enables personalized experiences, predictive analytics, and automated tasks, shaping the future of marketing through enhanced user experiences and ethical considerations (Kumar et al., 2024). Neurophysiological techniques were used to compare the cognitive, affective, and behavioral responses to visual communication elements of Foster's Hollywood and VICIO brands and found that they generate stronger impact on users' affective responses (De, 2024) The sensory, affective, behavioral, and intellectual facets of brand experience positively impact all four dimensions of brand equity: brand awareness, brand association, perceived quality, and brand loyalty (Catherine et al., 2024)

Proposed Research Model

A conceptual framework (Figure 1) was developed on the conceptual perspective and review of the literature. The constructive purpose of the study is to find the influence of neuromarketing strategies (brand positioning, brand awareness, brand prestige, performance, feeling, judgment, branding, advertisement, purchase decision, product design, and innovation) on brand equity as shown in Figure 2.

Figure 2. Conceptual framework

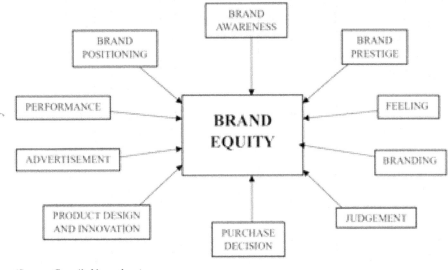

(Source: Compiled by authors)

Consumer preference, or why people choose one product over another, is one of the main areas of interest for businesses in today's market. This study's analysis of neuromarketing focuses on the brain's structure and operations, the significance of perception, and the actions of consumers during the buying process. The study aims to recognize and comprehend the concept of neuromarketing strategies that affect brand equity for customer choices during the purchase. Based on the literature review, the following hypothesis and objective are proposed.

Ho: The neuromarketing strategies do not influence the brand equity.

Research Objective: To find the role of neuromarketing strategies on brand equity.

RESEARCH METHODOLOGY

Data Collection

The primary data collection method utilized was a questionnaire, designed to address key factors influencing customer product choices. A survey instrument comprising two parts was developed for this purpose. The first part collected demographic information about the respondents, while the second part consisted of 39 statements related to product selection criteria to brand equity, brand positioning, brand awareness, brand prestige, performance, feeling, judgment, brand advertisement, purchase decision, product design, and innovation. The data was collected from the 162 consumers of the Kangra District of Himachal Pradesh using convenience sampling.

Measures

The variables were measured using an established scale. 39 item scale was considered to measure the constructs - brand equity (3 items), brand positioning (3 items), brand awareness (3 items), brand prestige (3 items), performance (3 items), feeling (3 items), judgment (3 items), branding (4 items) advertisement (6 items), purchase decision (4 items), product design, and innovation (4 items) on five-point Likert Scale with 1 representing strongly agree to 5 representing strongly disagree. The Cronbach's alpha value of all constructs exceeded the acceptable threshold value of 0.7, thereby reinforcing its reliability for further analysis and interpretation (Refer to table 3).

The demographic profile of the respondents included information related to gender, age, qualification, and income. Table 1 represents the demographic profile of the respondents where the majority of respondents are male (67.9%) in the age group of 18-25 years (74.1%) with a monthly income less than 25,000 (38.9%) graduation as the minimum qualification (59.3%).

Table 1. Demographic profile of respondents

Demographic Characteristics	Frequency	Percentage
Gender		
Female	52	32.1
Male	110	67.9
Age (in years)		
Below 18	8	4.9
18-25	120	74.1
25-35	24	14.8
35-45	3	1.9
45-55	6	3.7
Above 55	1	0.6
Qualification		
Primary	5	3.1
Secondary	14	8.6
Graduate	96	59.3
Post Graduate	33	20.4
PhD	2	1.2
Others	12	7.4
Monthly Income (in Rs)		
Below 25,000	63	38.9
25,000-50,000	19	11.7
50,000-75,000	30	18.5
Above 75000	50	30.9

The survey question aimed to identify the product that respondents had the greatest influence in creating an attachment with a brand. The results in Table 2 indicate that 29% of respondents considered food and beverages to be influential in brand attachment, while only 0.6% mentioned pharmacy to be influential in brand attachment.

Table 2. Respondent's response on the brand with the greatest influence for creating attachment

Items	Cosmetics	Dresses	Electronic items	Financial services	Food and beverages	Footwears	Home appliances	Pharmacy
Frequency	26	17	39	18	29	23	9	1
Percentage	16	10.5	24.1	11.1	17.9	14.2	5.6	0.6

Data Analysis

The data was statistically analyzed using the IBM SPSS version 22. Descriptive analysis and ANOVA were used to describe the role of neuromarketing strategies on brand equity.

DISCUSSION

Descriptive Statistics

The mean, standard deviation, and Cronbach's alpha values are presented in table 3 demonstrating the variations in the respondent's score.

Table 3. Descriptive statistics

Items	Variables	Mean	Standard Deviation	Cronbach alpha
Brand Positioning (BP)		**4.03**	**0.615**	
BP1	The brand makes the product active	4.04	0.73	0.774
BP2	Branded products safe to use	4.12	0.854	
BP3	Branded products are treatable	3.19	0.7	
Brand Awareness (BA)		**4.28**	**0.54**	
BA1	With awareness programs the brand is introduced among the consumers	4.2	0.629	
BA2	In social media, contents about the brand are circulated	4.44	0.61	0.795
BA3	The brand is popularized by repeated announcements in the advertisement	4.23	0.742	
Brand Prestige (BPR)		**3.88**	**0.72**	
BPR1	The price paid for the branded product is reasonable	3.76	0.847	
BPR2	Branded products are comfortable to use	4.03	0.784	0.781
BPR3	Branded products steal the confidence of the consumers	3.88	0.98	

continued on following page

Table 3. *Continued*

Performance (PR)		**3.88**	**0.672**	
PR1	Branded products are reliable to buy	3.82	0.779	**0.788**
PR2	I think branded products have special feature	3.84	0.877	
PR3	I buy branded product in spite of rise in price of the brand	3.59	0.867	
Feeling (FL)		**4.01**	**0.752**	
FL1	The brand gives me the feel of warmness	3.85	1.035	**0.752**
FL2	Brand gives me a sense of security	3.92	0.796	
FL3	Brands carries a self-respect in the market	4.08	0.856	
Judgement (JD)		**4.04**	**0.663**	
JD1	I think the manufactures are great thinkers	4.13	0.805	**0.823**
JD2	Brand carries a good value to the product	4.06	0.786	
JD3	Branded products are very innovative	3.81	0.858	
Branding (BR)		**4.01**	**0.687**	
BR1	Name	4.17	0.766	**0.703**
BR2	Term of the product	3.81	0.718	
BR3	Logo of the product	3.99	0.892	
BR4	Design of the product	4.2	0.763	
Advertisement (AD)		**4.01**	**0.619**	
AD1	Television	4.15	0.793	**0.718**
AD2	Magazine	3.62	0.819	
AD3	Cell Phone	4.03	0.942	
AD4	Internet	4.35	0.902	
AD5	Direct Mail	3.33	1.02	
AD6	Outdoor	3.66	0.979	
Purchase Decision (PD)		**4.18**	**0.609**	
PD1	Economic Condition	4.22	0.612	**0.79**
PD2	Personal Preference	4.17	0.752	
PD3	Group Influence	3.19	0.822	
PD4	Marketing Campaigns	3.85	0.969	
Product Design and Innovation (PDI)		**4.3**	**0.695**	
PDI1	The best quality of the product force to buy repeatedly	4.23	0.843	**0.736**
PDI2	Special features of the product is always picked up	4.2	0.651	
PDI3	The package of the product has glamorous product identity	4.03	0.751	
PDI4	Usually buy the product that carries an informative label	4.15	0.954	

The Cronbach's alpha value of 0.774, 0.795, 0.781, 0.788, 0.752, 0.823, 0.703, 0.718, 0.790, and 0.736 as observed in Table 3, surpasses the threshold of 0.7, suggesting a satisfactory level of dependability or internal consistency within the data, thereby enhancing its reliability for analysis purpose.

Data Analysis

Table 4. Correlation analysis

		BE	BP	BA	BPR	PE	FE	JD	BR	ADV	PD	PDI
BE	Pearson Correlation	1	.657**	.583**	.782**	.428**	-.428**	-.492**	.509**	-.691**	.321**	.510**
	Sig. (2-tailed)		0.000	0.000	0.000	0.000	0.000	0.000	0.000	0.000	0.000	0.000

**. Correlation is significant at the 0.01 level (2-tailed).

In Table 4, it is evident that there is a positive correlation of 0.657 between the variables BE and BP, 0.583 between variables BE and BA, 0.782 between variables BE and BPR, 0.428 between BE and PE, 0.509 between variables BE and BR, 0.321 between variables BE and PD, 0.510 between variables BE and PDI, suggesting that if one variable increase than other also tends to increase. The calculated data suggests a moderately strong positive relationship between BE and BP, BE and BA, BE and BPR, BE and PE, BE and, BE and JD, BE and PD, BE and PDI.

Whereas the variables FE, JD and ADV possess a negative correlation with the variable BE with vales of -.428, -492, and -691 This indicates a perfect negative correlation between the variables, implying that as one variable increases, the other variable consistently decreases.

Table 5. Model summary

Model		Sum of Squares	Df.	Mean Square	F	Sig.
1	Regression	250.157	10	25.016	8.808	.000b
	Residual	428.837	151	2.840		
	Total	678.994	161			

a. Dependent Variable: BE

b. Independent Variables (Constant): BP, BA, BPR, PR, FL, JD, BR, AD,PD, PDI

Table 5 indicates the model summary indicating the significant p value. Specifically, when considering a value of 8.808 with a degree of freedom of 1 (numerator) as 10 and a degree of freedom of 2 (denominator) as 151, along with a significance level (α) of 0.05 and a confidence level of 95%, the critical value from the F table is determined to be 2.79. However, the calculated F value (8.808) exceeds the critical F value (2.79). Consequently, the null hypothesis (Ho) is rejected, while the alternative hypothesis (H1) is accepted. This signifies that the neuromarketing strategies (BP, BA, BPR, PE, JD, PD, PDI, FE, JD, and ADV) significantly influence the brand equity.

CONCLUSION

In conclusion, neuromarketing facilitates the identification of consumer preferences, allowing businesses to more effectively comprehend and satisfy consumer requirements. The findings of the neuromarketing study have a significant influence and aid in improving customer understanding as the neuromarketing strategies - brand positioning, brand awareness, brand prestige, performance, feeling, judgment, branding, advertisement, purchase decision, product design, and innovation) influence the brand equity. The neuromarketing strategies BP, BA, BPR, PE, JD, ADV, PD, PDI are positively correlated with BE, whereas the variables FE, JD, and ADV possess a negative correlation with the variable BE. The retail customers are influenced psychologically to purchase a brand via neuromarketing methods. Therefore, neuromarketing can be a potent tool for forecasting customer behaviour when paired with other qualitative data.

PRACTICAL IMPLICATIONS

The marketing industry has undergone significant changes in recent years, placing a greater emphasis on understanding people and their needs. This shift has led to the emergence of a new subfield termed as "neuromarketing," which opens up opportunities for uncovering previously unknown data about decision-making and customer preferences. Neuromarketing assists in selecting advertisements that include essential elements tailored to consumers' needs.

Neuromarketing offers marketers with reliable data by facilitating interactions that address customers' requirements and desires. This paper recommends using neuromarketing to identify customer preferences. Through neuromarketing methods, retail customers can be psychologically influenced to choose a brand. To build brand equity among retail customers, marketers should adopt different strategies. These tactics will help in ensuring that retail customers prefer the brand over its competitors.

LIMITATIONS

The significant limitation of the study is small sample size, consisting 162 respondents raising the risk of sampling bias. Despite its diversity in age, gender, and educational level, makes it difficult to generalize the findings to a broader population. Financial constraints further complicate the research process, as resources are essential for purchasing tools, supplies, and covering data collection, analysis, and publication costs. Neuromarketing strategic fields require specialized equipment, advanced technology, and well-equipped facilities, which can limit the scope of potential study. Moreover, retail customers are particularly drawn to electronic goods brands, and in today's market, they are constantly inundated with information about numerous brands within the same category, adding complexity to accurately understanding their preferences.

REFERENCES

Aaker, D. A. (1991). *Managing brand equity: Capitalizing on the value of a brand name*. Free Press.

Aaker, D. A. (1992). The value of brand equity. *The Journal of Business Strategy*, 13(4), 27–32. 10.1108/eb039503

Agarwal, S., & Dutta, T. (2015). Neuromarketing and consumer neuroscience: Current understanding and the way forward. *Decision (Washington, D.C.)*, 42(4), 457–462. 10.1007/s40622-015-0113-1

Alsharif, A. H., Salleh, N. Z. M., Abdullah, M., Khraiwish, A., & Ashaari, A. (2023). Neuromarketing tools used in the marketing mix: A systematic literature and future research agenda. *SAGE Open*, 13(1), 21582440231156563. 10.1177/21582440231156563

Alsharif, A. H., Salleh, N. Z. M., Baharun, R., & Yusoff, M. E. (2021). Consumer behaviour through neuromarketing approach. *Journal of Contemporary Issues in Business and Government*, 27(3), 344–354.

Alsmadi, S., & Hailat, K. (2021). Neuromarketing and improved understanding of consumer behaviour through brain-based neuro activity. *Journal of Information & Knowledge Management*, 20(02), 2150020. 10.1142/S0219649221500209

Ambler, T., & Barwise, P. (1998). The trouble with brand valuation. *Journal of Brand Management*, 5(5), 367–377. 10.1057/bm.1998.25

Ariely, D., & Berns, G. S. (2010). Neuromarketing: The hope and hype of neuroimaging in business. *Nature Reviews. Neuroscience*, 11(4), 284–292. 10.1038/nrn279520197790

Arora, M. (2020). Post-truth and marketing communication in technological age. In *Handbook of research on innovations in technology and marketing for the connected consumer* (pp. 94–108). IGI Global., 10.4018/978-1-7998-0131-3.ch005

Arora, M. (2023). Encapsulating Role of Persuasion and Skill Development in Marketing Communication for Brand Building: A Perspective. In *International Handbook of Skill, Education, Learning, and Research Development in Tourism and Hospitality* (pp. 1–17). Springer Nature Singapore.

Arora, M. (2024). Virtual Reality in Education: Analyzing the Literature and Bibliometric State of Knowledge. *Transforming Education with Virtual Reality*, 379-402. 10.1002/9781394200498.ch22

Arora, M., & Sharma, R. L. (2021). Repurposing the Role of Entrepreneurs in the Havoc of COVID-19. In *Entrepreneurship and Big Data* (pp. 229-250). CRC Press.

Arora, M., & Sharma, R. L. (2023). Artificial intelligence and big data: Ontological and communicative perspectives in multi-sectoral scenarios of modern businesses. *Foresight*, 25(1), 126–143. 10.1108/FS-10-2021-0216

Barwise, P. (1993). Brand equity: Snark or boojum? *International Journal of Research in Marketing*, 10(1), 93–104. 10.1016/0167-8116(93)90036-X

Behl, A., Jayawardena, N., Shankar, A., Gupta, M., & Lang, L. D. (2024). Gamification and neuromarketing: A unified approach for improving user experience. *Journal of Consumer Behaviour*, 23(1), 218–228. 10.1002/cb.2178

Bhopal, R., & Devi, R. (2022). Digitalization and Its Role on Flexible Workforce. *National Journal Of Commerce And Management.*

Bhopal, R., & Devi, R. (2023). Emotional Intelligence for Effective Leadership: Future Research Trends Using Bibliometric Analysis. In *AI and Emotional Intelligence for Modern Business Management* (pp. 48-63). IGI Global. 10.4018/979-8-3693-0418-1.ch004

Casey, R. (2004). Designing brand identity: A complete guide to creating, building, and maintaining strong brands. *Journal of the Academy of Marketing Science*, 32(1), 100–101. 10.1177/0092070304321011

Catherine, S., Kiruthiga, V., Suresh, N. V., & Gabriel, R. (2024). Effective Brand Building in Metaverse Platform: Consumer-Based Brand Equity in a Virtual World (CBBE). In *Omnichannel Approach to Co-Creating Customer Experiences Through Metaverse Platforms* (pp. 39-48). IGI Global.

Chattopadhyay, T., Shivani, S., & Krishnan, M. (2009). Determinants of brand equity-A blue print for building strong brand: A study of automobile segment in India. *African Journal of Marketing Management*, 1(4), 109–121.

Cherubino, P., Martinez-Levy, A. C., Caratu, M., Cartocci, G., Di Flumeri, G., Modica, E., Rossi, D., Mancini, M., & Trettel, A. (2019). Consumer behaviour through the eyes of neurophysiological measures: State-of-the-art and future trends. *Computational Intelligence and Neuroscience*, 2019, 1–41. 10.1155/2019/197684731641346

Cronin, J. J.Jr, Smith, J. S., Gleim, M. R., Ramirez, E., & Martinez, J. D. (2011). Green marketing strategies: An examination of stakeholders and the opportunities they present. *Journal of the Academy of Marketing Science*, 39(1), 158–174. 10.1007/s11747-010-0227-0

De, A. D. L. I. V. (2024). Analysis Of Visual Brand Identity In The Fast-Food Sector: A Neuromarketing Study. *Revista de Ciencias*, 29, 1–20.

Devi, R. & Bhopal, R.(2023). A Review-Based Study on Opportunities and Challenges Of Start-Ups In India. *National Journal Of Commerce And Management.*

Dhiman, V., & Arora, M. (2024). Current State of Metaverse in Entrepreneurial Ecosystem: A Retrospective Analysis of Its Evolving Landscape. In *Exploring the Use of Metaverse in Business and Education* (pp. 73-87). IGI Global. 10.4018/979-8-3693-5868-9.ch005

Doyle, P., & Stern, P. (2006). *Marketing management and strategy.* Pearson Education.

Erdem, T., Imai, S., & Keane, M. P. (2003). Brand and quantity choice dynamics under price uncertainty. *Quantitative Marketing and Economics*, 1(1), 5–64. 10.1023/A:1023536326497

Erdem, T., & Swait, J. (2001). Brand equity as a signaling. *Journal of Consumer Psychology*, 7(2), 131–157. 10.1207/s15327663jcp0702_02

Farquhar, P. H. (1989). Managing brand equity. *Marketing research, 1*(3).

Fisher, C. E., Chin, L., & Klitzman, R. (2010). Defining neuromarketing: Practices and professional challenges. *Harvard Review of Psychiatry*, 18(4), 230–237. 10.3 109/10673229.2010.49662320597593

Ghorban, Z. S. (2012). Advertising and Brand Equity Creation: Examination of Product Market in Iran. *International Journal of Business and Management Tomorrow, 2*(7).

Hjorth-Andersen, C. (1984). The concept of quality and the efficiency of markets for consumer products. *The Journal of Consumer Research*, 11(2), 708–718. 10.1086/209007

Holbrook, M. B., & Batra, R. (1987). Assessing the role of emotions as mediators of consumer responses to advertising. *The Journal of Consumer Research*, 14(3), 404–420. 10.1086/209123

Hsu, C. L., & Chen, M. C. (2018). How gamification marketing activities motivate desirable consumer behaviors: Focusing on the role of brand love. *Computers in Human Behavior*, 88, 121–133. 10.1016/j.chb.2018.06.037

Ismajli, A., Ziberi, B., & Metushi, A. (2022). The impact of neuromarketing on consumer behaviour. *Corporate Governance and Organizational Behavior Review*, 6(2), 95–103. 10.22495/cgobrv6i2p9

Jamal Abad, S. G., & Hossein, J. S. (2013). Conceptualization Of Customer Based Brand Equity In Financial Service Sector. *Studies in Business & Economics*, 8(1).

Jangid, J., & Bhardwaj, B. (2024). Relationship Between AI and Green Finance: Exploring the Changing Dynamics. In *Leveraging AI and Emotional Intelligence in Contemporary Business Organizations* (pp. 211-218). IGI Global. 10.4018/979-8-3693-1902-4.ch012

Jedidi, K., Mela, C. F., & Gupta, S. (1999). Managing advertising and promotion for long-run profitability. *Marketing Science*, 18(1), 1–22. 10.1287/mksc.18.1.1

Kamakura, W. A., & Russell, G. J. (1989). A probabilistic choice model for market segmentation and elasticity structure. *JMR, Journal of Marketing Research*, 26(4), 379–390. 10.1177/002224378902600401

Kayaman, R., & Arasli, H. (2007). Customer based brand equity: Evidence from the hotel industry. *Managing Service Quality*, 17(1), 92–109. 10.1108/09604520710720692

Keller, K. L. (1993). Conceptualizing, measuring, and managing customer-based brand equity. *Journal of Marketing*, 57(1), 1–22. 10.1177/002224299305700101

Keller, K. L., & Lehmann, D. R. (2003). How do brands create value? *Marketing management, 12*(3), 26-26.

Khondakar, M. F. K., Sarowar, M. H., Chowdhury, M. H., Majumder, S., Hossain, M. A., Dewan, M. A. A., & Hossain, Q. D. (2024). A systematic review on EEG-based neuromarketing: Recent trends and analyzing techniques. *Brain Informatics*, 11(1), 17. 10.1186/s40708-024-00229-838837089

Kotler, P., & Armstrong, G. (2001). *Principles of Marketing* (9th ed.).

Kumar, J., Arora, M., & Erkol Bayram, G. (Eds.). (2024). *Exploring the Use of Metaverse in Business and Education*. IGI Global. 10.4018/979-8-3693-5868-9

Kumar, P., Chowdhury, S., & Madhavedi, S. (2024). Role of Neuromarketing and Artificial Intelligence in Futuristic Marketing Approach: An Empirical Study. *Journal of Informatics Education and Research.*, 4(2). 10.52783/jier.v4i2.809

Lhotáková, M., & Olšanová, K. (2013). The role of positioning in strategic brand management–case of home appliance market. *Global Journal of Commerce and Management Perspective*, 2(1), 71–81.

Lim, W. M. (2020). The sharing economy: A marketing perspective. *Australasian Marketing Journal*, 28(3), 4–13. 10.1016/j.ausmj.2020.06.007

Liyin, J. I. N. (2009). Dimensions and determinants of website brand equity: From the perspective of website contents. *Frontiers of Business Research in China, 3*(4), 514-542.

Loureiro, S., Ruediger, K., & Demetris, V. (2012). Brand emotional connection and loyalty. *Journal of Brand Management*, 20(1), 13–27. 10.1057/bm.2012.3

Mahajan, V., Rao, V. R., & Srivastava, R. K. (1994). An approach to assess the importance of brand equity in acquisition decisions. *Journal of Product Innovation Management*, 11(3), 221–235. 10.1111/1540-5885.1130221

Mariampolski, H. (2006). Ethnography for marketers: A guide to consumer immersion. *Sage (Atlanta, Ga.)*.

Mashrur, F. R., Rahman, K. M., Miya, M. T. I., Vaidyanathan, R., Anwar, S. F., Sarker, F., & Mamun, K. A. (2022). An intelligent neuromarketing system for predicting consumers' future choice from electroencephalography signals. *Physiology & Behavior*, 253, 113847. 10.1016/j.physbeh.2022.11384735594931

Morin, C., & Renvoisé, P. (2018). *The persuasion code: How neuromarketing can help you persuade anyone, anywhere, anytime.* John Wiley & Sons.

Nam, J., Ekinci, Y., & Whyatt, G. (2011). Brand equity, brand loyalty and consumer satisfaction. *Annals of Tourism Research*, 38(3), 1009–1030. 10.1016/j.annals.2011.01.015

Nazma, Bhopal, R., & Devi, R. (2023). Sustainable Development Using Green Finance and Triple Bottom Line: A Bibliometric Review. *IMIB Journal of Innovation and Management,* 1-22. 10.1177/ijim.231184138

Nemati, H., Bakhshinezhad, E., Madadkhah, M., Kamyab, M., Taati, R., Faegh, S., & Jan, N. K. L. (2013). Brand Equity From The Perspective Of Customers. [Oman Chapter]. *Arabian Journal of Business and Management Review*, 2(10), 13–19. 10.12816/0002326

Neumeier, M. (2005). *The brand gap.* Peachpit Press.

Nilashi, M., & Abumalloh, R. A. (2023). Neuromarketing and Metaverse. *Journal of Soft Computing and Decision Support Systems*, 10(1), 1–3.

Paquette, H. (2013). *Social media as a marketing tool: A literature review.*

Parchure, N. P., Parchure, S. N., & Bora, B. (2020, November). Role of neuromarketing in enhancing consumer behaviour. In *AIP Conference Proceedings* (Vol. 2273, No. 1). AIP Publishing. 10.1063/5.0024517

Perrachione, T. K., & Perrachione, J. R. (2008). Brains and brands: Developing mutually informative research in neuroscience and marketing. *Journal of Consumer Behaviour*, 7(4-5), 303–318. 10.1002/cb.253

Pouromid, B., & Iranzadeh, S. (2012). The evaluation of the factors affects on the brand equity of Pars Khazar household appliances based on the vision of female consumer. *Middle East Journal of Scientific Research*, 12(8), 1050–1055.

Rathore, S., & Arora, M. (2024). Sustainability Reporting in the Metaverse: A Multi-Sectoral Analysis. In *Exploring the Use of Metaverse in Business and Education* (pp. 147-165). IGI Global. 10.4018/979-8-3693-5868-9.ch009

Shocker, A. D., & Weitz, B. (1988). A perspective on brand equity principles and issues. *Report*, 88(104), 2–4.

Shukla, P., Awasthi, A., Kumari, S., Sahil, S., Gandh, N. K., Agustin, F. E., & Nneoma, N. R. (2024). The Role of Emotions in Consumer Brand Loyalty: A Neuromarketing Approach. [IJTHAP]. *International Journal of Tourism and Hospitality in Asia Pasific*, 7(1), 104–116. 10.32535/ijthap.v7i1.2901

Simon, C. J., & Sullivan, M. W. (1993). The measurement and determinants of brand equity: A financial approach. *Marketing Science*, 12(1), 28–52. 10.1287/mksc.12.1.28

Singh, K. S. D., & Islam, M. A. (2017). Validating an instrument for measuring brand equity of CSR driven organizations in Malaysia. *Management & Marketing*, 12(2), 237–251. 10.1515/mmcks-2017-0015

Singh, S. (2020). Impact of neuromarketing applications on consumers. *Journal of Business and Management*, 26(2), 33–52. 10.6347/JBM.202009_26(2).0002

Sohal, A., & Sharma, D. (2024). *Work-Family Conflict*. International Encyclopedia of Business Management., 10.1016/B978-0-443-13701-3.00061-X

Solnais, C., Andreu-Perez, J., Sánchez-Fernández, J., & Andréu-Abela, J. (2013). The contribution of neuroscience to consumer research: A conceptual framework and empirical review. *Journal of Economic Psychology*, 36, 68–81. 10.1016/j.joep.2013.02.011

Srinivasan, V. (1979). Network models for estimating brand-specific effects in multi-attribute marketing models. *Management Science*, 25(1), 11–21. 10.1287/mnsc.25.1.11

Srinivasan, V., Park, C. S., & Chang, D. R. (2005). An approach to the measurement, analysis, and prediction of brand equity and its sources. *Management Science*, 51(9), 1433–1448. 10.1287/mnsc.1050.0405

Srivastava, G., & Bag, S. (2024). Modern-day marketing concepts based on face recognition and neuro-marketing: A review and future research directions. *Benchmarking*, 31(2), 410–438. 10.1108/BIJ-09-2022-0588

Stoll, M., Baecke, S., & Kenning, P. (2008). What they see is what they get? An fMRI-study on neural correlates of attractive packaging. *Journal of Consumer Behaviour*, 7(4-5), 342–359. 10.1002/cb.256

Suomala, J., Palokangas, L., Leminen, S., Westerlund, M., Heinonen, J., & Numminen, J. (2012). *Neuromarketing: Understanding customers' subconscious responses to marketing.*

Swait, J., Erdem, T., Louviere, J., & Dubelaar, C. (1993). The equalization price: A measure of consumer-perceived brand equity. *International Journal of Research in Marketing*, 10(1), 23–45. 10.1016/0167-8116(93)90031-S

Thiripurasundari, U., & Natarajan, P. (2011). Determinants of brand equity in Indian car manufacturing firms. *International Journal of Trade. Economics and Finance*, 2(4), 346.

Wang, T., & Ji, P. (2010). Understanding customer needs through quantitative analysis of Kano's model. *International Journal of Quality & Reliability Management*, 27(2), 173–184. 10.1108/02656711011014294

Wood, W., & Neal, D. T. (2009). The habitual consumer. *Journal of Consumer Psychology*, 19(4), 579–592. 10.1016/j.jcps.2009.08.003

Yoo, B., Donthu, N., & Lee, S. (2000). An examination of selected marketing mix elements and brand equity. *Journal of the Academy of Marketing Science*, 28(2), 195–211. 10.1177/0092070300282002

Zurawicki, L. (2010). *Neuromarketing: Exploring the brain of the consumer.* Springer Science & Business Media. 10.1007/978-3-540-77829-5

Chapter 11
Does Your Brain Have a Buy Button?
A Neuro Marketing Approach With Sensory Branding

Surbhi Bhardwaj
National Institute of Technology, Kurukshetra, India

Neeraj Kaushik
https://orcid.org/0000-0003-2651-3448
National Institute of Technology, Kurukshetra, India

Manpreet Arora
Central University of Himachal Pradesh, India

ABSTRACT

In this competitive world, the human senses and their responsiveness play a vital role in influencing consumer behavior and purchase patterns. Brands are using neuromarketing to employ different sensory tactics to cover the maximum market share and connect with customers. Marketers use neurosciences techniques to connect with customers on emotional and behavioral aspects, known as the sensory branding approach. This trending approach of neuromarketing helps brands to create synergy in marketing with the creative use of psychology and neurosciences to make strategies for different customers at same time. The chapter aims to explore how brands use sensory emotional connections with customers to influence them to purchase. Using a conceptual approach for this chapter, it is explained what the sensory branding uses to create a powerful brand fit strategy for different customer profiles. The author observed that marketers faced challenges and used different kinds of techniques related to neuro sensory branding which help to understand consumer and make emotional bond.

DOI: 10.4018/979-8-3693-4236-7.ch011

INTRODUCTION

In today's competitive marketplace, the quest to understand consumer behavior has evolved beyond traditional market research methodologies. Enter the realm of neuro-marketing, a discipline that probes the depths of the human brain to decipher the underlying drivers of purchasing decisions. neuromarketing studies indicate how marketing tools can influence consumers' brains and, as a result, affect their choices, having as an aim the understanding of consumer psychology and behavior for the benefit of brands and the purchasing experience of customers also (Morin,2007;Ramsøy,2020). When the science of neurology combines with marketing practices then the concept of neuromarketing has developed (Hammou, et al., 2013; Murphy, et al.,2008). Several studies emphasize that the neuromarketing concept used the method of "selling to the brain not to the customer" for making detailed strategies of sales with neuroscience (Crespo-Pereira, et al; Renvoise, and Morin). The customer decision process has more complications because they have a variety of products in the market to satisfy a specific need (Vences, et al.,; Ariely and Berns). To consider this aspect of preference it is a must for the marketer to reach the customer's mind and act according to the solution key for this difficulty is only neuro-sensory marketing (Morin, 2007; Marcel, et al., 2009). Coupled with the innovative strategies of sensory branding, which leverage the power of sensory experiences to create lasting impressions, businesses gain a profound understanding of how to captivate and influence their target audience. Attention to sensory marketing has recently grown exponentially (Krishna, Cian, & Sokolova, 2016). Today, the targeted use of sensory cues is becoming increasingly important for marketing managers to effectively appeal to consumers (Chang & Chieng, 2006; Wiedmann, et al., 2013). According to a study about 95 percent of people are deciding with their subconscious minds only 5 percent make with their conscious mind which makes huge differences to identify the actual desire (Kumavat).

For Example, The success of the brand P&G with Febreze was achieved by using the techniques of neuromarketing as a solution key to predicting customer behavior (Al-Sharif, et al). Buick company increased their effort in neuromarketing by 9% to 40%. Same as Delta Airlines increased its success rate after putting extra effort into neuromarketing techniques to provide importance to the customer experience (Gurgu, et al; Juarez, et al). THQ is a video game manufacturer company and they designed different programs for customers' preferences to their brain pattern which they understood through using of neuromarketing techniques (Al-Sharif, et al, 2020; Vidal-Raméntol, 2020).

Looking inside the mind of the customer provides a competitive advantage to the marketer to understand their customers. In the dynamic landscape of consumer behavior, understanding the intricacies of neuro-marketing and sensory branding has become dominant for businesses seeking to unlock the indescribable buying pattern in the human brain. Marketers have only a single combination of neuroscience patterns with marketing strategies to explore how a comprehensive framework understands which is into the five core dimensions of human personality: Openness, Conscientiousness, Extraversion, Agreeableness, and Neuroticism brightens consumer preferences and responses. As we navigate the labyrinth of brand-product influence, we uncover the nuanced ways in which sensory stimuli shape customer behavior. Join us on a journey through the neural pathways of the modern marketplace, where insights from neuro-marketing and sensory branding converge to decode the mysteries behind consumer choices.

Problem of the Statement

Compared to other allied studies there is a lack of studies in the Indian market related to neuro-sensory branding. This article gives a bird's eye view to the Indian retailers to cover the gap and promote the neuro sensory techniques to create emotional bond with them.

REVIEW OF LITERATURE

Table 1. Review of literature

Year	Author with Title	Methodology	Finding
2023	Berman G.; Potgieter A.; Tait M. *"The influence of sensory branding strategies in-store on consumer preference: the south african skincare industry"*	Positivistic Research Paradigm and Descriptive Research	This study highlight that the stimuli had the positive influence on the customer shopping experience in skincare store. The study also indicates that use of fragrance testers and in-store beauticiany stimulation both uses as sensory branding strategies on the demographic profile of customer which helps marketers to understand the preferences.
2023	Gautam Srivastava, G; Bag, S. *"Modern-day marketing concepts based on face recognition and neuro-marketing: a review and future research directions"*	SLR	This study finds that thefive neuro-marketing and facial recognition techniques used in marketing as modern concepts. The findings also reflects that the usage of AI in marketing techniques provides a cognitive insights into human behavior which helps managers to design the policies accordingly which also boost conversion rates.

continued on following page

Table 1. Continued

Year	Author with Title	Methodology	Finding
2022	Bishnoi S.K.; Singh S. *"A study on consumer buying behaviour for fashion and luxury brands under emotional influence"*	Comprehensive Literature Study	This study conducted on fashion and luxury brands and the findings reflect the emotional need and connection of customers influence their buying decisions and they can take better and conscious decisions.
2021	Imamovic I.; De Azevedo A.J.A.; De Sousa B.M.B. *"The tourists' sensory experiences: Preliminary insights of urban areas of Porto, Portugal"*	Empirical	This study finds that the multisensory stimuli create a positive experience and rich memory in the mind of tourists which promote the sustainable development of particular area.
2020	Rodrigues C.; Skinner H.; Dennis C.; Melewar T.C. *"Towards a theoretical framework on sensorial place brand identity"*	Conceptual	This study refelects that the sensory place branding messages create a linkage between stakeholders and co-creators in terms of sensorial place identity, experiencescapes and multisensory place brand image, positively.

RESEARCH METHODOLOGY

Research Design

Research is designed with a Descriptive method of research to study the objectives. All descriptions highlighted the characteristics of relevant content.

Data Collection Method and Sources

Data Collection Method: Secondary data are used to design the Descriptive method of research.

Sources of Data Collection: The data is collected from available articles, published research, magazines, published journals, different websites, different published reports, etc.

DISCUSSION

Concept of Neuro-Marketing

The neuromarketing was first introduced by US-based Atlanta Advertising Company in June 2022. According to this advertising company report, a new department of marketing research using fMRI and stated neuromarketing as a technique of neuroscience including psychophysics and direct brain activity to predict and analyze the human behavior for marketing practices (Fisher et al.) (Lee et al.).

This is different from traditional marketing practices because it is the combination of two words 'neuro' which means brain i.e. related to neuroscience and 'marketing' which is stated to analysis the needs of customers and satisfy them.

Neuromarketing is the science of determining consumer behavior by using Neurometrics, Biometrics, and Psychometrics. Neurometrics measures neurological responses, Biometrics analysis, behavioral change, and Psychometrics understands psychological behavior.

Evolution

In 1991 neuromarketing techniques started to be developed in the United States by Paul Lauterbur and Peter Mansfield. They started some research and experiments on customers and their research was financed by several brands like Coca-Cola, L-mart, Levi-Strauss, and Ford (Ponnam, A). After that in 1996, Professor Gerald Zaltman applied for a patent for the Zaltman Metaphor Elicitation Technique (ZMET), was mainly used to explore the conscious and unconscious part of brain which checked the positive emotional responses of customers during their stimulate potential purchases thought process (Chi A.). One of the first recorded neuromarketing experiments was conducted by Professor of Neuroscience Read Montague at Baylor College of Medicine in 2003 (Chi A.)(Senior, C).

Table 2.

Time-Period	Stage	Description
Before 2000s	Early Years	The neuromarketing concept was derived from different techniques of neuroscience like fMRI, EEG for brain imaging, and biometrics techniques such as eye-tracking, and skin conductance to study consumer responses to marketing stimuli. At this stage, the neuromarketing technique was focused on understanding the neural processes to underline the pattern of consumer decision-making.
2000s -2010s	Validation Phase	This phase helps marketers to validate the effectiveness of demonstrated marketing strategies to predict consumer behavior. The usage of neuromarketing is treated as a tool to gain insights into consumer preferences.
Mid-2010s	Expansion and Diversification	This stage is an extension of neuromarketing from traditional neuroscience techniques to behavioral economics i.e. neuroeconomics, psychology, and big data analytics. This expansion helps companies to develop more comprehensive consumer profiles.
Late 2010s	Integration with Digital Marketing	This is the era of digital marketing and marketers adapt this change and use it with neuromarketing techniques to analyze online consumer behavior. Eye-tracking and EEG are used to track the assessment of user experience and engagement with digital content.
2010s-2020s	Ethical Considerations and Regulation	After digital marketing emergence privacy and ethical issues became challenges for marketers and the brain data of customers became a problem for them. So brand used the customer brain data under ethical guidelines and transparency standards.
2020s and Present	Personalization and AI	This is the time of personalized marketing experience. So all companies use AI- algorithms and ML tools to analyze customer taste and preferences and make marketing messages on real real-time basis which leads to more effective campaigns.

Concept of Sensory Branding

"People spend money when and where they feel good" (Walt Disney). Sensory branding provides a sound connection with their key customers in more interactive and personalized way. It is a marketing technique to provide multisensory (with the uses of all senses i.e. smell, touch, sound, taste, and sight) experience to the customers for creating interaction and additional value. Brands are using this technique to create the strong brand loyalty and a memorable or effective experience on site.

Tradition vs. Neuro-Sensory Marketing

Market is developed their shape according to need of customer because the consumers are the main element of shinning the market globally, so it is must to adapt the change according to their requirement and provide them more values at touch points to make them more comfortable and real feel. Below are some points which differentiate the traditional marketing to the neuro marketing:

Points of differentiation

Traditional Marketing	Neuro-Sensory Marketing
The main focus of traditional marketing was to create rational arguments related to product's features, price points, etc for consumers.	The neuro sensory marketing trigger the subconscious mind of the consumer which creates the decision patterns to buy a product.
The marketing strategies made on demographic profile and segmented market research of customers.	The marketing strateties creates with using the neuroscience and psychological patterns.
It was trigger the conscious mind of customers.	In this marketers target the subconscious part of mind.
In this surveys, focus groups, demographic analysis used as a techniques of marketing.	In this type of marketing strategies brain imaging, biometric measurements, sensory cues, multisensory experiences techniques are used.
This is emphasis on the customer trends and preferences, broadly.	In this brands are emphasis on emotional bond and sensory experiences.
The brand only provide information related to product and attract or convince the consumers	In this brand don't convenience the customer but they creates a memorable experiences for them to make and treate them more special. It helps to create an emotional bond with them.

Tools and Techniques

Techniques Used in Sensory Marketing

Customers are using their senses to make effective decisions regarding products for purchase. Marketers create a multisensory environment to gain the customer's attention because Multiple senses create several cues in the minds of customers.

1. **Sight:** The Pear Soap brand was the first brand who use visual advertisement to promote its brand in 1890. They buy original Egyptian artwork from artists after modification visualizing that artwork on the bar of Pear's soap. The main elements considered by marketers are given below which play a vital role in sensory branding practices:
   - Colours- Each colour indicates an emotion. According to psychology, red colour indicates passion, green colour indicates sustainability, and white indicates soberness and peace. According to the better color themes in advertisements marketers can gain a positive feeling for customers.
   - Images- Ordinary people's photos appeal that every customer is important to our brand. The images create an impression in the minds of customers, so marketers use those images which had a positive message for society, humanity, and the environment, making the advertisement more interesting and appealable.
   - Text- The writing pattern and combination of words also impacted the customer decision pattern significantly.
   - Graphics- In the era of AI it is important for marketer to used sound visual and graphics tools to attract the customer. It is a competitive advantage for the brand that how they uniquely illustrate and demonstrate their computer generated content at front of customer.
   - Light- In visual marketing lighting arrangement gives a nice feel and look for customers. Some retailers in India use the mood-lighting or lamps in their store to give a change to shoppers.
2. **Sounds:** Audio marketing came into the advertisement industry around the 1900s. In 1922, radio programs, and broadcasting techniques came into the market and around 1926, jingles got hit and gained popularity in the market. And now these days, advertisement music ramps up the entertainment values to the customers. The sounds are not only restricted to TV, and radio advertisements but now it become the tool to trigger the hearing sense of customers in retail stores also. Voiceovers, sound effects and thematic music became a trend to lighten the

mood of customers and provide them with a soft environment during shopping so that they can concentrate more on shopping and brand.

- **Smell:** Smell has direct link with human brain. Whenever we smell out any fragrance either good or bad, activate our neurosystem and our mood can change accordingly. Aroma is the aura of neurosystem. This technique rarely used by retailers. For example Abercrombie & Fitch, and Starbucks brand have used environmental fragrances, or aroma to lighten the mood as well as heighten the in-store experience of consumer.

Olfactory marketing and Nudge marketing are also involved in it.

3. **Touch:** Sensory branding is not only restricted with in store experiences but it brands are also used it in AI-based immersion techniques through AR,VR technique which give the interactive experience of customer's avatar in the virtual world also. For example, Apple VR-Vision Pro.

4. **Taste:** The definition of taste is very subjective but it is only sense which is directly related with the smell sense. Mainly food industry used this sensory technique to provide the samples and adding new flavors to taking the competitive advantage from market.

Neuro-Sensory Techniques With Their Elementary Features

For brand-product fitness, marketers used the AI enabled sensory practices with neurosciences techniques then the actual frame of customer perception and preference they can portray. The toos are used to experiment in lab and infere the real essence of specific segment and make strategy accordingly. Some techniques with their elementary features are discussed below:

- **Working of Techniques:**

fMRI (functional Magnetic Resonance Imaging)-

■ It detects blood flow in the brain associated with increased neural activity.

EEG (Electro-EncephaloGram)-

■ It records electrical signals on the scalp from neurons inside the brain

Eye Tracking: Gaze-

- It detects exactly where subjects direct their gaze

Eye Tracking: Pupilometry-

- It measures whether subjects' pupils are dilated

Biometrics-

- It measures skin conductance, heart rate, and respiration

Facial Coding-

- It is worked to identifies facial expressions
  - **Revealing From Customers**

fMRI (functional Magnetic Resonance Imaging)-

- It gives the detailed emotional responses,
- Level of engagement, and
- Brand recall.

EEG (Electro-EncephaloGram)-

- Level of engagement, and
- Brand recall.

Eye Tracking: Gaze-

- It indicates that what grabs the customer attention,
- It also shows what confuses the customers, and
- Speed of recognition

Eye Tracking: Pupilometry-

- Level of engagement

Biometrics-

- It shows the level of engagement whether the response is positive or negative.

Facial Coding-

- It indicates the general emotional response like happiness, sadness, surprise, fear, etc.
  - **Use**

fMRI (functional Magnetic Resonance Imaging)-

- It is using to set price and improve branding

EEG (Electro-EncephaloGram)-

- It is used to improve advertisement and brand image.

Eye Tracking: Gaze-

- It helps to improve the design of website, advertisement and packaging style or patterns.

Eye Tracking: Pupilometry, Biometrics, and Facial Coding-

- All these are used to improve the content of advertisement.
  - **Pros**

fMRI (functional Magnetic Resonance Imaging)-

- It is considered as the gold standard for measuring specific emotions
- must be performed in a lab

EEG (Electro-EncephaloGram)-

- It is helpful to measure changes over smaller increments of time.

Eye Tracking: Gaze and Pupilometry-

- It is inexpensive
- It is easy to control and manage
- It can provide the best results when used in combination with biometrics

Biometrics-

■ It is best used in conjunction with other methods, such as eye-tracking

Facial Coding-

■ Inexpensive.
  ● **Cons**

fMRI (functional Magnetic Resonance Imaging)-

■ It is most expensive and invasive technique
■ It gives less detailed than EEG

EEG (Electro-EncephaloGram)-

■ It is expensive and invasive technique
■

Eye Tracking: Gaze and Pupilometry-

■ It does not measure emotions

Challenges For Marketers to Understand Customer Behaviour

Neuro-sensory marketing used sensory stimuli to create a unique brand experience for customer. It is very difficult for marketers to deeply understand the consumer psychology and sensory perception, to evolving consumer preferences according to market dynamics. Experiment with new trends makes different difficult phase in the journey of adoption of trends. Traditional marketing faces significant challenges from the rise of digitalization, the metaverse, social media, and new entrepreneurial ventures in metaverse and virtual reality (VR) (Arora, 2024a; Arora & Sharma, 2023). Entrepreneurs foster growth by innovating new products and services, creating jobs, and driving competitive markets. Their ventures stimulate economic development and meet evolving consumer needs, contributing to overall societal progress. Digitalization compels entrepreneurs to adopt personalized, data-driven marketing strategies, enhancing customer targeting and engagement. This shift drives innovation and competitive advantage in the digital marketplace (Arora & Sharma, 2021; Arora 2016); Arora & Sharma,2022). Digitalization has shifted consumer behaviour towards online platforms, demanding more personalized and data-driven marketing strategies (Rathore & Arora, 2024; Chandel & Arora, M.,2024).The metaverse introduces a virtual realm where immersive, interactive brand experiences become the norm, challenging traditional media's reach and engagement capabilities (Dhiman & Arora 2024a; Kumar, Arora & Erkol Bayram,Eds. 2024a; Arora, 2024b). Meanwhile, entrepreneurial ventures in the metaverse and VR create innovative marketing opportunities that offer immersive experiences, further pushing the boundaries of how consumers interact with brands (Dhiman & Arora, (2024) b ; Kumar, J., Arora, M., & Erkol Bayram, G. Eds., 2024b). Social media has transformed communication, enabling direct, real-time interaction between brands and consumers, and making traditional one-way advertising less effective (Arora, 2020). These technological advancements demand that traditional marketing strategies evolve rapidly to stay relevant and effective in an increasingly digital world (Arora, M. 2023).

Some main challenges are discuss below particularly with understanding customer behaviour are listed below:

- **Multisensory Integration:** Marketers must ensure that all sensory elements align with the brand identity and message. Coordinating various sensory cues to create a coherent brand experience can be challenging, especially across different touchpoints.
- **Consistency Across Channels:** Maintaining consistency in sensory branding across various channels, such as physical stores, online platforms, and advertising, is crucial. Ensuring that the sensory experience evoked by the brand is consistent across all touchpoints can be difficult, especially when adapting to different mediums.
- **Cultural Sensitivity:** Sensory preferences can vary significantly across cultures. Marketers need to understand cultural nuances and adapt sensory elements accordingly to resonate with diverse audiences without causing offense or misunderstanding.
- **Individual Differences:** People have different sensory preferences and sensitivities. Marketers need to account for these individual differences and tailor the sensory experience to appeal to a broad range of consumers while avoiding sensory overload or alienation.
- **Regulatory Constraints:** Some sensory elements, such as certain scents or sounds, may be subject to regulatory restrictions or guidelines. Marketers must navigate these regulations while still effectively leveraging sensory branding to influence customer behavior.
- **Measuring Effectiveness:** Unlike traditional marketing metrics like sales or click-through rates, measuring the impact of sensory branding on customer behavior can be challenging. Marketers need to develop innovative methods

to assess the effectiveness of sensory stimuli in driving brand perception, loyalty, and purchase intent.

- **Adapting to Digital Platforms:** As more consumer interactions occur in digital environments, marketers must find ways to incorporate sensory elements into online experiences. This requires creativity in leveraging visual, auditory, and interactive elements to create immersive digital brand experiences.
- **Sensory Overload:** In today's fast-paced world, consumers are bombarded with sensory stimuli from various sources. Marketers need to strike a balance between capturing attention through sensory branding and avoiding sensory overload, which can lead to disengagement or negative perceptions of the brand.
- **Long-term Brand Building:** Building a strong sensory brand requires consistent effort over time. Marketers must resist the temptation to constantly change sensory elements and instead focus on building enduring associations between sensory cues and brand identity.

OCEAN Anaysis

Brands are not just predict the future behaviour of customer but they focus on to create the model for present with the combination of artificial intelligence tools. Marketers used the psychology based personality trait theory analysis i.e. most prominent analysis is OCEAN Analysis. On the basis of this analysis they create the customer profile and put flavor of neuro-sensory strategies on it to capture and cover maximum market in this cut-throat competition scenario.

Table 3. OCEAN analysis

Analysis	Traits	Description	Behaviour Influence
O	Openness to Experience	Intellectually curious, open to emotion, sensitive to beauty, and try new things.	Highly positive influence these type of customer because they are willingly ready to experience new things. So brand can easily accessed their brain patterns
C	Conscientioness	Self-disciplined, act dutifully, stubborn and focused.	Positive influence because these type of customer have fixed pattern in their brain which can change after seen and getting some unique but their zone related practices.
E	Exraversion	Enthusiastic and action-oriented	Highly influenced behaviour they have because this type of trait having very different patterns in their brain because they are highly social interactive customers.

continued on following page

Table 1: OCEAN analysis Continued

Analysis	Traits	Description	Behaviour Influence
A	Agreeableness	Concern for social harmony, kind, and trustworthy, They have an optimistic view of human nature.	Positively influence these type of customer because they are easily influence from other people so visual marketing strategy works on it.
N	Neuroticim	Emotional instable	Moderate effect they have because thes type of customer don't have or follow a specific pattern for decision. There past experiences affected them a lot.

OCEAN Analysis provide a mirror profile of customers to brand so brands can predict their range of outcome accordingly and check their relationship and success rate consistency in market. This analysis used to create the hyper personalized advertisement services(HyPAS) with the help of AI. HyPAS is an interactive advertisement board that detects a customers' gender, race, age and emotions with the use of facial analysing algorithm which directly or indirectly promoting the deep fake conveniencing which creates the negative impact on customers.

CONCLUSION

Neuromarketing is the newest edge of marketing, which having a human-centered approach. It combines various disciplines of science and marketing. Advertisers now focus more on tactics that affect our reptilian brain and hitting the "Buy" button within our brain. Human brain divided mainly into 3 sections and each sections has their own importance. The first section which is youngest part of human brain and generally used to take reational decision, the second middle section of brain hold by emotions and the last section ehivh is known as reptilian brain hold the unconscious activities of brain. Marketers always try to trigger out the middle and last section of brain. With the usage of multisensory experiences, companies takes decisions to inspire the right mood for boost brand awareness and drive the sale. Because 'the senses are a kind of reason, these are not merely a means to sensation, enjoyable or otherwise, but they are also a means to knowledge – and are, indeed, your only actual means to knowledge'. Given the challenges of realizing high sensory attributes–function congruence and the associated costs of implementation, this recommendation is good news for managers and should encourage them to tackle congruence-related challenges. The managers, who wish to plan their sensory marketing activities, they should carefully select and arrange the sensory attributes. Considering the recommendations in terms of level- and sense-related aspects can help them select the right sensory attributes to take full advantage of partial sensory attributes–function congruence. If properly designed, partial sensory attributes–

function congruence can serve as a similarly effective and even more efficient strategy than high sensory attributes–function congruence. The managers should keep in mind that not all sensory attributes need to be fully congruent with the product's primary function implies that sensory attributes also do not always have to be fully congruent with each other. Specifically, if the product-related sensory attributes are congruent with product's primary function. Marketing managers are advised to focus on the congruence of product-related (rather than non-product-related) sensory attributes with the product's primary function. Moreover, we recommend concentrating on the congruence of sensory attributes related to one sense (e.g., vision), such as product colour and ambient colour, rather than on the congruence of sensory attributes related to other senses (e.g., smell), such as ambient scent. In summary, this research offers new ways for managers to effectively and efficiently design a multisensory experience in retailing.

REFERENCES

Ahmed, R. R., Streimikiene, D., Channar, Z. A., Soomro, H. A., Streimikis, J., & Kyriakopoulos, G. L. (2022). The Neuromarketing Concept in Artificial Neural Networks: A Case of Forecasting and Simulation from the Advertising Industry. *Sustainability (Basel)*, 14(14), 8546. 10.3390/su14148546

Al-Sharif, A. H., Salleh, N. Z. M., Baharun, R., & Yusoff, M. F. (2021). Consumer Behaviour Through Neuromarketing Approach. [CrossRef]. *Journal of Contemporary Issues in Business and Government*, 27, 344–354.

Alexis, P. (2020). How Neuromarketing Will Revolutionise Luxury Brands. *The Review Magazine*https://www.thereviewmag.co.uk/how-neuromarketing-will-revolutionise-luxury-brands/

Ariely, D., & Berns, G. S. (2010). Neuromarketing: The hope and hype of neuroimaging in business. [CrossRef]. *Nature Reviews. Neuroscience*, 11(4), 284–292. 10.1038/nrn279520197790

Arora, M. (2016). Creative dimensions of entrepreneurship: A key to business innovation. *Pacific Business Review International*, 1(1), 255–259.

Arora, M. (2020). Post-truth and marketing communication in technological age. In *Handbook of research on innovations in technology and marketing for the connected consumer* (pp. 94–108). IGI Global. 10.4018/978-1-7998-0131-3.ch005

Arora, M. (2023). Encapsulating Role of Persuasion and Skill Development in Marketing Communication for Brand Building: A Perspective. In *International Handbook of Skill, Education, Learning, and Research Development in Tourism and Hospitality* (pp. 1–17). Springer Nature Singapore.

Arora, M. (2024). Virtual Reality in Education: Analyzing the Literature and Bibliometric State of Knowledge. *Transforming Education with Virtual Reality*, 379-402. 10.1002/9781394200498.ch22

Arora, M. (2024). Metaverse Metamorphosis: Bridging the Gap Between Research Insights and Industry Applications. In *Research, Innovation, and Industry Impacts of the Metaverse* (pp. 275-286).

Arora, M., & Sharma, R. L. (2021). Repurposing the Role of Entrepreneurs in the Havoc of COVID-19. In *Entrepreneurship and Big Data* (pp. 229-250). CRC Press.

Arora, M., & Sharma, R. L. (2022). Coalescing skills of gig players and fervor of entrepreneurial leaders to provide resilience strategies during global economic crises. In *COVID-19's Impact on the Cryptocurrency Market and the Digital Economy* (pp. 118–140). IGI Global. 10.4018/978-1-7998-9117-8.ch008

Arora, M., & Sharma, R. L. (2023). Artificial intelligence and big data: Ontological and communicative perspectives in multi-sectoral scenarios of modern businesses. *Foresight*, 25(1), 126–143. 10.1108/FS-10-2021-0216

Arora, M., & Sharma, R. L. (2023). Artificial intelligence and big data: Ontological and communicative perspectives in multi-sectoral scenarios of modern businesses. *Foresight*, 25(1), 126–143. 10.1108/FS-10-2021-0216

Berman, G., Potgieter, A., & Tait, M. (2023). The Influence of Sensory Branding Strategies In-Store on Consumer Preference: The South African Skincare Industry. *Journal of Brand Strategy*, 12(2), 194–220.

Bishnoi, S. K., & Singh, S. (2022). A Study on Consumer Buying Behaviour for Fashion and Luxury Brands Under Emotional Influence. *Research Journal of Textile and Apparel.*, 26(4), 405–418. 10.1108/RJTA-03-2021-0026

Chandel, M., & Arora, M. (2024). Metaverse Perspectives: Unpacking Its Role in Shaping Sustainable Development Goals-A Qualitative Inquiry. In *Research, Innovation, and Industry Impacts of the Metaverse* (pp. 62-75). IGI Global.

Chang, P. L., & Chieng, M. H. (2006). Building consumer-brand relationship: A cross-cultural experiential view. *Psychology and Marketing*, 23(11), 927–959. 10.1002/mar.20140

Chi, A. (2022). *A Brief History of Neuromarketing*. Boon Mind. https://www.boonmind.com/a-brief-history-of-neuromarketing/

Crespo-Pereira, V., Legerén-Lago, B., & Arregui-McGullion, J. (2020). Implementing Neuromarketing in the Enterprise: Factors That Impact the Adoption of Neuromarketing in Major Spanish Corporations. [CrossRef]. *Frontiers in Communication*, 5, 576789. 10.3389/fcomm.2020.576789

Dhiman, V., & Arora, M. (2024)b. Exploring the linkage between business incubation and entrepreneurship: understanding trends, themes and future research agenda. *LBS Journal of Management & Research*.

Dhiman, V., & Arora, M. (2024). Current State of Metaverse in Entrepreneurial Ecosystem: A Retrospective Analysis of Its Evolving Landscape. In *Exploring the Use of Metaverse in Business and Education* (pp. 73-87). IGI Global. 10.4018/979-8-3693-5868-9.ch005

Fisher, C. E., Chin, L., & Klitzman, R. (2010). Definiing Neuromarketing: Practices and Professional Challenges. *Harvard Review of Psychiatry*, 18(4), 230–237. 10.3 109/10673229.2010.49662320597593

Gurgu, R., Gurgu, I., & Tonis, R. (2020). Neuromarketing for a better understanding of consumer needs and emotions [CrossRef]. *Independent Journal of Management & Production*, 11(1), 208–235. 10.14807/ijmp.v11i1.993

Haase, J., & Wiedmann, K.-P. (2018). The sensory perception item set (SPI): An exploratory effort to develop a holistic scale for sensory marketing. *Psychology and Marketing*, 35(10), 727–739. 10.1002/mar.21130

Hammou, K. A., Galib, M. H., & Melloul, J. (2013). The Contributions of Neuro-marketing in Marketing Research. [CrossRef]. *Journal of Management Research*, 5(4), 20–33. 10.5296/jmr.v5i4.4023

Imamovic, I., De Azevedo, A. J. A., & De Sousa, B. M. B. (2021). The Tourists' Sensory Experiences: Preliminary Insights of Urban Areas of Porto, Portugal. *Iberian Conference on Information Systems and Technologies, CISTI*. IEEE. 10.23919/CISTI52073.2021.9476371

Juarez, D., Tur-Viñes, V., & Mengual, A. (2020). Neuromarketing Applied to Educational Toy Packaging. *Frontiers in Psychology*, 11, 2077. 10.3389/fpsyg.2020.0207732982857

Krishna, A., Cian, L., & Sokolova, T. (2016). The power of sensory marketing in advertising. *Current Opinion in Psychology*, 10, 142–147. 10.1016/j.copsyc.2016.01.007

Kumar, J., Arora, M., & Erkol Bayram, G. (Eds.). (2024). *Research, Innovation, and Industry Impacts of the Metaverse*. IGI Global.

Kumar, J., Arora, M., & Erkol Bayram, G. (Eds.). (2024). *Exploring the Use of Metaverse in Business and Education*. IGI Global. 10.4018/979-8-3693-5868-9

Kumar, J., Arora, M., & Erkol Bayram, G. (Eds.). (2024). *Exploring the Use of Metaverse in Business and Education*. IGI Global. 10.4018/979-8-3693-5868-9

Kumavat, R. (2023). Neuromarketing-current situation & available future trends in India with special reference to Jalgaon district. *International Journal of Contemporary Management*.

Kurtoğlu, A. L., & Ferman, A. M. (2020). An exploratory research among fashion business leaders and neuromarketing company executives on the perception of applied neuromarketing. [CrossRef]. *Pressacademia*, 11(1), 230–232. 10.17261/Pressacademia.2020.1274

Lee, N., Brandes, L., Chamberlain, L., & Senior, C. (2017). This is Your Brain on Neuromarketing: Reflections on a Decade of Research. *Journal of Marketing Management*, 33(11-12), 878–892. 10.1080/0267257X.2017.1327249

Marcel, P., Lacramioara, R., Maniu, I., & Zaharie, M. (2009). Neuromarketing—Getting inside the customer's mind. *Ann. Univ. Oradea Econ. Sci.*, 4, 804–807.

Morin, C. (2011). Neuromarketing: The new science of consumer behavior. *Society*, 48(2), 131–135. 10.1007/s12115-010-9408-1

Morin, C. (2011). Neuromarketing: The new science of consumer behavior. [Cross-Ref]. *Society*, 48(2), 131–135. 10.1007/s12115-010-9408-1

Murphy, E. R., Illes, J., & Reiner, P. B. (2008). Neuroethics of neuromarketing. [CrossRef]. *Journal of Consumer Behaviour*, 7(4-5), 293–302. 10.1002/cb.252

Ponnam, A. (2011). A case for customer based brand equity conceptualization within motivational perspective. *Academy of Marketing Studies Journal*, 15, 61–70.

Ramsøy, T. Z. (2020). *An Introduction to Consumer Neuroscience & Neuromarketing [MOOC]*. Coursera. https://www.coursera.org/learn/neuromarketing?=&page=1

Rathore, S., & Arora, M. (2024). Sustainability Reporting in the Metaverse: A Multi-Sectoral Analysis. In *Exploring the Use of Metaverse in Business and Education* (pp. 147-165). IGI Global. 10.4018/979-8-3693-5868-9.ch009

Renvoise, C., & Morin, P. (2007). *Neuromarketing: Understanding the "Buy Button" in Your Customer's Brain*. Thomas Nelson Publishers.

Rodrigues, C., Skinner, H., Dennis, C., & Melewar, T. C. (2020). Towards a Theoretical Framework on Sensorial Place Brand Identity. *Journal of Place Management and Development.*, 13(3), 273–295. 10.1108/JPMD-11-2018-0087

Srivastava, G., & Bag, S. (2023). Modern-Day Marketing Concepts Based on Face Recognition and Neuro-Marketing: A Review and Future Research Directions. *Benchmarking*. 10.1108/BIJ-09-2022-0588

Vences, N. A., Díaz-Campo, J., & Rosales, D. F. G. (2020). Neuromarketing as an Emotional Connection Tool Between Organizations and Audiences in Social Networks. A Theoretical Review. *Frontiers in Psychology*, 11, 1787. 10.3389/fpsyg.2020.0178732849055

Vidal-Raméntol, S. (2020). Neuromarketing and Sustainability. [CrossRef]. *Advances in Social Sciences Research Journal*, 7(12), 181–191. 10.14738/assrj.712.9360

Wiedmann, K.-P., Hennigs, N., Klarmann, C., & Behrens, S. (2013). Creating multi-sensory experiences in luxury marketing. *Marketing Review St. Gallen*, 30(6), 60–68. 10.1365/s11621-013-0300-4

Chapter 12
Sensory Storytelling:
Crafting Brand Narratives Through Sight, Sound, Smell, Touch, and Taste

Anchal Luthra
https://orcid.org/0000-0003-0559-1893
Amity University, Noida, India

Shivani Dixit
https://orcid.org/0000-0002-6936-4617
IMS Ghaziabad (University Courses Campus), India

Anamica Singh
https://orcid.org/0000-0002-0107-6627
Amity University, Noida, India

Seema Garg
https://orcid.org/0000-0002-4750-026X
Amity University, Noida, India

Sharad Khattar
Amity University, Noida, India

ABSTRACT

This chapter delves into the field of sensory marketing, a rapidly growing discipline. It primarily focuses on the increasing use of multi-sensory experiences as a powerful tool in modern marketing. The chapter emphasizes the significant influence that the five primary senses-sight, hearing, smell, touch, and taste-have on consumer behaviour. It also provides a detailed exploration of each sense and how marketers can

DOI: 10.4018/979-8-3693-4236-7.ch012

effectively use multiple sensory inputs to engage consumers emotionally and foster strong connections between their Brands and them. The chapter further examines various examples and current trends that deliberately incorporate points of contact with different sensory components, leading to enhanced brand differentiation in the dynamic landscape of contemporary marketing.

INTRODUCTION

In today's competitive business environment, companies constantly look for new ways to attract and build long-term customer relationships. Multisensory marketing has gained popularity in creating immersive brand experiences by incorporating sensory inputs such as sight, sound, smell, touch, and taste (Spence, 2022). This approach recognizes that consumers engage with brands through reason and their senses, which elicit emotions, enhance recall and affect behavior. As the digital era continues transforming consumer behaviors and patterns of interaction, brands have started including multisensory components in their storytelling and branding strategies more frequently (Zha *et al.*, 2022). This shift is supported by findings from market research agencies like Forrester Research (2023) and Nielsen (2022), which underline the growing importance of sensory marketing in driving consumer engagement and purchase decisions. This book chapter investigates how integrating sensory cues into narratives can increase people's understanding of brands while also fostering loyalty toward them. Through real-life examples backed up with empirical studies conducted across different industries and contexts worldwide, it seeks to equip marketers or brand managers with actionable insights into successfully implementing sensory storytelling approaches (Zha *et al.*, 2022). In line with prior literature on sensory marketing, however, there appears to be limited knowledge regarding when, where, why, and what kind of tactics should be used. Previous works have only touched lightly on some aspects but failed to dig deeper into all others, especially those related to affecting perception about products/services offered by brands among clients/consumers from diverse backgrounds such as children, teens, adults elderly, etc who may reside within urban rural areas domestically internationally feeling positive negative indifferent neutral excited satisfied bored confused curious surprised about these companies (Lindstrom, 2021).

This chapter adopts an interdisciplinary approach by drawing on experiential marketing theory from cognitive psychology, neuroaesthetics, and consumer behavior literature grounded in concepts such as involvement or engagement (Krishna, 2013; Spence & Gallace, 2011). Theoretical contributions provide insights into how different senses can influence perception formation processes relating to brands besides decision-making at various stages along the value chain toward purchase behavior, among other things. From a managerial point of view, this chapter provides practical assistance that will enable marketers to use sensory cues effectively in their storytelling efforts. Brands need to know what feelings are evoked, where, when, why, and how these should be employed to capture customers' hearts, minds, souls, spirits, thereby creating unforgettable experiences that connect deeply with them emotionally, psychologically, or even spiritually if possible (Velasco, and Spence, 2019). This chapter will also provide guidelines and relevant implementation strategies, based on which could help transform ordinary tales into powerful stories capable of profoundly touching people's lives.

MATERIALS AND METHODS

A systematic literature review was conducted to find academic papers, industry reports, and articles about sensory marketing, storytelling, and related concepts. Further, the main principles and patterns that affect sensory storytelling in branding were identified. In addition, case studies of companies that had successfully employed strategies of this kind were studied to establish best practices and challenges. Also, professionals and academicians specialized in marketing or consumer behavior were interviewed, therefore allowing the gathering of empirical knowledge based on their personal experiences while enriching the analysis with practical insights. A systematic structure was established for organizing various parts of the chapter, including main sections, subsections, critical points, etc., thus ensuring that all relevant Areas are covered holistically, boosting credibility through more detailed findings within each section.

LITERATURE REVIEW

Sensory Marketing: A significant effect on customer perception, feeling, and behavior is made by sensory experiences; thus, it is essential to know what sensory marketing is. It recognizes that people use rational criteria when selecting purchases and their sense organs, such as the eyes, ears, nose, or skin (Krishna, 2012). This involves setting up places that appeal to the senses, creating attractive packages, adding pleasant smells and sounds to products, and providing tactile contact points for enhancing the brand experience, among others (Hultén *et al.,* 2011). Understanding this concept enables businesses to connect with customers emotionally, differentiate themselves from competitors, and foster greater loyalty toward their brands while driving up engagement levels. Customers interact with the world through five basic senses: sight, hearing, smell, and taste, influencing their behavior as consumers significantly (Zha *et al.,* 2022). Each of these has a unique role in shaping our perceptions about things around us, including emotions and, eventually, decisions made by buyers. Marketing is visual mainly because humans have highly developed eyesight, so they say, 'seeing is believing.' How an item looks, its colors, shapes, or overall beauty can evoke certain feelings in someone's mind, influencing his choice (Jiménez-Marín *et al.,* 2022). In a business context, logos and packages act as the first point of contact between buyers and sellers; hence, the design should be eye-catching enough to create a desire for ownership among potential customers. What we hear also matters since auditory perception involves processing sound and music, whereas some tunes could leave lasting memories after being associated with particular brands. Rodgers *et al.,* (2021) added that jingles build positive moods and increase awareness about different products during shopping trips. Music played in retail spaces could make one feel like one belongs to a given enterprise through identification with familiar tunes, thereby boosting loyalty levels among clients towards the firms involved.

Olfactory marketing taps into the sense of smell, which is believed to be strongly linked to memory and emotions, hence making it a powerful tool for creating lasting impressions within people's minds. Positive emotions can be triggered by having pleasant odors around stores or even items themselves being scented. At the same time, some food brands may use fragrances that bring back the good old days to consumers. This approach has the potential of immersing customers into brands more deeply and fostering loyalty towards them in return. Touching things helps us know whether they are good or bad in quality; thus, this aspect should never be underestimated during the packaging stage because tactile sense plays a significant role in evaluating products by would-be users (Zha *et al.,* 2022). When individuals touch what belongs to them, they psychologically feel connected; hence, marketers need to capitalize on such experiences, if at all possible, through things like interactive displays featuring different textures alongside other forms, which allow for direct engagement with clients' hands, leading to stronger bonds between brand owners and purchasers. Taste perception comes last, though not frequently used compared to rest, but still plays a significant role, especially when dealing with the foodstuffs and beverages industry, where flavorings affect how we view things (Lindstrom, 2005). For instance, organizations could utilize gustatory encounters by giving samples introducing new flavors and hosting culinary events to establish positive associations with these types of businesses, encouraging repeat consumer buying behaviors over time.

Knowing each sense's role in consumer behavior enables marketers to design better strategies for creating multi-sensory brand experiences that connect more deeply with people. Sensory marketing has come a long way. It started as conventional advertising and is now recognized as an essential strategy for engaging people at a deeper level. Technological advancements, changes in consumer behavior, and awareness of the impact sensory experiences have on consumer perception have driven the growth of sensory marketing. Before, sensory marketing only focused on visual and auditory means of stimulation. Brands used print ads, radio jingles, and TV commercials to catch the attention of their target audience. However, as more studies about consumer psychology were conducted, marketers realized that it was necessary to appeal to multiple senses simultaneously if they wanted more robust brand experiences (Zha *et al.,* 2022). This marked a significant shift in the industry-multisensory marketing that came into play when companies started in-corporating smell, touch, and taste elements into their promotional activities. They did this because research had shown that these senses greatly influenced customer emotions, memory, and buying behavior. All this shows that over time, people have learned how important it is to use all five senses when communicating their brand message through advertising or other means. Looking ahead to future developments within customer preferences and technological advancements will further highlight the importance of sensory encounters in successful branding through marketing efforts.

The Power of Multisensory Experiences: The effectiveness of multimodal experiences lies in their ability to create immersive events that are hard to forget by involving different areas of Our brains in which such memories reside while attracting various mental faculties simultaneously. According to Mishra *et al.,* (2021), 'multisensory experiences work best because they engage more than one sense.' For this reason, such events must stimulate sight, sound, touch, taste, and smell concurrently to effectively involve all these organs with emotion centers, thereby creating lasting impressions upon individuals who go through them (Lindstrom, 2005). One study revealed that using multiple sensory cues can help people remember brands better, influence purchase choices, and foster loyalty toward a brand (Shahid *et al.,* 2022). Such events have the potential to evoke different types of emotions such as joy, excitement, longing, etc., however, companies can make them more potent by appealing to several senses concurrently, thus making it an immersive experience that will forever stay etched within one's mind (Krishna *et al.,* 2013). Another research found that involving various modalities boosts information processing in the brain, leading to a more robust formation of memories about brands, which supports future recall among customers (Spence, 2022). In addition, consumers' perception of value and quality may be enhanced through multi-sensory encounters. When people use many senses simultaneously, they perceive products or services offered by businesses as higher priced, luxurious, and attractive (Laukkanen *et al.,* 2022). Companies could also foster deeper connections with clients by engaging more than just one sense during interactions, resulting in a more substantial impact on individuals' lives and thus creating memorable moments. People with positive multisensory experiences with a particular company will likely become emotionally attached to it, hence developing loyalty to such enterprises. Brands using multi-modal marketing strategies can differentiate themselves in a competitive market and establish stronger bonds with their target audience. Here are some examples of successful multi-sensory advertising campaigns.

Starbucks Reserve Roastery: Starbucks Reserve Roastery gives visitors an engaging multi-sensory experience of coffee production's visual, auditory, and olfactory aspects. They have state-of-the-art roasting machines, interactive brewing stations, and attractive coffee samples that take one through a complete journey from the first bean to the final cup. According to Spence (2023), this has helped them differentiate their high-end Reserve brand and build a loyal customer base by adopting a multimodal approach.

IKEA Catalogs with Augmented Reality (AR): IKEA has transformed its traditional print catalogs into something more by using Augmented Reality (AR) technology, allowing shoppers to see furniture pieces and other home design items in their living spaces. Customers need to scan catalog pages using their smartphones or tablets. Then, they can view virtual 3D models of furniture integrated within their living environments, thus giving them a chance to have a multi-sensory experience before making a purchase decision. Introducing an interactive augmented reality (AR) experience significantly increased consumer engagement, leading to higher revenues for IKEA.

ScentAir's Scent Marketing Solutions: ScentAir is a scent marketing company that provides customized fragrance solutions to enhance brand experiences among customers. One good example is when Westin Hotels & Resorts teamed up with ScentAir to create unique scents for their hotels. The hotel lobbies and guest rooms are filled with Westin White Tea fragrance, creating calmness and freshness, mirroring wellness and tranquillity associated with the brand (Rottigni & Spence, 2024). Therefore, Westin employed multiple branding modes while improving the overall guest experience.

Bose's SoundTouch Wireless Speakers: To promote its SoundTouch wireless speakers, Bose launched an extensive marketing campaign emphasizing the power of captivating sound. They had interactive displays at stores, allowing buyers to have live demonstrations where they could hear the exceptional quality produced by these speakers. Additionally, through various narrative techniques and visually stunning content delivered via digital marketing platforms, the emotional aspect of music was effectively communicated. Bose used a multimodal strategy to successfully communicate the unique benefits associated with its products, thus driving sales.

Visual Sensory Marketing: This approach employs the visual sense to offer fascinating brand experiences that catch customers' attention and encourage them to interact. Visual sensory marketing refers to branding, packaging, and digital content strategically designed for specific visual senses, targeting and attracting consumers

(Spence, 2023). Brands use different visual cues such as bright colors, attractive images, beautiful designs, or layouts, among others, deliberately to communicate their identity; this, in turn, creates feelings and affects what people choose to buy. Visuals are important in branding because they often serve as a person's first contact point with any brand. Logos, color schemes, typography, and other visual elements help people understand a particular company is about (its principles, nature) and values (Lelis *et al.,* 2022). How packages have been designed plays a crucial role in how healthy brands represent themselves visually. Attractive package designs can attract consumer attention within crowded retail displays, thus influencing their purchasing decisions (Lindstrom, 2005). Businesses frequently utilize graphics to convey product features, benefits, and value propositions. In today's era, where everything revolves around digital technology, graphics Have become essential, especially regarding digital marketing strategies like web design, social media content creation, or online advertising. Moreover, visual materials, including pictures, videos, or even animated things, show up better as they are easily shareable, not forgetting that they capture one's eye, making them handy tools for drawing audience interest and fostering interaction among individuals (Spence, 2022). Visual marketing is an essential aspect of marketing because it attracts attention. However, it can also be complicated for various reasons, such as conveying emotions, showing brand identity or policies, etc. Metaverse has given a different dimension to the visual marketing perspectives which has multi sectoral business implications (Kumar, Arora & Erkol Bayram, G. Eds., 2024; Dhiman & Arora, 2024). Therefore, we shall look at some examples of visually driven marketing strategies and their effectiveness.

Apple's Product Launch Events: Apple is known for having visually stunning product launches that are carefully planned to engage audiences and generate excitement around new product releases. These events display sleek product designs, high-quality graphics, and engaging presentations highlighting the creativity and craftsmanship of Apple products. Using visually impactful elements like colorful graphics or polished product films helps reinforce Apple's identity as a design leader and a technological innovation pioneer. Furthermore, these types of marketing through visuals have proved very successful because they create media buzz, build customer anticipation, and ultimately drive sales volume (Lindstrom, 2005).

Dove's Real Beauty Campaign: The Real Beauty Campaign by Dove is another prime example of visual-based marketing that challenges conventional beauty standards and promotes body acceptance. The campaign features visually stunning ads and videos celebrating natural beauty in women of all shapes, sizes, and ethnicities. Through powerful imagery coupled with emotionally charged advertising, Dove has positioned itself as a champion for inclusivity and self-love among women. The effectiveness of this particular campaign can be seen from its extensive coverage by different media outlets, positive social media engagement, and awards recognition attained.

Red Bull's Sponsorships in Extreme Sports: Red Bull's marketing strategy focuses on visually oriented tactics, like sponsoring extreme sports and hosting events that capture the exciting passion of its target demographic. Red Bull creates mind-blowing movies and photographs that show fearless athletes pushing the limits of human performance in sports such as skateboarding, snowboarding, or skydiving. Such visually captivating content entertains viewers and establishes a strong link between the brand itself and energy, excitement, and adventure (Buhalis & Karatay, 2022).

Auditory Sensory Marketing: Auditory sensory marketing uses sound to create memorable brand encounters that resonate with consumers at a deeper level than other forms of marketing. Sound logos are auditory cues or musical motifs unique to a particular company. These audio identifiers serve as audio beacons that help customers recognize and recall brands faster than they would by relying solely on visual cues alone (Meyers-Levy *et al.*, 2011). Brands can use Catchy tunes or calming background noises strategically to strengthen their identity emotionally and appeal more directly to shape behavior among listeners. However, jingles usually consist of short, catchy melodies designed primarily for advertising purposes seeking to establish familiarity with target audiences, thereby enhancing the ability of people to remember them easily. Jingles can evoke positive feelings, attract attention, and leave lasting impressions on the minds of those who hear them frequently.

Appropriate usage of sound and music in marketing can significantly affect how customers see, feel, and react toward brands. Using jingles, sound logos, or even background melodies skillfully, businesses create memorable moments when consumers can genuinely connect with them. Emotions can be stirred, and consumer behavior can be influenced through auditory means. Music can evoke happiness, sadness, thrill, or nostalgia. Different elements like speed, rhythm, tune, or words in a song can make someone experience different emotions (Meyers-Levy *et al.,* 2011). Likewise, acoustic features like catchy tunes alongside sonic signatures summon memories, thus linking specific commodities with certain manufacturers. This repeated exposure to such sonic attributes leads a person's mind to easily recollect the brand every time they come across it, prompting strong brand awareness. Moreover, auditory cues influence purchase decisions and customer behavior; for example, retail environment studies have shown that background music affects factors like store dwell time, product choice variety, and propensity to buy (Rathee & Rajain *et al.,* 2017). The sound image created by these organizations can shape their character perception amongst clients and other stakeholders interested in knowing what values they stand for or how good they are at what they do. For instance, an intelligent luxury brand might want itself represented by calm, refined audio, while a vibrant, cheerful jingle may work best for a young, dynamic company. All these sonic stimuli contribute towards shaping overall encounters, further influencing peoples' understanding of different brands.

Olfactory Sensory Marketing: Olfactory sensory marketing uses scent to produce fascinating brand experiences that influence consumers for a long time (Herz, 2011). Brands create immersive atmospheres and foster impressions of their products by using scents like the They are enticing the aroma of fresh coffee brewing in a café or the delicate fragrance wafting through a store. Scent marketing is an intentional approach to enhancing brand experiences through creating more immersive environments. To properly implement scent marketing, it is necessary to understand its principles and strategies well enough. Frequently known as fragrance marketing or olfactory advertising, scent marketing is a deliberate strategy that employs our sense of smell to produce captivating encounters with brands. Aromachology refers to the use of smells or odors in order to evoke specific feelings, memories, and connections with a particular brand or product (Thangaleela *et al.,* 2022). A scent is a powerful tool for shaping customer behavior and perception because it can tap into solid emotional associations through the human brain. Fragrance shapes customers' perceptions of brands and enhances their overall brand experience. Therefore, immersive sensory experiences can be created in retail stores, among others, so that brands may connect with customers more profoundly through strategic selection and diffusion of certain scents in hotels, spas, etc. (DeSalle, 2018). What scent marketing does is that it allows firms to establish emotional bonds with clients by evoking positive emotions. Certain fragrances have been found to evoke feelings of happiness, nostalgia, or relaxation, thus making people develop more muscular attachments towards those brands, according to Herz (2011) studies. Additionally, the quality effectiveness worth evaluation stage for any given product/service can also be affected by its smell; this means that individuals are likely going associate cleanliness and freshness with cleaning agents based on their aromas, while beauty products having floral scents might indicate the use of natural ingredients luxuriousness. Furthermore, firms can increase the perceived value of their products and differentiate themselves from competitors by associating pleasant smells with desirable attributes. This implies that when customers perceive goods or services as being of high quality because they have been made better using some olfactory cues, such an eventuality will increase loyalty towards such brands, hence more sales revenue realization (Roy & Singh, 2023). There is ample evidence from research showing that scent marketing does influence consumer behavior; this includes what people buy and how much money they spend and it all also enhances persuasion (Arora, 2023). These findings indicate that pleasant smells could make individuals stay longer in stores, allowing them to make unplanned purchases and boosting overall sales figures. In addition, Companies can stand apart in crowded markets and leave a lasting impression on consumers by integrating scents into their marketing strategies.

Singapore Airlines: Singapore Airlines (SIA) is famous for its excellent service and meticulous attention to detail, including smell marketing. The airport lounges and cabins of SIA have Introduced a unique fragrance called "Stefan Floridian Waters" to enhance passengers' overall satisfaction. This scent mixes jasmine, lavender, and rosemary notes to create a calm atmosphere for travellers (Lindstrom, 2005). Many travellers were pleased with the new aroma, which made them feel more relaxed and refreshed during the flight. Moreover, customer satisfaction ratings went up, and customers repeated bookings themselves, which shows how much fragrance impacts consumer opinion and loyalty towards the airline.

Macy's Thanksgiving Day Parade: Every year, thousands gather along New York City streets or tune into their television sets across America–and worldwide–to watch Macy's Thanksgiving Day Parade. In 2009, Macy's partnered with International Flavors & Fragrances (IFF) to infuse the parade route with a custom scent called "Sweet Smell of Success." To disperse this perfume – which featured delightful vanilla scents mixed with caramel and pumpkin spice fragrances – unique scent cannons released bursts of aromatic mist along the procession path (Krishna, 2013). Adding smells into the mix made people more engaged while enjoying themselves so much that they never wanted it to end! Also, there was an increase in viewership ratings for this event, plus positive feedback from participants; all these things point out just how important smelling good can be when it comes to customer perception about any given occasion.

Tactile Sensory Marketing: Tactile sensory marketing utilizes the sensation of touch to provide captivating brand encounters that deeply connect with customers physically. In a more digitized society, where many encounters occur via screens and smartphones, tactile experiences provide a distinct chance for companies to distinguish themselves and have a profound influence. Tactile sensory marketing is a strategic approach that utilizes textures, materials, and tactile feedback to elicit sensory reactions and shape customer perceptions (Kim *et al.,* 2020). Brands use tactile signals such as sumptuous materials, ergonomic product designs, interactive touchscreens, and haptic interfaces to improve product experiences and establish emotional connections with their audience. Tactile elements, such as textures and materials, are crucial in shaping consumers' perceptions of product quality, luxury, and functionality. Brands use a variety of textures and materials in their products and packaging to create sensory-rich experiences that engage consumers on a tactile level (Hultén *et al.,* 2010). In the digital realm, tactile feedback refers to using tactile sensations, such as vibrations or pressure, to simulate the sense of touch in electronic devices. Brands leverage haptic or tactile feedback in smartphones, tablets, and gaming controllers to enhance user experiences and provide feedback in response to user interactions. Tactile elements are also integral to product Design, and ergonomics influence how products feel in consumers' hands and how they interact with them. Brands invest in ergonomic design principles to ensure that products are comfortable to hold, easy to use, and pleasant to touch (Biswas *et al.,* 2019). Tactile elements are essential in packaging design, influencing consumers' perceptions of product quality and value. Brands use embossing, debossing, varnishes, and other tactile finishes to create visually and tactilely appealing packaging that stands out on store shelves. By combining tangible components into the design of products, packaging, and digital interfaces, businesses can create immersive experiences that captivate customers on a profound level and distinguish themselves in the market.

Gustative Sensory Marketing: Gustatory sensory marketing is a strategic approach that uses flavors, food and beverage branding, product sampling, and cooking events to elicit emotions and shape consumer preferences (Nwachukwu *et al.,* 2022). Brands leverage tastes into an appetizing experience that lingers longer in people's minds, including tempting samples of foods or drinks and new combinations of flavors. Product sampling is among many widely applied marketing techniques by companies dealing with foodstuffs and beverages. It involves introducing clients to different items so they can try them out themselves. Marketers can show their offerings' superiority, deliciousness, or uniqueness through this method since customers can taste them before buying. These occasions may occur physically at retail outlets, during various gatherings such as parties, or online platforms where buyers directly come across products' taste profiles while evaluating their consistency, among other attributes. In food and beverage branding, taste differentiation is significant because it helps communicate quality levels and triggers emotional responses from consumers. To convey these unique sensations of flavor offered by its products, brands employ package design elements like ingredient narratives and descriptive panels that show the specific types of tastes associated with them. Culinary experiences, e.g., restaurant dining or participation in food festivals, greatly influence how people perceive flavors or tastes. Businesses use such moments to create impact around specific points, thus connecting emotionally with clients. Also, establishments selling edibles often collaborate with other firms/influencers to provide distinct flavor encounters and expand their audience reach further: cross-promotions and limited editions involving recipe-sharing joint ventures, among others (Nwachukwu *et al.,* 2022).

Food and drink marketing relies heavily on taste and flavor because they affect what consumers like, what they buy, and how loyal they are to certain brands. Companies can create captivating taste experiences and carve out unique market positions through product sampling, branding strategies, culinary events, and collaborations investigating the relationship between brand loyalty and customer preference regarding taste. Taste is closely linked with emotions and memories because flavors can evoke pleasurable or unpleasant feelings depending on previous encounters with them (Zhou & Tse, 2022). People who have enjoyed eating products from a particular company may develop strong emotional bonds with that firm and its offerings. For instance, taste is an essential indicator of any food item's authenticity or genuineness, influencing consumer perceptions towards such products, which affects their purchase decisions too. Conversely, failure by businesses to meet customers' expectations regarding flavor could lead to negative word-of-mouth publicity, thus making it hard for such enterprises to retain clients within crowded markets where many other options are available. In addition, brands should offer tastes that others cannot imitate easily since it makes them stand out from competitors' products, attracting more loyal buyers over time. This implies that companies need innovative ways to add value through unique flavors to attract attention and encourage people to try new things frequently. Sometimes, specialty food and beverage companies differentiate themselves by using artisanal inputs blended in different ratios, creating unexpected combinations that result in exciting flavors that most individuals have never experienced (Zhou & Tse, 2022). Positive gustatory encounters might lead to frequent buying plus advocacy since satisfied consumers tend to recommend these goods to their friends, thus creating a situation whereby even if pricing were higher than average still, many customers would remain loyal due to having gained trust after repeated satisfying experiences provided consistently every year without fail (Lindstrom, 2005). Alternatively, some organizations can keep customers returning year after year by introducing additional varieties. This, therefore, acts as an opportunity for consumers to try them all out, thereby enhancing attachment levels towards such brands at a personal level. Secondly, cultural and geographical aspects affect taste preferences because every culture or region has unique culinary traditions with specific flavor profiles through which people identify (Krishna, 2012). Such knowledge allows marketers to understand what works best when promoting products within particular localities. This may generate increased revenues over time due to heightened customer satisfaction arising from improved relevance created between fast food outlets' menus vis-à-vis individual needs based on locality-specific meals offered.

INTEGRATING MULTISENSORY EXPERIENCES

The procedure for integrating many experiences of the senses in marketing is to use several senses to invent immersive brand encounters that are profoundly committed to customers. In today's highly competitive business environment, where customers are constantly exposed to a lot of information and choices, firms are actively looking for innovative ways of attracting attention and building important relationships. Multisensory experiences allow companies to engage vision, sound, taste, touch, and smell. This technique results in comprehensive brand experiences simultaneously stimulating multiple senses (Cornelio *et al.*, 2021). By intentionally incorporating aspects of sensation into their products or services, a firm can create memorable and powerful experiences that evoke emotions, enhance brand identity, and influence consumer behavior. Sensory Branding is an inclusive sensory branding strategy that covers sensations such as sight, hearing, touch or feel, taste, and smell to provide immersive brand experiences (Shahid *et al.,* 2022). For example, maintaining similar sensory elements across all touchpoints, including packaging design such as advertising techniques, retail locations, and digital platforms, will help improve brand identification and enhance brand memory. Incorporate sensory stimuli into product design and packaging to appeal to different senses of consumers at once. Use tangible materials, visually pleasing attributes, nice smells, and distinct taste mixtures when creating products that capture clients' sensory experiences and differentiate themselves from other brands. Apply technology to create interactive digital interfaces capable of engaging multiple senses simultaneously. Auditory cues like music, tactile feedback like user interface elements, and stimulating visuals may be integrated into websites' mobile apps and virtual reality (VR), ensuring increased brand interaction (Spence, 2022). Beauty companies can employ augmented reality (AR) technology, allowing individuals to try cosmetics virtually, thus giving a multi-sensory shopping experience from their homes. Arrange experiential marketing events that excite customers' senses, leading them into life-long brand experiences. Use live demonstrations, product samples, interactive displays, and live music or performances to appeal to sight, sound, touch, taste, and smell (Lindstrom, 2005). Leading food and beverage companies could stage temporary sampling events or cooking classes to showcase their products and interact with customers in a multi-sensory setting. Integration across various channels: Integrate sensory components effortlessly across different marketing platforms for a consistent brand experience. Consistency in sensory cues should be maintained across print media, internet materials, social media avenues, in-store promotions, and outdoor advertising (Caissie *et al.,* 2021). Customise sensory experiences based on individual preferences and choices using personalization and customization tactics. Employ data analytics and consumer insights to discover preferences and deliver exacting sensory experiences that will strongly attract specific market segments. When adding sensations to marketing campaigns and brand experience, it is necessary to have a methodical strategy. Moreover, it is a comprehensive strategy that considers the distinct attributes and preferences of the target audience. Through sensory branding, multi-sensory product design, interactive digital experiences, experiential marketing events, cross-channel integration, and customization strategies, businesses can build immersive brand experiences that resonate with customers. Significant factors to consider when designing integrated multimodal experiences across many channels. Ensure that sensory aspects of the brand, such as visuals, sounds, and other sensory inputs, are aligned with the brand's identity, values, and positioning across all platforms and channels (Zha *et al.,* 2022). Maintaining uniformity on sensory cues like colors, textures, sounds, aromas, or tastes is vital in bolstering brand identification and fostering consumer trust. For each channel or environment being developed for multimodal experiences, one must consider its different characteristics and limitations. Customise sensory stimuli to match specific contexts and targeted audience profiles conveyed by each channel, be it a brick-and-mortar store or online platform, including social media sites or an event venue. Integrate several different touchpoints seamlessly to communicate any sensory element as part of a unified branding experience (Shahid *et al.,* 2022). Ensure a smooth transition from one channel to another without distortion to tell a consistent story effectively and logically about the brand. Create interactive content involving multiple senses, thus compelling people to participate actively. Use various media formats like movies/ animations/ virtual tours/ branded games, which engage individuals more fully within the narrative world created by brands. Multiple platforms are involved in increasing involvement across various platforms' use of auditory effects, visual animations, and tactile input points, therefore increasing participation gains (Arezes *et al.,* 2016). Data analytics and customer insights customize multimodal experiences based on individual preferences. Classify audiences into subgroups with the help of demographic, behavioral, and psychographic data to offer tailored sensory experiences targeting particular client groups. Continuously monitor and improve multimodal experiences using feedback, measurements, and emerging trends. Be updated on technical advancements, cultural shifts that may affect sensory marketing, and industry changes so that you can constantly create/modify sensory marketing concepts. Leverage innovative sensory stimuli, communication channels, and formats to keep abreast of current happenings and effectively capture customers in new and influential ways.

FUTURE TRENDS AND OPPORTUNITIES

Sensory marketing in the future is an enormous opportunity for businesses to change how they correspond with customers and create long-lasting impressions. With the advancement of technology and changing customer tastes, companies now have fresh opportunities to use sensory inputs creatively. From augmented reality and virtual reality experiences to individualized sensory messages and biometric feedback, the future of sensory marketing has no limit (Antunes & Veríssimo, 2024). Brands that embrace these emerging trends and Technologies will be able to create immersive, influential experiences that truly connect with consumers. Augmented Reality (AR) and Virtual Reality (VR) technologies captivate the senses by superimposing digital material on existing physical spaces or creating synthetic environments. Augmented reality (AR) and virtual reality (VR) are used by brands in interactive product demos, virtual try-on experiences, and immersive storytelling involving multiple senses at once (Hilken *et al.,* 2022). Beauty firms employ augmented reality (AR) applications, allowing clients to virtually test cosmetics and try different looks, enhancing their online shopping experience while influencing purchase decisions. Haptic technology lets someone feel touch through vibrating sensations, pressure, or motion. For example, haptic feedback is employed by brands in digital interfaces, wearable devices, and gaming peripherals to enhance user experience, resulting in more immersive interactions (Bhatia *et al.,* 2021). A case in point is fitness trackers, which provide users with haptic feedback, thus enabling immediate updates and motivating prompts during exercise, fostering increased engagement and commitment towards fitness goals. Scent delivery systems are devices dispersing fragrances or smells within physical environments that create immersive sensory experiences. In various settings, such as retail outlets, hotels, and entertainment places, where scents can enhance brand impression, marketers use scent marketing to evoke emotions that manipulate people's behavior (Lindstrom, 2005). Sophisticated fragrance delivery equipment permits precise control over dispersion intensity and the directionality of odors, enabling brands to create tailor-made olfactory encounters that meet particular circumstances and match the preferences of their target groups. Taste simulation technology imitates the taste experience by electrically or thermally stimulating taste receptors. Brands have begun using taste simulation technologies to provide virtual taste experiences in digital domains like online food and beverage platforms, gaming apps, and virtual dining (Spence, 2023). Researchers have developed devices that use electrical pulses to activate the taste buds to simulate sweet, sour, salty, or bitter tastes. This enables a person to experience the taste of a meal or drink virtually without actually eating anything physical. Sensory analytics and biometric monitoring involve studying physiological responses and sensory perceptions to evaluate customer engagement and emotional reactions in real time. To enhance marketing campaigns, product designs, and customer experiences, brands employ sensory analytics through consumer insights based on a data-driven understanding of consumer preferences and behaviors. Eye tracking monitors visual attention patterns, whereas galvanic skin response (GSR) sensors measure changes in skin conductance as indicators of arousal and stress during sensory experiences. Neuroscience and neuromarketing study the neurological mechanisms underpinning sensory perception, emotions, and decision-making. By leveraging neuroscience findings, companies develop more effective multimodal marketing approaches that subconsciously resonate with customers. Brain imaging studies reveal which brain areas are activated when distinct sensing stimuli are presented, offering valuable information about how these senses work during consumer processing.

The advancements in multisensory marketing provide companies with exciting opportunities to create immersive, impactful experiences that engage customers on multiple levels. By employing AR and VR, haptic technology, fragrance delivery systems, taste simulation technologies, sensory analytics, and neuroscience insights, brands can enhance their traditional marketing techniques, creating captivating sensory experiences for audiences that lead to commercial outcomes. Forecasts for the future of sensory and multisensory experiences in marketing indicate a persistent progression towards more immersive, customized, and technologically sophisticated approaches. Hyper-personalization is tailoring products, services, or experiences to meet individual users' needs and preferences. They will use data analytics and artificial intelligence to personalize sensory experiences according to an individual's preferences and profiles (Hilken *et al.,* 2022). Through real-time data collection and analysis, marketers can create highly personalized multi-sensory experiences that connect with individuals, resulting in more consumer engagement and, hence, more loyalty. Virtual Reality Shopping refers to using virtual reality (VR) technology to transform shopping by enabling customers to take part in fully immersive virtual shopping from the convenience of their homes (Laukkanen *et al.,* 2022). Virtual reality and artificial intelligence have brought a paradigm shift in almost every arena (Arora & Sharma, 2023; Arora, 2024). Consumers can roam through virtual storefronts, try out items, and interact with companies in realistic settings, thereby increasing convenience and widening access to international markets. The Sensory Internet of Things (IoT) is when an IoT network has been integrated with sensors. Combining these two marketing tools will enable marketers to develop intelligent, interconnected environments sensitive to consumers' changing tastes and habits (Okorie *et al.,* 2024). Thus, smart homes, retail businesses, public spaces, etc., may have sensors automatically adjusting illumination, temperature, and music based on occupants' preferences, among other stimuli, for higher comfort levels and personalized experience design. Brands will employ multi-sensory storytelling techniques to create immersive storylines that stimulate different senses and evoke emotional responses (Zha *et al.,* 2022). Brands will use different sensory tools- vision, sound, touch, taste, and smell – to engage their customers in the storylines of their narratives, thus creating a lasting impact through interactive digital content and experiential marketing events. Brands will employ biometric monitoring and emotional targeting approaches to evaluate and enhance sensory experiences' emotional power. Firms can track such aspects as heart rate, skin conductance, or facial muscle contractility that reflect consumers' moods. Such information helps businesses to tailor sensory stimuli for greater involvement and persuasion. Augmented Sensory Realities refer to using augmented reality (AR) technology to enhance real-world sensory experiences. This is done by superimposing digital material onto physical settings in real-time (Antunes & Veríssimo, 2024). Consumers will improve their sense of reality through augmented reality (AR) devices, which overlay product information, ratings, and suggestions on actual products in a store. This would facilitate seamless integration between digital and physical senses. With increased consumer awareness about environmental concerns, firms will emphasize sustainability and ethical issues in their sensory marketing initiatives (Okorie *et al.,* 2024). They use sustainable methods like carbon-neutral fragrance delivery systems or eco-friendly packaging materials, therefore appealing to environmentally concerned clients who can identify with their values. Many aspects might shape the way sensory and multisensory experiences will be done in marketing in the future: hyper-personalization, virtual reality shopping, sensory Internet of Things (IoT), multi-sensory storytelling, biometric feedback, augmented sensory realities, and commitment to environmental sustainability. Adopting these current trends and advances by companies creates engaging and influential sensory experiences that involve customers actively in meaningful ways and ultimately enhance the success of their business.

PRACTICAL AND MANAGERIAL IMPLICATIONS

Modern brand strategies heavily rely on sensory storytelling techniques, which offer new methods of increasing brand commitment, bettering brand remembering, differentiating competitive environments, and fostering customer loyalty (Lindstrom, 2021). Brands can use their immersive power by creating events that appeal to customers' feelings through visual images or auditory impressions, among other things, such as smells, tastes, textures, and even flavors sometimes too (Hultén et al., 2011).

By employing sensory storytelling methods, brands connect with their customers emotionally, making it easy for people to recall and choose those brands in the future. Brands may achieve this by appealing to more than one sense using visual aids, sounds, smells, textures, and tastes, which can create unforgettable experiences that do not quickly fade from a customer's mind. Later in life, if someone needs some goods or services again, he/she will probably remember the positive encounter with a specific product's brand.

Sensory storytelling is not just a valuable tool for managers looking to position their brands strategically within the market. It also presents opportunities for innovation in products and services while obtaining insights from consumers, which can be used for integrated marketing communications or increasing employee engagement. Sensory experiences should be used in such a way that they fit well with desired perceptions and values to shape consumers' perception of what it means to them; this will eventually influence where, among other things like price point or features people place these brands against each other (Velasco, & Spence, 2019). Additionally, packaging design is needed more than ever before, given current trends within the industry itself. Sensory Storytelling can affect thinking deeply; it interrupts the cognitive engagement of the customer. Hence, brands need to make a lasting impression that will serve next time.

CONCLUSION

In the future, businesses should focus on sensory marketing and invest in immersive and personalized technology. Understanding the senses, using the emotional impacts of sensory stimuli, and innovation that meets customer expectations could help brands grow and create enduring brand experiences. The future of brand communication lies in multimodal marketing. This kind of marketing enables companies to interact with their clients in ways that go beyond traditional advertising methods by creating enduring impressions beyond logic. Implementing the multisensory revolution allows companies to differentiate themselves from competitors and build strong consumer relationships, resulting in brand loyalty, advocacy, and financial success. Businesses can rise above the competition by exploiting multiple senses to evoke memories. Sensory discrimination helps firms stand out and connect with their target audience. Consumers respond emotionally to sensory stimulation. Enjoyable sensory experiences may help brands generate emotional loyalty and lasting relationships. Engaging several senses boosts consumer engagement and attention. This greater participation creates lasting effects and a deeper brand relationship. By changing their perception of these elements, sensory elements in marketing can influence consumers' perceptions, preferences, buying intentions, etc. Brands can differentiate themselves through multimodal experiences necessary for deep consumer involvement in today's competitive markets. They create distinctive identities for consumers via immersive experiences that appeal to consumers' emotions or tastes. A business can stimulate its clients using sensing devices, thus opening up latent wants and providing continuity. Then, brands that actively engage emotionally invested customers will likely enjoy loyal repeat buyers. Through personalized sensorial experiences and interactive touch points, consumers partake actively in a brand's story, making it easier to form their opinions. Customers remember to advocate for those brands offering unique sensory experiences, leading to increased brand visibility and market domination. Consumer products like food, film, or perfumed candles might leave an everlasting impact on people's minds. Finally, Multimodal Marketing sets organizations apart from one another in reaching out to customers, thereby achieving success. Sight Touch Hearing Taste Smell. By engaging customers' senses of sight, hearing, touch, taste, and smell in these experiences, brands may create unforgettable ones. This might be achieved through visually attractive packaging, captivating videography, product feel, and representative fragrances that tell stories. Multimodal marketing has the most remarkable ability to differentiate brands and engage customers due to consumer discernment and technological advancements. In competitive marketplaces where multiple products are vying for attention, brands that achieve an emotional connection with their audience using multimodal techniques will stand out.

REFERENCES

Agapito, D., Pinto, P., & Mendes, J. (2012). Sensory marketing and tourist experiences. *Spatial and Organizational Dynamics Discussions Papers*, 10, 7–19.

Antunes, I. F. S., & Veríssimo, J. M. C. (2024). A bibliometric review and content analysis of research trends in sensory marketing. *Cogent Business & Management*, 11(1), 2338879. 10.1080/23311975.2024.2338879

Arora, M. (2023). Encapsulating Role of Persuasion and Skill Development in Marketing Communication for Brand Building: A Perspective. In *International Handbook of Skill, Education, Learning, and Research Development in Tourism and Hospitality* (pp. 1–17). Springer Nature Singapore.

Arora, M. (2024). Virtual Reality in Education: Analyzing the Literature and Bibliometric State of Knowledge. *Transforming Education with Virtual Reality*, 379-402.

Arora, M., & Sharma, R. L. (2023). Artificial intelligence and big data: ontological and communicative perspectives in multi-sectoral scenarios of modern businesses. *foresight*, 25(1), 126-143.

Bhatia, R., Garg, R., Chhikara, R., Kataria, A., & Talwar, V. (2021). Sensory marketing–a review and research agenda. *Academy of Marketing Studies Journal*, 25(4), 1–30.

Biswas, D., Szocs, C., & Abell, A. (2019). Extending the boundaries of sensory marketing and examining the sixth sensory system: Effects of vestibular sensations for sitting versus standing postures on food taste perception. *The Journal of Consumer Research*, 46(4), 708–724. 10.1093/jcr/ucz018

Buhalis, D., & Karatay, N. (2022). Mixed reality (MR) for Generation Z in cultural heritage tourism towards metaverse. In *Information and communication technologies in tourism 2022:Proceedings of the ENTER 2022 eTourism conference,* (pp. 16-27). Springer International Publishing.

Caissie, A. F., Riquier, L., De Revel, G., & Tempere, S. (2021). Representational and sensory cues as drivers of individual differences in expert quality assessment of red wines. *Food Quality and Preference*, 87, 104032. 10.1016/j.foodqual.2020.104032

Cornelio, P., Velasco, C., & Obrist, M. (2021). Multisensory integration as per technological advances: A review. *Frontiers in Neuroscience*, 15, 652611. 10.3389/fnins.2021.65261134239410

DeSalle, R. (2018). *Our senses: An immersive experience*. Yale University Press.

Dhiman, V., & Arora, M. (2024). Current State of Metaverse in Entrepreneurial Ecosystem: A Retrospective Analysis of Its Evolving Landscape. In *Exploring the Use of Metaverse in Business and Education* (pp. 73-87). IGI Global. 10.4018/979-8-3693-5868-9.ch005

Erenkol, A. D., & Merve, A. K. (2015). Sensory marketing. *Journal of Administrative Sciences and Policy Studies*, 3(1), 1–26. 10.15640/jasps.v3n1a1

Forrester Research. (2023). *Forrester: Generative AI Dominates Top 10 Emerging Technologies In 2023 and Beyond*. Forrester Research. https://www.forrester.com/press-newsroom/forrester-top-10-emerging-technologies-2023/

Herz, R. S. (2011). The emotional, cognitive, and biological basics of olfaction: Implications and considerations for scent marketing. *Sensory marketing*, 87–107.

Hilken, T., Chylinski, M., Keeling, D. I., Heller, J., de Ruyter, K., & Mahr, D. (2022). How to strategically choose or combine augmented and virtual reality for improved online experiential retailing. *Psychology and Marketing*, 39(3), 495–507. 10.1002/mar.21600

Hultén, B. (2011). Sensory marketing: The multi-sensory brand-experience concept. *European Business Review*, 23(3), 256–273. 10.1108/09555341111130245

Hultén, B., Broweus, N., & van Dijk, M. (2010). *Sensory marketing: Research on the sensuality of products*. Routledge.

Hussain, S. (2019). Sensory marketing strategies and consumer behavior: Sensible selling using all five senses. *IUP Journal of Business Strategy, 16*(3).

Jiménez-Marín, G., Alvarado, M. D. M. R., & González-Oñate, C. (2022). Application of Sensory Marketing Techniques at Marengo, a Small Sustainable Men's Fashion Store in Spain: Based on the Hulten, Broweus and van Dijk Model. *Sustainability (Basel)*, 14(19), 12547. 10.3390/su141912547

Kim, W. H., Lee, S. H., & Kim, K. S. (2020). Effects of sensory marketing on customer satisfaction and revisit intention in the hotel industry: The moderating roles of customers' prior experience and gender. *Anatolia*, 31(4), 523–535. 10.1080/13032917.2020.1783692

Koszembar-Wiklik, M. (2019). Sensory marketing–sensory communication and its social perception. *Communication Today*, 10(2), 146–156.

Krishna, A. (2012). An integrative review of sensory marketing: Engaging the senses to affect perception, judgment, and behavior. *Journal of Consumer Psychology*, 22(3), 332–351. 10.1016/j.jcps.2011.08.003

Krishna, A. (2013). *Customer sense: How the 5 senses influence buying behavior.* Springer. 10.1057/9781137346056

Kumar, J., Arora, M., & Erkol Bayram, G. (Eds.). (2024). *Exploring the Use of Metaverse in Business and Education.* IGI Global. 10.4018/979-8-3693-5868-9

Laukkanen, T., Xi, N., Hallikainen, H., Ruusunen, N., & Hamari, J. (2022). Virtual technologies supporting sustainable consumption: From a single-sensory stimulus to a multi-sensory experience. *International Journal of Information Management,* 63, 102455. 10.1016/j.ijinfomgt.2021.102455

Lelis, C., Leitao, S., Mealha, O., & Dunning, B. (2022). Typography: The constant vector of dynamic logos. *Visual Communication,* 21(1), 146–170. 10.1177/1470357220966775

Lindstrom, M. (2011). *Brand sense: Sensory secrets behind the stuff we buy.* Simon and Schuster.

Meyers-Levy, J., Bublitz, M. G., & Peracchio, L. A. (2011). The sounds of the marketplace: The role of audition in marketing. In *Sensory marketing.* Routledge.

Mishra, A., Shukla, A., Rana, N. P., & Dwivedi, Y. K. (2021). From "touch" to a "multisensory" experience: The impact of technology interface and product type on consumer responses. *Psychology and Marketing,* 38(3), 385–396. 10.1002/mar.21436

Nadanyiova, M., Kliestikova, J., & Kolencik, J. (2018). Sensory marketing from the perspective of a support tool for building brand value. *Economics and culture,* 15(1), 96-104.

Nielsen. (2022). *The need for consistent measurement in a digital-first landscape.* Nielsen. https://www.nielsen.com/insights/2023/need-for-consistent-measurement -2023-nielsen-annual-marketing-report/

Nwachukwu, D., Nwadighoha, E. E., Chukwu, E. N., & Udo, I. M. (2022). Gustative marketing strategy and customer patronage of restaurant businesses in Port Harcourt. *International Journal of Business & Entrepreneurship Research,* 13(6), 189–202.

Okorie, G. N., Udeh, C. A., & Adaga, E. M. (2024). Digital marketing in the age of IoT: A review of trends and impacts. *International Journal of Management & Entrepreneurship Research,* 6(1), 104–131. 10.51594/ijmer.v6i1.712

Randhir, R., Latasha, K., Tooraiven, P., & Monishan, B. (2016). Analysing the impact of sensory marketing on consumers: A case study of KFC. *Journal of US-China Public Administration,* 13(4), 278–292.

Rathee, R., & Rajain, P. (2017). Sensory marketing-investigating the use of five senses. *International Journal of Research in Finance and Marketing*, 7(5), 124–133.

Raz, C., Piper, D., Haller, R., Nicod, H., Dusart, N., & Giboreau, A. (2008). From sensory marketing to sensory design: How do consumers' input drive formulation? *Food Quality and Preference*, 19(8), 719–726. 10.1016/j.foodqual.2008.04.003

Rodgers, W., Yeung, F., Odindo, C., & Degbey, W. Y. (2021). Artificial intelligence-driven music biometrics influencing customers' retail buying behaviour. *Journal of Business Research*, 126, 401–414. 10.1016/j.jbusres.2020.12.039

Rottigni, F., & Spence, C. (2024). Crying over food: An extraordinary response to a multisensory eating experience. *International Journal of Gastronomy and Food Science*, 36, 100943. 10.1016/j.ijgfs.2024.100943

Roy, S., & Singh, P. (2023). The olfactory experience (in retail) scale: Construction, validation and generalisation. *Journal of Service Management*, 34(3), 403–432. 10.1108/JOSM-05-2021-0173

Rupini, R. V., & Nandagopal, R. (2015). A Study on the Influence of Senses and the Effectiveness of Sensory Branding. *Journal of Psychiatry*, 18(2), 236.

Shahid, S., Paul, J., Gilal, F. G., & Ansari, S. (2022). The role of sensory marketing and brand experience in building emotional attachment and brand loyalty in luxury retail stores. *Psychology and Marketing*, 39(7), 1398–1412. 10.1002/mar.21661

Singhal, S., & Khare, K. (2015). Does sense react for marketing–Sensory marketing. *International Journal of Management, IT and Engineering (IJMIE)*, 2249-0558.

Spence, C. (2022). Gastrophysics: Getting creative with pairing flavours. *International Journal of Gastronomy and Food Science*, 27, 100433. 10.1016/j.ijgfs.2021.100433

Spence, C. (2022). On the use of ambient odours to influence the multisensory experience of dining. *International Journal of Gastronomy and Food Science*, 27, 100444. 10.1016/j.ijgfs.2021.100444

Spence, C. (2022). Sensehacking the guest's multisensory hotel experience. *Frontiers in Psychology*, 13, 1014818. 10.3389/fpsyg.2022.101481836600704

Spence, C. (2023). Explaining visual shape–taste crossmodal correspondences. *Multisensory Research*, 36(4), 313–345. 10.1163/22134808-bja1009637080553

Spence, C. (2024). Multisensory sweetness enhancement: Comparing olfaction and vision. *Smell, Taste, Eat: The Role of the Chemical Senses in Eating Behaviour*, 17–28.

Spence, C., & Gallace, A. (2011). Multisensory design: Reaching out to touch the consumer. *Psychology and Marketing*, 28(3), 267–308. 10.1002/mar.20392

Spence, C., & Van Doorn, G. (2022). Visual communication via the design of food and beverage packaging. *Cognitive Research: Principles and Implications*, 7(1), 42. 10.1186/s41235-022-00391-935551542

Thangaleela, S., Sivamaruthi, B. S., Kesika, P., Bharathi, M., Kunaviktikul, W., Klunklin, A., Chanthapoon, C., & Chaiyasut, C. (2022). Essential oils, phytoncides, aromachology, and aromatherapy—A review. *Applied Sciences (Basel, Switzerland)*, 12(9), 4495. 10.3390/app12094495

Velasco, C., & Spence, C. (2019). The multisensory analysis of product packaging framework. *Multisensory packaging: Designing new product experiences*, 191-223.

Wala, A., Czyrka, K., & Frąś, J. (2019). Sensory branding and marketing stimulate the relationship between the buyer and the brand. *Organizacja i Zarządzanie: kwartalnik naukowy*, (1), 109-120.

Zha, D. (2021). Gustative signatures as corporate brand identifiers: exploring the sensuality of taste as a marketing strategy. In *Corporate Brand Design* (pp. 251–263). Routledge. 10.4324/9781003054153-21

Zha, D., Foroudi, P., Melewar, T. C., & Jin, Z. (2022). Experiencing the sense of the brand: The mining, processing and application of brand data through sensory brand experiences. *Qualitative Market Research*, 25(2), 205–232. 10.1108/QMR-09-2021-0118

Zhang, M., & Park, J. (2023). A Study of "Five Senses" in Application of Packaging Design of Products. *Studies in Art and Architecture*, 2(4), 43–49. 10.56397/SAA.2023.12.07

Zhou, Y., & Tse, C. S. (2022). Sweet taste brings happiness, but happiness does not taste sweet: The unidirectionality of taste-emotion metaphoric association. *Journal of Cognitive Psychology*, 34(3), 339–361. 10.1080/20445911.2021.2020797

Chapter 13
Behaviour Examining Sensorimotor and Affective Responses to Marketing Stimuli Through Neuropsychology

Rishi Prakash Shukla
https://orcid.org/0000-0003-0854-7302
Jaipuria Institute of Management, Jaipur, India

Sanjay Taneja
https://orcid.org/0000-0002-3632-4053
Graphic Era University, India

Prashant S. Gundawar
Sasmira Group, India

Ravi Kumar Jain
https://orcid.org/0000-0001-9912-8730
Sparsh Global Business School, India

Priya Shukla
Independent Researcher, India

ABSTRACT

Neuromarketing integrates neuroscience, psychology, and marketing to explore

DOI: 10.4018/979-8-3693-4236-7.ch013

consumers' subconscious and emotional reactions to marketing stimuli. This inter-disciplinary approach utilizes advanced neuroimaging and psychophysiological techniques to provide deeper insights into consumer behavior. The research employs a comprehensive literature review and bibliometric analysis, revealing significant trends, gaps, and advancements in the field. The findings underscore the importance of integrating neuromarketing into advertising practices to create more compelling campaigns that resonate with consumers' subconscious motivations. The study also highlights the evolution of neuromarketing technologies and methodologies, em-phasizing their practical applications in branding, pricing, advertising, packaging, and decision-making. By addressing research gaps and considering cultural and individual differences, this research contributes to both theoretical knowledge and practical marketing strategies, offering actionable insights for developing effective and engaging marketing campaigns.

INTRODUCTION

Neuromarketing is an advertising method that focuses on a person's feelings and emotions and part of the mind to establish a strong bond between both the client and the good or service. It is regarded as a multidisciplinary segment since it includes several different subjects like as psychological, sociological, advertising, and neu-rology. It takes into account the examination of emotional emotions or responses, as well as an (Shaw & Bagozzi, 2018) individual's overall activity, to different advertising methods. . Neuromarketing is the on-the-ground use of neuroscien-tific technique in the marketing profession. Neuromarketing is the use of 7 direct neuroimaging, measuring technology, scans to identify a participant's response to certain items, labeling, advertisements, and different advertising factors. Because the respondent may not always comprehend the brain reactions analyzed (Barlow et al., 2004) by these approaches, they can be more illuminating than information acquired through interviews, focus group discussions, and other methods. The term neuro-culture relates to neuro-biology fields. It is the cradle of new scientific dis-ciplines like neuroethology and neuro-philosophy, which merge neuroscience with other scientific disciplines.

Neuromarketing, as explored in the chapter, represents a crucial evolution in advertising and consumer behavior research due to its ability to uncover sub-conscious responses and emotional triggers that traditional methods often miss. Unlike conventional market research techniques like surveys or focus groups, neuromarketing utilizes advanced neuroscientific tools such as EEG, fMRI, and eye-tracking to directly measure brain activity and physiological responses. This approach provides marketers with deeper insights into how consumers perceive and react to marketing stimuli on a neurological level, revealing implicit preferences, decision-making processes, and emotional engagement that influence purchasing behavior. By understanding these underlying neural mechanisms, advertisers can optimize their strategies to create more compelling campaigns that resonate with consumers' subconscious desires and motivations. Thus, integrating neuromarketing into advertising practices is essential not only for enhancing effectiveness and ROI but also for staying ahead in an increasingly competitive marketplace where understanding consumer psychology is paramount.

Background

Neuromarketing is an interdisciplinary field that merges neuroscience, psychology, and marketing to investigate the subconscious reactions and emotional responses of consumers to various marketing stimuli. This innovative approach leverages advanced neuroimaging techniques and psychophysiological measurements to gain deeper insights into consumer behavior. By analyzing brain activity, eye movements, and other physiological responses, neuromarketing aims to uncover the underlying mechanisms that drive consumer decisions, thereby allowing marketers to tailor their strategies more effectively. *Approaches of*

Neuromarketing

Electroencephalography (EEG) is an electrical representation of brain function. An electroencephalogram (EEG) is a test that uses tiny metal discs (electrodes) connected to your scalp to detect electrical activity in your brain. Your brain cells communicate by electrical impulses and are always active, even when you're sleeping(Waterlander et al., 2015) . The electrodes are wearable and may be worn on the head. A helmet or cap containing electrodes is placed on the individual's head, followed by a display of productsand services. Brain activity can be utilized to assess a product's relative attractiveness to consumers. Functional Magnetic Resonance Imaging (fMRI) is an approach that investigates the anatomic anatomy of the brain as well as blood flow regulation. (An MRI scan is performed conducted in order to determine blood oxygen levels. It is characterized by an increase in neural activity in that area (van Herpen et al., 2009). FMRI is a neuromarketing technology that examines differences in brain activity (Krampe et al., 2018) between different people. Eye-tracking has been used to assess the major emphasis of a person's visual attention, as well as their reaction to visual stimulation. Sensations, gazing movements, ability to concentrate, and pupils' alterations are all examples of pupil changes. The amount of time spent focusing, the item targeted, and the duration of concentration are all measured by the eye-tracking.

1. Application of Neuromarketing
    a.   . Branding

To begin with, as contrasted to other producers, the consumer's branding and attachment to the favoured company are tied to the powerful emotions formed throughout the judgement process. This highlights the importance of brand engagement, and advertisers should seize the. As per fMRI studies, favoured brands exhibited more brainwave activity than popular brands. As a result, strategic plan and very well trademarks are significant parts of marketing, advertising, and marketing tactics that marketers' assets must heed (Boccia et al., 2019).

b. Pricing

It is an important factor that may influence a customer's buying decision. Setting a suitable price for an outcome, whether it is a service or a product, is a key part of purchasing choices. The most challenging aspect of marketing is determining a product's pricing and its relevance to a customer's purchasing decision. Many advertising and marketing studies have lately been undertaken since pricing is a key component in selecting how to present items to customers and display them to customers. Price is an important consideration since, in most circumstances, costs and benefits are considered.

c. Advertising

Several areas of the brain are stimulated by advertisements. Advertisements that are effective activate the medial striatum and dorsomedial frontal cortex in the brain. The research found that good face features in advertising have a beneficial impact. On an interpersonal basis, neuromarketing tools can accurately analyses an advertisement's response and effectiveness. Advertisements can influence the midline frontal cortex's judgement region, leading to greater revenue.

d. Packaging

As everyone is fascinated in packaging(Armstrong et al., 2006) that is particularly well-placed or enticing. Advertisers have long realized that whatever is on the exterior isn't usually what is on the inside, but neuroscience has pushed (Barlow et al., 2004)this to a whole new level. Customers were shown in trials to package, and their responses have indeed been recorded as positive, negative, or neutral. Additionally, they have indeed been extremely well enquired about color, language, and pictures. According to this survey, customers had a negative reaction to smooth packaging but a positive one to matte packaging.

e.   Decision making

There are 5 stages of decision-making in neuromarketing. Identifying the challenge, examining the alternative options, take a choice after weighing the possibilities, considering the likely consequences of actions(Van Kerrebroeck et al., 2017), and benefiting from the decision-making process in the future[are all part of this process(Heilbronner et al., 2009). As previously said, this type of decision-making is a branding and marketing method that may be investigated using functional magnetic resonance imaging neuromarketing strategies.

Justification of the Topic

The increasing complexity and competitiveness of today's market necessitates more sophisticated tools for understanding consumer behavior. Traditional methods such as surveys and focus groups, while valuable, often fail to capture the subconscious processes that significantly influence purchasing decisions. Neuromarketing fills this gap by providing a direct window into the brain's responses to marketing stimuli. This capability is critical for developing marketing campaigns that resonate on a deeper emotional level, enhancing the efficacy of advertising efforts and driving higher engagement and sales.

Research Gap

The research gap in neuromarketing pertaining to sensorimotor and affective responses to marketing stimuli necessitates further exploration to enrich our understanding and application of consumer behavior insights. Current studies predominantly focus on cognitive and emotional responses, overlooking the influence of sensorimotor interactions and failing to adequately account for cultural and individual differences in consumer responses. Addressing these gaps would not only deepen our theoretical understanding but also enhance the practical relevance of neuromarketing in developing targeted and effective marketing strategies. By integrating sensorimotor responses, considering cultural nuances, and conducting longitudinal studies in real-world settings, neuromarketing can offer more robust insights into consumer behavior, thereby empowering marketers to create more engaging and impactful marketing campaigns tailored to diverse consumer demographics and preferences.

Evolution

Neuromarketing has evolved significantly since its inception, with advancements in technology playing a pivotal role. Early studies relied heavily on basic neuroimaging techniques, but the field has since expanded to incorporate a variety of tools, including Electroencephalography (EEG), Functional Magnetic Resonance Imaging (fMRI), and eye-tracking. These technologies enable researchers to observe real-time brain activity, measure blood flow changes, and track eye movements, providing a comprehensive view of how consumers interact with marketing stimuli. Over time, the integration of these techniques has led to more nuanced insights into consumer behavior, paving the way for more targeted and effective marketing strategies.

Expected Contribution

This research aims to enhance the field of neuromarketing by examining sensorimotor and affective responses to marketing stimuli through a neuropsychological lens. By incorporating sensorimotor interactions and considering cultural and individual differences, the study will provide a more comprehensive understanding of consumer behavior. The findings are expected to contribute to both theory and practice by:

- Expanding Theoretical Knowledge: Providing new insights into the sensorimotor aspects of consumer responses and their interplay with affective reactions.
- Practical Applications: Offering actionable insights for marketers to design more engaging and impactful campaigns tailored to diverse consumer groups.
- Methodological Advancements: Demonstrating the value of integrating multiple neuroimaging and psychophysiological techniques in neuromarketing research.

By addressing these aspects, the study aims to enrich the neuromarketing literature and offer practical guidance for developing more effective marketing strategies that resonate with consumers on a deeper, subconscious level.

LITERATURE REVIEW AND METHODOLOGY

Literature Review: The literature review (LR) was conducted by systematically identifying and synthesizing recent studies that contribute to understanding consumer behavior and marketing strategies through neuropsychological and related methodologies. Key academic databases and journals were searched using relevant keywords such as "neuromarketing," "consumer behavior," "EEG," "fMRI," "virtual reality," and "marketing communication." Peer-reviewed articles were selected based on their relevance to the topic and quality of research methodology. Each study was critically reviewed to extract key findings, methodologies employed (such as experimental designs, neuroscientific techniques, and data analysis methods), and theoretical contributions to the field. The synthesis of these studies aimed to provide a comprehensive overview of current trends, gaps, and advancements in neuromarketing and consumer behavior research. By integrating findings from diverse disciplines including neuroscience, psychology, and marketing, the LR offers insights into how neuroscientific methods and virtual reality are utilized to enhance understanding of consumer responses to marketing stimuli in both traditional and digital environments.

Methodology: There are five major phases to this study: search, discoveries, analysis, and firms., result and conclusion. The method of this investigation begins with the use of the core term "neuromarketing" in the Scopus database. Following that, the outcome phase was able to obtain a total of 362 articles published from 2007 to 2022. We concentrated on unearthing the facts in the next step of our research. We concentrated on several elements, such as document kinds, authors, sources, and nations. The final stage of our research involved doing bibliometric analysis and retrieving the data. The neuromarketing bibliometric analysis in this research was built using R, an open-source statistical tool. Specifically, we installed and utilized bibliometric, which is accessible in the R library, and then we used bibliophagy to perform our study. We also utilize Excel to ensure the visualization of our research.

BIBLIOMETRIC ANALYSIS

Bibliometrics is a useful method for assessing research output and understanding the level of knowledge in a specific topic (Dhiman & Arora (2024)a; Dhiman & Arora (2024) b; Dhiman & Arora (2024)c; Dhiman & Arora, (2024)d. Our study's bibliometric analysis is organized into many categories, each with many sub-categories. The primary categories include article descriptive statistics, author analysis, country analysis, citation analysis, co-word analysis, cooperation network, and thematic mapping. To make a collaboration network we use the Louvain method of clustering with association normalization. To get more clear networks we use minimum 3 edges with 0.3 repulsion force and uses 50 nodes. For doing our co-words analysis we use authors keywords only. The articles were published in 223 different journals, booklets, conferences, and sessions. The number of keywords mentioned in the articles was thrice. There are a total of 1018 authors' keywords in 262 articles. There were 1035 authors in all, 46 of whom were single authors throughout all publications, and the remaining 989 papers each contained multiple authors. There were 2.86 authors per document, 0.35 authors per document, and 3.57 co-authors per document. The average number of documents per author was 0.35. Avoid combining SI and CGS units, such as a magnetic field in oersteds and current in amperes. Due to the fact that equations do not balance dimensionally, this frequently causes confusion. If mixed units must be used, be sure to specify them for each quantity you include in an equation.

ANNUAL SCIENTIFIC PRODUCTION

InFigure 1, Our research included 362 publications published between 2015 and 2022 in 233 different sources, he vast majority of which were from journals. The application of neuroscience techniques in marketing is a relatively new phenomenon.

Figure 1. Articles published per year

For the first time, in 2007, FUGATE DL in the United States identified the potential of neuroscience in marketing and coined the word NEUROMARKETING. This researcher began exploring the issue, and people were interested in it. The research activities were modest in the beginning, but from 2015 forward, the number of papers increased rapidly, with 66 being the most published paper in 2021. In the first quarter of this year, we already record published 12 papers.

a)   Average Citations per Year

The average number of citations per article and per year are shown in the **Table 1**, with the last column listing the years that were cited. The year with the most MeanTCperArt (127.75) was 2007, accompanied by 2008 and 2010 with MeanTCperArt of 65 and 61.81, respectively. Whereas the greatest number of MeanTCperYear(8.51) was in 2007, it was followed by 2017 and 2012, which had numbers of 6.05 and 5.4, respectively.

Table 1. Average citations per year

Year	Number of articles	Mean TC per Art	Mean TC per Year	Citable Years
2007	4	127.75	8.516666667	15
2008	4	65	4.642857143	14
2009	5	52.4	4.030769231	13
2010	11	61.81818182	5.151515152	12
2011	8	54.25	4.931818182	11
2012	17	54	5.4	10
2013	12	42.33333333	4.703703704	9
2014	15	29.4	3.675	8
2015	22	18.27272727	2.61038961	7
2016	23	18.04347826	3.007246377	6
2017	36	30.25	6.05	5
2018	31	15.16129032	3.790322581	4
2019	44	6.727272727	2.242424242	3
2020	52	4.442307692	2.221153846	2
2021	66	0.803030303	0.803030303	1
2022	12	0.083333333		0

b)   Most Relevant Sources

Figure 2 graph depicts the most recent sources where articles about neuro-marketing have been published. The most writers utilized the journal FRONTIERS IN PSY-CHOLOGY

Figure 2. Top ten most relevant sources

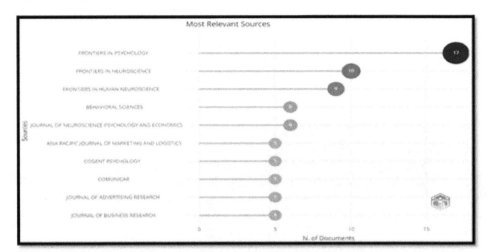

This journal published 17 papers, followed by Frontiers in neuroscience, which published 10 articles. We can see that there are journals of business and marketing where neuro-marketing papers were published, such as JOURNAL OF NEURO-SCIENCE, PSYCHOLOGY, AND ECONOMICS. We had seen 5 documents in JOURNAL OF ADVERTISING RESEARCH. As a result, journals are beginning to recognize neuroscience in marketing

c)   Source clustering through Bradford's Law

In **Figure 3**, Locating journals in a statistical literature is a significant feature of bibliometric analysis research, particularly Bradford's law of clustering which has applications in journal acquisitions policies in library and information. Bradford's law of clustering explains how publications on a specific (Hunt, 1983) subject is dispersed or transmitted in different journals, and he proposed that "if a scientific journal is arranged in order of decreasing productivity of articles on a given subject, they may be divided into a core of periodicals more particularly dedicated to the subject and several groups or zones containing the same number of articles as the nucleus." In our analysis we had 3 zone and major core sources follow in the zone 1 with highest frequency op paper in FRONTIERS IN PSYCHOLOGY.

Figure 3. Source clustering through Bradford's Law

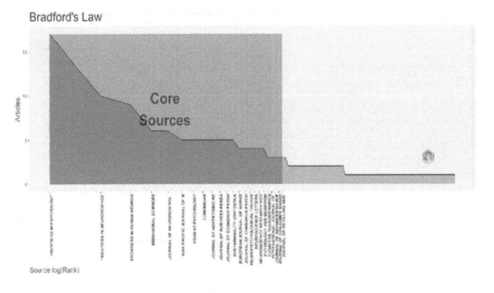

I.   Most Relevant Authors

In **Figure 4**, The top ten writers who produced research in the field of neuro-marketing are depicted in the column chart above. The most well-known and reputable author name is Babilonfi, who wrote the most papers in the neuroscience sector throughout the years. He has 11 research articles to his name, with MAQ coming in second with 9 papers published in this discipline. There were around 1035 authors that worked in this topic, but these were the most successful, having at least 5 research papers centered on neuro-marketing.

Figure 4. Top ten authors based on the number of articles

AUTHOR'S ESTIMATION

Author Productivity Through Lotka's Law

In **Table 2**, Lotka's law is concerned with the frequency and percentage of an author's production in a certain field. The current study attempts to investigate the application of Lotka's law in the application of neuroscience in marketing. The number of documents produced by the author is represented in the aforementioned documents, and the number of authors informs us of the frequency of publications. In our study, we had a total of 1035 writers, of which 878 only wrote one research article and had a probability of 0.848, and only 110 wrote two research papers and had a probability of 0.106. Out of the 1035 authors, only 47 wrote more than two research papers in the field of neuroscience.

Table 2. Author productivity through Lotka's law

Documents written	No. of Authors	Proportion of Authors
1	878	0.848
2	110	0.106

continued on following page

Table 2. Continued

Documents written	No. of Authors	Proportion of Authors
3	23	0.022
4	12	0.012
5	6	0.006
6	2	0.002
7	1	0.001
8	1	0.001
9	1	0.001
11	1	0.001

Figure 5. Frequency distribution of scientific productivity

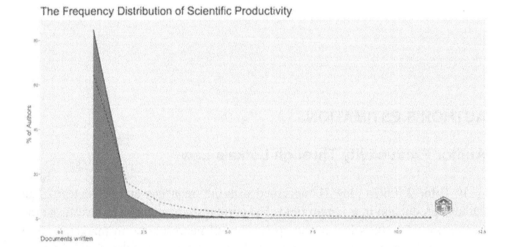

Authors' Production over Time

Figure 6. Top Authors' Production over time

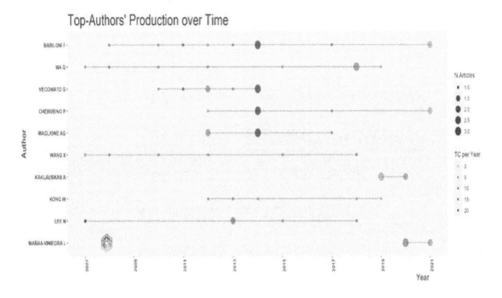

Figure 6. depicts the top ten authors' output over time. This is a timeline of top writers and their contributions to this field. In 2014, BABILONI F, VECCHIATO G, CHERUBINO P, and MAGLIONE AG each published three articles. BABILONI F, CHERUBINO P, MAAS-VINIEGRA L wrote two papers in the field of neuro-marketing last year in 2021.

Most Relevant Affiliations

Figure 7 depicts the top ten universities and the number of papers produced by their faculty and students. Most articles on neuro-marketing were published by Vilnius Gediminas Technical University. In this field, Zhejiang University has published 31 research papers. Three universities contributed 13 publications namely Complutense University Of Madrid, Sapienza University Of Rome, and Sungkyunkwan University

Figure 7. Top ten organisations based on the number of articles

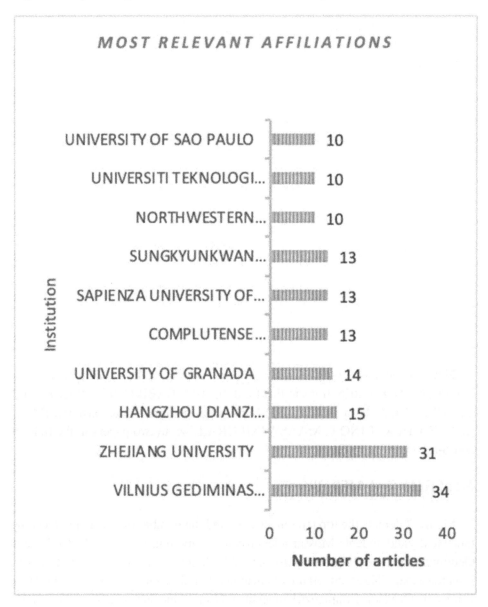

Country Scientific Production

The number of articles disseminated by different nations throughout the world is shown in the column chart above. The United States tops the list, with 134 publications in neuro-marketing submitted. Italy and Spain, two well-known European countries, were also strongly motivated to perform research in this field, with 129 and 128 published papers, respectively. China was just another prominent country, with 103 publications published working in this emerging topic.

Figure 8. Top ten countries based on the number of articles

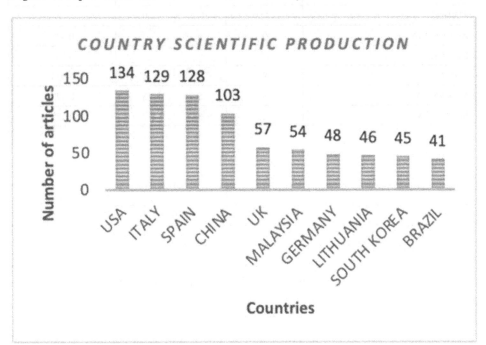

Corresponding Author's Country

The **Table 3** examines neuro-marketing articles for each nation in terms of single and multiple publications. It also attempts to examine the collaborative network that is taking place in various nations when it comes to publishing neuro-marketing publications. It demonstrates that certain nations, such as Turkey, India, and Iran, solely published in their own country without working with other countries.

Table 3. Neuro-marketing articles for each nation in terms of single and multiple publications

Country	Articles	SCP	MCP	MCP_Ratio
USA	31	24	7	0.226
SPAIN	30	25	5	0.167
CHINA	23	20	3	0.13
ITALY	17	10	7	0.412
UNITED KINGDOM	16	12	4	0.25
GERMANY	15	13	2	0.133
KOREA	12	9	3	0.25
TURKEY	11	11	0	0
AUSTRALIA	9	6	3	0.333
BRAZIL	9	6	3	0.333
JAPAN	9	5	4	0.444
MALAYSIA	8	5	3	0.375
SLOVAKIA	8	5	3	0.375
LITHUANIA	7	5	2	0.286
NETHERLANDS	7	4	3	0.429
IRAN	6	6	0	0
INDIA	5	5	0	0
POLAND	5	5	0	0
PORTUGAL	4	3	1	0.25
ROMANIA	4	4	0	0

Almost all authors from other nations like to collaborate with authors from other countries. According to the table, the top three leading countries are the United States, Spain, and China. Looking at the MCP ratio column, we can see that most nations operate alone or have few publications with many countries, with the exception of Italy and Japan. In this country, the ratio is more than 0.4, implying that half of total publications were produced in collaboration with other nations.

Figure 9. Corresponding author's country

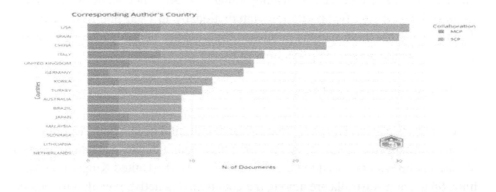

Figure 9 Corresponding Author's Country provides more impressive visual and simpler insights. It gives an insight into data that includes both single country publications (SCP) and multiple country publications (MCP) (MCP).

Most Cited Countries

Table 4. Country with a total of citations

Country	Total Citations	Average Article Citations
USA	1526	49.23
UNITED KINGDOM	618	38.62
ITALY	528	31.06
BRAZIL	463	51.44
AUSTRALIA	420	46.67
CHINA	324	14.09
POLAND	277	55.4
FRANCE	250	125
SPAIN	222	7.4
GERMANY	213	14.2

Table 4, displays the top ten cities and nations in the globe according to the number of citations that neuromarketing articles have earned from other academics. The total and average number of article citations are displayed in the table. From greatest to least, the results are arranged according to the total number of citations. There is a list in it. First place went to the United States, then the United Kingdom, then Italy. The table demonstrates that while some countries received less citations overall than others, their average article citations were generally higher.. Poland

(277–55.4), Brazil (463–51.44), and Australia (420–46.6) are the nations involved. This data reveals that, despite publishing a small number of publications, these three nations obtained significant citations internationally in each publication. It also demonstrates that these nations published high-quality neuro-marketing research publications rather than a large number of them.

Collaboration World Map

The map displays country collaboration across the globe, with blue indicating that partnership happens in that nation. The dark blue colour indicates a greater frequency of partnership with other nations. The United States, the United Kingdom, China, Italy, Spain, and Australia are among the countries that actively work with others.

Figure 10. Country collaboration map

Country Collaboration Map

The United States, China, and a few European nations follow China as the countries that collaborate the most in the release of neuro-marketing research, according to the map. It suggests that, in comparison to publications in a single country, multinational cooperation can increase the number of publications.

Most Global Cited Documents

Table 5. Top ten global cited documents

Paper	Total Citations	TC per Year	Normalized TC
LOPES AT, 2017, PATTERN RECOGN	437	72.8333	14.44628
LEE N, 2007, INT J PSYCHOPHYSIOL	356	22.25	2.78669
KHUSHABA RN, 2013, EXPERT SYS APPL	252	25.2	5.95276
REIMANN M, 2010, J CONSUM PSYCHOL	249	19.1538	4.02794
PLASSMANN H, 2012, J CONSUM PSYCHOL	235	21.3636	4.35185
DIMOKA A, 2011, INF SYST RES	179	14.9167	3.29954
FALK EB, 2012, PSYCHOL SCI	177	16.0909	3.27778
BERNS GS, 2012, J CONSUM PSYCHOL	153	13.9091	2.83333
BOKSEM MAS, 2015, J MARK RES	152	19	8.31841
OHME R, 2009, J NEUROSCI PSYCHOL ECON	141	10.0714	2.69084

Table 5: lists the author's names with the sources or journals that obtained a high citations from other publications and were ranked in the top 10. This data revealed that particular papers earned a high number of citations in specific years. Lopes AT article was perhaps the most cited paper, with 437 total citations and a mean of 72.83 per year. LEE N's work in the international journal of Psychophysiology received the second most citations, with 256 total citations at a rate of 22.25 per year.

Author's Keywords

The connection between keywords and neuromarketing is covered in **Table 6**. In their study publications, the researchers included several keywords and linked them to neuro--marketing. This is a crucial element since we need to examine trends in research, make appropriate referrals in the neuro-marketing sector, and identify fields of research where they are interested in combining with neuromarketing.

Table 6. Top ten author's keywords

Words	Occurrences
neuromarketing	254
EEG	37
consumer neuroscience	32
neuroscience	31

continued on following page

Table 6. Continued

Words	Occurrences
marketing	26
emotion	20
neuroeconomics	20
advertising	19
eye tracking	19
FRMI	19

The table above shows the total number of the author's keywords that rank in the top ten. The list is dominated by neuro-marketing with 254 occurrences, followed by electroencephalography with 37 occurrences, and consumer neuroscience and neuroscience with 32 and 31 occurrences, respectively. We've also seen authors begin to combine the term "neuro" with other fields such as "neuro-economics" and "neuro-advertising."

WORD CLOUD

Figure 11 illustrates a word cloud of author keywords from neuromarketing article research publications. The graphic highlights general terminology in neuromarketing, such as neuroscience, eye tracking, decision-making, emotion, and FRMI. Aside from these broad categories, some of the most popular keywords include consumer behaviour, brand, marketing, and artificial intelligence.

Figure 11. Word cloud of keywords plus

Figure 12 that shows the hierarchical relationship between the keywords produced by hierarchical clustering is explained in the illustration. By measuring the height of multiple objects that are linked together in branches, it is used to allocate objects to clusters. Initially, the researchers are represented by social media in the dendrogram figure. Other than social media, the keywords in Neuromarketing publications are neuro-management(Baños et al., 2008). The graphic demonstrates that neuro-management topics are distinct from market research areas.

Figure 12. Author's keywords Tree map

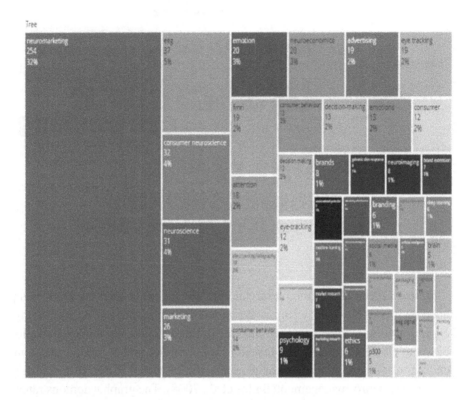

THREE-FIELDS PLOT BETWEEN COUNTRIES, AFFILIATION AND KEYWORDS

Figure 14 Three field plots show us images of universities from various nations focusing on certain keywords in the neuromarketing discipline. China's Zhejiang University was the most engaged in the field of neuromarketing. Northwest University in the United States is now focusing on two important fields known as marketing and economics, both of which are linked to neuroscience. Sapienza University of Rome in Italy is developing advanced technology known as electroencephalography.

Figure 13. Multi-fields plot between countries, affiliations, and keywords

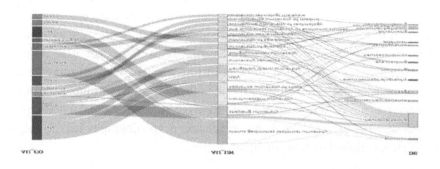

Trend Topic Analysing From Keywords

Figure 14 depicts the year's trend themes in this field. In 2019, the most popular keyword was "neuromarketing." The goal of research in 2020 is to create an eye-tracking gadget. When neuroscience became a popular topic in 2017, the neuromarketing notion began to gain traction. Last year, 2021, machine learning drew a lot of attention because everyone understands ML and Ai are the future.

Figure 14 Trend Topics of author's keywords over time

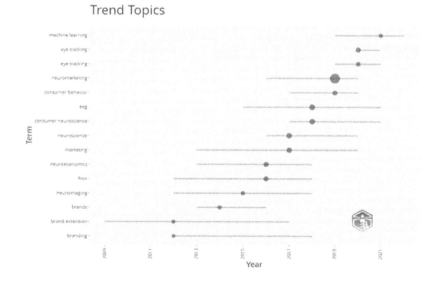

Authors' Keyword Co-Occurrences Network

Figure 15 It is critical for each author to incorporate keywords following the abstract in their research papers. These keywords are made up of the research fields that were used in the publications. The figure shows which fields were associated with neuromarketing study. It establishes the network's co-occurrences of the author's keywords. The network is separated into four distinct clusters, with neuromarketing as the dominant term in the red cluster, and the other keywords forming a network. Neuroscience was the most important keyword in the blue cluster, and it was linked to consumer neuroscience in the red cluster. Electroencephalography led the purple cluster, which was linked to neuroimaging.

Figure 15. Authors Keyword co-occurrences network

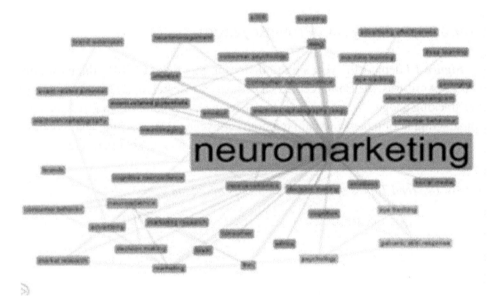

Institutions Collaboration Network

Figure 16. Institutions co-occurrences network

Authors Collaboration Network

Figure 16 To better comprehend the structure of academic contributions in this area, the author cooperation network was employed. The author Collaboration Network determines the presence of five key network clusters and estimates the number of collaborative publications between authors that contribute to knowledge progress in this field of study. There are two major clusters highlighted in red and purple that are very well related to each other. The largest circle in the red cluster is Babiloni F, who has the most articleas, while Mattia D leads the purple group.

Figure 17. Network of authors

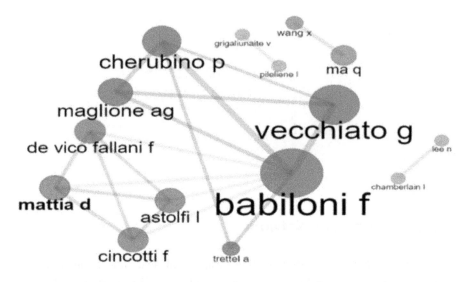

Countries Collaboration Network

Figure 17 Countries collaboration network connects writers from various countries and shows which countries collaborated. There were seven clusters in the above picture, with the largest cluster represented in red and led by the United States. We may deduce that nations such as Australia, India, Canada, and Mexico collaborated with the United States in the field of neuromarketing. The majority of European nations are clustered in blue and have tight ties with China, whereas Italy is linked to Spain, which is clustered in green. The purple cluster was led by the United Kingdom, and various Middle Eastern countries collaborated in this subject.

Figure 18. Countries collaboration network

Thematic mapping

Figure 18 Thematic mapping provides the display of 4 distinct topic categorisations, as illustrated in figure. The themed map makes advantage of the author's keyword field. The upper-right corner of the screen displays the motor themes. These are distinguished by their great centrality and density. The key worry among the "motor themes" that have received the most attention in the literature is eye tracking. The driving topic in our analysis is, of course, electroencephalography and cognitive neuroscience. This subject is linked to a variety of themes, including brand expansion, emotion, and advertising. In terms of neuro management it is linked to both neuroeconomics and neuromarketing. The upper-left quadrant exhibits high density themes but negligible external links, indicating that they are of low importance to the field (low centrality).It is possible to identify highly particular themes in this quadrant, which will restrict the branches to deal with. The subject of our study area is Multi criteria analysis video advertising.

Figure 19. Thematic map

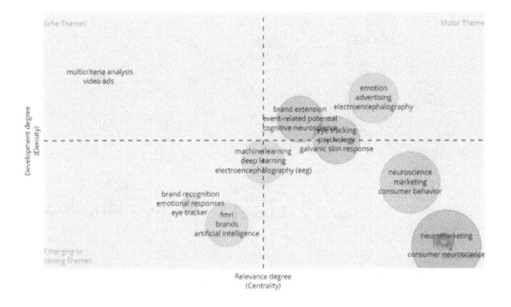

Figure 19 The emerging or declining themes are located in the lower-left quadrant. The concept of sensation emerges in this research, and it is linked again with artificial intelligence, fmri, and eye tracker. It's worth noting that one of the most frequently occurring words related with the concept of engagement is brand recognition. The need for brand recognition in order to manage business brand trust and loyalty, as employed in neuromarketing.

Historical Direct Citation Network

A historical direct citation network that employs a chronological citation network creates the intellectual structure. It does, after all, "provide a temporal map of the most relevant citations deriving from a bibliographic collection. The most intriguing feature of this visualisation is not the author/s' names per se, but rather their areas of interest in neuromarketing and the subsequent discussion that researchers open in the scientific field.

Figure 20. Historical direct citation network

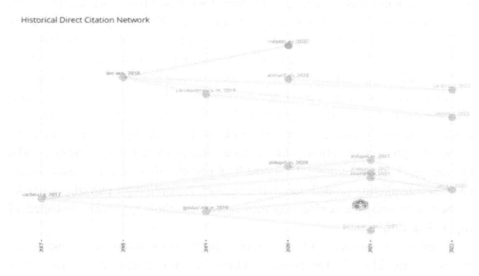

Finally, **Figure 20** the lower-right quadrant displays the fundamental and transversal themes. These themes tackle significant challenges that span the field's various subject areas.. Neuroscience, marketing, and consumer behaviour are emerging issues in this field. While the words machine learning and deep learning are used in every industry since these technologies will improve humanity's future, Certainly, the bibliometric research demonstrates that the topic of neuromarketing is highly associated with the phrase consumer happiness, which is assessed by analysing customer behaviour using various IT technologies.

DISCUSSION AND FUTURE RESEARCH DIRECTIONS

This study employed a descriptive and bibliometric analysis of published scientific papers on neuro-marketing in the Scopus database. For analysis, we use bibliometric: an r-tool for undertaking in-depth scientific mapping analysis. According to our research, the majority of publications focus on neuro-marketing implementation techniques such as EEG, FRMI, and eye tracking with the focus on consumer behaviour and purchasing patterns to do the right kind of advertising to make their brand more popular. We conducted a search for neuro-marketing using the title abstract and keyword search criteria to select suitable materials. We also performed bibliometric analysis to determine the worldwide neuro-marketing patterns include annual production with citations of the most productive sources, nations, and academic institutions over the years. Institutions, writers, and other types of keyword analysis are all examples of this. According to our findings, this is a fairly new issue that has been attracting researchers for the past five years, and the yearly production of publications has been steadily increasing. The most productive country is the United States, which has 134 documents and 1526 total citations. Italy was next, followed by Italy came in second with 129 papers, while Spain came in third with 128. The United States is presently collaborating with almost every country, including Australia, China, and European countries. Vilnius Gediminas technical university in Lithuania was the most productive university in terms of publishing articles in neuro-marketing, followed by Zhejiang University in China. Babilonfi is the most productive author, with 11 documents produced, and followed by MA Q, who has 9 papers published. Almost 84.8 percent of writers have only written one neuro-marketing-related paper. The authors' top option for publishing articles connected to neuro-marketing was Frontiers In Psychology, which published 17 papers linked to it.

Based on our analysis, we determined the topic for future study and which researcher should do it. The growing subject in neuro-marketing was the use of neuro-marketing to build brand recall in the brains of customers. Second is employing an eye tracking gadget to collect client feedback in order to develop a marketing strategy. Learn and uncover additional strategies for emotional marketing by studying neuroscience. In terms of technology, there is a lot of room for advancement in the EEG and FRMI processes.

CONCLUSION

This investigation give an outline of Neuro-marketing research and the number of publications, providing 362 articles from Scopus database. We learned from the studies that the corporation is transitioning from traditional marketing techniques to a new phenomenon known as neuro-marketing with the support of developing IT technologies and advancements in the medical area. Companies begin adopting EEG, FRMI, and eye tracking techniques to optimise pricing and packaging, raise brand awareness, and use selective approach advertising approaches. Neuro-marketing field approaches inform companies about their customers' patterns and behaviours, as well as the psychology underlying their decision-making criteria, allowing them to employ the most effective marketing strategies to increase sales. This work sought to minimise technique flaws, yet there are still shortcomings that present potential for further academic research. For example, this study focuses on articles in the neuro-marketing sector that have been published in English. One of the other constraints is that we only use data from the Scopus database. There might be articles in other databases as well.

REFERENCES

Armstrong, K. M., Fitzgerald, J. K., & Moore, T. (2006). Changes in Visual Receptive Fields with Microstimulation of Frontal Cortex. *Neuron*, 50(5), 791–798. 10.1016/j.neuron.2006.05.01016731516

Baños, R. M., Botella, C., Rubió, I., Quero, S., García-Palacios, A., & Alcañiz, M. (2008). Presence and emotions in virtual environments: The influence of stereoscopy. *Cyberpsychology and Behavior, 11*(1), 1–8. 10.1089/cpb.2007.9936

Barlow, A. K. J., Siddiqui, N. Q., & Mannion, M. (2004). Developments in information and communication technologies for retail marketing channels. *International Journal of Retail & Distribution Management, 32*(3), 157–163. 10.1108/09590550410524948

Boccia, F., Malgeri Manzo, R., & Covino, D. (2019). Consumer behavior and corporate social responsibility: An evaluation by a choice experiment. *Corporate Social Responsibility and Environmental Management, 26*(1), 97–105. 10.1002/csr.1661

Casado-Aranda, L. A., Liébana-Cabanillas, F., & Sánchez-Fernández, J. (2018). A Neuropsychological Study on How Consumers Process Risky and Secure E-payments. *Journal of Interactive Marketing, 43*, 151–164. 10.1016/j.intmar.2018.03.001

Dhiman, V., & Arora, M. (2024). Exploring the linkage between business incubation and entrepreneurship: understanding trends, themes and future research agenda. *LBS Journal of Management & Research.*

Dhiman, V., & Arora, M. (2024). Current State of Metaverse in Entrepreneurial Ecosystem: A Retrospective Analysis of Its Evolving Landscape. In *Exploring the Use of Metaverse in Business and Education* (pp. 73-87). IGI Global.

Heilbronner, R. L., Sweet, J. J., Morgan, J. E., Larrabee, G. J., & Millis, S. R. (2009). American academy of clinical neuropsychology consensus conference statement on the neuropsychological assessment of effort, response bias, and malingering. In *Clinical Neuropsychologist, 23*(7). 10.1080/13854040903155063

Hunt, S. D. (1983). General Theories and the Fundamental Explananda of Marketing. *Journal of Marketing, 47*(4), 9–17. 10.1177/002224298304700402

Krampe, C., Strelow, E., Haas, A., & Kenning, P. (2018). The application of mobile fNIRS to "shopper neuroscience" – first insights from a merchandising communication study. *European Journal of Marketing, 52*(1–2), 244–259. 10.1108/EJM-12-2016-0727

Shaw, S. D., & Bagozzi, R. P. (2018). The neuropsychology of consumer behavior and marketing. *Consumer Psychology Review, 1*(1), 22–40. 10.1002/arcp.1006 van Herpen, E., Pieters, R., & Zeelenberg, M. (2009). When demand accelerates demand: Trailing the bandwagon☆. *Journal of Consumer Psychology, 19*(3), 302–312. 10.1016/j.jcps.2009.01.001

van Kerrebroeck, H., Brengman, M., & Willems, K. (2017). When brands come to life: experimental research on the vividness effect of Virtual Reality in transformational marketing communications. *Virtual Reality, 21*(4), 177–191. 10.1007/s10055-017-0306-3

Waterlander, W. E., Jiang, Y., Steenhuis, I. H. M., & Ni Mhurchu, C. (2015). Using a 3D virtual supermarket to measure food purchase behavior: A validation study. *Journal of Medical Internet Research, 17*(4), e107. 10.2196/jmir.3774

Chapter 14
Neurological Pathways to Impulse Buying in Virtual Reality

Roop Kamal
RIMT University, India & Chandigarh University, India

Yashmin Sofat
A.S. College, Khanna, India

Shipra
RIMT University, India

ABSTRACT

The objective of this chapter is to gain an understanding of how the immersive quality of virtual reality (VR) affects customer perception, emotional engagement, and brand memory. Furthermore, the chapter investigates the physiological responses that are triggered by virtual reality advertising. This chapter investigates the neurological correlates that are linked with virtual reality (VR) experiences. These correlates include activation patterns in regions of the brain that are involved in attention, memory encoding, and emotional processing. Additionally, this chapter addresses the potential for virtual reality (VR) advertising to elicit stronger emotional responses and boost brand memorability in comparison to traditional advertising forms. The ethical considerations are addressed. This chapter, in its entirety, makes a contribution to our understanding of the neurological mechanisms that are responsible for consumer responses to virtual reality advertising and offers insights into the consequences that this phenomenon has for both consumers and marketers.

DOI: 10.4018/979-8-3693-4236-7.ch014

INTRODUCTION

Virtual reality, or VR, is a simulated three-dimensional (3D) environment that lets users explore and interact with a virtual surrounding in a way that approximates reality, as it's perceived through the users' senses (Adeola et al., 2022). Virtual reality is the use of computer technology to create simulated environments (Kumar, Arora & Erkol Bayram, Eds., 2024). Virtual reality places the user inside a three-dimensional experience. Instead of viewing a screen in front of them, users are immersed in and interact with 3D worlds (Alsharif, 2023).

The evolution of marketing strategies has led to the incorporation of cutting-edge technology to captivate audiences with unprecedented experiences (Cardoso et al., 2022). Central to this technological revolution is the use of virtual reality (VR), which has emerged as an essential tool in engaging and delivering innovative content to consumers (Dhiman & Arora, 2024). VR's unique capability to create immersive environments makes it an ideal platform for marketers to distinguish their campaigns in a highly competitive environment (Garzón-Paredes 2023; Rathore & Arora,2024).

This marketing concept that used to be considered as a large fantasy is now growing and evolving in front of our eyes, getting the shape of a new technology called Virtual Reality. In fact, compared to other forms of marketing, the use of VR enables a consumer literally to 'immerse' himself in a world that is simulated with products and services, therefore, giving them a real feel of the product (Bhardwaj et al., 2023). This technology allows the spirit of marketing storytelling and can encourage experiential, involving campaigns that elicit an emotional response and thus are easier to recall. For instance, virtual showrooms to promote products using virtual reality enables the clients to navigate through a product in a 3D manner, travel through the world virtually can be an ideal example of a VR human experience. In addition, it strongly supports the creation of training and virtual tours necessary for preparing efficient travel and other services for consumers (Ismajli et al., 2022). Hence as technology advances and makes VR more available then more marketers will be using it as another effective tool in reaching consumers and distinguishing their brand from the rest. Through the use of virtual reality, there is a possibility of creating better marketing messages, more effective and memorable marketing communication and experiences hence a better way of consumer interest and consumer commitment (Ambika et al., 2023). Exemplary businesses and future oriented business take a lot of care on their business communication (Arora & Sharma, 2017). Further, artificial intelligence revolutionizes marketing and business operations by enabling data-driven decision-making, personalized customer experiences, and efficient process automation. It enhances targeting accuracy, optimizes campaigns, and improves overall operational efficiency across various industries ((Arora & Sharma, 2023). Big data plays a crucial role by providing actionable insights that drive strategic decision-making, enhance customer experiences, and optimize business processes (Arora & Sharma, 2021).

Types of Virtual Reality

Figure 1. Types of virtual reality

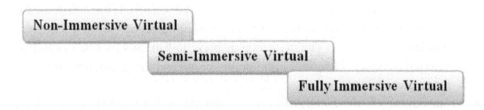

i.   **Non-Immersive Virtual Reality**: This category is often overlooked as VR simply because it's so common. Non-immersive VR technology features a computer-generated virtual environment where the user simultaneously remains aware and controlled by their physical environment (Alsharif et al.,2023). Video games are a prime example of non-immersive VR.

ii. **Semi-Immersive Virtual Reality**: This type of VR provides an experience partially based in a virtual environment (Cenizo,2022). This type of VR makes sense for educational and training purposes with graphical computing and large projector systems, such as flight simulators for pilot trainees.

iii. **Fully Immersive Virtual Reality:** Right now, there are no completely immersive VR technologies, but advances are so swift that they may be right around the corner. This type of VR generates the most realistic simulation experience, from sight to sound to sometimes even olfactory sensations (Goel, 2023). Car racing games are an example of immersive virtual reality that gives the user the sensation of speed and driving skills (Gill & Singh J 2022). Developed for gaming and other entertainment purposes, VR use in other sectors is increasing.

Hardware in Virtual Reality

Virtual reality hardware includes sensory accessories such as controllers, as well as headsets, hand trackers, treadmills and, for creators, 3D cameras.

1. **VR Headsets:** A VR headset is a head-mounted device, such as goggles. A VR headset is a visual screen or display. Headsets often include state-of-the-art sound, eye or head motion-tracking sensors or cameras.

   There are three main types of headsets:

   - PC-Based VR Headsets: PC headsets tend to be the highest-priced devices because they offer the most immersive experiences. These headsets are usually cable-tethered from the headset and powered by external hardware (Garima et al., 2021). The dedicated display, built-in motion sensors and an external camera tracker offer high-quality sound and image and head tracking for greater realism.
   - Standalone VR Headsets: All-in-one or standalone VR headsets are wireless, integrated pieces of hardware, such as tablets or phones (Kamal et al., 2024). Wireless VR headsets are not always standalone. Some systems transmit information wirelessly from consoles or PCs in proximity, and others use wired packs carried in a pocket or clipped to clothing.
   - Mobile Headsets: These shell devices use lenses that cover a smartphone. The lenses separate the screen to create a stereoscopic image that transforms a smartphone into a VR device. Mobile headsets are relatively inexpensive (Manpreet and Malhan, 2024)]. Wires are not needed because the phone does the processing. Phones don't offer the best visual experiences and are underpowered by game console- or PC-based VR (Gupta et al., 2023). They provide no positional tracking. The generated environment displays from a single point, and it is not possible to look around objects in a scene (Ambika et al., 2023).

2. **VR Accessories:** VR accessories are hardware products that facilitate VR technology. New devices are always in development to improve the immersive experience (Hazari & Sethna, 2023). Today's accessories include the 3D mouse, optical trackers, wired gloves, motion controllers, bodysuits, treadmills, and even smelling devices.

These are some of the accessories used today in VR:

- 3D Mouse: A 3D mouse is a control and pointing device designed for movement in virtual 3D spaces (Manpreet et al., 2023). 3D mice employ several methods to control 3D movement and 2D pointing, including accelerometers, multi-axis sensors, IR sensors and lights.

- Optical Trackers: Visual devices monitors the user's position (Massa and Ladhari 2023). The most common method for VR systems is to use one or multiple fixed video cameras to follow the tracked object or person.
- Wired Gloves: This type of device, worn on the hands, is also known as cyber gloves or data gloves. Various sensor technologies capture physical movement data (Misra 2023). Like an inertial or magnetic tracking device, a motion tracker attaches to capture the glove's rotation and global position data (Vinay et al., 2023). The glove software interprets movement. High-end versions provide haptic feedback or tactile stimulation, allowing a wired glove to be an output device.
- Motion Controllers: These accessories allow users to act in mixed reality. Controllers allow for fine-grained interaction with digital objects because they have a precise position in space (Sangeeta and Tondon, 2021).
- Omnidirectional Treadmills (ODTs): This accessory machine gives users the ability to move in any direction physically (Russo, 2022). ODTs allow users to move freely for a fully immersive experience in VR environments.
- Smelling Devices: Smell devices are one of the newer accessories in the VR world. Vaqso, a Tokyo-based company, offers a headset attachment that emits odors to convey the size and shape of a candy bar (Raji et al., 2024). The fan-equipped device holds several different smells that can change intensity based on the screen action.

Advantages of Virtual Reality

One of the primary significances of VR is its ability to create immersive experiences that can help individuals learn, practice, and explore in a safe and controlled environment.

1. **Time flexibility and location independence**: Virtual Reality makes it possible to hold meetings, training sessions, or conferences in virtual rooms. This eliminates the need to travel to the respective locations.
2. **Supports the personalization of virtual experiences**: Haptic and auditory stimuli are important in this context. In the long run, VR should allow for the customization of the user experience (Adeola et al., 2022). This would open up entirely new possibilities in the areas of marketing, entertainment, and education.
3. **Enhance Collaboration:** VR could make collaboration in companies much easier. At the same time, employees from various locations would be able to meet directly in the digital space.

4. **Immersive Gaming Experience:** Moreover, Virtual Reality technology has the potential to transform the entertainment industry, creating immersive gaming experiences that allow players to become fully immersed in a virtual world (Sood et al., 2022).

Applications of Virtual Reality

The following are some of the applications of virtual reality:

1. Industries: VR simulations have a wide range of applications, including training simulation, prototyping, designing, and testing tools and objects.

    Examples: Driving simulators, flight simulators for pilots, and combat simulators for military personnel are some of the most commonly used VR simulations in the industrial domain.

2. Healthcare: Virtual Reality is making a significant impact in healthcare. In 2021, the FDA approved prescription-use EaseVRx for the treatment of pain reduction in adults (Sood et al., 2022). The system uses cognitive behavioural therapy and other behavioural principles such as deep relaxation, attention-shifting, and others, to aid in the reduction of chronic pain.
3. Education: VR headsets are also useful in blocking out visual and auditory distractions, allowing teachers to interact one-on-one with students.

    For example: During the COVID-19 pandemic, there was a surge in virtual learning, with many classes held via online meeting platforms.

4. Social Interaction: Virtual Reality enables interaction with other users which provides an opportunity to create social connections. It also helps to create skill development (Arora, 2023).
5. Users can participate in virtual cognition training to improve their social skills, such as emotion recognition, social attribution, and analogical reasoning.
6. Travel and tourism: Users can enjoy immersive tourism in simulated environments based on real landscapes or locations with virtual tourism (Kajla et al., 2024). Virtual museum visits and navigating areas using apps such as Google Street View are examples of VR tourism.

VR Marketing

The concept of marketing in virtual reality isn't hard to grasp because it is exactly what it sounds like. Using VR technologies for promoting your product can come in various forms (Verma, 2023). For example, instead of reading a text about a certain business brand, you can watch and listen to a 3D avatar telling you about it and showing it to you in real-time. We call it VR customer engagement, which leads to increased brand awareness and generates interest in potential customers (Kajla et al., 2024). Marketing in VR involves the use of VR headsets, 3D environments, and interactive content to captivate and immerse the audience in a brand's message or products. Unlike traditional marketing channels, such as television or print, VR marketing allows customers to actively participate in the marketing campaign, providing a more memorable and personalized experience (Kim et al., 2023). Together with the technology of augmented reality, VR has become a powerful tool for realistic simulations in businesses. The idea is to transport users into a digital environment where they can interact with products, explore virtual showrooms, or take part in training and learning experiences.

Figure 2. Uses of virtual reality in marketing

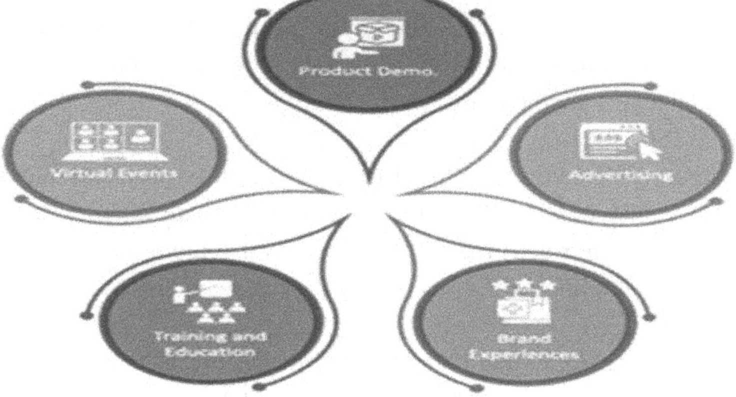

Source: https://www.sketchbubble.com/en/presentation-virtual-reality-vr-marketing.html

Existing and Possible Use Cases of Virtual Reality Marketing 2024 VR technology is used in different ways for marketing purposes, and here are some use cases that can be implemented inside the virtual reality market (Nilashi and Abumalloh, 2023).

1. Virtual Demos: In 2024, businesses can leverage VR technology to create immersive and engaging experiences for their customers. From automotive companies like Volvo showcasing their latest models to tech firms highlighting new gadgets, virtual product demonstrations offer a unique way to captivate audiences and drive sales.

2. Virtual Events and Conferences: Through VR technology, businesses can host virtual gatherings that offer the same level of user engagement as in-person events. Attendees can navigate virtual conference halls, interact with exhibitors, and attend keynote sessions, all from the comfort of their homes.

3. Virtual Store Experiences: In 2024, retailers are embracing VR and spatial computing applications to create digital storefronts that replicate the physical shopping experience. From browsing shelves to trying on virtual clothing, customers can enjoy a personalized and immersive shopping journey from anywhere in the world (Raj et al., 2023). This type of VR experience creates a desired lasting impression and can be considered a personalized experience.

4. Branding Through Virtual Influencers: Don't be surprised, as virtual influencers indeed exist! These digital ambassadors embody brand values and resonate with tech-savvy consumers, contributing to effective brand storytelling and customer engagement (Alvi, 2023).

5. Product Visualization: Now companies are leveraging VR to create lifelike 3D models of their products, giving customers a realistic preview of what to expect (Ambika et al., 2023). Whether its furniture placement in a virtual room or previewing a new smartphone design, product visualization is a real benefit of virtual reality marketing.

Incorporating VR into marketing strategies, known as VR marketing, has shown substantial effectiveness in captivating audiences (Ismajli 2022). For instance, in VR advertising, brands can create interactive ads that are more engaging than traditional media. The interactivity of VR ads increases consumer engagement and retention rates.

One notable area is virtual reality digital marketing, where digital campaigns are enhanced through the immersive capabilities of VR (Gupta et al., 2023). Such an approach offers a novel way for brands to interact with their digital audience, making marketing campaigns more memorable and impactful.

Companies Using VR Marketing

Virtual reality in marketing is not just a concept; it is a rapidly growing trend with numerous successful VR marketing examples. For instance, real estate companies use VR to offer virtual tours of properties, providing a realistic experience of the space without physical presence. Retail brands leverage VR to allow customers to try on clothes or preview products in a virtual space.

1. **Lenskart: Try New Specs**

Introducing Lenskart's Virtual Augmented Reality experience — a one-of-a-kind tool that makes it seamless to buy sunglasses and eyeglasses online (Gupta et al., 2023). Keeping the current pandemic in mind, we've designed a feature that lets you try and buy eyeglasses at the comfort of your home. This tool allows you to scan and analyze your face, detect your face shape and temple size, thereby suggesting frames that suit you the best (Adeola et al., 2022).

2. CaratLane: Mirror, mirror, on the wall, an interactive experience for them all

To address the customers' problem of not being able to see how a product looks on them while shopping online, CaratLane introduced the world's first virtual 3D jewellery Try-on app. The app uses facial recognition and 3D imaging technologies to provide a life-like immersive try-on experience for customers to discover a range of jewelry designs, try on earrings and buy jewelry. Once the app is downloaded, a user's laptop or mobile turns into a handy mirror and shows you how those earrings look when worn, from all sides.

3. Dulux and Asian Paint: Color Visualizer

These companies provide their users with a Color visualizer app to let them choose the best color combinations for their walls. The customers can try out different combinations virtually, decide which one looks the best, then save it. They can, then, purchase the same color in any store using the color codes (Adeola et al., 2022). This feature especially comes in handy for marketing during COVID-19 crisis when you cannot have people over your home to decide the color for your walls.

This virtual reality marketing worked really well for Asian Paints and Dulux. As a result, a lot of companies are following their heels and launching similar apps for determining the best look for their homes (Gupta et al., 2023). IKEA, for instance, introduced a similar app to let anyone choose multiple sets of furniture that suit their space.

VR and Customer Perception

The immersive quality of virtual reality (VR) significantly impacts customer perception across various dimensions, including product experience, brand engagement, and overall satisfaction in the following ways:

1. Enhanced Product Experience: VR offers consumers the opportunity to engage with products or services in a simulated environment that closely mimics real-world experiences. This immersive experience allows customers to interact with products in ways that traditional media cannot replicate. For example, trying on clothes virtually, experiencing travel destinations, or test-driving vehicles (Ismajli 2022). The heightened sensory experience in VR fosters a stronger emotional connection with the product, leading to more positive perceptions and increased purchase intentions.

2. Increased Brand Engagement: VR provides brands with a unique platform to create memorable and interactive experiences for consumer. By immersing customers in branded virtual environments, companies can deliver compelling narratives, showcase their values, and forge deeper connections with their target audience. The immersive nature of VR captivates attention and fosters greater engagement, leading to enhanced brand recall and positive brand associations (Bhardwaj et al., 2023).

3. Perceived Value and Differentiation: The immersive quality of VR can elevate the perceived value of products or services by offering customers novel and engaging experiences. Brands that leverage VR effectively can differentiate themselves from competitors and position their offerings as innovative and cutting-edge (Adeola et al., 2022). As a result, customers may perceive VR-enabled products or services as more desirable and be willing to pay a premium for the added value they provide.

4. Empowerment and Personalization: VR empowers customers to personalize their experiences based on their preferences and interests (Gupta et al., 2023).. Through customizable settings and interactive features, users can tailor their VR experiences to align with their individual tastes and needs. This sense of empowerment enhances customer satisfaction and fosters positive perceptions of the brand, as customers feel valued and understood.

5. Reduced Perceived Risk: In certain industries, such as real estate or tourism, VR can help mitigate the perceived risk associated with high-involvement purchases by allowing customers to preview products or services before making a commitment (Nilashi and Abumalloh 2023). By providing an immersive preview of the offering, VR enables customers to make more informed decisions, thereby reducing uncertainty and increasing confidence in their purchase.

Overall, the immersive quality of VR has a profound impact on customer perception by elevating product experiences, fostering brand engagement, enhancing perceived value, empowering customers, and reducing perceived risk. As VR technology continues to evolve, its potential to shape customer perceptions and drive business outcomes will only grow stronger.

VR and Emotional Engagement of Customers

Virtual reality (VR) has the potential to significantly enhance emotional engagement among customers through its immersive and interactive nature. Here's how VR can impact emotional engagement:

1. Emotional Immersion: VR creates a sense of presence and immersion by transporting users to virtual environments where they can interact with objects and experiences in a realistic manner (Nilashi and Abumalloh 2023). This immersion allows users to emotionally engage with the content on a deeper level, as they feel more connected to the virtual world and the experiences within it. Whether it's exploring a virtual art gallery, interacting with characters in a story, or experiencing a thrilling adventure, VR elicits emotions such as excitement, awe, and joy that enhance the overall engagement of users.

2. Empathy and Perspective-taking: VR can facilitate empathy and perspective-taking by enabling users to see the world from different viewpoints or inhabit the experiences of others. For example, immersive VR simulations can transport users to unfamiliar environments or place them in the shoes of individuals facing challenging circumstances, such as refugees or patients undergoing medical treatment. By allowing users to embody different perspectives, VR fosters empathy and emotional connection, leading to a more profound understanding of others' experiences (Adeola et al., 2022).

3. Personalized and Memorable Experiences: VR experiences can be personalized to cater to individual preferences, interests, and emotions. Whether it's customizing virtual environments, tailoring storytelling narratives, or incorporating interactive elements, VR allows brands to create experiences that resonate with users on a personal level (Bhardwaj et al., 2023). These personalized experiences leave a lasting impression on users and evoke strong emotional responses, making them more memorable and impactful.

4. Emotional Storytelling: VR provides a powerful platform for emotional storytelling, allowing brands to convey narratives in a highly immersive and compelling manner. By leveraging interactive storytelling techniques, such as branching narratives or user-driven experiences, brands can engage users emotionally and involve them in the unfolding story (Nilashi and Abumalloh 2023). Whether it's

evoking feelings of suspense, empathy, or inspiration, VR storytelling captivates users' attention and elicits emotional responses that deepen their engagement with the content.

5. Enhanced Social Connection: VR enables social interactions and shared experiences in virtual environments, fostering a sense of presence and connection among users. Whether it's collaborating on projects, attending virtual events, or interacting with friends in virtual spaces, VR facilitates meaningful social interactions that evoke emotions such as camaraderie, belonging, and solidarity. These social connections enhance emotional engagement and contribute to a sense of community among users.

Overall, VR has the potential to profoundly impact emotional engagement among customers by creating immersive experiences, fostering empathy and perspective-taking, personalizing content, leveraging emotional storytelling, and facilitating social connections (Ismajli 2022). As VR technology continues to advance, its ability to evoke emotions and create meaningful experiences will only grow stronger, making it a valuable tool for brands seeking to engage and connect with their audience on a deeper level (Ambika et al., 2023).

VR and Brand Memorability

Virtual Reality (VR) offers unique opportunities for brands to boost memorability through immersive and interactive experiences. Here's how VR can enhance brand memorability:

1. Multi-Sensory Engagement: VR engages users through multiple senses, including sight, sound, and sometimes touch. By immersing users in a 3D environment and providing audio-visual stimuli, VR creates a memorable experience that appeals to different sensory modalities (Ismajli 2022). This multi-sensory engagement enhances brand memorability by creating vivid and lasting impressions in users' minds.

2. Experiential Learning: VR allows users to learn about a brand, product, or service through experiential learning rather than passive consumption of information. Whether it's exploring a virtual showroom, interacting with product prototypes, or experiencing a branded virtual event, VR enables users to actively engage with the brand in a hands-on manner (Nilashi and Abumalloh 2023). This experiential learning approach facilitates deeper encoding of brand-related information in users' memory, leading to improved recall and memorability.

3. Emotional Connection: VR has the power to evoke strong emotions and create emotional connection with user. By immersing users in emotionally compelling narratives, virtual experiences, or branded environments, VR triggers emotional responses that enhance brand memorability (Ambika et al., 2023). Whether its excitement, awe, or nostalgia, the emotions elicited by VR leave a lasting impression on users and contribute to their memory of the brand.

4. Interactive Storytelling: VR enables brands to tell stories in a highly interactive and immersive manner. Through interactive storytelling experiences, users can actively participate in the narrative, make choices that shape the outcome, and explore different story paths. This interactivity not only engages users more deeply but also enhances their involvement and investment in the brand narrative, making it more (Adeola et al., 2022).

5. Personalized Experiences: VR experiences can be personalized to cater to individual preferences, interests, and demographics. By tailoring content and interactions based on user profiles or preferences, brands can create personalized experiences that resonate with users on a personal level (Kajla et al., 2024). These personalized experiences leave a stronger impression on users and increase the likelihood of brand memorability.

6. Novelty and Innovation: VR is still a relatively novel technology for many consumers, which makes VR experiences inherently memorable. Brands that leverage VR effectively can capitalize on this novelty factor to create memorable experiences that stand out in users' minds. By positioning themselves as innovators and early adopters of VR technology, brands can enhance their memorability and differentiate themselves from competitors.

Overall, VR boosts brand memorability by engaging users through multi-sensory experiences, facilitating experiential learning, evoking emotions, enabling interactive storytelling, offering personalized experiences, and capitalizing on novelty and innovation. The success of various entrepreneurial ventures depends upon innovation and creativity (Arora, 2016; Dhiman & Arora 2024; Arora & Sharma, 2021). In boosting new entrepreneurial business ventures and strengthening the existing ones, the AR and VR can play an important role. By leveraging the unique capabilities of VR, brands can create memorable experiences that leave a lasting impression on users and strengthen their brand identity and recall (Nilashi and Abumalloh, 2023).

VR and Metaverse

The metaverse is considered to be the further development of the concept of VR or the Virtual Reality, which is a set of connected large spaces where people can live, work, communicate and relax (Jeetesh et al., 2024). Therefore, as a virtual environment the metaverse is centralized to transform industries by allowing for unique interactions and experiences. Thus, it is especially important and valuable in VR for the improvement of users' experiences, for changes in social relationships, and for the generation of new types of economic activities.

An essential advantage that the metaverse conveys in VR is the one of offering rather realistic and engaging experiences. Regarding the type of the application, it is basically noted that the metaverse is conceptually drastically different from isolated and detached task-oriented traditional VR applications. It also increases possibilities of more diverse and interesting interactions that makes it possible to move around the vast virtual space, be in real life events, or be able to share in complex and multi-user events (Arora, 2024). For example, music concerts or sports games are equally accessible in the metaverse for millions of users from different parts of the world and let them feel numerous as if everyone is together.

Furthermore, the metaverse improves social relations in virtual reality by extending a way to find a reliable friend or a business partner. In the metaverse, people can build their own characters, communicate directly with others, and organize groups with similar objectives and interests. This capability redeems VR from being an isolated experience to a socially connected event thereby increasing a sense of fraternity. For example, avatars in the metaverse help the remote workers to collaborate better holding meetings, brainstorming and water cooler conversations in a virtual office setting. It also raises the level of efficiency and contributes to the strengthening of interpersonal relationships among the employees (Ambika et al., 2023).

Another area of relevance of the metaverse to the economy relates to the use of virtual reality. It also becomes very apparent that the metaverse is a very rich environment for business and entrepreneurship, given that it is primarily a digital economy in question. Assets in the metaverse include virtual lands, products, and services can be bought, traded, and sold thus opening new forms of commerce. Advertisers can have stores in the form of virtual stores, create unique and one-off events and have adverts within the metaverse that are immersive to users (Adeola et al., 2022). Furthermore, it means that content creators can make money on the contribution to the metaverse: for example, on the creation of objects or on the production of game elements, therefore encouraging a dense cycle of invention and trading in the social space.

The metaverse increases the capacities and uses of virtual reality exponentially through its unified, integrated and interactive nature. It is important in that it changes users' experiences, develops new types of social connections, and produces new types of value. Sure, as the metaverse grows, it will be instrumental in defining the further development of VR and expanding the opportunity to use it in different industries (Amran, 2022). Through adoption and use of the metaverse, everyone and anything from people to companies to society in large can benefit from virtual reality and enhance the manner in which people interact especially on the virtual platform.

Neurological Basis of VR Advertising Response

Understanding the neurological mechanisms underlying consumer responses to virtual reality (VR) advertising can provide valuable insights into the effectiveness of immersive marketing strategies. While research in this area is still evolving, several neurological processes likely play a role in shaping consumer reactions to VR advertising:

1. Emotional Processing: VR advertising has the potential to elicit strong emotional responses from viewers due to its immersive nature. Neuroimaging studies have shown that emotional stimuli activate regions of the brain associated with emotion processing, such as the amygdala and insula. When exposed to emotionally engaging VR content, these brain regions may be activated, leading to heightened emotional arousal and engagement with the advertising message (Adeola et al., 2022).

2. Presence and Immersion: Presence refers to the feeling of "being there" in a virtual environment, while immersion refers to the extent to which users feel engaged and absorbed in the VR experience. Neuroscientific research suggests that presence and immersion in VR are associated with activation of brain regions involved in spatial navigation, such as the hippocampus and parietal cortex, as well as regions associated with attention and executive control, such as the prefrontal cortex. These brain areas may contribute to the sense of presence and immersion experienced by viewers of VR advertising, enhancing their receptivity to brand messages.

3. Memory Encoding and Retrieval: VR advertising has the potential to enhance memory encoding and retrieval by providing multisensory and interactive experiences that engage multiple cognitive processes (Kajla et al., 2024). Neuroimaging studies have shown that encoding and retrieval of memories involve activation of brain regions such as the hippocampus, prefrontal cortex, and medial temporal lobe. When consumers engage with VR advertising, these brain regions may be activated, leading to more effective encoding and retrieval of brand-related information.

4. Reward Processing: Neuroscientific research suggests that reward processing plays a crucial role in motivating consumer behavior. VR advertising can activate brain regions associated with reward processing, such as the ventral striatum and orbitofrontal cortex, by providing enjoyable and engaging experiences. When

consumers find VR advertising rewarding, they may be more likely to develop positive attitudes toward the brand and engage in purchase behavior.

5. Mirror Neuron System: The mirror neuron system is involved in social cognition and empathy, allowing individuals to understand and resonate with the experiences of others. VR advertising that features relatable characters or scenarios may activate the mirror neuron system, leading to increased empathy and emotional connection with the brand message.

Overall, the neurological mechanisms underlying consumer responses to VR advertising involve complex interactions between emotional processing, presence and immersion, memory encoding and retrieval, reward processing, and social cognition. By gaining a better understanding of these mechanisms, marketers can design more effective VR advertising campaigns that resonate with consumers on a deeper level.

Limitations of Virtual Reality

Even though virtual reality is a powerful and versatile tool, current VR technology has some obvious limitations and drawbacks.

1. Privacy concern: A key VR privacy issue is the highly personal nature of the collected data i.e., biometric data such as iris or retina scans, fingerprints and handprints, face geometry, and voiceprints.
2. Technological limitations: Because of the lack of standardisation, it is difficult to troubleshoot bugs and receive proper support for any issues (Ambika et al., 2023). Other issues include Virtual Reality development software tends to take up a lot of data space on computers and has high power consumption.
3. Cyber sickness: Cyber sickness is a phenomenon where users will feel symptoms similar to motion sickness (i.e., nausea, and dizziness) as a result of using a VR device. A conflict occurs when there is an excessive mismatch between the motion a user perceives visually and the lack of the corresponding movement in their body.
4. Accessibility: The cost of VR headsets and VR-ready computers on the market is still higher making this out of reach for most people.
5. Security concern: If a hacker gains access to a VR headset's motion-tracking data, they can potentially use it to create a digital replica (also known as deep fakes) and thus undermine Virtual Reality security.

CONCLUSION

The study of the process of impulse buying at the neural level in the context of VR needs to be understood as an important contribution to the analysis of consumer behavior and the opportunity to create better marketing interventions. The inclusion of sensors in VR improves haptic feedback; this makes Virtual Reality more realistic and present. It is for this reason that the sense of being-present gets amplified and causes emotional reactions that can greatly affect the buying-decision.

Other studies show that impulse buying is strongly correlated with the stimulation of brain's pleasure center, related to dopamine or 'feel good' chemical. This is made even worse by VR environments, as they are immersive and presents the information in a very engaging and interesting manner that grabs one's attention and stirs up emotions. For instance, semi-automated VR buying or virtual shopping expeditions excite the brain's reward circuit far more than a typical e-shopping. The concept of experience zones wherein products can be tested from a distance, visit a store and the like increases the perception and actualization of possible purchases.

Besides, VR can appeal to social proof or the tendency to conform to large groups, another factor that affects impulse buying. The use of virtual social platforms and social presence in an actual or parallel reality environment ensures that the targeted audience is compelled to make purchases impulsively within environments that mimic the real world. From the information above, it can be also understood that using the possibility of individual approach to VR activities – choice of objects, preference, and behavior, it is possible to stimulate purchase impulse by showing the necessary product and promos at the best time.

Thus, knowing these neurological pathways, marketers can create VR experiences and build VR environments which would stimulate markets' impulse purchase, engage the viewers into more active, personalized, and socially interacting while shopping in VR. In the future, as technology in the VR system improves the chances are likely to heighten of changing consumer behaviour and thereby the chances of impulse buying are also expected to rise substantially thus proffering excellent opportunities in the domains of marketing and retail sale. Engaging the consumer, satisfying them and, consequently, increasing the rate of sales are possible by applying the VR technique.

REFERENCES

Adeola, O., Evans, O., Ndubuisi Edeh, J., & Adisa, I. (2022). The future of marketing: artificial intelligence, virtual reality, and neuromarketing. *Marketing communications and brand development in emerging economies Volume I: Contemporary and future perspectives*, 253-280.

Alsharif, A. H., Salleh, N. Z. M., Abdullah, M., Khraiwish, A., & Ashaari, A. (2023). Neuromarketing tools used in the marketing mix: A systematic literature and future research agenda. *SAGE Open*, 13(1), 21582440231156563. 10.1177/21582440231156563

Alvi, I. (2023). Investigating students' adoption of virtual reality for L2-learning in India. *Education and Information Technologies*, 1–22.

Ambika, A., Shin, H., & Jain, V. (2023). Immersive technologies and consumer behavior: A systematic review of two decades of research. *Australian Journal of Management*, •••, 03128962231181429. 10.1177/03128962231181429

Amran, A. S., Ibrahim, S. A. S., Malim, N. H. A. H., Hamzah, N., Sumari, P., Lutfi, S. L., & Abdullah, J. M. (2022). Data Acquisition and Data Processing using Electroencephalogram in Neuromarketing: A Review. *Pertanika Journal of Science & Technology*, 30(1), 19–33. 10.47836/pjst.30.1.02

Arora, M. (2016). Creative dimensions of entrepreneurship: A key to business innovation. *Pacific Business Review International*, 1(1), 255–259.

Arora, M. (2024). Virtual Reality in Education: Analyzing the Literature and Bibliometric State of Knowledge. *Transforming Education with Virtual Reality*, 379-402. 10.1002/9781394200498.ch22

Arora, M., & Sharma, R. L. (2017). Decoding diverse dimensions of entrepreneurial leadership with special emphasis on persuasive communication. *Management Dynamics*, 17(1), 70–77. 10.57198/2583-4932.1063

Arora, M., & Sharma, R. L. (2021). Repurposing the Role of Entrepreneurs in the Havoc of COVID-19. In *Entrepreneurship and Big Data* (pp. 229-250). CRC Press.

Arora, M., & Sharma, R. L. (2021). Neutralizing Maleficent Effects of COVID-19 Through Entrepreneurship: Peeping Through the Lens of Communication. In *Effective Strategies for Communicating Insights in Business* (pp. 67-86). IGI Global.

Arora, M., & Sharma, R. L. (2023). Artificial intelligence and big data: Ontological and communicative perspectives in multi-sectoral scenarios of modern businesses. *Foresight*, 25(1), 126–143. 10.1108/FS-10-2021-0216

Bhardwaj, S., Rana, G. A., Behl, A., & de Caceres, S. J. G. (2023). Exploring the boundaries of Neuromarketing through systematic investigation. *Journal of Business Research*, 154, 113371. 10.1016/j.jbusres.2022.113371

Cardoso, L., Chen, M. M., Araújo, A., de Almeida, G. G. F., Dias, F., & Moutinho, L. (2022). Accessing neuromarketing scientific performance: Research gaps and emerging topics. *Behavioral Sciences (Basel, Switzerland)*, 12(2), 55. 10.3390/bs1202005535200306

Casado-Aranda, L. A., Sánchez-Fernández, J., Bigne, E., & Smidts, A. (2023). The application of neuromarketing tools in communication research: A comprehensive review of trends. *Psychology and Marketing*, 40(9), 1737–1756. 10.1002/mar.21832

Cenizo, C. (2022). Neuromarketing: Concept, historical evolution and challenges. *Journal ICONO*, 14(20), 1.

Dhiman, V., & Arora, M. (2024). Current State of Metaverse in Entrepreneurial Ecosystem: A Retrospective Analysis of Its Evolving Landscape. In *Exploring the Use of Metaverse in Business and Education* (pp. 73-87). IGI Global. 10.4018/979-8-3693-5868-9.ch005

Dhiman, V., & Arora, M. (2024). Exploring the linkage between business incubation and entrepreneurship: understanding trends, themes and future research agenda. *LBS Journal of Management & Research*.

Garzón-Paredes, A. R., & Royo-Vela, M. (2023). Emotional and cognitive responses to cultural heritage: A neuromarketing experiment using virtual reality in the tourist destination image model context. *Journal of Positive Psychology and Wellbeing*, 7(2), 630–651.

Gill, R., & Singh, J. (2022). A study of neuromarketing techniques for proposing cost effective information driven framework for decision making. *Materials Today: Proceedings*, 49, 2969–2981. 10.1016/j.matpr.2020.08.730

. Goel, P., Mahadevan, K., & Punjani, K. K. (2023). Augmented and virtual reality in apparel industry: a bibliometric review and future research agenda. *foresight*, 25(2), 167-184.

Grima, S., Kizilkaya, M., Sood, K., & ErdemDelice, M. (2021). The perceived effectiveness of blockchain for digital operational risk resilience in the European Union insurance market sector. *Journal of Risk and Financial Management*, 14(8), 363. 10.3390/jrfm14080363

Gupta, M., Shalender, K., Singla, B., & Singh, N. (Eds.). (2023). *Applications of Neuromarketing in the Metaverse*. IGI Global. 10.4018/978-1-6684-8150-9

Hazari, S., & Sethna, B. N. (2023). A comparison of lifestyle marketing and brand influencer advertising for generation Z Instagram users. *Journal of Promotion Management*, 29(4), 491–534. 10.1080/10496491.2022.2163033

Ismajli, A., Ziberi, B., & Metushi, A. (2022). The impact of neuromarketing on consumer behaviour. *Corporate Governance and Organizational Behavior Review*, 6(2), 95–103. 10.22495/cgobrv6i2p9

Kajla, T., Raj, S., Kansra, P., Gupta, S. L., & Singh, N. (2024). Neuromarketing and consumer behavior: A bibliometric analysis. *Journal of Consumer Behaviour*, 23(2), 959–975. 10.1002/cb.2256

Kamal, R. (2024). *Artificial Intelligence-Powered Political Advertising: Harnessing Data-Driven Insights for Campaign Strategies*. IGI Global. 10.4018/979-8-3693-2964-1.ch006

Kaur, M. (2023). *Adapting to Technological Disruption: Challenges and Opportunities for Employment*. IEEE. .10.1109/ICCCIS60361.2023.10425266

Kaur, M., & Malhan, S. (2024). The Role of the Manufacturing Sector in Driving India's Long-Term Growth. Kumar, N., Sood, K., Özen, E. & Grima, S. (Ed.) *The Framework for Resilient Industry: A Holistic Approach for Developing Economies (Emerald Studies in Finance, Insurance, and Risk Management)*, Emerald Publishing Limited. 10.1108/978-1-83753-734-120241021

Kim, J. H., Kim, M., Park, M., & Yoo, J. (2023). Immersive interactive technologies and virtual shopping experiences: Differences in consumer perceptions between augmented reality (AR) and virtual reality (VR). *Telematics and Informatics*, 77, 101936. 10.1016/j.tele.2022.101936

Kumar, J., Arora, M., & Erkol Bayram, G. (Eds.). (2024). *Exploring the Use of Metaverse in Business and Education*. IGI Global. 10.4018/979-8-3693-5868-9

Massa, E., & Ladhari, R. (2023). Augmented reality in marketing: Conceptualization and systematic review. *International Journal of Consumer Studies*, 47(6), 2335–2366. 10.1111/ijcs.12930

Misra, L. (2023). Neuromarketing insights into consumer behavior. *IUJ Journal of Management*, 11(1), 143–163.

Mittal, A., Mantri, A., Tandon, U., & Dwivedi, Y. K. (2022). A unified perspective on the adoption of online teaching in higher education during the COVID-19 pandemic. *Information Discovery and Delivery*, 50(2), 117–132. 10.1108/IDD-09-2020-0114

Nilashi, M., & Abumalloh, R. A. (2023). Neuromarketing and Metaverse. *Journal of Soft Computing and Decision Support Systems*, 10(1), 1–3.

Raj, S., Sampat, B., Behl, A., & Jain, K. (2023). Understanding senior citizens' intentions to use virtual reality for religious tourism in India: A behavioural reasoning theory perspective. *Tourism Recreation Research*, 48(6), 983–999. 10.1080/02508281.2023.2246735

Raji, M. A., Olodo, H. B., Oke, T. T., Addy, W. A., Ofodile, O. C., & Oyewole, A. T. (2024). Business strategies in virtual reality: A review of market opportunities and consumer experience. *International Journal of Management & Entrepreneurship Research*, 6(3), 722–736. 10.51594/ijmer.v6i3.883

Rathore, S., & Arora, M. (2024). Sustainability Reporting in the Metaverse: A Multi-Sectoral Analysis. In *Exploring the Use of Metaverse in Business and Education* (pp. 147-165). IGI Global. 10.4018/979-8-3693-5868-9.ch009

Russo, V., Bilucaglia, M., & Zito, M. (2022). From virtual reality to augmented reality: A neuromarketing perspective. *Frontiers in Psychology*, 13, 965499. 10.3389/fpsyg.2022.96549936160557

Sangeeta, & Tandon, U. (2021). Factors influencing adoption of online teaching by school teachers: A study during COVID-19 pandemic. *Journal of Public Affairs, 21*(4).

Singh, V., Nanavati, B., Kar, A. K., & Gupta, A. (2023). How to maximize clicks for display advertisement in digital marketing? A reinforcement learning approach. *Information Systems Frontiers*, 25(4), 1621–1638. 10.1007/s10796-022-10314-0

Sood, K., Kaur, B., & Grima, S. (2022). Revamping Indian non-life insurance industry with a trusted network: Blockchain technology. In *Big Data: A game changer for insurance industry* (pp. 213-228). Emerald Publishing Limited.

Verma, J. (2023). Impact of Augmented Reality and Virtual Reality on Customer Purchase Behavior in the Virtual World. In *Applications of Neuromarketing in the Metaverse* (pp. 258–270). IGI Global.

Chapter 15
Modernizing Customer Experience Through Augmented– Virtual Reality in Emerging Markets:
Sensible Selling Towards Transforming Neuromarketing

Bhupinder Singh
https://orcid.org/0009-0006-4779-2553
Sharda University, Noida, India

Christian Kaunert
https://orcid.org/0000-0002-4493-2235
Dublin City University, Ireland

Rishabha Malviya
Galgotias University, India

ABSTRACT

The retail sector is experiencing a significant transformation through the integration of augmented reality (AR) and virtual reality (VR) technologies. The convergence of AR and VR is driving a substantial change in the dynamic and ever-evolving retail business. This integration is ushering in a new era of immersive and personalized shopping experiences, fundamentally altering how consumers engage with products and environments. Through AR applications, customers can effortlessly use their

DOI: 10.4018/979-8-3693-4236-7.ch015

smartphones to locate items, receive real-time promotions, and gain additional information about them. Augmented reality enables a virtual try-on experience, allowing buyers to visualize products in a virtual setting. This chapter explores the various applications, challenges and potential implications of AR and VR in the retail sector, highlighting the substantial transformations these technologies bring to the industry. Augmented reality is revolutionizing in-store navigation, providing consumers with an engaging and user-friendly navigational experience.

Introduction

The blending of augmented reality (AR) and virtual reality (VR) with the customer experience landscape has eliminated the boundaries between online and offline buying and created a plethora of opportunities to reach previously unheard-of levels of consumer happiness (Singha & Singha, 2024). The retail sector is experiencing a significant transformation through the integration of Augmented Reality (AR) and Virtual Reality (VR) technologies. The current retail landscape is undergoing a profound shift due to the incorporation of AR and VR technologies. The convergence of AR and VR is driving a substantial change in the dynamic and ever-evolving retail business. This integration is ushering in a new era of immersive and personalized shopping experiences, fundamentally altering how consumers engage with products and environments. Even though conventional retail has rebounded since the pandemic, a sizable percentage of consumers still choose to purchase online via e-commerce sites (Abrokwah-Larbi, 2024).

Through AR applications, customers can effortlessly use their smartphones to locate items, receive real-time promotions, and gain additional information about them. Augmented reality enables a virtual try-on experience, allowing buyers to visualize products in a virtual setting. Realistic AR simulations enable customers to virtually try on items and arrange furniture in their living spaces, enabling more informed purchasing decisions. The use of augmented reality has empowered retailers to offer highly tailored product recommendations. As a result, businesses in the e-commerce space that use technology innovations like augmented reality (AR) to enhance the user experience have been successful in drawing in new customers (Caboni & Hagberg, 2019). Before making a purchase, consumers may use Augmented Reality (AR) to see things in their real-world environments and get a virtual preview of ownership and use (Yang et al., 2024). From the seller's point of view, augmented reality (AR) is a novel way to communicate with customers by giving them individualized 3D product experiences and a contactless interface that allows them to interact with things in real time (Xue, 2022). Through realistic modeling of 3D virtual and actual things, this interaction takes place at the junction of the physical and virtual worlds (Moorhouse et al., 2018).

Digital technologies such as cloud computing, analytics, social media, mobile platforms, artificial intelligence and the Internet of Things have completely changed how businesses interact with their customers (Wang et al., 2024). AR is characterized as an interactive experience that takes place in the real world and augments real-world items with computer-generated perceptual information that covers a range of sensory modalities, including audio, visual, haptic, somatosensory and olfactory stimuli (Baltierra, 2023). Customers are spending more time online and less time on in-person visits. The amount of groceries purchased online has grown by double digits (Plotkina et al., 2022). AR applications can provide personalized suggestions based on consumer preferences and past purchase history, enhancing the overall shopping experience and increasing customer satisfaction. This chapter explore into the various applications, challenges and potential implications of AR and VR in the retail sector, highlighting the substantial transformations these technologies bring to the industry. Augmented reality is revolutionizing in-store navigation, providing consumers with an engaging and user-friendly navigational experience. In addition, when customers choose their favorite local shopping venues, cost is becoming less important. Prominent international Fortune companies like Google, Amazon, Facebook and Twitter have transformed their operational frameworks to deliver outstanding client experiences, going beyond simple tweaks to customer care and support (Peukert, 2019).

Background of Study

Customers are changing, thus providing "customer service" alone is no longer adequate (Halid et al., 2024; Syed et al., 2021). Creating engaging and relevant customer experiences is essential in this age of elevated expectations (Zhang, 2020; Carton, 2019; Soliman & Al Balushi, 2023). In addition to meeting this need, brands now need to deal with consumer" attention spans which are getting shorter by the day and they only have eight seconds currently (Mohamed, 2024). People reduce the number of brands they are considering during the consumer journey and therefore marketers need to work to influence those choices by offering experiences that are pertinent to the customer (Bhatnagar, 2022). Any ambiguous strategy runs the risk of not reaching the appropriate customers at the right time (Singh, 2023).

Customers want consistently excellent and pertinent experiences whether they are engaging with your contact center, website, mobile application, or self-service choices (Henke & Jacques Bughin, 2016). The cerebral cortex encodes both physical and cognitive processes mostly through the motor cortex (Kaushal & Yadav, 2023). Thus, neurofeedback training may be helpful for those who have trouble understanding the order in which cognitive activities should be performed; it is especially useful for training the left hemisphere's sensorimotor cortex (C3). As an alternative, training targeted at the sensorimotor cortex (C4) of the right hemisphere may elicit feelings of tranquility or arousal (Singh, 2023). Training in intermediate areas may result in a mix of outcomes. Training along the sensorimotor cortex (C3) is commonly advised for epileptics in order to improve SMR (sensorimotor rhythm) (King, 2022). Also, the stroke, epilepsy, paralysis and illnesses involving the integration of senses and motor skills may benefit from training targeted at the sensorimotor cortex (Savickaite, 2024).

Objectives of the Chapter

This chapter has the following objectives to:

1. Examine the state of customer experience in emerging regions at the moment and pinpointing areas that need work.
2. Investigate how augmented and virtual reality technology might improve consumer happiness and engagement.
3. Evaluate how customer behavior and purchase decisions are affected by augmented and virtual reality in emerging regions.
4. Specify how augmented-virtual reality tactics are developed and implemented in relation to neuromarketing concepts.
5. Offers doable tactics to help companies in developing nations successfully incorporate augmented and virtual reality technology into their marketing and sales strategies in order to gain a competitive edge and long-term growth.

Figure 1. Highlights the objectives of this chapter

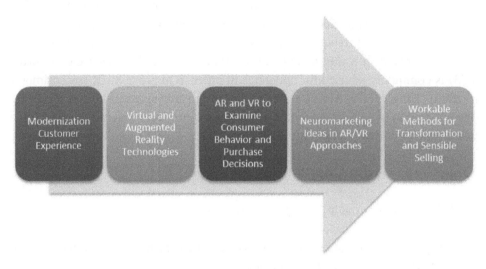

Structure of the Chapter

This chapter deeply dives in the Modernizing Customers Experience through Augmented-Virtual Reality in Emerging Market: Sensible Selling towards Transforming Neuromarketing. Section 2 elaborates the Augmented Reality and Virtual Reality for Modernizing Customer Experience. Section 3 expresses the Augmented-Virtual Reality in Emerging Markets. Section 4 lays down the Sensible Selling: Optimizing Marketing Strategies. Section 5 specifies the Transforming Neuromarketing through AR/VR. Section 6 highlights the Challenges. Finally, Section 7 Conclude the Chapter with Future Scope.

Figure 2. Highlights the flow of the chapter

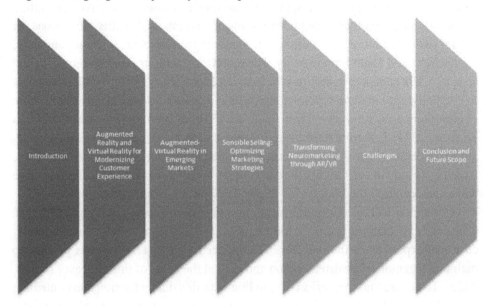

AUGMENTED REALITY AND VIRTUAL REALITY FOR MODERNIZING CUSTOMER EXPERIENCE

Augmented reality (AR) allows users to see and interact with computer-generated items by superimposing them over the actual world (Babet, 2020). Augmented Reality (AR) allows customers, especially in retail, to see a product as it would look in their house before deciding to buy it (Sadowski, 2023). In the meanwhile, virtual reality (VR) provides users with an immersive experience that allows them to easily browse a virtual store and make purchases while on the go (Sharma & Singh, 2022). Virtual Reality (VR) is a computer-generated environment that allows users to interact with a synthetic 3D world in real life by employing sensors-equipped electronic gear such as gloves, headphones, and hand-operated consoles (Gao & Liu, 2022). Virtual reality (VR) creates the illusion of a tangible experience by digitizing the user's physical presence (Rajamannar, 2021). With the use of aural and visual cues to enhance realism, virtual reality (VR) allows users to see and engage with a simulated world that is similar to actual situations. Virtual reality (VR) replaces reality entirely with a digital simulation designed to provide a life-changing experience (Singh, 2022). Artificial intelligence is also a game changer in multi sectorial business scenario (Arora & Sharma, 2023). Marketing communication in virtual environments and the emerging metaverse is a dynamic frontier, redefining how brands engage with audiences. In these digital realms, immersive experiences and interactive storytelling are paramount. Whether through virtual events, augmented reality activations, or virtual reality simulations, marketers leverage these platforms to create authentic connections and foster brand loyalty. The metaverse, with its interconnected virtual spaces, offers endless possibilities for branded experiences, from virtual storefronts to interactive advertisements embedded within virtual worlds or in any other sphere of entrepreneurial ecosystem (Kumar, Arora & Erkol Bayram, Eds. 2024; Dhiman & Arora, 2024). Effective marketing communication in these environments requires a deep understanding of digital culture, user behavior, and emerging technologies, enabling brands to craft compelling narratives and engage audiences in innovative ways, transcending the boundaries of physical space (Arora, 2023).

A common feeling of commitment and purpose towards satisfying customers' wants and expectations is crucial for the successful implementation of a compelling customer experience (Ancillai, 2019). Employees must first have a clear purpose to maintain a genuine, consistent vision and goal at the heart of this endeavor (Singh, 2022). To ensure that their efforts are in line with this distinct vision and contribute to the delivery of authentic client experiences, company executives should create a customer-centric vision and efficiently convey it to brand and marketing managers. In addition, this vision must to include methods for exceeding client expectations (George, 2023). Customer-focused companies need to stay aware of the changing demands of their customers and work hard to deliver unique and worthwhile experiences if they want to stay competitive (Kuusinen, 2019).

Figure 3. Highlights the significance of AR and VR in uplifting customer experiences

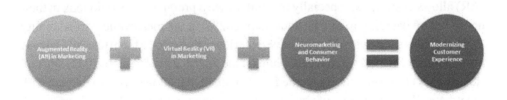

Augmented Reality (AR) in Marketing

The augmented reality (AR) consumer experience makes use of advanced technology to let users interact with goods or services and see things in their own environment (Singh, 2022). Customers are assisted in making knowledgeable purchases through this engaging and participatory experience which also adds excitement to the process. AR expands its applicability to a number of industries, including immersive retail displays, virtual try-ons, interactive user guides and interactive packaging (Wheeler, 2023). Using augmented reality technology in your marketing materials is known as augmented reality marketing. On the other hand, it may be viewed as a powerful marketing tactic that allows companies to customize their interactions with customers (Sedkaoui, 2018).

This technology allows consumers to examine goods and services in a unique, immersive way which can boost brand recognition in conjunction with other marketing strategies (Neuwirth, 2023). Compared to traditional advertising approaches, augmented reality offers firms a competitive edge through immersive marketing by stimulating multiple senses and creating stronger emotional connections (Schaeffer, 2017). Through the provision of more personalized customer experiences with goods and services, this marketing strategy fosters long-lasting memories that increase perceived value, brand recognition, and loyalty. Solutions utilizing augmented reality may expedite buying choices, efficiently engage and retain consumers and save time (Singh, 2019).

Virtual Reality (VR) in Marketing

Businesses may close the gap between experience and action by implementing VR into their marketing campaigns. Virtual reality (VR) presents the possibility of presenting digital experiences in place of actual ones, so efficiently advertising goods and services (Venkatesh, 2021). Virtual reality (VR) may be used to display new product development in addition to showcasing current items. Customers are involved in the creation process and can offer insightful feedback as a result (Reviglio della Venaria, 2020). Most importantly, virtual reality changes how consumers and companies interact. People actively seek out VR brand encounters rather than passively encountering adverts or utilizing ad blockers (Maes, 2018). Customers in this situation approach brands directly, changing the conventional dynamic of a brand attracting customers to one in which people approach the brand (Berman & Pollack, 2021). With the use of VR headsets or multi-projected settings, users may access immersive digital worlds through the frontier of technology known as virtual reality (VR). This invention makes it possible to create virtual experiences that could either perfectly mimic or completely deviate from actual events (Bug & Bernd, 2020).

Virtual reality (VR) finds use in a wide range of industries, including marketing, education, healthcare, and entertainment (Deshbhratar et al., 2023; Arora, 2024). Virtual reality (VR) marketing a term used to describe the integration of VR into marketing strategies has shown to be a very successful tactic for drawing in viewers (Lycett et al., 2024). For example, companies may create interactive VR advertisements that have higher levels of engagement than traditional media. VR advertisements' interactive format increases viewer engagement and retention rates. The noteworthy use is in virtual reality digital marketing, where the immersive qualities of VR are used to enhance digital advertisements (Meibner et al., 2020). This strategy gives businesses a new way to interact with their online audience, making marketing efforts more memorable and effective. The use of virtual reality in marketing is not just a theoretical idea; it is a quickly growing trend that is backed by several effective VR marketing cases (Semeradova, & Weinlich, 2022). For example, real estate companies use virtual reality (VR) to provide virtual tours of their properties, giving potential buyers a realistic impression of the area without having to visit in person. After Covid-19, the concept of virtual tours and marketing in sectors like tourism have seen a profound shift (Arora, Kumar & Valeri (2023). Retail firms also use virtual reality (VR) technology to let shoppers virtually try on garments or sample items in a virtual environment (Sengupta & Cao, 2022).

Figure 4. Virtual reality (VR) in marketing

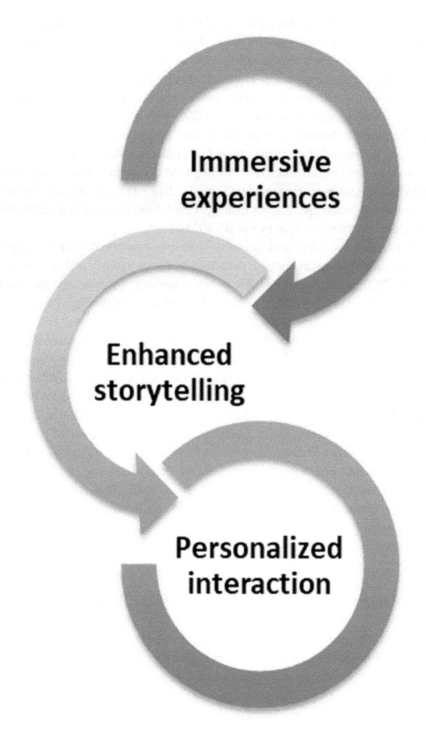

Neuromarketing and Consumer Behavior

The advent of neuromarketing has revolutionized the marketing landscape. This interdisciplinary field amalgamates principles from neuroscience, psychology and marketing to comprehend consumer behavior better and devise more impactful marketing strategies. Neuromarketing employs a diverse array of tools and techniques to gauge the brain's reactions to marketing stimuli and glean insights into the consumer's decision-making process (Lombart et al., 2020). With this, eye-tracking devices are utilized to pinpoint the specific stimulus eliciting the response at any given moment. Also, some neuromarketing firms utilize GSR (galvanic skin response) sensors to measure skin electrical conductivity, offering further insights into consumers' reactions to various commercial messages (Santulli, 2019). This presents an overview of neuromarketing, encompassing its historical evolution, theoretical underpinnings, and practical applications (Lavoye et al., 2023).

The experiences, ideas and concepts that it has gathered over the lives are stored in our brains and impact our decisions, both consciously and unconsciously (Thomas, 2021). Understanding these decision-making processes and successfully adjusting to them is made easier with the help of neuromarketing. To understand the psychology of the consumer, a great deal of study and analysis is done in the field of digital marketing (Abdelmaged, 2021). The goal is to get inside their heads and feel what they are thinking in order to comprehend what motivates them to buy particular goods or services and how they come to their decisions. While a lot of marketing gurus think that emotional elements are what really influence customers when they purchase, occasionally the numbers don't match up (Akhtar, 2018). For example, a Statista poll on the characteristics that lead customers to trust a shop found those excellent reviews on blogs and forums, ethical methods, and pricing all rate higher than emotional triggers (Lavoye, 2023). However, other inputs that elicit strong emotions, like as colors, slogans, or store displays, frequently serve as the catalyst for the inclination to enter a business. It's interesting to note that when asked in polls, people are more likely to provide logical answers than emotional ones (Yim & Park, 2019).

AUGMENTED-VIRTUAL REALITY IN EMERGING MARKETS

Incorporating engagement functions into the website or mobile app may improve the user experience for customers. It is not ideal for clients to have to call the telephone contact center. Rather, companies have to become contemporary by letting clients communicate with them through web, mobile, or in-app branded apps that are already loaded on clients' digital devices. Engaging clients proactively at pivotal points in their unique journeys is important. It's out of date to wait for customers to make contact (Zhu, 2024). In order to provide customers with an outstanding experience, brands need to be proactive in monitoring the context of the in-app customer journey and encouraging them to interact with ease at the right times, like during new user registration or when they have problems that need prompt assistance, all with a single click or touch (Marr, 2021). Consumers hate wasting time on IVR systems and conversing with scripted operators that lack sufficient knowledge. Make efficient use of your staff to guarantee that qualified employees interact with clients (Fan et al., 2022). Customers should be easily linked to the right expert to handle their needs on the first call by applying business rules and contextual routing, which is achieved by evaluating online and in-app consumer Behaviour (Collins, 2019). Businesses may provide one-click direct interactions with these specialists by leveraging the customer journey context that comes from web and mobile activity (Chen & Lin, 2022).

SENSIBLE SELLING: OPTIMIZING MARKETING STRATEGIES

Using techniques such as Customer Journey Maps or Experience Maps, marketers may map the emotional journey of their consumers with the goal of strengthening the relationship and engaging them with personalized content (Pietronudo & Leone, 2022). An illustration of a customer's experiences as they develop over time, covering several phases and touchpoints, is provided by a customer journey map. These exchanges establish the perceived worth of a good or service as well as the state of the customer base's association with the brand. Personas also help to define various audience segments (Pamuru et al., 2021). There are several advantages to applying customer journey mapping and a design thinking methodology. It is fast, flexible, and iterative, providing for instant customer input and allowing marketers to quickly hone their efforts. In the end, the collaborative aspect of the process creates a culture where everyone is concerned about the client experience (Machairidis & Mourmouras, 2020).

Assist consumers with their context to help the customer journey move forward. The majority of customer journeys begin on the website or app, and voice calls to the contact center frequently have no relationship to these platforms (Raghavan & Pai, 2021). Asking security questions while a consumer is already signed into the website or app is not something associates should do. Additionally, by having pertinent information about the caller and the background of their current customer journey, they should be better prepared to manage calls. Contextual awareness and machine learning are key components of modern technological systems that provide this capacity. Also, associates should be equipped to offer human touch support, be able to switch between voice and video channels with ease, and use interactive and visual technologies like screen sharing (Schwarz, 2022).

Personalized Customer Engagements

Customer engagement extends beyond simple online interactions or behaviors like liking and sharing content on social media or visiting websites and downloading whitepapers (Lavuri & Akram, 2023). It centers on determining compatibility and figuring out how people and organizations may live in harmony with one another (Caliskan et al., 2023). It may establish meaningful and regular relationships with your consumers and show them how much you respect them by utilizing insights. Consumers of today are drawn to companies that make an effort to get to know them personally and show gratitude for their efforts to provide better services (Kacprzak & Hensel, 2023). Take a personalized approach to show your consumers that you genuinely care about them, instead of just responding to their generic social media posts or automatically sending thank-you cards after a transaction (Vinaykarthik, 2022). Customize experiences for customers that prefer human connection over automatic answers. It is critical to keep current and consistent across all customer touch-points in order to stay relevant and consistent throughout people's customer journeys (Kamal & Himel, A2023). Make use of primary and secondary research to pinpoint the social elements affecting your audience and be ready to adjust when your environment shifts. With the use of social media, you may gain important insights into past demands, present interests, and future wants of your clientele, both present and prospective (Ahmed, 2022).

TRANSFORMING NEUROMARKETING THROUGH AR/VR

Proactively and successfully include consumers at key junctures in their unique journeys. Nowadays, the customer journey usually starts online, where buyers browse products, read reviews, compare costs and look for live customer support before deciding what to buy (Vuong & Mai, 2023). Developing a dynamic customer journey and using interaction opportunities with relevant insights are critical (Singh, 2024). Customer journey maps must to be designed with clarity in mind, enabling marketers to quickly choose where to spend their efforts (Auttri et al., 2023). They ought to enable marketers to swiftly translate the broad and nebulous field of customer experience strategy into concrete projects. Increased customer satisfaction and loyalty will result from being able to use contemporary communication tools to quickly respond to and answer customers' problems (Zaki, 2022). Make use of Internet of Things, mobile point-of-sale, social listening, marketing automation tools, customer analytics platforms, and collaborative workforce management (Soliman & Al Balushi, 2023). These developments in digital technology will surely be crucial to creating better customer experiences, evaluating the influence of CX and maximizing efforts (Bhatnagar, 2022). Customers are putting more and more pressure on companies to provide them with relevant and interesting experiences that go beyond simple transactional exchanges and have components that genuinely satisfy and excite them. Many businesses agree that a positive customer experience has a big impact on a loyal client base (Singh, 2023). It is crucial to incorporate next-generation technologies like artificial intelligence (AI), the Internet of Things (IoT), and machine learning into current business operations in order to fulfill these changing expectations (Henke & Jacques Bughin, 2016).

Achieving a balance between updating current apps and implementing more effective cloud delivery strategies for new applications is necessary to meet these new expectations (Kaushal & Yadav, 2023). However, a sizable segment of IT experts and decision-makers voice worries over the growing intricacy of multi-cloud setups and the difficulties in properly utilizing emerging technologies (Singh, 2023). So, comprehending the complexities of the multi-cloud environment is essential for incorporating cutting-edge infrastructures that drive contemporary apps. Choosing the right application modernization base is essential to providing creative client experiences (King, 2022). The following important elements are outlined in this whitepaper to help lay this foundation: establishing objectives and specifications to guarantee that modernization initiatives improve the client experience; figuring out the best combination of infrastructure technologies to support the ecosystem of applications that drive the consumer experience; evaluating application preparedness to determine which workloads are most suited for deployment in cloud environments- public, private and hybrid (Babet, 2020).

Understanding Consumer Behavior in Immersive Environments

Consumer expectations have never been higher, and as consumers gain more power, they want companies to go above and beyond in order to succeed (Sadowski, 2023). Customer experience necessitates ongoing nurturing and optimization, which calls for a customer-centric approach that embraces the new standard of mobile and digital engagements. Businesses who grasp this chance and create a long-term plan will have an advantage over their competitors (Sharma & Singh, 2022). Utilize digital technology as instruments to accomplish company goals rather than attempting to incorporate new technologies into antiquated processes. Positive results from this strategy will include better client loyalty, retention rates, and revenue. At the center of your strategy, it is imperative that the customer comes before technology (Mashood et al., 2023).

Neurofeedback and Emotional Response Analysis of Customers

Neurofeedback is a type of biofeedback that teaches people how to control their brain waves and sends messages back to them, usually in the form of visual or auditory cues (Gao & Liu, 2022). The effectiveness of neurofeedback treatment in treating a range of illnesses has been the subject of several researches. Despite being thought of as non-invasive, the absence of solid scientific proof has caused some to doubt its veracity (Rajamannar, 2021). There are also drawbacks, such cost, time commitment and fleeting advantages; notable advancements may take months to materialize. Neurofeedback is acknowledged as a supplemental and alternative treatment for a variety of brain dysfunctions despite these disadvantages. There are currently insufficient data to draw firm judgments on its efficacy. For desired or undesired brain activity, feedback is either positive or negative (Singh, 2022). The clinical and technical aspects of a number of subjects, including: (1) Various protocols for treating neurofeedback such as- alpha, beta, alpha/theta, delta, gamma, and theta; (2) Electrode placements in the frontal, temporal, central and occipital lobes using standard recording channels; (3) Electrode montages, such as unipolar and bipolar configurations; (4) Neurofeedback types, such as frequency, power, slow cortical potential, and functional magnetic resonance imaging; (5) Neurofeedback software options; (6) Clinical applications including learning disabilities, dyslexia, dyscalculia, depression, anxiety, ADHD, epilepsy, insomnia, drug addiction and autism spectrum disorders; and other applications like pain management and improving athletic and musical performance (Ancillai et al., 2019).

Predictive Analytics and Consumer Insights

Getting new customers is essential to the expansion and success of any organization. In the current era of data-driven initiatives, predictive analytics becomes an indispensable tool for businesses looking to grow their clientele (Singh, 2022). Predictive analytics uses machine learning algorithms and historical data to identify trends and project future events. This gives companies the ability to deliberately target the best clients, maximizing the effect of their acquisition efforts (George, 2023). The area of data science called predictive analytics uses statistical algorithms, machine learning techniques, and historical data to predict future events (Wind & Hays, 2016). It facilitates the use of data to guide corporate results through well-informed decision-making and action-taking. Gaining expertise in predictive analytics is essential for those who want to use this powerful tool for acquiring new clients (Kuusinen, 2019). Predictive analytics is essentially analyzing data to find connections and trends that help in prediction-making. For example, a business may use predictive analytics to look at demographic information and past purchases to identify characteristics of its most valued customers (Singh, 2022). This information may then be used to develop targeted marketing campaigns that are designed for comparable consumer demographics, increasing the likelihood of gaining new clients (Naji et al., 2024).

Challenges

Many current consumers have grown up in a digital environment where ordered goods are delivered quickly to their homes and services have made on-demand services the norm (Wheeler, 2023). As a result, many businesses are finding it difficult to connect with these customers (Sedkaoui, 2018). Consumers of today have high standards when it comes to connecting with brands through mobile devices, yet many businesses find it difficult to meet these demands for a smooth, integrated experience. This problem affects a number of industrial sectors, including retail, telecommunications, financial services and others. Creating immersive AR/VR experiences is exciting and challenging; it requires following best practices and overcoming significant challenges (Neuwirth, 2023). Understanding the technology, defining the user experience, choosing appropriate platforms, creating engaging content and carrying out extensive testing and iteration are important aspects of developing AR/VR content. The potential for AR/VR development is enormous, despite the obstacles, and it offers businesses the chance to provide customers with engaging and interactive experiences (Schaeffer, 2017).

Technological Infrastructure

Organizations need to modify their business strategies in this new digital era to make sure that the customer experience is not only more effective but also prioritizes building a personal connection with the brand (Singh, 2019). Consumers indicated in a recent survey that they would get the desired level of personal contact by combining automated technologies with new techniques for in-app brand engagements, like personalized interactions through video, screen sharing, chat, and other contextual voice communications (Venkatesh, 2021). In the age of nearly infinite customer alternatives, companies who can't find this balance run the danger of falling behind. Even if most companies understand that they must change, in order to develop and maintain strong customer connections, they must act quickly to put in place an efficient digital strategy (Reviglio della Venaria, 2020).

Content Creation: Creating High-Quality, Culturally Appropriate AR/VR Content Requires Investment and Expertise

The creating of engaging material is crucial to an immersive experience's success. Interactive, aesthetically pleasing, and relevant to the needs of the user are the three main qualities of content 9Duan, et al., 2024). When creating content, it's also imperative to give the user's journey first priority. For example, making sure the material is understandable and simple to navigate might improve customer happiness (Tzampazaki et al., 2024). A crucial part of developing AR and VR is experimentation and refining. Developers may identify and fix any problems or faults in the experience through experimentation. Refinement is adding user input to improve the experience as a whole. To make sure that the immersive experience meets user expectations and demands, it is imperative to conduct regular testing and modification. Creating AR/VR experiences that are immersive comes with significant challenges (Hanafiah et al., 2024). The biggest obstacle is the high cost of development because of the specialized hardware and software needed. Furthermore, there is a need for competent developers with the knowledge and abilities needed for AR/VR development. To improve accessibility even further, there's a need for more broadly available, reasonably priced, and user-friendly equipment (Tembrevilla et al., 2024).

Data Privacy: Customer Data Collection Through AR/VR

The moral implications of AR and VR technology are numerous and intricate. Virtual reality (VR) technology raises concerns about privacy, health risks, and autonomy restrictions. AR technologies may be interpreted in ways that ignore worker surveillance and exploitation in work environments Lauer-(Schmaltz et al., 2024). The use of virtual reality (VR) in training programs and educational environments raises ethical questions about the effects on individuals and society as a whole, calling for careful consideration and recommendations for its ethical use (Bala & Gupta, 2024). Ethical norms need to be reevaluated since VR journalism raises ethical questions about how to accurately convey facts and audience impressions (Hazarika & Rahmati, 2023). When assessing XR technologies which include AR and VR and it is necessary to apply the same moral standards to them as to other applications, take into consideration their effectiveness and examine them using well-established evaluation frameworks (Varela et al., 2024).

Figure 5. Highlights the challenges

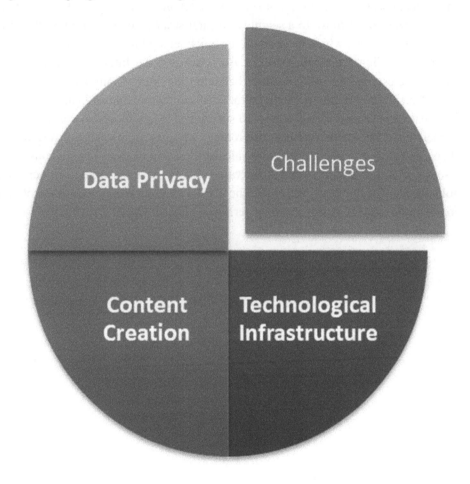

CONCLUSION AND FUTURE RESEARCH DIRECTIONS

The improving of customer experiences requires a thorough understanding of the consumer. It is important to try to understand the consumers' identities, interests, and actual requirements. To become genuinely customer-centric, companies must create customer personas in order to better identify and comprehend their target demographic. Use cloud technologies to promote digital learning across channels. It is imperative for organizations to enhance their capacity to record, examine and derive insights from every client interaction channel, encompassing audio, video, and screen sharing. By capturing all interactions and media kinds in real-time, organizations may obtain important information that help them enhance consumer engagement scenarios and future experiences. Cloud technology makes it simpler for organizations to move to a seamless, digital strategy by streamlining the integration of channels, which is essential for quick adaptability and agility. Utilizing cutting-edge digital technologies like Big Data and the Internet of Things may yield priceless insights on consumer behavior, changing wants and preferences, and efficient ways to interact with them. Creating memorable and engaging client experiences is crucial for a business to succeed in the tech-driven world of today. Immersion technologies, like as virtual reality (VR) and augmented reality (AR), are changing how we connect with companies and present chances to give consumers a sense of empowerment and distinct value. Using these technologies to create a holistic plan for the customer experience (CX) may encourage strong emotional connections with the brand and long-term consumer loyalty.

REFERENCES

Abdelmaged, M. A. M. (2021). *Implementation of virtual reality in healthcare, entertainment, tourism, education, and retail sectors.*

Abrokwah-Larbi, K. (2024). Transforming metaverse marketing into strategic agility in SMEs through mediating roles of IMT and CI: theoretical framework and research propositions. *Journal of Contemporary Marketing Science.*

Ahmed, A. (2022). Marketing 4.0: The Unseen Potential of AI in Consumer Relations. *International Journal of New Media Studies: International Peer Reviewed Scholarly Indexed Journal*, 9(1), 5–12.

Akhtar, O. M. A. R. (2018). Understanding use cases for augmented, mixed and virtual reality. *Altimeter. Online verfügbar unter* https://marketing. prophet. com/acton/ct/33865/p-00b2/Bct/l-00a9/l-00a9: 17b/ct16_0/1.

Ancillai, C., Terho, H., Cardinali, S., & Pascucci, F. (2019). Advancing social media driven sales research: Establishing conceptual foundations for B-to-B social selling. *Industrial Marketing Management*, 82, 293–308. 10.1016/j.indmarman.2019.01.002

Ancillai, C., Terho, H., Cardinali, S., & Pascucci, F. (2019). Advancing social media driven sales research: Establishing conceptual foundations for B-to-B social selling. *Industrial Marketing Management*, 82, 293–308. 10.1016/j.indmarman.2019.01.002

Arora, M. (2023). Encapsulating Role of Persuasion and Skill Development in Marketing Communication for Brand Building: A Perspective. In *International Handbook of Skill, Education, Learning, and Research Development in Tourism and Hospitality* (pp. 1–17). Springer Nature Singapore.

Arora, M. (2024). Virtual Reality in Education: Analyzing the Literature and Bibliometric State of Knowledge. *Transforming Education with Virtual Reality*, 379-402.

Arora, M., Kumar, J., & Valeri, M. (2023). Crises and Resilience in the Age of Digitalization: Perspectivations of Past, Present and Future for Tourism Industry. In *Tourism Innovation in the Digital Era* (pp. 57-74). Emerald Publishing Limited.

Arora, M., & Sharma, R. L. (2023). Artificial intelligence and big data: ontological and communicative perspectives in multi-sectoral scenarios of modern businesses. *foresight*, 25(1), 126-143.

Auttri, B., Chaitanya, K., Daida, S., & Jain, S. K. (2023). Digital Transformation in Customer Relationship Management: Enhancing Engagement and Loyalty. [EEL]. *European Economic Letters*, 13(3), 1140–1149.

Babet, A. (2020). Utilization of personalization in marketing automation and email marketing.

. Bala, R., & Gupta, P. (2024). Virtual Reality in Education: Benefits, Applications and Challenges. *Transforming Education with Virtual Reality*, 165-180.

Baltierra, S. (2023, January). Virtual Reality and Augmented Reality Applied to E-Commerce: A Literature Review. In *Human-Computer Interaction: 8th Iberoamerican Workshop, HCI-COLLAB 2022* (p. 201). Springer Nature.

Berman, B., & Pollack, D. (2021). Strategies for the successful implementation of augmented reality. *Business Horizons*, 64(5), 621–630. 10.1016/j.bushor.2021.02.027

Bhatnagar, S. (2022). *Digital Disruptions and Transformation of Bank Marketing*.

Bug, P., & Bernd, M. (2020). The future of fashion films in augmented reality and virtual reality. *Fashion and film: moving images and consumer behavior*, 281-301.

Caboni, F., & Hagberg, J. (2019). Augmented reality in retailing: A review of features, applications and value. *International Journal of Retail & Distribution Management*, 47(11), 1125–1140. 10.1108/IJRDM-12-2018-0263

. Çalışkan, G., Yayla, İ., & Pamukçu, H. (2023). The use of augmented reality technologies in tourism businesses from the perspective of UTAUT2. *European Journal of Innovation Management*.

Carton, S. (2019). *What impact will immersive technologies such as augmented and virtual reality have on the retail sector?* [Doctoral dissertation, Dublin, National College of Ireland].

Chen, Y., & Lin, C. A. (2022). Consumer behavior in an augmented reality environment: Exploring the effects of flow via augmented realism and technology fluidity. *Telematics and Informatics*, 71, 101833. 10.1016/j.tele.2022.101833

Collins, R. (2019). *Marketing Implications of Utilizing Augmented Reality for In-Store Retailing*.

Deshbhratar, S., Joshi, S., Alwaali, R. N., Saear, A. R., & Marhoon, H. A. (2023, September). Augmented reality of online and physical retailing: A study of applications and its value. In *AIP Conference Proceedings* (*Vol. 2736*, No. 1). AIP Publishing. 10.1063/5.0170917

Dhiman, V., & Arora, M. (2024). Current State of Metaverse in Entrepreneurial Ecosystem: A Retrospective Analysis of Its Evolving Landscape. In *Exploring the Use of Metaverse in Business and Education* (pp. 73-87). IGI Global. 10.4018/979-8-3693-5868-9.ch005

Duan, W., Khurshid, A., Khan, K., & Calin, A. C. (2024). Transforming industry: Investigating 4.0 technologies for sustainable product evolution in china through a novel fuzzy three-way decision-making process. *Technological Forecasting and Social Change*, 200, 123125. 10.1016/j.techfore.2023.123125

Fan, X., Jiang, X., & Deng, N. (2022). Immersive technology: A meta-analysis of augmented/virtual reality applications and their impact on tourism experience. *Tourism Management*, 91, 104534. 10.1016/j.tourman.2022.104534

. Gao, Y., & Liu, H. (2022). Artificial intelligence-enabled personalization in interactive marketing: a customer journey perspective. *Journal of Research in Interactive Marketing*, (ahead-of-print), 1-18.

George, A. S. (2023). Future Economic Implications of Artificial Intelligence. *Partners Universal International Research Journal*, 2(3), 20–39.

Halid, H., Ravesangar, K., Mahadzir, S. L., & Halim, S. N. A. (2024). Artificial Intelligence (AI) in Human Resource Management (HRM). In *Building the Future with Human Resource Management* (pp. 37–70). Springer International Publishing. 10.1007/978-3-031-52811-8_2

Hanafiah, M. H., Asyraff, M. A., Ismail, M. N. I., & Sjukriana, J. (2024). Understanding the key drivers in using mobile payment (M-Payment) among Generation Z travellers. *Young Consumers*. 10.1108/YC-08-2023-1835

Hazarika, A., & Rahmati, M. (2023). Towards an evolved immersive experience: Exploring 5G-and beyond-enabled ultra-low-latency communications for augmented and virtual reality. *Sensors (Basel)*, 23(7), 3682. 10.3390/s2307368237050742

Henke, N., & Jacques Bughin, L. (2016). *The age of analytics: Competing in a data-driven world*.

Kacprzak, A., & Hensel, P. (2023). Exploring online customer experience: A systematic literature review and research agenda. *International Journal of Consumer Studies*, 47(6), 2583–2608. 10.1111/ijcs.12966

Kamal, M., & Himel, A. S. (2023). Redefining Modern Marketing: An Analysis of AI and NLP's Influence on Consumer Engagement, Strategy, and Beyond. *Eigenpub Review of Science and Technology*, 7(1), 203–223.

Kaushal, V., & Yadav, R. (2023). Learning successful implementation of Chatbots in businesses from B2B customer experience perspective. *Concurrency and Computation*, 35(1), e7450. 10.1002/cpe.7450

Kaushal, V., & Yadav, R. (2023). Learning successful implementation of Chatbots in businesses from B2B customer experience perspective. *Concurrency and Computation*, 35(1), e7450. 10.1002/cpe.7450

King, K. (2022). *AI Strategy for Sales and Marketing: Connecting Marketing, Sales and Customer Experience*. Kogan Page Publishers.

King, K. (2022). *AI Strategy for Sales and Marketing: Connecting Marketing, Sales and Customer Experience*. Kogan Page Publishers.

Kumar, J., Arora, M., & Erkol Bayram, G. (Eds.). (2024). *Exploring the Use of Metaverse in Business and Education*. IGI Global. 10.4018/979-8-3693-5868-9

Kuusinen, M. (2019). *Scenarios for digital marketing: a Delphi-based analysis for 2028.*

Lauer-Schmaltz, M. W., Cash, P., Hansen, J. P., & Maier, A. (2024). Towards the Human Digital Twin: Definition and Design—A survey. *arXiv preprint arXiv:2402.07922.*

Lavoye, V. (2023). *Augmented reality in consumer retail: a presence theory approach.*

Lavoye, V., Tarkiainen, A., Sipilä, J., & Mero, J. (2023). More than skin-deep: The influence of presence dimensions on purchase intentions in augmented reality shopping. *Journal of Business Research*, 169, 114247. 10.1016/j.jbusres.2023.114247

Lavuri, R., & Akram, U. (2023). Role of virtual reality authentic experience on affective responses: Moderating role virtual reality attachment. *Journal of Ecotourism*, 1–19. 10.1080/14724049.2023.2237704

Lombart, C., Millan, E., Normand, J. M., Verhulst, A., Labbé-Pinlon, B., & Moreau, G. (2020). Effects of physical, non-immersive virtual, and immersive virtual store environments on consumers' perceptions and purchase behavior. *Computers in Human Behavior*, 110, 106374. 10.1016/j.chb.2020.106374

Lycett, M., Meechao, K., & Reppel, A. (2024). *Materializing Design Fictions for Metaverse Services.*

. Machairidis, E., & Mourmouras, N. (2020). *The impact of augmented, virtual and mixed reality technologies on consumer purchase decision, in the Greek market.*

Maes, P. (2018). *Disruptive Selling: A New Strategic Approach to Sales, Marketing and Customer Service*. Kogan Page Publishers.

Marr, B. (2021). *Extended reality in practice: 100+ amazing ways virtual, augmented and mixed reality are changing business and Society*. John Wiley & Sons.

Mashood, K., Kayani, H. U. R., Malik, A. A., & Tahir, A. (2023). ARTIFICIAL INTELLIGENCE RECENT TRENDS AND APPLICATIONS IN INDUSTRIES. *Pakistan Journal of Science*, 75(02). 10.57041/pjs.v75i02.855

Meißner, M., Pfeiffer, J., Peukert, C., Dietrich, H., & Pfeiffer, T. (2020). How virtual reality affects consumer choice. *Journal of Business Research*, 117, 219–231. 10.1016/j.jbusres.2020.06.004

Mohamed, Ů. (2024). *Integrating Digital Techniques/Technologies in Developing Egyptian Museums (Case Study: Alexandria Library Museums-Alexandria City).* Sohag Engineering Journal.

. Moorhouse, N., tom Dieck, M. C., & Jung, T. (2018). Technological innovations transforming the consumer retail experience: a review of literature. *Augmented Reality and Virtual Reality: Empowering Human, Place and Business*, 133-143.

Naji, K. K., Gunduz, M., Alhenzab, F., Al-Hababi, H., & Al-Qahtani, A. (2024). A Systematic Review of the Digital Transformation of the Building Construction Industry. *IEEE Access : Practical Innovations, Open Solutions*, 12, 31461–31487. 10.1109/ACCESS.2024.3365934

Neuwirth, R. J. (2023). Prohibited artificial intelligence practices in the proposed EU artificial intelligence act (AIA). *Computer Law & Security Report*, 48, 105798. 10.1016/j.clsr.2023.105798

Pamuru, V., Khern-am-nuai, W., & Kannan, K. (2021). The impact of an augmented-reality game on local businesses: A study of Pokémon go on restaurants. *Information Systems Research*, 32(3), 950–966. 10.1287/isre.2021.1004

Peukert, C., Pfeiffer, J., Meißner, M., Pfeiffer, T., & Weinhardt, C. (2019). Shopping in virtual reality stores: The influence of immersion on system adoption. *Journal of Management Information Systems*, 36(3), 755–788. 10.1080/07421222.2019.1628889

Pietronudo, M. C., & Leone, D. (2022). The Power of Augmented Reality for Smart Environments: An Explorative Analysis of the Business Process Management. In *Machine Learning for Smart Environments/Cities: An IoT Approach* (pp. 73–91). Springer International Publishing. 10.1007/978-3-030-97516-6_4

Plotkina, D., Dinsmore, J., & Racat, M. (2022). Improving service brand personality with augmented reality marketing. *Journal of Services Marketing*, 36(6), 781–799. 10.1108/JSM-12-2020-0519

Raghavan, S., & Pai, R. (2021). Changing Paradigm of Consumer Experience Through Martech–A Case Study on Indian Online Retail Industry. *International Journal of Case Studies in Business* [IJCSBE]. *IT and Education*, 5(1), 186–199.

Rajamannar, R. (2021). *Quantum marketing: mastering the new marketing mindset for tomorrow's consumers*. HarperCollins Leadership.

Rajamannar, R. (2021). *Quantum marketing: mastering the new marketing mindset for tomorrow's consumers*. HarperCollins Leadership.

Reviglio della Venaria, U. (2020). Personalization in Social Media: Challenges and Opportunities for Democratic Societies.

Sadowski, J. (2023). Total life insurance: Logics of anticipatory control and actuarial governance in insurance technology. *Social Studies of Science*, 03063127231186437.37427796

Santulli, M. (2019). *The influence of augmented reality on consumers' online purchase intention: the Sephora Virtual Artist case* [Doctoral dissertation].

Savickaite, S. (2024). *Using Virtual Reality to explore individual differences in perception due to neurodiversity* [Doctoral dissertation, University of Glasgow].

Schaeffer, E. (2017). *Industry X. 0: Realizing digital value in industrial sectors*. Kogan Page Publishers.

Schwarz, M. (2022). *Augmented Reality in Online Retail: Generational Differences Between Millennials and Generation Z Using Virtual Try-On's*.

Sedkaoui, S. (Ed.). (2018). *Big data analytics for entrepreneurial success*. IGI Global.

Semerádová, T., & Weinlich, P. (2022). The place of virtual reality in e-retail: Viable shopping environment or just a game. In *Moving businesses online and embracing e-commerce: Impact and opportunities caused by COVID-19* (pp. 92–117). IGI Global. 10.4018/978-1-7998-8294-7.ch005

Sengupta, A., & Cao, L. (2022). Augmented reality's perceived immersion effect on the customer shopping process: Decision-making quality and privacy concerns. *International Journal of Retail & Distribution Management*, 50(8/9), 1039–1061. 10.1108/IJRDM-10-2021-0522

Sharma, A., & Singh, B. (2022). Measuring Impact of E-commerce on Small Scale Business: A Systematic Review. *Journal of Corporate Governance and International Business Law*, 5(1).

Singh, B. (2019). Profiling Public Healthcare: A Comparative Analysis Based on the Multidimensional Healthcare Management and Legal Approach. *Indian Journal of Health and Medical Law*, 2(2), 1–5.

Singh, B. (2022). Understanding Legal Frameworks Concerning Transgender Healthcare in the Age of Dynamism. *ELECTRONIC JOURNAL OF SOCIAL AND STRATEGIC STUDIES*, 3(1), 56–65. 10.47362/EJSSS.2022.3104

Singh, B. (2022). Relevance of Agriculture-Nutrition Linkage for Human Healthcare: A Conceptual Legal Framework of Implication and Pathways. *Justice and Law Bulletin*, 1(1), 44–49.

Singh, B. (2022). COVID-19 Pandemic and Public Healthcare: Endless Downward Spiral or Solution via Rapid Legal and Health Services Implementation with Patient Monitoring Program. *Justice and Law Bulletin*, 1(1), 1–7.

Singh, B. (2022). Understanding Legal Frameworks Concerning Transgender Healthcare in the Age of Dynamism. *ELECTRONIC JOURNAL OF SOCIAL AND STRATEGIC STUDIES*, 3(1), 56–65. 10.47362/EJSSS.2022.3104

Singh, B. (2022). Relevance of Agriculture-Nutrition Linkage for Human Healthcare: A Conceptual Legal Framework of Implication and Pathways. *Justice and Law Bulletin*, 1(1), 44–49.

Singh, B. (2022). COVID-19 Pandemic and Public Healthcare: Endless Downward Spiral or Solution via Rapid Legal and Health Services Implementation with Patient Monitoring Program. *Justice and Law Bulletin*, 1(1), 1–7.

Singh, B. (2023). Blockchain Technology in Renovating Healthcare: Legal and Future Perspectives. In *Revolutionizing Healthcare Through Artificial Intelligence and Internet of Things Applications* (pp. 177-186). IGI Global.

Singh, B. (2023). Federated Learning for Envision Future Trajectory Smart Transport System for Climate Preservation and Smart Green Planet: Insights into Global Governance and SDG-9 (Industry, Innovation and Infrastructure). *National Journal of Environmental Law*, 6(2), 6–17.

Singh, B. (2023). Blockchain Technology in Renovating Healthcare: Legal and Future Perspectives. In *Revolutionizing Healthcare Through Artificial Intelligence and Internet of Things Applications* (pp. 177-186). IGI Global.

Singh, B. (2024). Legal Dynamics Lensing Metaverse Crafted for Videogame Industry and E-Sports: Phenomenological Exploration Catalyst Complexity and Future. *Journal of Intellectual Property Rights Law*, 7(1), 8–14.

Singha, R., & Singha, S. (2024). Building Capabilities and Workforce for Metaverse-Driven Retail Formats. In *Creator's Economy in Metaverse Platforms: Empowering Stakeholders Through Omnichannel Approach* (pp. 111-131). IGI Global. 10.4018/979-8-3693-3358-7.ch007

Soliman, M., & Al Balushi, M. K. (2023). Unveiling destination evangelism through generative AI tools. *ROBONOMICS: The Journal of the Automated Economy*, 4(54), 1.

Syed, A. A., Gaol, F. L., Pradipto, Y. D., & Matsuo, T. (2021). Augmented and virtual reality in e-commerce—A survey. *ICIC Express Letters*, 15, 1227–1233.

Tembrevilla, G., Phillion, A., & Zeadin, M. (2024). Experiential learning in engineering education: A systematic literature review. *Journal of Engineering Education*, 113(1), 195–218. 10.1002/jee.20575

Thomas, S. (2021). Investigating interactive marketing technologies-adoption of augmented/virtual reality in the Indian context. *International Journal of Business Competition and Growth*, 7(3), 214–230. 10.1504/IJBCG.2021.116266

Tzampazaki, M., Zografos, C., Vrochidou, E., & Papakostas, G. A. (2024). Machine Vision—Moving from Industry 4.0 to Industry 5.0. *Applied Sciences (Basel, Switzerland)*, 14(4), 1471. 10.3390/app14041471

Varela, L., Putnik, G., & Romero, F. (2024). Collaborative manufacturing and management contextualization in the Industry 4.0 based on a systematic literature review. *International Journal of Management Science and Engineering Management*, 19(1), 78–95. 10.1080/17509653.2023.2174200

Venkatesh, D. N. (2021). *Winning with employees: Leveraging employee experience for a competitive edge*. SAGE Publishing India.

Vinaykarthik, B. C. (2022, October). Design of Artificial Intelligence (AI) based User Experience Websites for E-commerce Application and Future of Digital Marketing. In *2022 3rd International Conference on Smart Electronics and Communication (ICOSEC)* (pp. 1023-1029). IEEE.

Vuong, N. A., & Mai, T. T. (2023). Unveiling the Synergy: Exploring the Intersection of AI and NLP in Redefining Modern Marketing for Enhanced Consumer Engagement and Strategy Optimization. *Quarterly Journal of Emerging Technologies and Innovations*, 8(3), 103–118.

Wang, J., Sun, Y., Zhang, L., Zhang, S., Feng, L., & Morrison, A. M. (2024). Effect of display methods on intentions to use virtual reality in museum tourism. *Journal of Travel Research*, 63(2), 314–334. 10.1177/00472875231164987

Wheeler, J. (2023). *The Digital-First Customer Experience: Seven Design Strategies from the World's Leading Brands*. Kogan Page Publishers.

Wind, Y. J., & Hays, C. F. (2016). *Beyond advertising: Creating value through all customer touchpoints*. John Wiley & Sons.

Xue, L. (2022). *Designing effective augmented reality platforms to enhance the consumer shopping experiences* [Doctoral dissertation, Loughborough University].

Yang, L., Kumar, R., Kaur, R., Babbar, A., Makhanshahi, G. S., Singh, A., Kumar, R., Bhowmik, A., & Alawadi, A. H. (2024). Exploring the role of computer vision in product design and development: A comprehensive review. [IJIDeM]. *International Journal on Interactive Design and Manufacturing*, 1–48. 10.1007/s12008-024-01765-7

Yim, M. Y. C., & Park, S. Y. (2019). "I am not satisfied with my body, so I like augmented reality (AR)": Consumer responses to AR-based product presentations. *Journal of Business Research*, 100, 581–589. 10.1016/j.jbusres.2018.10.041

Zaki, H. O. (2022). The Impact Of Artificial Intelligence On Content Marketing. *Journal of Strategic Digital Transformation In Society*, 2(3).

. Zhang, J. (2020). *A systematic review of the use of augmented reality (AR) and virtual reality (VR) in online retailing.*

Zhu, W., Owen, C. B., Li, H., & Lee, J. H. (2024). Personalized in-store e-commerce with the promopad: An augmented reality shopping assistant. *Electronic Journal for E-commerce Tools and Applications*, 1(3), 1–19.

Chapter 16
Boosting Wellbeing Leveraging Virtual Communities Through Innovative Digital Marketing Strategies

Swati Sharma
University School of Business, Chandigarh University, Punjab, India

Kavita Sharma
University School of Business, Chandigarh University, Punjab, India

Anupal Mongia
https://orcid.org/0009-0002-4224-7725
Mody University of Science and Technology, India

Reena Malik
https://orcid.org/0000-0002-1645-3667
Chitkara Business School, Chitkara University, Punjab, India

ABSTRACT

The well-being of individuals has taken precedence in the new era that Covid-19 has brought. Numerous viewpoints on medical care technology and the social sciences have been used to analyse the topic of wellbeing in digital communities. This chapter is a review of the literature that explains how understanding the comfort, happiness, and quality of life of members of virtual communities can help businesses develop their digital communication and marketing strategies.

DOI: 10.4018/979-8-3693-4236-7.ch016

INTRODUCTION

An Overview of the Digital Era's Effects on Wellness and Community Development

The rapid advances in technology and the ubiquitous availability of the internet that define the digital age have completely changed the way people interact and connect with one another. Community development and wellbeing have been significantly impacted by this transition in a number of ways:

- **Access and Connectivity:** Individuals may now connect with individuals anywhere in the world and access information and communication channels never before possible thanks to the internet, which has also eliminated geographical limitations(Ayachi et al.,2022). People with similar identities, hobbies, or aspirations can now congregate on social media platforms, online forums, and virtual communities to create support systems and communities.
- **Multicultural Groups:** Online communities have made it easier for different groups to emerge around a range of interests, occupations, identities, and health issues.

People who might face feelings of alienation or exclusion in their physical surroundings can discover a sense of acceptance and assistance in virtual communities that comprehend and affirm their realities (Hunter et al., 2012).

- **Assistance and Materials:** A multitude of support tools are available in online forums, from peer support and emotional validation to professional guidance and educational content (Martimnez et al.,2016). In virtual spaces, people dealing with difficulties like mental health disorders, long-term illnesses, or life transitions can get support and direction from others who have gone through similar things.
- **Increased Awareness and Protest:** Individuals and groups may now advocate for change, raise awareness of social concerns, and mobilize support for causes thanks to digital platforms that amplify their voices. Online campaigns and social media activism have sparked movements for mental health awareness, social justice, and other worthwhile causes, encouraging cooperation and a sense of camaraderie (Hercheui and M. D,2011).

The Significance of Online Networks in Promoting Wellbeing

Online communities are essential for promoting wellbeing because they offer spaces for social interaction, encouragement, and empowerment. Here are a few crucial elements emphasizing their significance:

- **Social Attachment and Integration:** People might find a sense of support and belonging in virtual communities, especially those who might feel alone or ostracized in their offline settings. Members can build a helpful network that improves mental and emotional welfare by exchanging experiences, giving counsel, and offering emotional support to one another.
- **Diversification and Easy access:** People from different places and cultures can come together in virtual communities based on common identities, interests, or experiences, even though these communities are not physical. Online resources provide accessible and inclusive environments for those with disabilities, chronic diseases, or mobility limits who may find it difficult to participate in traditional offline communities.
- **Data and Sources:** Virtual communities are invaluable information and resource centers that provide members with access to a wealth of knowledge, professional guidance, and helpful hints on a range of subjects pertaining to wellness, personal growth, and health (Chan,2015). Through information sharing, best practices, and experience sharing, members enable people to make well-informed decisions regarding their own well-being.
- **Self-determination and Protest:** Virtual communities offer forums for activism, advocacy, and group action, empowering people to confront stigma, bring attention to significant issues, and promote constructive change. Virtual communities provide members the tools they need to confront structural issues, advance social justice, and fight toward a more inclusive and fair society by amplifying voices and rallying support.
- **A clear mission and involvement in the community:** Virtual communities encourage a feeling of purpose and community involvement by giving people the chance to meaningfully participate to group objectives, projects, or initiatives.

Members can strengthen their sense of identity and connection to the community via cooperative activities and shared experiences, which has a good effect on their general welfare.

CONCEPTUAL FRAMEWORK

According to research, virtual communities provide important social support for mental health. These communities provide a sense of belonging and alleviate feelings of loneliness, particularly for those with specific interests or who face similar issues (Wright & Bell, 2003). Virtual communities frequently act as information exchange centers, providing members with access to useful resources and assistance. This can be especially useful in health-related communities, where people can learn about managing diseases, treatments, and healthy lifestyle habits (Coulson, 2005). To attract and engage community members, effective content marketing methods call for the creation and distribution of good, relevant information. Content related to wellbeing can include articles, films, and webinars on health, exercise, mental health, and other topics (Holliman & Rowley, 2014). Social media platforms are critical for growing virtual communities (Kumar, J., et al.2024). Targeted advertising, influencer collaborations, and engaging posts are all effective strategies for attracting and retaining members. Social media also allows for real-time connection and interaction, which strengthens the sense of community (Kaplan & Haenlein, 2010). Gamification aspects, such as challenges, incentives, and leaderboards, can boost participation and motivation in online groups. Gamification has been found to improve user experience and encourage healthy behavior (Deterding et al., 2011). Innovative digital marketing methods can boost engagement and participation in online communities. Higher levels of participation are associated with increased support, more robust information exchange, and improved wellbeing outcomes (Ridings & Gefen, 2004). Digital marketing can influence behavior change by encouraging healthy behaviors and offering continuing incentive and support. Campaigns that use social proof, success stories, and interactive information can motivate members to live healthier lives (Bull et al., 2010). Virtual communities can provide emotional assistance through peer engagement and professional counsel. Digital marketing tactics that provide a friendly and happy community environment can benefit members' mental wellness and emotional well-being (Naslund et al., 2016). Privacy and security concerns are key hurdles to interacting with virtual communities. Effective internet advertising approaches have to tackle these concerns by providing secure platforms and open data procedures (Krasnova et al., 2010). Individuals' ability to join in virtual communities can be influenced by their access to electronic devices and computer literacy levels. Strategies that close the digital gap are critical for promoting inclusive wellness (van Deursen & Van Dijk, 2014). Virtual groups are online environments where people who share similar interests or objectives interact, communicate, and form relationships. Communities like these have the ability to greatly improve members' well-being by offering social support, data, and a sense of community (Ridings & Gefen, 2004). According to research, virtual communities can give significant social assistance, which is essential for emotional and mental health. Members frequently receive encouragement, compassion, and advice from their peers, which helps to alleviate emotions of isolation and loneliness (Oh, Ozkaya, and LaRose, 2014). Creating and distributing important, relevant, and consistent material helps attract and maintain a specific audience inside virtual community. Content that informs, provides entertainment and inspires can improve people's overall well-being (Pulizzi, 2012). The proper use of social networking platforms can increase community engagement and promote a supportive environment. Positive interactions, user-generated material, and real-time communication can all help to enhance community relationships and improve well-being (Ashley & Tuten, 2015). Ensuring the confidentiality and safety of people's data is critical. To preserve sensitive information and retain confidence, digital marketers must follow ethical guidelines and regulations (Trepte et al., 2017). Misinformation can have a negative impact on people's well-being. Digital marketers must promote accurate and truthful information inside virtual communities to protect members' well-being and security (Vraga & Bode, 2020; Arora, 2020).

COMPREHENDING WELLBEING IN DIGITAL COMMUNITIES

Acknowledging the complex nature of wellness and its online manifestations is essential to comprehending wellbeing in virtual communities. Here are important things to think about:

- **Mental Health:** A person's emotional stability, sense of self-worth, and general mental health are all considered aspects of psychological wellbeing.

Psychological well-being in virtual communities can be impacted by things like the strength of social bonds, a feeling of community, and chances for personal development and self-expression (Arora & Sharma, 2021).

- **Welfare of Society:** The quality of a person's connections and social interactions is referred to as social wellness. Social welfare in virtual communities can be promoted by deep relationships, common interests, and chances for cooperation and support from one another. Feelings of connectivity and belonging are facilitated by supportive social networks, active participation in community events, and involvement in other activities.
- **Welfare of the Emotions:** The capacity to recognize and effectively control one's emotions is a necessary component of emotional wellness.

Emotional well-being in virtual communities can be impacted by things like affirmation, empathy, and the ability to express feelings in a safe space (Caplan,2002). Positive emotional wellbeing is more common among community members who feel appreciated, understood, and welcomed.

- **Wellness of the Body:** Physical well-being includes things like diet, exercise, rest, and general physical health. Virtual communities can help members achieve their wellness objectives by offering support, accountability, and encouragement—even though they might not have a direct influence on physical health. Members' awareness and motivation to focus their physical wellbeing can be increased through discussions on fitness challenges, healthy lifestyle choices, and the sharing of health-related materials.

Case Studies of Effective Online Communities That Enhance Wellbeing

Examples of effective health-focused online networks, such as Patientlike and Fitocracy, show how innovative digital marketing methods may boost participation and wellbeing. These platforms improve the user experience through content marketing, gamification, and personalization (Frost & Massagli, 2008).

Corporate wellness programs that use virtual communities and digital marketing have improved employee health and productivity. Companies such as Virgin Pulse employ these tactics to build supportive, engaging wellness communities (Parks & Steelman, 2008).

7 Cups is an online platform that employs certified therapists and trained listeners to offer emotional support and counselling. Does It Advance Well-Being? Members can communicate discreetly with professional listeners who provide active listening and sympathetic assistance. The website also provides a number of forums and support groups where users may talk about their experiences and get encouragement from others going through comparable difficulties.7 Cups has established a helpful online community where people may seek consolation, affirmation, and direction for a variety of mental health issues. Headspace Community: Guided meditation sessions, sleep stories, and mindfulness activities are all available on the Headspace app for meditation and mindfulness. How Does It Advance Well-Being? Apart from offering meditation sessions, Headspace also offers a virtual community where users may interact with other mindfulness enthusiasts, exchange stories about their meditation experiences. Those who are interested in mindfulness, meditation, and mental wellness can feel connected, at home, and supported by one another through the Headspace Community.

Those looking to reach their fitness and health objectives can find tools, resources, and support at SparkPeople, an online community and weight loss program.

How Does It Advance Well-Being? Meal planning, activity monitoring, fitness and nutrition articles, and community forums for users to discuss obstacles they've faced and accomplished are just a few of the tools offered by the platform. Additionally, SparkPeople provides events, challenges, and virtual teams to promote responsibility and togetherness.

SparkPeople has established a thriving online community where participants can get inspiration, guidance, and useful assistance on their path to better health and wellness. Online support groups offered by the Anxiety and Depression Association of America (ADAA):

For those dealing with depression and anxiety problems, ADAA provides online support groups. How It Promotes Wellbeing: Participants can take part in online support groups led by certified therapists, where they can meet people who are understanding of their issues, learn coping mechanisms, and get validation. People can share their stories, obtain understanding, and get encouragement in ADAA's online support groups, which offer a secure and encouraging environment for those pursuing recovery and better mental health. The Mighty is a digital health community that offers tools and assistance to those dealing with a range of health issues. How Does It Advance Well-Being? In addition to accessing articles, videos, and forums covering a broad range of health topics, members can interact with people who share. By fostering empathy, understanding, and camaraderie among those managing health issues, the Mighty network enables people to find strength and resilience in their quest for enhanced wellness. The community of Nike Run Club (NRC): Nike's strategy involves utilizing its NRC app to establish an online running community where members can log their runs, establish objectives, and take part in challenges. By promoting accountability, incentive, and companionship among runners globally, the NRC community promotes physical activity and general welfare. The mindfulness and meditation software Headspace provides a virtual community where users can meet other people who are also interested in meditation, exchange stories, and take part in challenges with other users. Through peer support and shared mindfulness practices, the Headspace community encourages resilience, emotional wellbeing, and stress reduction. Fitbit's virtual community encourages users to establish and meet fitness goals, share accomplishments, and provide encouragement to one another through challenges, groups, and social features. Fitbit users experience better physical health and wellbeing as a result of the community's encouragement of motivation, accountability, and a sense of belonging.

The examples provided show how businesses and brands use online communities and cutting-edge digital marketing techniques to support different aspects of well-being, such as stress management, mental health, physical fitness, and emotional equilibrium. These companies enable people to put their health first and lead better, more fulfilled lives by developing healthy online communities and user interactions.

POSSIBLE DRAWBACKS AND THREATS OF USING ONLINE FORUMS FOR DIGITAL MARKETING

Although using virtual communities for digital marketing has many advantages, there are a number of risks and difficulties that companies must be aware of. Here are a few possible difficulties and dangers:

- **Privacy Issues:** Members of virtual communities frequently communicate with one another and share personal information. It is imperative for brands to guarantee the safeguarding of user privacy and adhere to pertinent data protection laws (Bakalu et al.,2019)
- **Authenticity and Trust:** It can be difficult to establish trust in online communities, particularly if users feel that marketing communications are invasive or deceptive. In order to cultivate trust among community members, brands must build credibility, openness, and authenticity in their communications.
- **Community Standards and Moderating:** Efficient moderation techniques and well-defined guidelines are necessary to sustain a constructive and encouraging community atmosphere. Establishing and enforcing community guidelines is crucial for brands in order to prevent spam, harassment, and other inappropriate behavior that may negatively impact the user experience.
- **Juggling Engagement and Promotion:** Valuable material and meaningful connections are the lifeblood of virtual communities. It's important for brands to find a balance between useful and interesting conversations and promotional content to avoid offending community members or appearing excessively promotional.
- **Handling Unfavorable Comments**: Brands may be at danger of damage to their reputation if community members provide unfavorable reviews or criticism. It's critical to address concerns, correct problems, and take the necessary steps to restore confidence in the wake of unfavorable remarks or complaints.
- **Sustaining Interest and Relevance:** It takes constant work and ingenuity to keep users interested and engaged over time. It is imperative for brands to consistently offer community members value by means of pertinent material, interactive experiences, and avenues for feedback and involvement.
- **Platform Variations and Dependencies**: Virtual communities frequently rely on social media networks or other third-party platforms, which occa-

sionally change their features, policies, or algorithms. To reduce the chance of disruptions, brands must diversify their presence across several channels and adjust to platform changes.

FUTURE DIRECTIONS AND SUGGESTIONS

Future predictions for virtual communities and digital marketing must take into account new developments in technology, customer behavior, and developing trends. The prospects of virtual Communities and virtual world, holds enormous potential as entrepreneurs, employing innovations in the metaverse, artificial intelligence (AI), and virtual reality (VR) education, have the potential to redefine marketing paradigms (Arora & Sharma, 2023); (Kumar, Arora & Erkol Bayram, (Eds.). (2024)). They have the potential to promote well-being in various aspects. Startups are the driving forces of economic growth and innovation (Arora & Sharma, 2021; Arora,2016). Entrepreneurs have the ability to utilise virtual world in order to develop brand experiences that are immersive and transcend traditional boundaries, thereby engaging customers and enhancing their satisfaction (Arora, 2023). The metaverse provides a virtual environment in which brands can build interactive and persistent presences, thereby fostering deeper connections with audiences all over the world (Dhiman & Arora, 2024 a; Rathore & Arora, 2024). If the wellbeing aspects are taken care in this scenario, it can prove to be a fruitful tool. This experience is enhanced by artificial intelligence, which personalises interactions based on vast data analytics. This ensures that each encounter is both relevant and meaningful. Additionally, virtual reality education gives business owners the ability to teach their personnel remotely and immerse customers in virtual product experiences, which has the potential to revolutionise customer engagement and brand loyalty as well as taking care of their wellbeing (Arora, 2024; Dhiman & Arora, 2024b). These advances, when taken as a whole, foreshadow a future in which virtual world not only improves the experiences of consumers but also promotes unparalleled growth and competition in the global marketplace.

Here are a few future projections:

- **Growth of Micro- and Niche Communities:** Virtual communities will keep developing into increasingly focused, niche markets that serve particular identities, interests, or affinity groups. There will be the emergence of micro-communities that provide individualized experiences and stronger bonds amongst individuals who have similar interests or goals.
- **Combining virtual reality (VR) and augmented reality (AR):** With the ability to create immersive experiences that meld the real and virtual worlds

together, augmented reality and virtual reality technology will be incorporated into virtual communities and digital marketing tactics more and more. In order to engage consumers in new ways, brands will use AR and VR to develop interactive storytelling, product demos, and virtual events.

- **AI-powered personalization and marketing: More** customization in digital marketing will be facilitated by AI-powered algorithms and machine learning, which will give hyper-targeted content, recommendations, and offers based on user preferences, behaviors, and context. In order to predict client demands and provide more pertinent and timely messaging, brands will make use of predictive modeling and data analytics.

- **Community-Driven Content Development:** Members of virtual communities will co-create and co-curate information that represents their interests, experiences, and viewpoints, taking an increasingly active part in the content creation process. In order to boost user-generated content, encourage authenticity, and forge closer bonds with consumers, brands will work in tandem with community members.

- **Growth of Influencer Marketing and Social Commerce:** E-commerce features will be more deeply incorporated into social media platforms, allowing for smooth buying experiences inside of social networks. Influencer marketing is going to become more and more important as brands collaborate with community leaders and micro-influencers to increase conversions, trust, and engagement.

- **Focus on Mental Health and Community Well-Being:** More focus will be placed on fostering mental health and community welfare in virtual communities by offering tools, support systems, and resources for resilience and self-care. Initiatives that promote inclusivity, empathy, and excellent mental health outcomes within their communities will be given top priority by brands.

Suggestions for businesses and marketers who want to improve well-being in online communities by using creative digital marketing techniques.

Suggestions for businesses and advertisers hoping to improve well-being in online communities by implementing creative digital marketing techniques:

- **Recognize Your Audience:** To fully comprehend the needs, tastes, and habits of your target audience in virtual communities, conduct in-depth research. To effectively adapt your marketing strategy, ascertain your target audience's wellbeing-related pain points.

- **Encourage Genuine Connections:** Put openness and sincerity first while interacting with members of the virtual community. Establish sincere bonds based on mutual respect, empathy, and trust to create a welcoming atmosphere.

- **Offer Content with Extra Value:** Provide insightful and timely content that focuses on community members' overall wellbeing. Assist people in prioritizing their physical, mental, and emotional well-being by providing them with informative materials, useful advice, and motivational tales.

- **Take Part in Active Hearing:** Pay close attention to the opinions and needs of those involved in the virtual community. Show them that you understand, care about, and are prepared to attend to their needs by actively responding to their remarks, inquiries, and worries.

- **Utilize content that users have created (UGC):** Invite people in the community to share their success stories, wellness-related experiences, and perspectives. Use case studies, social media, and testimonies to enhance user-generated material that highlights the benefits of your goods and services.

- **Encourage peer cooperation and support:** Provide people in the community the chance to interact, lend a hand to one another, and exchange resources for bettering their well-being. Lead peer-led activities, group conversations, and cooperative projects that encourage empowerment and unity.

- **Spreading Positive Narratives and Positive Role Models:** Within virtual communities, digital marketing methods highlight good tales, testimonials, and role models, inspiring and pushing members to strive for similar accomplishments. Through the display of real-life success stories and the accomplishment of wellness objectives by individuals who have surmounted obstacles, companies have the ability to inspire hope, optimism, and a sense of possibilities among citizens.

- **Encouraging Collaboration and Peer Support:** Digital marketing tactics foster peer-to-peer assistance and cooperation in online communities, allowing participants to impart knowledge, exchange best practices, and provide support. Brands may leverage the community's combined wisdom, experiences, and skills to boost wellness by fostering meaningful interactions and relationships among members.

CONCLUSION

Cutting-edge digital marketing techniques act as catalysts, encouraging partici-pation, establishing credibility, and enabling users to reach their wellness objectives in online groups. By utilizing state-of-the-art technologies and data-driven insights, these tactics enable customized interactions, individualized experiences, and personal access to resources that are meaningful to community members. Digital marketing tactics facilitate cross-border connections, experience sharing, and mutual assistance among individuals by surmounting geographical borders and accessibility constraints. Brands provide community members with the knowledge and resources they need to make wise decisions and take constructive action to enhance their happiness and well-being through instruction, knowledge exchange, and professional guidance. Digital marketing tactics also make it easier to build welcoming and inclusive online communities where participants feel validated, encouraged, and like they belong. Through showcasing success stories, emphasizing good role models, and encouraging peer-to-peer assistance and cooperation, companies leverage the community's pooled knowledge, skills, and abilities to motivate positive behavior changes, goal attainment, and enhanced well-being. In the end, these creative approaches help to build thriving, resilient, and empowered online communities where people connect, develop, and support one another on their path to overall wellbeing. Moreover, creative digital marketing techniques enable the development of welcoming and encouraging online communities where participants receive inspiration, encouragement, and validation. Brands can encourage people to strive for similar accomplishments by highlighting positive tales and highlighting role models in the community through storytelling, testimonials, and user-generated material. Through group conversations, challeng-es, and cooperative projects, brands may also encourage peer-to-peer support and collaboration. By doing this, they can take advantage of the community's aggregate knowledge, skills, and abilities to boost wellbeing.

Furthermore, digital marketing tactics used in online communities provide people the knowledge and resources they need to make wise decisions and take constructive action to enhance their happiness and well-being. Brands may use their knowledge, connections, and power to offer instructional materials, helpful hints, and professional counsel on a range of wellbeing-related subjects, from diet and exercise to mental health and self-care. Brands gain credibility and authority within the community by positioning themselves as reliable allies in the pursuit of holistic wellbeing by providing helpful tools and advice. All things considered, creative digital marketing techniques are essential for creating positive effects in online communities by encouraging participation, self-determination, and networks of support that enable people to live longer, better, and more fulfilled lives. Brands have the ability to significantly improve the well-being of their virtual community members by utilizing technology, creativity, and data-driven insights. This can be achieved by building lively, resilient, and empowered communities where people can connect, thrive, and support one another on their path to holistic wellbeing.

Future study and application should concentrate on understanding the long-term consequences of virtual community engagement, meeting the needs of various populations, integrating new technologies, leveraging behavioral data for customization, ensuring ethical practices, gauging health outcomes, and encouraging collaborations. By addressing these issues, digital marketing tactics can better use virtual communities to improve health and foster friendly, vibrant online environments. Form strategic alliances with medical organizations, mental health practitioners, and wellness businesses to provide a comprehensive approach to well-being. Give members the opportunity to utilize professional guidance, resources, and services via the virtual communities platform.

REFERENCES

Arora, M. (2016). Creative dimensions of entrepreneurship: A key to business innovation. *Pacific Business Review International*, 1(1), 255–259.

Arora, M. (2020). Post-truth and marketing communication in technological age. In *Handbook of research on innovations in technology and marketing for the connected consumer* (pp. 94–108). IGI Global., 10.4018/978-1-7998-0131-3.ch005

Arora, M. (2023). Encapsulating Role of Persuasion and Skill Development in Marketing Communication for Brand Building: A Perspective. In *International Handbook of Skill, Education, Learning, and Research Development in Tourism and Hospitality* (pp. 1-17). Singapore: Springer Nature Singapore.

Arora, M. (2024). Virtual Reality in Education: Analyzing the Literature and Bibliometric State of Knowledge. *Transforming Education with Virtual Reality*, 379-402. 10.1002/9781394200498.ch22

Arora, M., & Sharma, R. L. (2021). Post-Pandemic Psycho-Social Wellbeing in India: Challenges and the Way Ahead. *Alina COSTIN, 2021*.

Arora, M., & Sharma, R. L. (2023). Artificial intelligence and big data: Ontological and communicative perspectives in multi-sectoral scenarios of modern businesses. *Foresight*, 25(1), 126–143. 10.1108/FS-10-2021-0216

Ayachi, Zeineb & Jallouli, Rim. (2022). Digital Marketing Strategies Driven by Wellbeing in Virtual Communities: Literature Review. *Journal of Telecommunications and the Digital Economy*.

Barak, A., Boniel-Nissim, M., & Suler, J. (2008). Fostering empowerment in online support groups. *Computers in Human Behavior*, 24(5), 1867–1883. 10.1016/j.chb.2008.02.004

Bekalu, M. A., McCloud, R. F., & Viswanath, K. (2019). Association of social media use with social well-being, positive mental health, and self-rated health: Disentangling routine use from emotional connection to use. *Health Education & Behavior*, 46(2_suppl, 2S), 69S–80S. 10.1177/10901981198637683174 2462

Bull, S. S., Levine, D. K., Black, S. R., Schmiege, S. J., & Santelli, J. S. (2010). Social media-delivered sexual health intervention: A cluster randomized controlled trial. *American Journal of Preventive Medicine*, 39(5), 512–519.23079168

Caplan, S. E. (2002). Problematic internet use and psychosocial well-being: Development of a theory-based cognitive–behavioral measurement instrument. *Computers in Human Behavior*, 18(5), 553–575. 10.1016/S0747-5632(02)00004-3

Chan, M. (2015). Multimodal connectedness and quality of life: Examining the influences of technology adoption and interpersonal communication on well-being across the life span. *Journal of Computer-Mediated Communication*, 20(1), 3–18. 10.1111/jcc4.12089

Couldry, N., Rodriguez, C., Bolin, G., Cohen, J., Volkmer, I., Goggin, G., Kraidy, M., Iwabuchi, K., Qiu, J. L., Wasserman, H., Zhao, Y., Rincón, O., Magallanes-Blanco, C., Thomas, P. N., Koltsova, O., Rakhmani, I., & Lee, K.-S. (2018). Media, communication and the struggle for social progress. *Global Media and Communication*, 14(2), 173–191. 10.1177/1742766518776679

Coulson, N. S. (2005). Receiving social support online: An analysis of a computer-mediated support group for individuals living with irritable bowel syndrome. *Cyberpsychology & Behavior*, 8(6), 580–584. 10.1089/cpb.2005.8.58016332169

Deterding, S., Dixon, D., Khaled, R., & Nacke, L. (2011). From game design elements to gamefulness: defining "gamification". *Proceedings of the 15th International Academic MindTrek Conference: Envisioning Future Media Environments*, (pp. 9-15). ACM. 10.1145/2181037.2181040

Dhiman, V., & Arora, M. (2024)a. Current State of Metaverse in Entrepreneurial Ecosystem: A Retrospective Analysis of Its Evolving Landscape. In *Exploring the Use of Metaverse in Business and Education* (pp. 73-87). IGI Global. 10.4018/979-8-3693-5868-9.ch005

Dhiman, V., & Arora, M. (2024)b. Exploring the linkage between business incubation and entrepreneurship: understanding trends, themes and future research agenda. *LBS Journal of Management & Research*.

Diener, E., Emmons, R. A., Larsen, R. J., & Griffin, S. (1985). The satisfaction with life scale. *Journal of Personality Assessment*, 49(1), 71–75. 10.1207/s15327752jpa4901_1316367493

Diener, E., Oishi, S., & Tay, L. (2018a). Advances in subjective well-being research. *Nature Human Behaviour*, 2(4), 253–260. 10.1038/s41562-018-0307-630936533

Diener, E., Suh, E. M., Lucas, R. E., & Smith, H. L. (1999). Subjective well-being: Three decades of progress. *Psychological Bulletin*, 125(2), 276–302. 10.1037/0033-2909.125.2.276

Dienlin, T., & Johannes, N. (2020). The impact of digital technology use on adolescent well-being. *Dialogues in Clinical Neuroscience*, 22(2), 135–142. 10.31887/DCNS.2020.22.2/tdienlin32699513

Duradoni, M., Innocenti, F., & Guazzini, A. (2020). Well-being and social media: A systematic review of Bergen Addiction Scales. *Future Internet*, 12(2), 24. 10.3390/fi12020024

Elwert, F., & Winship, C. (2014). Endogenous selection bias: The problem of conditioning on a collider variable. *Annual Review of Sociology*, 40(1), 31–53. 10.1146/annurev-soc-071913-04345530111904

Frost, J. H., & Massagli, M. P. (2008). Social uses of personal health information within PatientsLikeMe, an online patient community: What can happen when patients have access to one another's data. *Journal of Medical Internet Research*, 10(3), e15. 10.2196/jmir.105318504244

Gigerenzer, G. (2010). Personal reflections on theory and psychology. *Theory & Psychology*, 20(6), 733–743. 10.1177/0959354310378184

Griffioen, N., Scholten, H., Lichtwarck-Aschoff, A., van Rooij, M., & Granic, I. (2021). Everyone does it–differently: A window into emerging adults' smartphone use. *Humanities & Social Sciences Communications*, 8(1), 1–11. 10.1057/s41599-021-00863-138617731

Gui, M., Fasoli, M., & Carradore, R. (2017). 'Digital well-being': Developing a new theoretical tool for media literacy research. *Italian Journal of Sociology of Education*, 9(1), 155–173.

Hargittai, E. (2008). The digital reproduction of inequality. In Grusky, D. (Ed.), *Social Stratification* (pp. 936–944). Westview Press.

Hedström, P., & Ylikoski, P. (2010). Causal mechanisms in the social sciences. *Annual Review of Sociology*, 36(1), 49–67. 10.1146/annurev.soc.012809.102632

Hercheui, M. D. (2011). A literature review of virtual communities: The relevance of understanding the influence of institutions on online collectives. *Information Communication and Society*, 14(1), 1–23. 10.1080/13691181003663593

Holliman, G., & Rowley, J. (2014). Business to business digital content marketing: Marketers' perceptions of best practice. *Journal of Research in Interactive Marketing*, 8(4), 269–293. 10.1108/JRIM-02-2014-0013

Hunter, M. G., & Stockdale, R. (2012). A framework for analyzing online communities. *International Journal of Sociotechnology and Knowledge Development*, 2(3), 11–25. 10.4018/jskd.2010070102

Jansen, R. A., Rafferty, A. N., & Griffiths, T. L. (2021). A rational model of the Dunning–Kruger effect supports insensitivity to evidence in low performers. *Nature Human Behaviour*, 5(6), 756–763. 10.1038/s41562-021-01057-033633375

Kaplan, A. M., & Haenlein, M. (2010). Users of the world, unite! The challenges and opportunities of social media. *Business Horizons*, 53(1), 59–68. 10.1016/j.bushor.2009.09.003

Kardefelt-Winther, D., Rees, G., & Livingstone, S. (2020). Contextualising the link between adolescents' use of digital technology and their mental health: A multi-country study of time spent online and life satisfaction. *Journal of Child Psychology and Psychiatry, and Allied Disciplines*, 61(8), 875–889. 10.1111/jcpp.1328032634259

Krasnova, H., Spiekermann, S., Koroleva, K., & Hildebrand, T. (2010). Online social networks: Why we disclose. *Journal of Information Technology*, 25(2), 109–125. 10.1057/jit.2010.6

Kumar, J., Arora, M., & Erkol Bayram, G. (Eds.). (2024). *Exploring the Use of Metaverse in Business and Education*. IGI Global. 10.4018/979-8-3693-5868-9

Kushlev, K. (2018). Media technology and well-being: a complementarity-interference model. In Diener, E., Oishi, S., & Tay, L. (Eds.), *Handbook of Well-Being* (pp. 970–982). DEF Publishers.

Martínez-López, F. J., Anaya-Sánchez, R., Aguilar-Illescas, R., & Molinillo, S. (2016). Types of virtual communities and virtual brand communities. In *Online Brand Communities* (pp. 125–140). Progress in IS. 10.1007/978-3-319-24826-4_8

Muniz, A. M.Jr, & O'Guinn, T. C. (2001). Brand Community. *The Journal of Consumer Research*, 27(4), 412–432. 10.1086/319618

Naslund, J. A., Aschbrenner, K. A., Marsch, L. A., & Bartels, S. J. (2016). The future of mental health care: Peer-to-peer support and social media. *Epidemiology and Psychiatric Sciences*, 25(2), 113–122. 10.1017/S204579601500106726744309

Oh, H. J., Ozkaya, E., & LaRose, R. (2014). How Does Online Social Networking Enhance Life Satisfaction? The Relationships Among Online Supportive Interaction, Affect, Perceived Social Support, Sense of Community, and Life Satisfaction. *Computers in Human Behavior*, 30, 69–78. 10.1016/j.chb.2013.07.053

Parks, K. M., & Steelman, L. A. (2008). Organizational wellness programs: A meta-analysis. *Journal of Occupational Health Psychology*, 13(1), 58–68. 10.1037/1076-8998.13.1.5818211169

Pulizzi, J. (2012). The Rise of Storytelling as the New Marketing. *Publishing Research Quarterly*, 28(2), 116–123. 10.1007/s12109-012-9264-5

Rathore, S., & Arora, M. (2024). Sustainability Reporting in the Metaverse: A Multi-Sectoral Analysis. In *Exploring the Use of Metaverse in Business and Education* (pp. 147-165). IGI Global. 10.4018/979-8-3693-5868-9.ch009

Ridings, C. M., & Gefen, D. (2004). Virtual community attraction: Why people hang out online. *Journal of Computer-Mediated Communication*, 10(1), JCMC1010. 10.1111/j.1083-6101.2004.tb00229.x

Ridings, C. M., & Gefen, D. (2004). Virtual Community Attraction: Why People Hang Out Online. *Journal of Computer-Mediated Communication*, 10(1), JCMC10110. 10.1111/j.1083-6101.2004.tb00229.x

Ridings, C. M., & Gefen, D. (2004). Virtual Community Attraction: Why People Hang Out Online. *Journal of Computer-Mediated Communication*, 10(1), JCMC10110. 10.1111/j.1083-6101.2004.tb00229.x

Samuels, M. (2019). *The Power of Live Streaming in Social Media*. Social Media Today.

Smith, A. N. (2012). Shifting landscapes: The implications of social media for social marketing. *Journal of Marketing Theory and Practice*, 20(3), 239–253.

Trepte, S., Reinecke, L., & Juechems, K. (2017). The Social Media Privacy Model: Privacy and Communication in the Light of Social Media Affordances. *Communication Theory*, 27(4), 239–258.

van Deursen, A. J., & van Dijk, J. A. (2014). The digital divide shifts to differences in usage. *New Media & Society*, 16(3), 507–526. 10.1177/1461444813487959

Vraga, E. K., & Bode, L. (2020). Defining Misinformation and Understanding its Bounded Nature: Using Expertise and Evidence for Describing Misinformation. *Political Communication*, 37(1), 136–144. 10.1080/10584609.2020.1716500

Wright, K. B., Bell, S. B., Wright, K. B., & Bell, S. B. (2003). Health-related support groups on the Internet: Linking empirical findings to social support and computer-mediated communication theory. *Journal of Health Psychology*, 8(1), 39–54. 10.1177/1359105303008001429221113899

Chapter 17
The Right Color Attracts the Right Customer:
The Art of Selling Smartly With Neuromarketing and Color Psychology

Rajneesh Ahlawat
Chaudhary Devi Lal University, India

Pooja Swami
Chaudhary Devi Lal University, India

ABSTRACT

Neuromarketing is emerging as the next game-changing branch of marketing that applies the principles of neuroscience to better understand the customer's conscious and subconscious mind while deciding to purchase any product or service as well as during his choice-making processes. Color psychology is a key technique of neuromarketing that explores how people perceive different colors and how it affects their emotions and their purchasing decisions. By studying the subconscious associations and sensory responses to various colors, neuromarketers can develop a significant understanding of how color influences consumer choices and thereby, by leveraging color psychology and integrating it into each stage of their marketing process, they can boost their sales to the targeted segment. By reviewing the existing literature, this chapter aims to portray the interplay between neuromarketing, color psychology, and consumer behavior, and also highlights how the strategic use of colors can attract the right customer and enhance sales effectiveness.

DOI: 10.4018/979-8-3693-4236-7.ch017

INTRODUCTION

With the winds of globalization and the intensely competitive nature of today's marketplace, companies are constantly looking for new ways to stand out and attract customers. While there is no doubt that traditional marketing methods have been and will be at the top most priority when it comes to advertising, but they often fail to hit the target customer base when it comes to understanding the nuanced details of how consumers make purchases. To address this gap, neuromarketing has emerged as an innovative discipline that integrates marketing, psychology, and neuroscience to gain deeper insights into the subconscious drivers of consumer behavior (Singh et al., 2023). Neuromarketing is based on the understanding that the human brain is programmed to react to specific stimuli, with color being a particularly influential one. Color psychology is a branch of psychology that studies the influence of colors on human emotions and actions and it significantly affects consumer perceptions and influences purchase choices (Valdez & Mehrabian, 1994). This chapter aims to provide a review of the psychological implications of colors in marketing. The research reveals that, in the first 90 seconds, people form opinions about products and people, and colors alone account for between 62% to 90% of how we evaluate products and people. It also has been studied that 84.7% of people cite that colors are one of the primary reasons that they buy a particular product and when they buy a particular product 93% of the purchase is driven by colors only, 6% looks at the texture and 1% is dependent on the sound or smell of the product (Morton, n.d.). So, colors are not only used by companies to differentiate their products from the competitors, but they also influence the moods and emotions of the purchasers, thus colors play a very important role in the formation of attitudes towards a certain brand or product. Incorporating color psychology in the marketing offers companies a powerful tool for attracting the right customers and optimizing sales strategies. From branding and product packaging to advertising and retail environments, the strategic use of colors helps in creating memorable brand experiences with customers, thereby increases consumer engagement, which further drive their purchasing decisions and assists companies in exceeding their sales targets (Bortolotti et al., 2023; Song et al., 2022). The synergy between neuromarketing and color psychology opens up a wealth of opportunities for savvy marketers seeking to upscale their sales strategies and drive sales success. Through a comprehensive examination of theory, research findings, and real-world examples, this chapter shall elucidate the practical applications of color psychology in various aspects of marketing. This chapter shall help the readers to understand how by leveraging color psychology of neuromarketing brands can create a dominance on consumer's mind and can successfully multiply their number of sales along with building long-term brand loyalty.

Neuromarketing

Neuromarketing is a multidisciplinary field that has emerged from the amalgamation of two fields i.e. neuroscience and marketing and by combining the principles from both the fields, it studies consumers' sensory, cognitive, and affective responses to the marketing stimuli (Agarwal & Dutta 2015). Neuroscience is the study of the nervous system of the human brain and it explores how it functions, what is its structure, how it responds to various stimulus etc. Neuroscience provides the foundational knowledge and tools necessary to study the brain's response to marketing stimuli. And techniques such as functional magnetic resonance imaging (fMRI), electroencephalography (EEG), and eye-tracking allow researchers to observe brain activity in real-time and measure physiological responses to various marketing stimuli such as brand logo, color of product, website interface etc. (Antonenko, 2019; Hakim & Levy 2018). On the other hand, marketing brings a wealth of expertise in understanding consumer preferences, market trends, and effective communication strategies. Neuromarketing is the product of culmination of neuroscience, neuropsychology and marketing and integrating these multiple scientific disciplines, this approach provides marketers with a unique understanding of the neurocognitive mechanisms that influence consumer purchasing process.

Figure 1. Neuromarketing composition

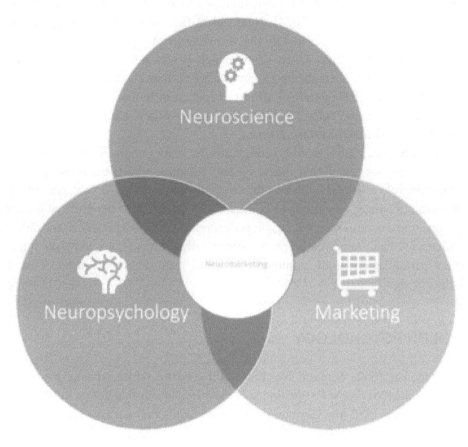

Neuromarketing is a strategy that uses neuroscience and cognitive science to study how people's brains react to advertising and other brand-related messages. It's also known as consumer neuroscience.

Neuromarketing and Color Perception

The relationship between neuroscience and human's perception of colors is very important for the neuromarketers to understand deeply to strategically utilize the psychology of colors. At the heart of color perception is the visual system, a complex network of neural pathways responsible for processing visual information from the eyes to the brain. The retina, located at the back of the eye, contains specialized cells called photoreceptors that detect light and convert it into electrical signals.

These signals are then transmitted to the brain via the optic nerve, where they are processed and interpreted in various regions of the visual cortex (Cohen-Duwek et al., 2022; Maitlo et al., 2024). Neuroscientific research has shown that color perception is impacted not just by the wavelengths of light reflected off objects, but also by the neural processing of these signals within the brain. Different parts of the visual cortex are dedicated to processing various elements of color, such as hue, saturation, and brightness. Furthermore, neurons in the visual cortex respond selectively to specific colors, allowing the brain to differentiate between a variety of colors and shades (Conway, 2014).

Neuroscience has revealed how higher-order brain regions influence our sense of color and how emotional, memory, and attention-related brain areas play an important role in modifying our subjective perception of color. For example, the amygdala mediates emotional responses to colors, whereas the prefrontal cortex evaluates and assigns meaning to colors depending on past experiences and cultural influences. Thus, neuromarketers by strategically utilizing color in marketing can elicit particular emotions, communicate brand messages, and impact consumer behavior significantly.

COLOR PSYCHOLOGY

In the late 1600s, Sir Isaac Newton is said to be the pioneer of color psychology who studied the color spectrum and how the different wavelengths of light describe each color. In 1810, the German poet Johann Wolfgang von Goethe released the theory of colors, one of the earliest books on color psychology (Parkinson, 2023). Goethe wrote on the significance of various colors and believed that they could evoke specific emotions. According to color psychology, also termed chromotherapy, or color healing, the frequencies and hues of certain colors can influence how we feel and what we do physically (Jonauskaite et al., 2020). These days, marketing and advertising are among the primary industries that apply color psychology. The study of ways in which particular colors influence human behavior is referred to as color psychology. Different colors have their own distinct meanings, connotations, and neurological effects which vary greatly from culture to culture. In addition to cultural variations, color psychology is also greatly affected by personal choice. Color psychology is the practical application of color theory, which is the study of how colors look together when different color combinations are created, and how they are perceived by people (Ciotti, 2020). There is scientific evidence that suggests using specific colors can increase brand awareness and boost sales by as much as 80%. It is important to keep in mind that when potential customers visit the website or store, the first thing they do is look at the visual contents. Therefore, it is crucial to study how colors influence your customers' tastes and action. Take a look at the following table which shows the emotions evoked by each color in the human and how they are utilized by marketers to boost their marketing and sales program.

Table 1. Strategic application of color psychology in marketing

Color	Emotion	Application in Marketing
Red	Excitement, Passion, Urgency, Strength	This color is often used to create a sense of urgency in sales promotions and its application can be seen in the food industry to evoke appetite and impulse buying. It is also generally seen associated with clearance sales and discounts.
Blue	Trust, Calmness, Serenity, Loyalty	This color is seen frequently used by banks, healthcare, and tech companies to convey trustworthiness and reliability. It is used for promoting relaxation and focus in advertising for wellness products or services.
Yellow	Happiness, Optimism, Positivity, Enthusiasm	This color draws people's attention and promotes a positive mood. It is found used in retail settings to grab attention and stimulate impulse purchases. It works effectively for grabbing attention of children or promoting summer-related products.
Green	Growth, Harmony, Nature, Freshness	This color is associated with nature and environmental consciousness. It is mostly used by eco-friendly brands and health-related products to convey freshness and vitality. It is also used in food packaging to symbolize natural ingredients.
Orange	Energy, Optimism, Friendly, Warm	This color grabs attention and creates a sense of excitement. It is commonly used by retailers to promote sales and discounts and also to evoke feelings of warmth and friendliness.
Purple	Luxury, Creativity, Royal, Mystery	This color is associated with royalty and sophistication. It is highly used by luxury brands to convey exclusivity and elegance. It is also used in beauty and cosmetic products to imply luxury and indulgence.
Black	Elegance, Authority, Formal, Power	This color conveys sophistication and authority and is used in luxury branding and high-end products to imply exclusivity and quality. It generally creates a sense of mystery and intrigue.

Source: Author

It is essential for brands to make smart choices by carefully analyzing these colors. This allows them to ensure that their color selections are in line with their brand ethos, that they resonate with their target audience, and that they can withstand the competition.

Must-Have Color Palettes for Any Brand

The below mentioned are the essential combinations of colors that are carefully chosen to represent a brand's identity and evoke specific emotions, ensuring consistency and recognition across all marketing materials and platforms. These palettes play a crucial role in brand differentiation, customer engagement, and overall brand success.

Primary Colors

These are the colors that are used to symbolize a brand, and they are the ones that are most easily recognizable. The majority of brands typically use not more than three primary colors. Primary colors are vibrant and eye-catching, making them effective for grabbing attention and creating brand recognition. They are often used as dominant colors in branding to convey boldness, energy, and excitement (Romanchuk, 2023). For example, popular brands like Coca-Cola and Canon prominently feature the primary color red in their branding. The brands utilize this vivid red color in its logo, packaging, and advertising to evoke emotions of energy and passion, making it more noticeable on shelves which helps in boosting their sales.

Secondary Colors

These colors provide support and complement the primary colors. While they may not be as immediately recognizable as primary colors, but nonetheless are crucial to a brand's identity. The quantity of secondary colors might vary but usually falls between two and four (Picmonkey, n.d.). For example, the primary colors of Google's logo are red, blue, yellow, and green, but the company also incorporates a range of secondary colors in its various Google products, such as Gmail, Google Drive, and Google Calendar. These secondary colors provide flexibility and visual interest while maintaining a cohesive brand identity across Google's diverse range of products and services.

Neutral Colors

The neutral colors consist of various tones of black, white, gray, and occasionally brown or beige. These colors offer contrast and balance. They are utilized for text, backdrops, and other practical aspects that need readability or simplicity (Lange, 2023). For example, Apple is world-wide known for its minimalist design aesthetic, which incorporates neutral colors such as white, black, and grey. These colors create a sleek and modern look, enhancing the perceived value of Apple products and contributing to increased sales.

Accent Colors

Accent colors are used selectively to add visual appeal and bring attention to key branding aspects. They can elicit specific emotions or associations and are commonly used to promote brand messaging (Saffronavenue, n.d.). For example, Amazon uses the accent color orange within its branding, particularly in its logo and marketing materials. Orange color is associated with enthusiasm and innovation which shows Amazon's drive to provide innovative solutions and improve the shopping experience, resulting in more sales on their site.

Experts and studies agree that brands should avoid using too many colors in their designs. The use of too many colors in a color palette might weaken brand awareness and provide the impression of inconsistency. As a general rule of thumb, it is recommended that brands must avoid using more than two or three primary colors and instead broaden their color palette with secondary and neutral hues as required. The key is to use it consistently and choose carefully based on the values of the business, the customers it's trying to reach, and industry standards.

Figure 2. Color psychology in branding: The Persuasive power of color

Note: *This infographic shows how worldwide popular brands have utilized color psychology in their branding. From Brand & Trademark Colours by D. O'Connor, 2019, https://www.whiteriverdesign.com/brand-and-trademark-colours/*

The figure 2. illustrates how various world-wide popular brands have strategically utilized the colors in their branding. To better understand the significance of color psychology in logo designing, it is important to look at successful brand color strategies. Colors have been a powerful tool for many famous brands in communicating their ideals and building their identities. Marketers can deliberately use color psychology in logo designing to develop visually appealing, strong, and memorable logos that capture the soul of a brand by acknowledging the importance of colors in brand identity.

THE 7 PS OF COLOR-BASED MARKETING FOR SMARTER SALES

Color psychology can be used to improve several parts of marketing strategy by applying it to the 7Ps of marketing: Product, Price, Place, Promotion, People, Process, and Physical Evidence. By incorporating color psychology into marketing campaigns, "The 7 Ps of Color-Based Marketing for Smarter Sales" lays out a thorough plan to boost sales performance where each "P" represents a pivotal aspect of product design, packaging, marketing, and presentation that uses colors to evoke specific emotions and feelings. The following are some ways that a marketer could integrate color psychology into each of the seven principles:

Product

In marketing, a product is defined as any tangible good, intangible service, or idea that is offered to meet a consumer's need or want. It includes both tangible goods and services that are designed to satisfy individual wants or desires.

Product Design: Product engineers can use specific colors that draw attention to particular useful features or benefits of product which improves the product's aesthetic appeal and its overall functionality and generates targeted sales (Hagtvedt, 2020). For instance, a refrigerator with blue LED lights on the shelves isn't just for looks, it subconsciously reinforces the key feature of the product, which is keeping the food cool. The color blue is often linked to calmness and coolness, that aligns with the fridge's main purpose.

Packaging: Neuromarketers can choose colors for product packaging based on the product's purpose, target audience preferences, and desired emotional reactions. For example, green packaging can be opted for organic food that provides a sense of naturalness, whereas red packaging for a sports drink that conveys a sense of vitality and enthusiasm (Martinez et al., 2021). It is also suggested that as color preference varies by age and gender, so these factors should also be considered while deciding packaging color.

Price

Price refers to the monetary value assigned to a product or service that customers are required to pay in exchange for acquiring it. Neuromarketers can leverage color psychology to influence consumer perceptions of price, ultimately impacting their purchasing decisions.

Price tags: When the price tag is displayed in a contrasting color, such as red on a black background, it might attract attention to the price and possibly give the impression that it is lower than it actually is. Price tags can be used to influence perception of product quality for instance, black and gold colored price tags is often used by luxury brands to represent sophistication and class, thereby justifying high price points (Bettiga et al., 2021).

Discount and Signage: Applying eye-catching colors for discount and sale advertising is a strategic psychological approach which can increase foot traffic, boost sales, and create a sense of excitement and urgency among consumers that encourages them to make spontaneous purchasing decisions (Grandi et al., 2022). For example, the color red is commonly used in discount and sale signage due to its strong link with clearance sales and discounts.

Place

Place refers to the distribution channels via which products and services are made available to consumers. It encompasses all activities and processes involved in moving goods or services from the producer to the consumer, such as the location of sales outlets, distribution routes, logistics, and inventory control.

Retail Environment: The psychological use of colors in curating a retail environment is creating store designs with colors that make customers feel more at ease and influence their purchasing decisions (Cho & Suh, 2020). For example, warm colors like orange and yellow can be used to create a welcoming and inviting atmosphere, which may instantly uplift the mood of customers as they step into the store.

Store Layout and Signage: Color can also be effectively used in store layout and signage to guide customers through the store and highlight key areas such as product displays, checkout counters, and promotional sections. Color-coded pathways are an excellent example of this, using different colors to identify pathways or aisles within the store allows customers to navigate more quickly and locate what they're looking for (Khan et al., 2022).

Promotion

In marketing, promotion refers to the activities and methods used to communicate the value of a product or service to potential customers and encourage them to buy it. Promotion involves various elements such as (advertising, sales promotions, personal selling, public relation, direct marketing, digital marketing) where keeping in mind and tactfully using nuances of colors can strategically drive sales and revenue growth.

Advertising Materials: When designing advertising materials (business cards, brochures, letterhead, signage, websites, billboards etc.) it is important to incorporate colors that create the desired emotions and strengthen communication about the brand. For instance, the color green may be used in environmental campaigns to communicate the ideas of sustainability and eco-friendliness (Adam et al., 2022; Wenting et al., 2022).

Direct Marketing: Colors can create engaging and more effective direct marketing campaigns such as for successful email marketing campaigns using eye-catching colors in email subject lines, headers, and call-to-action buttons can improve open rates and click-through rates. Furthermore, vibrant colors can be utilized into direct mail pieces to make them stand out in recipients' mailboxes, which encourages recipients to open and read the mail piece.

People

The fifth P of the marketing mix is "People" that represents the employees, salespeople, and other individuals who work for the company. It recognizes the significant role that people play in delivering value to consumers and shaping the overall experience that customers have with an organization.

Employee Uniforms and Attires: It is important to select such colors for employee uniforms and attire that are reflective of the image and values of the brand as it can significantly impact how brand and its employees are perceived by its customers (Wu et al., 2020). A great example of this is the uniform colors of the food delivery boys of the popular companies Zomato and Swiggy in India. Zomato's delivery boys are often seen wearing red shade uniforms on the other hand Swiggy delivery boys are seen wearing orange color uniforms. These consistent uniform colors not only help Zomato and Swiggy delivery boys stand out but also serve as a visual representation of the respective brands' identities and values.

Personal Branding: Personal branding is the activity of promoting oneself and one's career as a brand. Consistency is the key to personal branding. People should use consistent colors across all platforms, including LinkedIn, business cards, websites, and social media profiles, to build a cohesive and recognizable brand identity.

This reinforces their personal brand message and creates a lasting impression on potential clients, employers, and competitors.

Process

In the context of marketing, process refers to the systematic series of steps or activities undertaken in delivering a product or service to the end-user and achieving marketing objectives.

Website and App User Interface (UI/UX): In digital marketing and user experience (UX) design, optimizing the color scheme of websites and digital platforms is an essential aspect of the marketing process. Marketers can benefit from color psychology principles when picking colors while designing company website or creating user interface that stimulate specific emotions, convey brand attributes, and affect user behavior (Jongmans et al., 2022). For example, using contrasting colors for buttons and links can enhance navigation and conversion rates by making interactive elements more visible and engaging to users.

Customer Relationship Management: Color selection in communication materials such as emails and newsletters is a crucial element of the marketing process, particularly in customer relationship management (CRM) and content marketing. Marketers must maintain brand identification and recognition by ensuring consistency in color usage across all communication materials. This includes using brand colors and design elements consistently in emails, newsletters, social media posts, and other marketing collateral to create a cohesive and recognizable brand experience for customers (Suriadi et al., 2022).

Physical Evidence

Physical evidence is the tangible components that customers experience while interacting with a product or service. For instance, Physical evidence in a restaurant includes the surroundings, staff uniform, menus, and internet reviews, which indicate the expected customer experience. Color psychology in physical evidence across multiple touchpoints can improve brand impression, affect customer emotions and actions, and boost company success.

Branded Materials: Branded materials are a diverse group of tangible assets that represent the personality of a brand and its values. These could include business cards, packaging materials, stationery, promotional products, and signage (Xiao et al., 2021). When branded materials share a consistent color palette, they create a cohesive and unified brand image, which differentiates it from competitors and allows it to stand out in the minds of customers and fetch the sales.

Event Branding: Event branding involves the strategic use of colors, logos, and visually appealing elements to create a consistent and memorable brand experience for the event attendees. The colors must represent the theme or objectives of the event. Whether it's a corporate conference, product launch, or charity fundraiser, the chosen colors should reflect the mood, tone, and purpose of the event. For example, vibrant and energetic colors may be used for a celebratory event, while muted and sophisticated colors may be more appropriate for a professional conference (Sublimeeventsdesign, 2023).

To sum up, it can be said that including color psychology in the 7Ps of marketing provides neuromarketers with a powerful tool to enhance numerous facets of their marketing strategy. For enhanced sales strategies and increased sales, it gives a magical wand to neuromarketers to effectively influence consumer perceptions, behaviors, and purchase decisions throughout the marketing mix by understanding the psychological associations and emotional responses evoked by different colors and hues.

OPPORTUNITIES AND CHALLENGES IN IMPLEMENTING COLOR PSYCHOLOGY IN MARKETING

Color psychology is one of the many techniques used in neuromarketing that has a lot of potential to help marketers make their sales campaigns more effective. Through a culture of risk-taking, problem-solving, and the production of exclusive products and services that are tailored to the requirements of the market, entrepreneurship is a driving force behind creativity and innovation (Arora & Sharma, (2021); Arora (2016); Arora & Sharma, (2022)). The role of artificial intelligence is very important in the changing paradigms of diverse businesses operating in various sectors and the marketing advancements in this regard (Arora & Sharma, (2023). When it comes to the world of business, this results in advantages over competitors and economic expansion (Dhiman & Arora, (2024) b). The expansion of these opportunities within the metaverse is made possible by entrepreneurship, which makes it feasible to create totally new virtual experiences, business models, marketplaces and without any doubt colors also play an important role in this world of virtual reality. This pushes the frontiers of what is possible in a digital economy Within the metaverse, entrepreneurship expands these opportunities by enabling the creation of entirely new virtual experiences, business models, and marketplaces, pushing the boundaries of what is possible in a digital economy (Rathore & Arora (2024)). By providing immersive, virtual environments in which firms may develop new ideas, engage with audiences all over the world, and create novel sources of income, the metaverse is causing a revolution in the world of entrepreneurship. Through the setting up of virtual stores, arranging of events, and the engagement of clients in ways that transcend physical boundaries, it enables entrepreneurs to create opportunities for growth and creativity that have never been achieved before (Kumar, Arora & Erkol Bayram (Eds.). (2024) b; Dhiman & Arora (2024) a; Kumar, Arora & Erkol Bayram, (Eds.). (2024) a; Arora (2024) b; Chandel & Arora, (2024)). Customers can be educated through the use of virtual reality by giving them with immersive, colorful, hands-on experiences that simplify difficult concepts and make them easier to think about and recall. It provides clients with the opportunity to interact with items in a virtual environment, providing them with thorough demonstrations which are attractive, tutorials, and personalized learning experiences that boost engagement and retention. (Arora, (2024) a; Arora (2023)). Entrepreneurs, as key drivers of growth and innovation, can play a pivotal role in integrating color psychology in marketing by fostering collaboration among marketers, designers, psychologists, and neuroscientists. They can spearhead initiatives that bring together these diverse experts to develop effective color strategies, ensuring that the incorporation of color information into various marketing channels and touchpoints, such as packaging, ads, and stores, is both impactful and efficient. By investing in this multidisciplinary approach, entrepreneurs can enhance brand perception, evoke desired emotional responses, and ultimately drive consumer engagement and loyalty, despite the costs and time involved.

Despite the potential benefits, incorporating color psychology into marketing presents a few challenges for neuromarketers. These challenges stems from the complex nature of human perception, cultural diversity, and ethical concerns which are mentioned below:

- One of the greatest challenges that neuromarketers have to deal with is that people see and react to colors in different ways. People's color preferences and associations vary depending on various factors, such as their age, gender, cultural background, and personal situations. Therefore, it's tricky to come up with color schemes that work for all groups of people.
- Another major challenge is that, different countries have different perceptions about regarding colors. In one society, something that is seen as neutral or positive might be seen negatively in another. For example, in some Eastern cultures, the color white indicates death or grief, while in Western cultures it means purity and cleanliness. Neuromarketers have to be very aware of these cultural differences to make sure that the colors they choose don't offend the people they are trying to approach.
- Integrating color psychology in marketing requires collaboration among marketers, designers, psychologists, and neuroscientists so it can be costly and time-consuming to incorporate color information into all the different

marketing channels and touchpoints, including packaging, ads, and stores. Moreover, ensuring consistency and coherence in color strategies across different contexts and platforms adds another layer of complexity.

- With the shift to digital marketing channels, neuromarketers must adapt their color strategy to online platforms and digital experiences. Screen brightness, device settings, and platform-specific design constraints all have an impact on color perception. Neuromarketers must evaluate these digital nuances and optimize color selection accordingly.

Although color psychology provides neuromarketers with valuable insights into consumer preferences and behavior, the effective implementation of color strategies in marketing presents a number of obstacles. Overcoming these challenges requires a nuanced understanding of human perception, cultural context, ethical considerations, and practical limitations, along with interdisciplinary collaboration and continuous adaptation to evolving consumer trends and technologies.

CONCLUSION

Neuromarketing, an interdisciplinary field that integrates neuroscience, neuropsychology, and marketing principles is capable of providing useful insights into consumer behavior and decision-making. Neuromarketing represents a paradigm shift in marketing research, offering a more nuanced understanding of consumer preferences and responses through the lens of neuroscience. Neuromarketers can gain insights into the inner workings of the human brain by utilizing advanced neuroscientific techniques such as functional magnetic resonance imaging (fMRI), electroencephalography (EEG), and eye-tracking. Considering this growing phenomenon, this chapter has focused and discussed how this color psychology can be leveraged by today's neuromarketers while designing their marketing campaigns to generate maximum of sales of their product or services and to show this we have proposed 7Ps of color integrated marketing which is the novel approach for smartly increasing the sales figures of the company. This novel approach can also be use utilized by the brands to establish their competitive advantage. Along with suggesting practical recommendations for leveraging color psychology to enhance sales performance in today's competitive marketplace, we have also presented few challenges that may be faced by neuromarketers while implementing this integrated framework which should be taken into consideration while employing these approaches. At last, it can be said that understanding how colors influence emotions, perceptions, and purchasing decisions of customers allows neuromarketers to modify their marketing campaigns to better connect with their target audiences thereby resulting in massive number of sales for the brand or company.

REFERENCES

Adam, M., Al-Sharaa, A., Ab Ghafar, N., Mundher, R., Abu Bakar, S., & Alhasan, A. (2022). The effects of colour content and cumulative area of outdoor advertisement billboards on the visual quality of urban streets. *ISPRS International Journal of Geo-Information*, 11(12), 630. 10.3390/ijgi11120630

Agarwal, S., & Dutta, T. (2015). Neuromarketing and consumer neuroscience: Current understanding and the way forward. *Decision (Washington, D.C.)*, 42(4), 457–462. 10.1007/s40622-015-0113-

Antonenko, P. D. (2019). Educational Neuroscience: Exploring Cognitive Processes that Underlie Learning. In Parsons, T. D., Lin, L., & Cockerham, D. (Eds.), *Mind, Brain and Technology. Educational Communications and Technology: Issues and Innovations*. Springer., 10.1007/978-3-030-02631-8_3

Arora, M. (2023). Encapsulating Role of Persuasion and Skill Development in Marketing Communication for Brand Building: A Perspective. In *International Handbook of Skill, Education, Learning, and Research Development in Tourism and Hospitality* (pp. 1–17). Springer Nature Singapore.

Arora, M. (2024) a. Virtual Reality in Education: Analyzing the Literature and Bibliometric State of Knowledge. *Transforming Education with Virtual Reality*, 379-402. 10.1002/9781394200498.ch22

Arora, M. (2024) b. Metaverse Metamorphosis: Bridging the Gap Between Research Insights and Industry Applications. In *Research, Innovation, and Industry Impacts of the Metaverse* (pp. 275-286). Research Gate.

Arora, M., & Sharma, R. L. (2021). Repurposing the Role of Entrepreneurs in the Havoc of COVID-19. In *Entrepreneurship and Big Data* (pp. 229-250). CRC Press.

Arora, M., & Sharma, R. L. (2023). Artificial intelligence and big data: Ontological and communicative perspectives in multi-sectoral scenarios of modern businesses. *Foresight*, 25(1), 126–143. 10.1108/FS-10-2021-0216

Bettiga, D., Mandolfo, M., Lolatto, R., & Lamberti, L. (2021, December). Investigating the effect of price tag colours on cortical, cardiac and ocular responses. In *2021 4th International Conference on Bio-Engineering for Smart Technologies (BioSMART)* (pp. 1-5). IEEE. 10.1109/BioSMART54244.2021.9677671

Bortolotti, A., Cannito, L., Anzani, S., & Palumbo, R. (2023). The promise of color in marketing: Use, applications, tips and neuromarketing. *Cultura e Scienza del Colore-Color Culture and Science*, 15(01), 76–85. 10.23738/CCSJ.150110

Chandel, M., & Arora, M. (2024). Metaverse Perspectives: Unpacking Its Role in Shaping Sustainable Development Goals-A Qualitative Inquiry. In *Research, Innovation, and Industry Impacts of the Metaverse* (pp. 62-75). IGI Global.

Cho, J. Y., & Suh, J. (2020). Spatial color efficacy in perceived luxury and preference to stay: An eye-tracking study of retail interior environment. *Frontiers in Psychology*, 11, 516274. 10.3389/fpsyg.2020.0029632296358

Ciotti, G. (2020). *Color Psychology in Marketing and Branding is All About Context*. Helpscout. https://www.helpscout.com/blog/psychology-of-color/#:~:text=so%20unwaveringly%20shallow?-,What%20is%20color%20psychology?be%20based%20on%20color%20alone

Cohen-Duwek, H., Slovin, H., & Ezra Tsur, E. (2022). Computational modeling of color perception with biologically plausible spiking neural networks. *PLoS Computational Biology*, 18(10), e1010648. 10.1371/journal.pcbi.101064836301992

Conway, B. R. (2014). Color signals through dorsal and ventral visual pathways. *Visual Neuroscience*, 31(2), 197–209. 10.1017/S0952523813000038224103417

Dhiman, V., & Arora, M. (2024)b. Exploring the linkage between business incubation and entrepreneurship: understanding trends, themes and future research agenda. *LBS Journal of Management & Research*.

Dhiman, V., & Arora, M. (2024)a. Current State of Metaverse in Entrepreneurial Ecosystem: A Retrospective Analysis of Its Evolving Landscape. In *Exploring the Use of Metaverse in Business and Education* (pp. 73-87). IGI Global. 10.4018/979-8-3693-5868-9.ch005

Grandi, B., & Cardinali, M. G. (2022). Colours and price offers: How different price communications can affect sales and customers' perceptions. *Journal of Retailing and Consumer Services*, 68, 103073. 10.1016/j.jretconser.2022.103073

Hagtvedt, H. (2020). Dark is durable, light is user-friendly: The impact of color lightness on two product attribute judgments. *Psychology and Marketing*, 37(7), 864–875. 10.1002/mar.21268

Hakim, A., & Levy, D. J. (2019). A gateway to consumers' minds: Achievements, caveats, and prospects of electroencephalography-based prediction in neuromarketing. *Wiley Interdisciplinary Reviews: Cognitive Science*, 10(2), e1485. 10.1002/wcs.148530496636

Jonauskaite, D., Tremea, I., Bürki, L., Diouf, C. N., & Mohr, C. (2020). To see or not to see: Importance of color perception to color therapy. *Color Research and Application*, 45(3), 450–464. 10.1002/col.22490

Jongmans, E., Jeannot, F., Liang, L., & Dampérat, M. (2022). Impact of website visual design on user experience and website evaluation: The sequential mediating roles of usability and pleasure. *Journal of Marketing Management*, 38(17-18), 2078–2113. 10.1080/0267257X.2022.2085315

Khan, M. A., Vivek, , Minhaj, S. M., Saifi, M. A., Alam, S., & Hasan, A. (2022). Impact of Store Design and Atmosphere on Shoppers' Purchase Decisions: An Empirical Study with Special Reference to Delhi-NCR. *Sustainability (Basel)*, 15(1), 95. 10.3390/su15010095

Kumar, J., Arora, M., & Erkol Bayram, G. (Eds.). (2024) b. *Research, Innovation, and Industry Impacts of the Metaverse*. IGI Global.

Kumar, J., Arora, M., & Erkol Bayram, G. (Eds.). (2024)a. *Exploring the Use of Metaverse in Business and Education*. IGI Global. 10.4018/979-8-3693-5868-9

Lange, C. (2023). The Science of Color in Marketing: How to Use Color Psychology to Boost Your Brand. *Medium*. https://bootcamp.uxdesign.cc/the-science-of-color-in-marketing-how-to-use-color-psychology-to-boost-your-brand-299db0c8a3b2

Maitlo, N., Noonari, N., Ghanghro, S. A., Duraisamy, S., & Ahmed, F. (2024). Color Recognition in Challenging Lighting Environments: CNN Approach. *arXiv preprint arXiv:2402.04762*. https://doi.org//arXiv.2402.0476210.1109/I2CT61223.2024.10543537

Martinez, L. M., Rando, B., Agante, L., & Abreu, A. M. (2021). True colors: Consumers' packaging choices depend on the color of retail environment. *Journal of Retailing and Consumer Services*, 59, 102372. 10.1016/j.jretconser.2020.102372

Morton, J. (n.d.). *Substantial research shows why color matters and how color plays a pivotal role in all our visual experiences*. Colorcom. https://www.colorcom.com/research/why-color-matters#:~:text=Research%20reveals%20people%20make%20a,is%20based%20on%20color%20alone.&text=3.,are%20now%20made%20in%2Dstore

O'connor, D. (2019). *Brand & Trademark Colours [Infographic]*. Whiteriverdesign. https://www.whiteriverdesign.com/brand-and-trademark-colours/

Parkinson, N. (2023). *The History of Color: A Universe of Chromatic Phenomena*. Frances Lincoln. https://www.google.co.in/books/edition/The_History_of_Color/FHu-EAAAQBAJ?hl=en&gbpv=1

Picmonkey. (n.d.). *Spice Up Your Branding with Secondary Color Palettes*. PicMonkey. https://www.picmonkey.com/blog/spice-up-your-branding-with-secondary-color-palettes

Rathore, S., & Arora, M. (2024). Sustainability Reporting in the Metaverse: A Multi-Sectoral Analysis. In *Exploring the Use of Metaverse in Business and Education* (pp. 147-165). IGI Global. https://doi.org/10.4018/979-8-3693-5868-9.ch009

Romanchuk, J. (2023). *Brand Colors — Everything You Need to Know*. Hubspot. https://blog.hubspot.com/marketing/brand-colors#:~:text=Primary%20color%3A%20The%20main%20color,the%20primary%20and%20secondary%20colors

Saffronavenue. (n.d.). *How to Use Accent Colors in Your Brand.* Saffronavenue. https://saffronavenue.com/blog/logo-branding/how-to-use-accent-colors-within -your-brand/#:~:text=Accent%20Colors%20in%20Print%20Marketing&text=Be %20it%20business%20cards%2C%20stationery,tangible%20touchpoint%20a%20 memorable%20interaction

Singh, P., Alhassan, I., & Khoshaim, L. (2023). What Do You Need to Know? A Systematic Review and Research Agenda on Neuromarketing Discipline. *Journal of Theoretical and Applied Electronic Commerce Research*, 18(4), 2007–2032. 10.3390/jtaer18040101

Song, J., Xu, F., & Jiang, Y. (2022). The colorful company: Effects of brand logo colorfulness on consumer judgments. *Psychology and Marketing*, 39(8), 1610–1620. 10.1002/mar.21674

Sublimeeventdesigns. (2023). *The Wow Factor: Use of Color in Event Design.* Sublimeeventsdesign. https://www.sublimeeventdesigns.com/the-wow-factor-use -of-color-in-event-design/

Suriadi, J., Mardiyana, M., & Reza, B. (2022). The concept of color psychology and logos to strengthen brand personality of local products. *Linguistics and Culture Review*, 6(S1), 839–856. 10.21744/lingcure.v6nS1.2168

Valdez, P., & Mehrabian, A. (1994). Effects of color on emotions. *Journal of Experimental Psychology. General*, 123(4), 394–409. 10.1037/0096-3445.123.4.394 7996122

Wenting, F., Yuelong, Z., Xianyun, S., & Chenling, L. (2022). Green advertising is more environmentally friendly? The influence of advertising color on consumers' preferences for green products. *Frontiers in Psychology*, 13, 959746. 10.3389/ fpsyg.2022.95974636389554

Wu, L., King, C. A., Lu, L., & Guchait, P. (2020). Hospitality aesthetic labor management: Consumers' and prospective employees' perspectives of hospitality brands. *International Journal of Hospitality Management*, 87, 102373. 10.1016/j. ijhm.2019.102373

Xiao, C., Zhu, H., Wang, X., & Wu, L. (2021). Vividly warm: The color saturation of logos on brands' customer sensitivity judgment. *Color Research and Application*, 46(6), 1347–1359. 10.1002/col.22682

Compilation of References

. Bala, R., & Gupta, P. (2024). Virtual Reality in Education: Benefits, Applications and Challenges. *Transforming Education with Virtual Reality*, 165-180.

. Çalışkan, G., Yayla, İ., & Pamukçu, H. (2023). The use of augmented reality technologies in tourism businesses from the perspective of UTAUT2. *European Journal of Innovation Management.*

. Dhiman, V., & Arora, M. (2024). Exploring the linkage between business incubation and entrepreneurship: understanding trends, themes and future research agenda. *LBS Journal of Management & Research.*

. Dhiman, V., & Arora, M. (2024)b. Exploring the linkage between business incubation and entrepreneurship: understanding trends, themes and future research agenda. *LBS Journal of Management & Research.*

. Gao, Y., & Liu, H. (2022). Artificial intelligence-enabled personalization in interactive marketing: a customer journey perspective. *Journal of Research in Interactive Marketing*, (ahead-of-print), 1-18.

. Goel, P., Mahadevan, K., & Punjani, K. K. (2023). Augmented and virtual reality in apparel industry: a bibliometric review and future research agenda. *foresight, 25*(2), 167-184.

. Hussain, S. (2019). Sensory marketing strategies and consumer behavior: Sensible selling using all five senses. *IUP Journal of Business Strategy, 16*(3).

. Machairidis, E., & Mourmouras, N. (2020). *The impact of augmented, virtual and mixed reality technologies on consumer purchase decision, in the Greek market.*

. Moorhouse, N., tom Dieck, M. C., & Jung, T. (2018). Technological innovations transforming the consumer retail experience: a review of literature. *Augmented Reality and Virtual Reality: Empowering Human, Place and Business*, 133-143.

. Zhang, J. (2020). *A systematic review of the use of augmented reality (AR) and virtual reality (VR) in online retailing.*

Aaker, D. A. (1991). *Managing brand equity: Capitalizing on the value of a brand name.* Free Press.

Aaker, D. A. (1992). The value of brand equity. *The Journal of Business Strategy*, 13(4), 27–32. 10.1108/eb039503

Abdelmaged, M. A. M. (2021). *Implementation of virtual reality in healthcare, entertainment, tourism, education, and retail sectors.*

Abdolmohamad Sagha, M., Seyyedamiri, N., Foroudi, P., & Akbari, M. (2022). The one thing you need to change is emotions: The effect of multi-sensory marketing on consumer behavior. *Sustainability (Basel)*, 14(4), 2334. 10.3390/su14042334

Abrokwah-Larbi, K. (2024). Transforming metaverse marketing into strategic agility in SMEs through mediating roles of IMT and CI: theoretical framework and research propositions. *Journal of Contemporary Marketing Science.*

Adam, M., Al-Sharaa, A., Ab Ghafar, N., Mundher, R., Abu Bakar, S., & Alhasan, A. (2022). The effects of colour content and cumulative area of outdoor advertisement billboards on the visual quality of urban streets. *ISPRS International Journal of Geo-Information*, 11(12), 630. 10.3390/ijgi11120630

Adeola, O., Evans, O., Ndubuisi Edeh, J., & Adisa, I. (2022). The future of marketing: artificial intelligence, virtual reality, and neuromarketing. *Marketing communications and brand development in emerging economies Volume I: Contemporary and future perspectives*, 253-280.

Agapito, D., Pinto, P., & Mendes, J. (2012). Sensory marketing and tourist experiences. *Spatial and Organizational Dynamics Discussions Papers*, 10, 7–19.

Agarwal, S., & Dutta, T. (2015). Neuromarketing and consumer neuroscience: Current understanding and the way forward. *Decision (Washington, D.C.)*, 42(4), 457–462. 10.1007/s40622-015-0113-1

Ahmed, A. (2022). Marketing 4.0: The Unseen Potential of AI in Consumer Relations. *International Journal of New Media Studies: International Peer Reviewed Scholarly Indexed Journal*, 9(1), 5–12.

Ahmed, R. R., Streimikiene, D., Channar, Z. A., Soomro, H. A., Streimikis, J., & Kyriakopoulos, G. L. (2022). The Neuromarketing Concept in Artificial Neural Networks: A Case of Forecasting and Simulation from the Advertising Industry. *Sustainability (Basel)*, 14(14), 8546. 10.3390/su14148546

Akhtar, O. M. A. R. (2018). Understanding use cases for augmented, mixed and virtual reality. *Altimeter. Online verfügbar unter*https://marketing. prophet. com/acton/ct/33865/p-00b2/Bct/l-00a9/l-00a9: 17b/ct16_0/1.

Al Sharif, A. H., Salleh, N. Z. M., Baharun, R. O., & Yusoff, M. E. (2021). Consumer behaviour through neuromarketing approach. *Journal of Contemporary Issues in Business and Government*, 27(3), 344–354.

Alexis, P. (2020). How Neuromarketing Will Revolutionise Luxury Brands. *The Review Magazine*https://www.thereviewmag.co.uk/how-neuromarketing-will-revolutionise-luxury-brands/

Alsharif, A. H., Salleh, N. Z. M., Abdullah, M., Khraiwish, A., & Ashaari, A. (2023). Neuro-marketing tools used in the marketing mix: A systematic literature and future research agenda. *SAGE Open*, 13(1), 21582440231156563. 10.1177/21582440231156563

Alsharif, A. H., Salleh, N. Z. M., Alrawad, M., & Lutfi, A. (2024). Exploring global trends and future directions in advertising research: A focus on consumer behavior. *Current Psychology (New Brunswick, N.J.)*, 43(7), 6193–6216. 10.1007/s12144-023-04812-w37359681

Alsharif, A. H., Salleh, N. Z. M., & Baharun, R. (2021). Neuromarketing: Marketing research in the new millennium. *Neuroscience Research Notes*, 4(3), 27–35. 10.31117/neuroscirn.v4i3.79

Alsharif, A. H., Salleh, N. Z. M., Baharun, R., Hashem, E. A. R., Mansor, A. A., Ali, J., & Abbas, A. F. (2021). Neuroimaging techniques in advertising research: Main applications, development, and brain regions and processes. *Sustainability (Basel)*, 13(11), 6488. 10.3390/su13116488

Al-Sharif, A. H., Salleh, N. Z. M., Baharun, R., & Yusoff, M. F. (2021). Consumer Behaviour Through Neuromarketing Approach. [CrossRef]. *Journal of Contemporary Issues in Business and Government*, 27, 344–354.

Alsharif, A. H., Salleh, N. Z. M., Hashem, E. A. R., Khraiwish, A., Putit, L., & Arif, L. S. M. (2023). Exploring factors influencing neuromarketing implementation in malaysian universities: Barriers and enablers. *Sustainability (Basel)*, 15(5), 4603. 10.3390/su15054603

Alsharif, A., Salleh, N. Z. M., Pilelienė, L., Abbas, A. F., & Ali, J. (2022). Current Trends in the Application of EEG in Neuromarketing: A Bibliometric Analysis. *Scientific Annals of Economics and Business*, 69(3), 393–415. 10.47743/saeb-2022-0020

Alsmadi, S., & Hailat, K. (2021). Neuromarketing and improved understanding of consumer behaviour through brain-based neuro activity. *Journal of Information & Knowledge Management*, 20(02), 2150020. 10.1142/S0219649221500209

Alvi, I. (2023). Investigating students' adoption of virtual reality for L2-learning in India. *Education and Information Technologies*, 1–22.

Alvino, L., Constantinides, E., & Franco, M. (2018). Towards a better understanding of consumer behavior: Marginal utility as a parameter in neuromarketing research. *International Journal of Marketing Studies*, 10(1), 90–106. 10.5539/ijms.v10n1p90

Ambika, A., Shin, H., & Jain, V. (2023). Immersive technologies and consumer behavior: A systematic review of two decades of research. *Australian Journal of Management*, ●●●, 03128962231181429. 10.1177/03128962231181429

Ambler, T., & Barwise, P. (1998). The trouble with brand valuation. *Journal of Brand Management*, 5(5), 367–377. 10.1057/bm.1998.25

American Marketing Association. (2022). *The Four Ps of Marketing*. AMA. https://www.ama.org/marketing-news/the-four-ps-of-marketing/

Amran, A. S., Ibrahim, S. A. S., Malim, N. H. A. H., Hamzah, N., Sumari, P., Lutfi, S. L., & Abdullah, J. M. (2022). Data Acquisition and Data Processing using Electroencephalogram in Neuromarketing: A Review. *Pertanika Journal of Science & Technology*, 30(1), 19–33. 10.47836/pjst.30.1.02

Ancillai, C., Terho, H., Cardinali, S., & Pascucci, F. (2019). Advancing social media driven sales research: Establishing conceptual foundations for B-to-B social selling. *Industrial Marketing Management*, 82, 293–308. 10.1016/j.indmarman.2019.01.002

Antonenko, P. D. (2019). Educational Neuroscience: Exploring Cognitive Processes that Underlie Learning. In Parsons, T. D., Lin, L., & Cockerham, D. (Eds.), *Mind, Brain and Technology. Educational Communications and Technology: Issues and Innovations*. Springer., 10.1007/978-3-030-02631-8_3

Antunes, I. F. S., & Veríssimo, J. M. C. (2024). A bibliometric review and content analysis of research trends in sensory marketing. *Cogent Business & Management*, 11(1), 2338879. 10.1080/23311975.2024.2338879

Ariely, D., & Berns, G. S. (2010). Neuromarketing: The hope and hype of neuroimaging in business. *Nature Reviews. Neuroscience*, 11(4), 284–292. 10.1038/nrn279520197790

Armstrong, K. M., Fitzgerald, J. K., & Moore, T. (2006). Changes in Visual Receptive Fields with Microstimulation of Frontal Cortex. *Neuron*, 50(5), 791–798. 10.1016/j.neuron.2006.05.01016731516

Arora, M. (2023). Encapsulating Role of Persuasion and Skill Development in Marketing Communication for Brand Building: A Perspective. In *International Handbook of Skill, Education, Learning, and Research Development in Tourism and Hospitality* (pp. 1-17). Singapore: Springer Nature Singapore.

Arora, M. (2024) b. Metaverse Metamorphosis: Bridging the Gap Between Research Insights and Industry Applications. In *Research, Innovation, and Industry Impacts of the Metaverse* (pp. 275-286). Research Gate.

Arora, M. (2024). Metaverse Metamorphosis: Bridging the Gap Between Research Insights and Industry Applications. In *Research, Innovation, and Industry Impacts of the Metaverse* (pp. 275-286).

Arora, M. (2024). Metaverse Metamorphosis: Bridging the Gap Between Research Insights and Industry Applications. In *Research, Innovation, and Industry Impacts of the Metaverse* (pp. 275-286). Research Gate.

Arora, M. (2024). Virtual Reality in Education: Analyzing the Literature and Bibliometric State of Knowledge. *Transforming Education with Virtual Reality*, 379-402.

Arora, M. (2024). Virtual Reality in Education: Analyzing the Literature and Bibliometric State of Knowledge. *Transforming Education with Virtual Reality*, 379-402. 10.1002/9781394200498.ch22

Arora, M., & Sharma, R. L. (2021). Neutralizing Maleficent Effects of COVID-19 Through Entrepreneurship: Peeping Through the Lens of Communication. In *Effective Strategies for Communicating Insights in Business* (pp. 67-86). IGI Global.

Arora, M., & Sharma, R. L. (2021). Post-Pandemic Psycho-Social Wellbeing in India: Challenges and the Way Ahead. *Alina COSTIN, 2021.*

Arora, M., & Sharma, R. L. (2021). Repurposing the Role of Entrepreneurs in the Havoc of COVID-19. In *Entrepreneurship and Big Data* (pp. 229-250). CRC Press.

Arora, M., & Sharma, R. L. (2023). Artificial intelligence and big data: ontological and communicative perspectives in multi-sectoral scenarios of modern businesses. *foresight, 25*(1), 126-143.

Arora, M., Kumar, J., & Valeri, M. (2023). Crises and Resilience in the Age of Digitalization: Perspectivations of Past, Present and Future for Tourism Industry. In *Tourism Innovation in the Digital Era* (pp. 57-74). Emerald Publishing Limited.

Arora, M. (2016). Creative dimensions of entrepreneurship: A key to business innovation. *Pacific Business Review International, 1*(1), 255–259.

Arora, M. (2020). Post-truth and marketing communication in technological age. In *Handbook of research on innovations in technology and marketing for the connected consumer* (pp. 94–108). IGI Global. 10.4018/978-1-7998-0131-3.ch005

Arora, M. (2023). Encapsulating Role of Persuasion and Skill Development in Marketing Communication for Brand Building: A Perspective. In *International Handbook of Skill, Education, Learning, and Research Development in Tourism and Hospitality* (pp. 1–17). Springer Nature Singapore.

Arora, M., & Sharma, R. L. (2017). Decoding diverse dimensions of entrepreneurial leadership with special emphasis on persuasive communication. *Management Dynamics, 17*(1), 70–77. 10.57198/2583-4932.1063

Arora, M., & Sharma, R. L. (2022). Coalescing skills of gig players and fervor of entrepreneurial leaders to provide resilience strategies during global economic crises. In *COVID-19's Impact on the Cryptocurrency Market and the Digital Economy* (pp. 118–140). IGI Global. 10.4018/978-1-7998-9117-8.ch008

Arora, M., & Sharma, R. L. (2023). Artificial intelligence and big data: Ontological and communicative perspectives in multi-sectoral scenarios of modern businesses. *Foresight, 25*(1), 126–143. 10.1108/FS-10-2021-0216

Aslan, R., & Özbeyaz, A. (2022). Analysis of brand visibility on smartphone images with three-stage model using eye-tracking and EEG: A decision-making study in neuromarketing. *Middle East Journal of Management, 9*(4), 417–434. 10.1504/MEJM.2022.123727

Auttri, B., Chaitanya, K., Daida, S., & Jain, S. K. (2023). Digital Transformation in Customer Relationship Management: Enhancing Engagement and Loyalty. [EEL]. *European Economic Letters, 13*(3), 1140–1149.

Compilation of References

Auvray, M., & Spence, C. (2008). The multisensory perception of flavor. *Consciousness and Cognition*, 17(3), 1016–1031. 10.1016/j.concog.2007.06.00517689100

Ayachi, Zeineb & Jallouli, Rim. (2022). Digital Marketing Strategies Driven by Wellbeing in Virtual Communities: Literature Review. *Journal of Telecommunications and the Digital Economy*.

Babet, A. (2020). Utilization of personalization in marketing automation and email marketing.

Baek, E., Jung, H., Hwan, S., & Lee, M. (2018). Using warmth as the visual design of a store : Intimacy, relational needs, and approach intentions. *Journal of Business Research*, 88(March), 91–101. 10.1016/j.jbusres.2018.03.013

Bakardjieva. E., & Kimmel. A (2017). Neuromarketing Research Practices: Attitudes, Ethics, and Behavioral Intentions. *Ethics and Behavior,27*(3), 179-200.

Bakardjieva, E., & Kimmel, A. J. (2017). Neuromarketing research practices: Attitudes, ethics, and behavioral intentions. *Ethics & Behavior*, 27(3), 179–200. 10.1080/10508422.2016.1162719

Baltierra, S. (2023, January). Virtual Reality and Augmented Reality Applied to E-Commerce: A Literature Review. In *Human-Computer Interaction:8th Iberoamerican Workshop, HCI-COLLAB 2022* (p. 201). Springer Nature.

Baños, R. M., Botella, C., Rubió, I., Quero, S., García-Palacios, A., & Alcañiz, M. (2008). Presence and emotions in virtual environments: The influence of stereoscopy. *Cyberpsychology and Behavior, 11*(1), 1–8. 10.1089/cpb.2007.9936

Barak, A., Boniel-Nissim, M., & Suler, J. (2008). Fostering empowerment in online support groups. *Computers in Human Behavior*, 24(5), 1867–1883. 10.1016/j.chb.2008.02.004

Barloso, K. (2023, December 21). *How to use sensory marketing to boost brand appeal*. Thrive Internet Marketing Agency. https://thriveagency.com/news/sensory-marketing/

Barlow, A. K. J., Siddiqui, N. Q., & Mannion, M. (2004). Developments in information and communication technologies for retail marketing channels. *International Journal of Retail & Distribution Management, 32*(3), 157–163. 10.1108/09590550410524948

Baron, A. S., Zaltman, G., & Olson, J. (2017). Barriers to advancing the science and practice of marketing. *Journal of Marketing Management*, 33(11-12), 893–908. 10.1080/0267257X.2017.1323839

Barsalou, L. W. (1999). *Perceptual symbol systems*.

Barsalou, L. W. (2008). Grounded Cognition. *Annual Review of Psychology, 59*. 10.1146/annurev.psych.59.103006.093639

Barwise, P. (1993). Brand equity: Snark or boojum? *International Journal of Research in Marketing*, 10(1), 93–104. 10.1016/0167-8116(93)90036-X

Bastiaansen, M., Straatman, S., Driessen, E., Mitas, O., Stekelenburg, J., & Wang, L. (2016). My destination in your brain : A novel neuromarketing approach for evaluating the effectiveness of destination marketing. *Journal of Destination Marketing & Management*. 10.1016/j. jdmm.2016.09.003

Bazzani, A., Ravaioli, S., Trieste, L., Faraguna, U., & Turchetti, G. (2020). Is EEG suitable for marketing research? A systematic review. *Frontiers in Neuroscience*, 14, 594566. 10.3389/ fnins.2020.59456633408608

Behl, A., Jayawardena, N., Shankar, A., Gupta, M., & Lang, L. D. (2024). Gamification and neuromarketing: A unified approach for improving user experience. *Journal of Consumer Behaviour*, 23(1), 218–228. 10.1002/cb.2178

Bekalu, M. A., McCloud, R. F., & Viswanath, K. (2019). Association of social media use with social well-being, positive mental health, and self-rated health: Disentangling routine use from emotional connection to use. *Health Education & Behavior*, 46(2_suppl, 2S), 69S–80S. 10.117 7/1090198119863768 31742462

Berman, B., & Pollack, D. (2021). Strategies for the successful implementation of augmented reality. *Business Horizons*, 64(5), 621–630. 10.1016/j.bushor.2021.02.027

Berman, G., Potgieter, A., & Tait, M. (2023). The Influence of Sensory Branding Strategies In-Store on Consumer Preference: The South African Skincare Industry. *Journal of Brand Strategy*, 12(2), 194–220.

Bettiga, D., Mandolfo, M., Lolatto, R., & Lamberti, L. (2021, December). Investigating the effect of price tag colours on cortical, cardiac and ocular responses. In *2021 4th International Conference on Bio-Engineering for Smart Technologies (BioSMART)* (pp. 1-5). IEEE. 10.1109/ BioSMART54244.2021.9677671

Bhardwaj, S., Rana, G. A., Behl, A., & de Caceres, S. J. G. (2023). Exploring the boundaries of Neuromarketing through systematic investigation. *Journal of Business Research*, 154, 113371. 10.1016/j.jbusres.2022.113371

Bhatia, K. (2014). Neuromarketing: Towards a better understanding of consumer behavior. *Optimization*, 6(1), 52–62.

Bhatia, R., Garg, R., Chhikara, R., Kataria, A., & Talwar, V. (2021). Sensory marketing–a review and research agenda. *Academy of Marketing Studies Journal*, 25(4), 1–30.

Bhatnagar, S. (2022). *Digital Disruptions and Transformation of Bank Marketing*.

Bhopal, R., & Devi, R. (2022). Digitalization and Its Role on Flexible Workforce. *National Journal Of Commerce And Management*.

Bhopal, R., & Devi, R. (2023). Emotional Intelligence for Effective Leadership: Future Research Trends Using Bibliometric Analysis. In *AI and Emotional Intelligence for Modern Business Management* (pp. 48-63). IGI Global. 10.4018/979-8-3693-0418-1.ch004

Compilation of References

Biocca, F., & Delaney, B. (1995). Immersive virtual reality technology. In Biocca, F., & Levy, M. R. (Eds.), *Communication in the age of virtual reality* (pp. 57–124). Lawrence Erlbaum Associates.

Bishnoi, S. K., & Singh, S. (2022). A Study on Consumer Buying Behaviour for Fashion and Luxury Brands Under Emotional Influence. *Research Journal of Textile and Apparel.*, 26(4), 405–418. 10.1108/RJTA-03-2021-0026

Biswas, D., Labrecque, L. I., & Lehmann, D. R. (2021). Effects of sequential sensory cues on food taste perception: Cross-modal interplay between visual and olfactory stimuli. *Journal of Consumer Psychology*, 31(4), 746–764. 10.1002/jcpy.1231

Biswas, D., & Szocs, C. (2019). The smell of healthy choices: Cross-modal sensory compensation effects of ambient scent on food purchases. *JMR, Journal of Marketing Research*, 56(1), 123–141. 10.1177/0022243718820585

Biswas, D., Szocs, C., & Abell, A. (2019). Extending the boundaries of sensory marketing and examining the sixth sensory system: Effects of vestibular sensations for sitting versus standing postures on food taste perception. *The Journal of Consumer Research*, 46(4), 708–724. 10.1093/jcr/ucz018

Boccia, F., Malgeri Manzo, R., & Covino, D. (2019). Consumer behavior and corporate social responsibility: An evaluation by a choice experiment. *Corporate Social Responsibility and Environmental Management, 26*(1), 97–105. 10.1002/csr.1661

Bortolotti, A., Cannito, L., Anzani, S., & Palumbo, R. (2023). The promise of color in marketing: Use, applications, tips and neuromarketing. *Cultura e Scienza del Colore-Color Culture and Science*, 15(01), 76–85. 10.23738/CCSJ.150110

Boston Consultancy Group. (2024). *Three Ways GenAI Will Transform Customer Experience.* Boston Consultancy Group. https://www.bcg.com/publications/2024/three-ways-genai-will-transform-customer-experience

Braeutigam, S., & Kenning, P. (2022). Ethics of Consumer Neuroscience. In *Oxford University Press eBooks* (pp. 211–220). 10.1093/oso/9780198789932.003.0012

Bug, P., & Bernd, M. (2020). The future of fashion films in augmented reality and virtual reality. *Fashion and film: moving images and consumer behavior*, 281-301.

Buhalis, D., & Karatay, N. (2022). Mixed reality (MR) for Generation Z in cultural heritage tourism towards metaverse. In *Information and communication technologies in tourism 2022:Proceedings of the ENTER 2022 eTourism conference,* (pp. 16-27). Springer International Publishing.

Bull, S. S., Levine, D. K., Black, S. R., Schmiege, S. J., & Santelli, J. S. (2010). Social media-delivered sexual health intervention: A cluster randomized controlled trial. *American Journal of Preventive Medicine*, 39(5), 512–519.23079168

Caboni, F., & Hagberg, J. (2019). Augmented reality in retailing: A review of features, applications and value. *International Journal of Retail & Distribution Management*, 47(11), 1125–1140. 10.1108/IJRDM-12-2018-0263

Caissie, A. F., Riquier, L., De Revel, G., & Tempere, S. (2021). Representational and sensory cues as drivers of individual differences in expert quality assessment of red wines. *Food Quality and Preference*, 87, 104032. 10.1016/j.foodqual.2020.104032

Calvert, G. A., Spence, C., & Stein, B. E. (Eds.). (2004). *Handbook of multisensory processes.* MIT press. 10.7551/mitpress/3422.001.0001

Campelo, A. (2017). Smell it, taste it, hear it, touch it and see it to make sense of this place. In *Handbook on place branding and marketing* (pp. 124–144). Edward Elgar Publishing. 10.4337/9781784718602.00018

Canniford, R., Riach, K., & Hill, T. (2018). Nosenography: How smell constitutes meaning, identity and temporal experience in spatial assemblages. *Marketing Theory*, 18(2), 234–248. 10.1177/1470593117732462

Caplan, S. E. (2002). Problematic internet use and psychosocial well-being: Development of a theory-based cognitive–behavioral measurement instrument. *Computers in Human Behavior*, 18(5), 553–575. 10.1016/S0747-5632(02)00004-3

Cardoso, L., Chen, M. M., Araújo, A., de Almeida, G. G. F., Dias, F., & Moutinho, L. (2022). Accessing neuromarketing scientific performance: Research gaps and emerging topics. *Behavioral Sciences (Basel, Switzerland)*, 12(2), 55. 10.3390/bs1202005535200306

Carton, S. (2019). *What impact will immersive technologies such as augmented and virtual reality have on the retail sector?* [Doctoral dissertation, Dublin, National College of Ireland].

Casado-Aranda, L. A., Liébana-Cabanillas, F., & Sánchez-Fernández, J. (2018). A Neuropsychological Study on How Consumers Process Risky and Secure E-payments. *Journal of Interactive Marketing, 43*, 151–164. 10.1016/j.intmar.2018.03.001

Casado-Aranda, L. A., Sánchez-Fernández, J., Bigne, E., & Smidts, A. (2023). The application of neuromarketing tools in communication research: A comprehensive review of trends. *Psychology and Marketing*, 40(9), 1737–1756. 10.1002/mar.21832

Casey, R. (2004). Designing brand identity: A complete guide to creating, building, and maintaining strong brands. *Journal of the Academy of Marketing Science*, 32(1), 100–101. 10.1177/0092070304321011

Castro, W. R. A., Montes, L. S. P., & Vera, G. R. (2015). Auditory Stimuli in Neuro-marketing Practices; Case: Unicentro Shopping Mall in Cúcuta, Colombia. *Cuadernos de administración, 31*(53), 117-129.

Catherine, S., Kiruthiga, V., Suresh, N. V., & Gabriel, R. (2024). Effective Brand Building in Metaverse Platform: Consumer-Based Brand Equity in a Virtual World (CBBE). In *Omnichannel Approach to Co-Creating Customer Experiences Through Metaverse Platforms* (pp. 39-48). IGI Global.

Cenizo, C. (2022). Neuromarketing: Concept, historical evolution and challenges. *Journal ICONO*, 14(20), 1.

Compilation of References

Chandel, M., & Arora, M. (2024). Metaverse Perspectives: Unpacking Its Role in Shaping Sustainable Development Goals-A Qualitative Inquiry. In *Research, Innovation, and Industry Impacts of the Metaverse* (pp. 62-75). IGI Global.

Chang, P. L., & Chieng, M. H. (2006). Building consumer-brand relationship: A cross-cultural experiential view. *Psychology and Marketing*, 23(11), 927–959. 10.1002/mar.20140

Chan, M. (2015). Multimodal connectedness and quality of life: Examining the influences of technology adoption and interpersonal communication on well-being across the life span. *Journal of Computer-Mediated Communication*, 20(1), 3–18. 10.1111/jcc4.12089

Chattopadhyay, R. (2020). Journey of neuroscience: Marketing management to organizational behavior. *Management Research Review*, 43(9), 1063–1079. 10.1108/MRR-09-2019-0387

Chattopadhyay, T., Shivani, S., & Krishnan, M. (2009). Determinants of brand equity-A blue print for building strong brand: A study of automobile segment in India. *African Journal of Marketing Management*, 1(4), 109–121.

Chen, Y., & Lin, C. A. (2022). Consumer behavior in an augmented reality environment: Exploring the effects of flow via augmented realism and technology fluidity. *Telematics and Informatics*, 71, 101833. 10.1016/j.tele.2022.101833

Cherubino, P., Martinez-Levy, A. C., Caratù, M., Cartocci, G., Di Flumeri, G., Modica, E., Rossi, D., Mancini, M., & Trettel, A. (2019). Consumer behaviour through the eyes of neurophysiological measures: State-of-the-art and future trends. *Computational Intelligence and Neuroscience*, 2019(1), 1976847. 10.1155/2019/197684731641346

Chi, A. (2022). *A Brief History of Neuromarketing*. Boon Mind. https://www.boonmind.com/a-brief-history-of-neuromarketing/

Chi, A. (2022, June 5). *A brief history of neuromarketing*. Boonmind. https://www.boonmind.com/a-brief-history-of-neuromarketing/

Cho, J. Y., & Suh, J. (2020). Spatial color efficacy in perceived luxury and preference to stay: An eye-tracking study of retail interior environment. *Frontiers in Psychology*, 11, 516274. 10.3389/fpsyg.2020.0029632296358

Ciotti, G. (2020). *Color Psychology in Marketing and Branding is All About Context*. Helpscout. https://www.helpscout.com/blog/psychology-of-color/#:~:text=so%20unwaveringly%20shallow?-,What%20is%20color%20psychology?be%20based%20on%20color%20alone

Clark, K. R. (2020). A field with a view: Ethical considerations for the fields of consumer neuroscience and neuromarketing. In *Developments in neuroethics and bioethics* (Vol. 3, pp. 23–61). Academic Press.

Cohen, J. B., Pham, M. T., & Andrade, E. B. (2018). The nature and role of affect in consumer behavior. In *Handbook of consumer psychology* (pp. 306-357). Routledge., Duerrschmid, K., & Danner, L. (2018). Eye tracking in consumer research. In *Methods in Consumer Research,* (pp. 279-318). Woodhead Publishing.

Cohen-Duwek, H., Slovin, H., & Ezra Tsur, E. (2022). Computational modeling of color perception with biologically plausible spiking neural networks. *PLoS Computational Biology*, 18(10), e1010648. 10.1371/journal.pcbi.101064836301992

Collins, R. (2019). *Marketing Implications of Utilizing Augmented Reality for In-Store Retailing.*

Conway, B. R. (2014). Color signals through dorsal and ventral visual pathways. *Visual Neuroscience*, 31(2), 197–209. 10.1017/S0952523813000382241034 17

Cornelio, P., Velasco, C., & Obrist, M. (2021). Multisensory integration as per technological advances: A review. *Frontiers in Neuroscience*, 15, 652611. 10.3389/fnins.2021.65261134239410

Costa, J., Freitas, C., & Paiva, T. (2016). Brain imaging during advertising: A neuromarketing study of sound and pictures. *The Marketing Review*, 15(4), 405–422. 10.1362/146934715X1450349053594

Couldry, N., Rodriguez, C., Bolin, G., Cohen, J., Volkmer, I., Goggin, G., Kraidy, M., Iwabuchi, K., Qiu, J. L., Wasserman, H., Zhao, Y., Rincón, O., Magallanes-Blanco, C., Thomas, P. N., Koltsova, O., Rakhmani, I., & Lee, K.-S. (2018). Media, communication and the struggle for social progress. *Global Media and Communication*, 14(2), 173–191. 10.1177/1742766518776679

Coulson, N. S. (2005). Receiving social support online: An analysis of a computer-mediated support group for individuals living with irritable bowel syndrome. *Cyberpsychology & Behavior*, 8(6), 580–584. 10.1089/cpb.2005.8.58016332169

Crespo-Pereira, V., Legerén-Lago, B., & Arregui-McGullion, J. (2020). Implementing Neuromarketing in the Enterprise: Factors That Impact the Adoption of Neuromarketing in Major Spanish Corporations. [CrossRef]. *Frontiers in Communication*, 5, 576789. 10.3389/fcomm.2020.576789

Cronin, J. J. Jr, Smith, J. S., Gleim, M. R., Ramirez, E., & Martinez, J. D. (2011). Green marketing strategies: An examination of stakeholders and the opportunities they present. *Journal of the Academy of Marketing Science*, 39(1), 158–174. 10.1007/s11747-010-0227-0

Cruz, C. M. L., Medeiros, J. F. D., Hermes, L. C. R., Marcon, A., & Marcon, É. (2016). Neuromarketing and the advances in the consumer behaviour studies: A systematic review of the literature. *International Journal of Business and Globalisation*, 17(3), 330–351. 10.1504/IJBG.2016.078842

Dangwal, A., Bathla, D., Kukreti, M., Mehta, M., Chauhan, P., & Sarangal, R. (2023). Neuromarketing science: A road to a commercial start-up. In *Applications of Neuromarketing in the Metaverse* (pp. 223–232). IGI Global. 10.4018/978-1-6684-8150-9.ch017

De Marco, M., Fantozzi, P., Fornaro, C., Laura, L., & Miloso, A. (2021). Cognitive analytics management of the customer lifetime value: An artificial neural network approach. *Journal of Enterprise Information Management*, 34(2), 679–696. 10.1108/JEIM-01-2020-0029

De, A. D. L. I. V. (2024). Analysis Of Visual Brand Identity In The Fast-Food Sector: A Neuromarketing Study. *Revista de Ciencias*, 29, 1–20.

Deroy, O., & Spence, C. (Eds.). (2013). *Multisensory flavor perception: From fundamental neuroscience through to the marketplace.* Frontiers Media SA.

Compilation of References

DeSalle, R. (2018). *Our senses: An immersive experience.* Yale University Press.

Deshbhratar, S., Joshi, S., Alwaali, R. N., Saear, A. R., & Marhoon, H. A. (2023, September). Augmented reality of online and physical retailing: A study of applications and its value. In *AIP Conference Proceedings* (*Vol. 2736*, No. 1). AIP Publishing. 10.1063/5.0170917

Deterding, S., Dixon, D., Khaled, R., & Nacke, L. (2011). From game design elements to game-fulness: defining "gamification". *Proceedings of the 15th International Academic MindTrek Conference: Envisioning Future Media Environments*, (pp. 9-15). ACM. 10.1145/2181037.2181040

Devi, R. & Bhopal, R.(2023). A Review-Based Study on Opportunities and Challenges Of Start-Ups In India. *National Journal Of Commerce And Management.*

Dhiman, V., & Arora, M. (2024). Current State of Metaverse in Entrepreneurial Ecosystem: A Retrospective Analysis of Its Evolving Landscape. In *Exploring the Use of Metaverse in Business and Education* (pp. 73-87). IGI Global.

Dhiman, V., & Arora, M. (2024). Current State of Metaverse in Entrepreneurial Ecosystem: A Retrospective Analysis of Its Evolving Landscape. In *Exploring the Use of Metaverse in Business and Education* (pp. 73-87). IGI Global. 10.4018/979-8-3693-5868-9.ch005

Dhiman, V., & Arora, M. (2024). Exploring the linkage between business incubation and entrepreneurship: understanding trends, themes and future research agenda. *LBS Journal of Management & Research.*

Dhiman, V., & Arora, M. (2024)b. Exploring the linkage between business incubation and entrepreneurship: understanding trends, themes and future research agenda. *LBS Journal of Management & Research.*

Diener, E., Emmons, R. A., Larsen, R. J., & Griffin, S. (1985). The satisfaction with life scale. *Journal of Personality Assessment*, 49(1), 71–75. 10.1207/s15327752jpa4901_1316367493

Diener, E., Oishi, S., & Tay, L. (2018a). Advances in subjective well-being research. *Nature Human Behaviour*, 2(4), 253–260. 10.1038/s41562-018-0307-630936533

Diener, E., Suh, E. M., Lucas, R. E., & Smith, H. L. (1999). Subjective well-being: Three decades of progress. *Psychological Bulletin*, 125(2), 276–302. 10.1037/0033-2909.125.2.276

Dienlin, T., & Johannes, N. (2020). The impact of digital technology use on adolescent well-being. *Dialogues in Clinical Neuroscience*, 22(2), 135–142. 10.31887/DCNS.2020.22.2/tdienlin32699513

Dierichsweiler, K. (2014). *Ethical issues in neuromarketing.* https://essay.utwente.nl/65384/

Doucé, L., & Adams, C. (2020). Sensory overload in a shopping environment: Not every sensory modality leads to too much stimulation. *Journal of Retailing and Consumer Services*, 57, 102154. 10.1016/j.jretconser.2020.102154

Doyle, P., & Stern, P. (2006). *Marketing management and strategy.* Pearson Education.

Duan, W., Khurshid, A., Khan, K., & Calin, A. C. (2024). Transforming industry: Investigating 4.0 technologies for sustainable product evolution in china through a novel fuzzy three-way decision-making process. *Technological Forecasting and Social Change*, 200, 123125. 10.1016/j.techfore.2023.123125

Ducu, C. (2017). *Topoi in neuromarketing ethics. Ethics and Neuromarketing: Implications for Market Research and Business Practice*, (pp. 31-64). Research Gate.

Du, P., & MacDonald, E. F. (2014). Eye-tracking data predict importance of product features and saliency of size change. *Journal of Mechanical Design*, 136(8), 081005. 10.1115/1.4027387

Duradoni, M., Innocenti, F., & Guazzini, A. (2020). Well-being and social media: A systematic review of Bergen Addiction Scales. *Future Internet*, 12(2), 24. 10.3390/fi12020024

Elder, R. S., & Krishna, A. (2010). The effects of advertising copy on sensory thoughts and perceived taste. *The Journal of Consumer Research*, 36(5), 748–756. 10.1086/605327

Elder, R. S., & Krishna, A. (2022). A review of sensory imagery for consumer psychology. *Journal of Consumer Psychology*, 32(2), 293–315. 10.1002/jcpy.1242

Elwert, F., & Winship, C. (2014). Endogenous selection bias: The problem of conditioning on a collider variable. *Annual Review of Sociology*, 40(1), 31–53. 10.1146/annurev-soc-071913-04345530111904

Erdem, T., Imai, S., & Keane, M. P. (2003). Brand and quantity choice dynamics under price uncertainty. *Quantitative Marketing and Economics*, 1(1), 5–64. 10.1023/A:1023536326497

Erdem, T., & Swait, J. (2001). Brand equity as a signaling. *Journal of Consumer Psychology*, 7(2), 131–157. 10.1207/s15327663jcp0702_02

Erenkol, A. D., & Merve, A. K. (2015). Sensory marketing. *Journal of Administrative Sciences and Policy Studies*, 3(1), 1–26. 10.15640/jasps.v3n1a1

Erickson, G. S. (2017). *New methods of market research and analysis*. Edward Elgar Publishing. 10.4337/9781786432698

Ernst, M. O., Lange, C., & Newell, F. N. (2007). Multisensory recognition of actively explored objects. *Canadian Journal of Experimental Psychology*, 61(3), 242–253. 10.1037/cjep200702517974318

Eser, Z., Isin, F., & Tolon, M. (2011). Perceptions of marketing academics, neurologists, and marketing professionals about Neuromarketing. *Journal of Marketing Management, 27*(7- 8), 854-868.

Fan, X., Jiang, X., & Deng, N. (2022). Immersive technology: A meta-analysis of augmented/virtual reality applications and their impact on tourism experience. *Tourism Management*, 91, 104534. 10.1016/j.tourman.2022.104534

Compilation of References

Farah, M. J. (2012). Neuroethics: The ethical, legal, and societal impact of neuroscience. *Annual Review of Psychology*, 63(1), 571–591. 10.1146/annurev.psych.093008.10043819575613

Farquhar, P. H. (1989). Managing brand equity. *Marketing research, 1*(3).

Felder, R. M., & Silverman, L. K. (1988). Learning and teaching styles in engineering education. *Engineering Education*, 78(7), 674–681.

Fisher, C. E., Chin, L., & Klitzman, R. (2010). Defining neuromarketing: Practices and professional challenges. *Harvard Review of Psychiatry*, 18(4), 230–237. 10.3109/10673229.2010.49662320597593

Forbes. (2022). Are Multisensory Experiences The Next Frontier Of Building Brands In The Metaverse? *Forbes*.https://www.forbes.com/sites/forbescommunicationscouncil/2022/05/10/are-multisensory-experiences-the-next-frontier-of-building-brands-in-the-metaverse/?sh=abc199d28852

Forrester Research. (2023). *Forrester: Generative AI Dominates Top 10 Emerging Technologies In 2023 and Beyond*. Forrester Research. https://www.forrester.com/press-newsroom/forrester-top-10-emerging-technologies-2023/

Fortunato, V. C. R., Giraldi, J. D. M. E., & de Oliveira, J. H. C. (2014). A review of studies on neuromarketing: Practical results, techniques, contributions and limitations. *Journal of Management Research*, 6(2), 201. 10.5296/jmr.v6i2.5446

Frost, J. H., & Massagli, M. P. (2008). Social uses of personal health information within PatientsLikeMe, an online patient community: What can happen when patients have access to one another's data. *Journal of Medical Internet Research*, 10(3), e15. 10.2196/jmir.105318504244

Fürst, A., Pečornik, N., & Binder, C. (2021). All or nothing in sensory marketing: Must all or only some sensory attributes be congruent with a product's primary function? *Journal of Retailing*, 97(3), 439–458. 10.1016/j.jretai.2020.09.006

Gakhal, B., & Senior, C. (2008). Examining the influence of fame in the presence of beauty: An electrodermal 'neuromarketing'study. *Journal of Consumer Behaviour*, 7(4-5), 331–341. 10.1002/cb.255

Garcia, J. R., & Saad, G. (2008). Evolutionary neuromarketing: Darwinizing the neuroimaging paradigm for consumer behavior. *Journal of Consumer Behaviour*, 7(4-5), 397–414. 10.1002/cb.259

Garzón-Paredes, A. R., & Royo-Vela, M. (2023). Emotional and cognitive responses to cultural heritage: A neuromarketing experiment using virtual reality in the tourist destination image model context. *Journal of Positive Psychology and Wellbeing*, 7(2), 630–651.

George, A. S. (2023). Future Economic Implications of Artificial Intelligence. *Partners Universal International Research Journal*, 2(3), 20–39.

Ghorban, Z. S. (2012). Advertising and Brand Equity Creation: Examination of Product Market in Iran. *International Journal of Business and Management Tomorrow, 2*(7).

Gigerenzer, G. (2010). Personal reflections on theory and psychology. *Theory & Psychology*, 20(6), 733–743. 10.1177/0959354310378184

Golnar-Nik, P., Farashi, S., & Safari, M. S. (2019). The application of EEG power for the prediction and interpretation of consumer decision-making: A neuromarketing study. *Physiology & Behavior*, 207, 90–98. 10.1016/j.physbeh.2019.04.02531047949

Gonçalves, M., Hu, Y., Aliagas, I., & Suárez, L. M. C. (2024). Neuromarketing algorithms' consumer privacy and ethical considerations: Challenges and opportunities. *Cogent Business & Management*, 11(1), 2333063. Advance online publication. 10.1080/23311975.2024.2333063

Gonchigjav, B. (2020). Results of neuromarketing study of visual attention and emotions of buyers in retail store environment. *Proceedings of the Mongolian Academy of Sciences*, 52-64. Research Gate.10.5564/pmas.v60i1.1337

González-Mena, G., Del-Valle-Soto, C., Corona, V., & Rodríguez, J. (2022). Neuromarketing in the digital age: The direct relation between facial expressions and website design. *Applied Sciences (Basel, Switzerland)*, 12(16), 8186. 10.3390/app12168186

Grandi, B., & Cardinali, M. G. (2022). Colours and price offers: How different price communications can affect sales and customers' perceptions. *Journal of Retailing and Consumer Services*, 68, 103073. 10.1016/j.jretconser.2022.103073

Griffioen, N., Scholten, H., Lichtwarck-Aschoff, A., van Rooij, M., & Granic, I. (2021). Everyone does it–differently: A window into emerging adults' smartphone use. *Humanities & Social Sciences Communications*, 8(1), 1–11. 10.1057/s41599-021-00863-138617731

Grima, S., Kizilkaya, M., Sood, K., & ErdemDelice, M. (2021). The perceived effectiveness of blockchain for digital operational risk resilience in the European Union insurance market sector. *Journal of Risk and Financial Management*, 14(8), 363. 10.3390/jrfm14080363

Gui, M., Fasoli, M., & Carradore, R. (2017). 'Digital well-being': Developing a new theoretical tool for media literacy research. *Italian Journal of Sociology of Education*, 9(1), 155–173.

Gupta, M., Sharma, S., & Bansal, S. (2022, April). Neuromarketing: An Emerging Domain in the Formal Education System. In *2022 3rd International Conference on Intelligent Engineering and Management (ICIEM)* (pp. 53-58). IEEE.

Gupta, R., Verma, H., & Kapoor, A. P. (2024). Neuromarketing in predicting voting behavior: A case of National elections in India. *Journal of Consumer Behaviour*, 23(2), 336–356. 10.1002/cb.2191

Gupta, S. D., Shah, M. M. A. D., Prasad, K. H., & Vishwaja, P. (2022). Effect of auditory signals in sensory marketing: Evidence from India. *International Journal of Business Excellence*, 28(1), 75–89. 10.1504/IJBEX.2022.125765

Gupta, T., & Bansal, S. (2023). Deciphering the Mind: Advancing Consumer Insights through Brain-Computer Interfaces in Neuromarketing for the Digital Age. *European Journal of Advances in Engineering and Technology*, 10(3), 25–35.

Gurgu, E., Ioana-Andreea, G., & Rocsana, B. (2020). Neuromarketing for a better understanding of consumer needs and emotions. *Independent Journal of Management & Production, 11.* 10.1016/j.matpr.2020.08.730

Gurgu, E., Gurgu, I. A., & Tonis, R. B. M. (2020). Neuromarketing for a better understanding of consumer needs and emotions. *Independent Journal of Management & Production*, 11(1), 208–235. 10.14807/ijmp.v11i1.993

Gvili, Y., Levy, S., & Zwilling, M. (2018). The sweet smell of advertising: The essence of matching scents with other ad cues. *International Journal of Advertising*, 37(4), 568–590. 10.1080/02650487.2017.1339584

Haase, J., Wiedmann, K. P., & Bettels, J. (2020). Sensory imagery in advertising: How the senses affect perceived product design and consumer attitude. *Journal of Marketing Communications*, 26(5), 475–487. 10.1080/13527266.2018.1518257

Haase, J., & Wiedmann, K.-P. (2018). The sensory perception item set (SPI): An exploratory effort to develop a holistic scale for sensory marketing. *Psychology and Marketing*, 35(10), 727–739. 10.1002/mar.21130

Hagtvedt, H. (2020). Dark is durable, light is user-friendly: The impact of color lightness on two product attribute judgments. *Psychology and Marketing*, 37(7), 864–875. 10.1002/mar.21268

Ha, J., Choi, K. M., & Im, C. H. (2022). Feasibility of using electrooculography-based eye-trackers for neuromarketing applications. *IEEE Transactions on Instrumentation and Measurement*, 71, 1–10. 10.1109/TIM.2022.3217849

Hakim, A., & Levy, D. J. (2019). A gateway to consumers' minds: Achievements, caveats, and prospects of electroencephalography-based prediction in neuromarketing. *Wiley Interdisciplinary Reviews: Cognitive Science*, 10(2), e1485. 10.1002/wcs.148530496636

Halid, H., Ravesangar, K., Mahadzir, S. L., & Halim, S. N. A. (2024). Artificial Intelligence (AI) in Human Resource Management (HRM). In *Building the Future with Human Resource Management* (pp. 37–70). Springer International Publishing. 10.1007/978-3-031-52811-8_2

Hammou, K. A., Galib, M. H., & Melloul, J. (2013). The Contributions of Neuromarketing in Marketing Research. [CrossRef]. *Journal of Management Research*, 5(4), 20–33. 10.5296/jmr.v5i4.4023

Hanafiah, M. H., Asyraff, M. A., Ismail, M. N. I., & Sjukriana, J. (2024). Understanding the key drivers in using mobile payment (M-Payment) among Generation Z travellers. *Young Consumers*. 10.1108/YC-08-2023-1835

Hargittai, E. (2008). The digital reproduction of inequality. In Grusky, D. (Ed.), *Social Stratification* (pp. 936–944). Westview Press.

Harris, J. M., Ciorciari, J., & Gountas, J. (2018). Consumer neuroscience and digital/social media health applications: Ethical considerations. *Journal of Consumer Behaviour*, 17(1), 179–189.

Hattula, J. D., Herzog, W., & Dhar, R. (2023). The impact of touchscreen devices on consumers' choice confidence and purchase likelihood. *Marketing Letters*, 34(1), 35–53. 10.1007/s11002-022-09623-w

Hazarika, A., & Rahmati, M. (2023). Towards an evolved immersive experience: Exploring 5G-and beyond-enabled ultra-low-latency communications for augmented and virtual reality. *Sensors (Basel)*, 23(7), 3682. 10.3390/s2307368237050742

Hazari, S., & Sethna, B. N. (2023). A comparison of lifestyle marketing and brand influencer advertising for generation Z Instagram users. *Journal of Promotion Management*, 29(4), 491–534. 10.1080/10496491.2022.2163033

Hedström, P., & Ylikoski, P. (2010). Causal mechanisms in the social sciences. *Annual Review of Sociology*, 36(1), 49–67. 10.1146/annurev.soc.012809.102632

Heilbronner, R. L., Sweet, J. J., Morgan, J. E., Larrabee, G. J., & Millis, S. R. (2009). American academy of clinical neuropsychology consensus conference statement on the neuropsychological assessment of effort, response bias, and malingering. In *Clinical Neuropsychologist, 23*(7). 10.1080/13854040903155063

Heller, J., Chylinski, M., de Ruyter, K., Mahr, D., & Keeling, D. I. (2019). Touching the untouchable: Exploring multi-sensory augmented reality in the context of online retailing. *Journal of Retailing*, 95(4), 219–234. 10.1016/j.jretai.2019.10.008

Helmefalk, M. (2019). Browsing behaviour as a mediator: The impact of multi-sensory cues on purchasing. *Journal of Consumer Marketing*, 36(2), 253–263. 10.1108/JCM-10-2017-2392

Henke, N., & Jacques Bughin, L. (2016). *The age of analytics: Competing in a data-driven world.*

Hensel, D., Wolter, L., & Znanewitz, J. (2016). A Guideline for Ethical aspects in conducting Neuromarketing studies. In *Springer eBooks* (pp. 65–87). 10.1007/978-3-319-45609-6_4

Hensel, D., Iorga, A. M., Wolter, L., & Znanewitz, J. (2017). Conducting neuromarketing studies ethically-practitioner perspectives. *Cogent Psychology*, 4(1), 1320858. 10.1080/23311908.2017.1320858

Henshaw, V., Medway, D., Warnaby, G., & Perkins, C. (2016). Marketing the 'city of smells'. *Marketing Theory*, 16(2), 153–170. 10.1177/1470593115619970

Hercheui, M. D. (2011). A literature review of virtual communities: The relevance of understanding the influence of institutions on online collectives. *Information Communication and Society*, 14(1), 1–23. 10.1080/13691181003663593

Herz, R. S. (2011). The emotional, cognitive, and biological basics of olfaction: Implications and considerations for scent marketing. *Sensory marketing,* 87–107.

Hilken, T., Chylinski, M., Keeling, D. I., Heller, J., de Ruyter, K., & Mahr, D. (2022). How to strategically choose or combine augmented and virtual reality for improved online experiential retailing. *Psychology and Marketing*, 39(3), 495–507. 10.1002/mar.21600

Hjorth-Andersen, C. (1984). The concept of quality and the efficiency of markets for consumer products. *The Journal of Consumer Research*, 11(2), 708–718. 10.1086/209007

Holbrook, M. B., & Batra, R. (1987). Assessing the role of emotions as mediators of consumer responses to advertising. *The Journal of Consumer Research*, 14(3), 404–420. 10.1086/209123

Holliman, G., & Rowley, J. (2014). Business to business digital content marketing: Marketers' perceptions of best practice. *Journal of Research in Interactive Marketing*, 8(4), 269–293. 10.1108/JRIM-02-2014-0013

Hsu, M. Y. T. (2018). *Cognitive systems research for neuromarketing assessment on evaluating consumer learning theory with fMRI*. Science Direct.

Hsu, C. L., & Chen, M. C. (2018). How gamification marketing activities motivate desirable consumer behaviors: Focusing on the role of brand love. *Computers in Human Behavior*, 88, 121–133. 10.1016/j.chb.2018.06.037

Hsu, M. Y. T., & Cheng, J. M. S. (2018). fMRI neuromarketing and consumer learning theory: Word-of-mouth effectiveness after product harm crisis. *European Journal of Marketing*, 52(1/2), 199–223. 10.1108/EJM-12-2016-0866

Huddleston, P. T., Behe, B. K., Driesener, C., & Minahan, S. (2018). Inside-outside: Using eye-tracking to investigate search-choice processes in the retail environment. *Journal of Retailing and Consumer Services*, 43, 85–93. 10.1016/j.jretconser.2018.03.006

Hultén, B. (2011). Sensory marketing: The multi-sensory brand-experience concept. *European Business Review*, 23(3), 256–273. 10.1108/09555341111130245

Hultén, B., Broweus, N., & van Dijk, M. (2010). *Sensory marketing: Research on the sensuality of products*. Routledge.

Hunt, S. D. (1983). General Theories and the Fundamental Explananda of Marketing. *Journal of Marketing*, 47(4), 9–17. 10.1177/002224298304700402

Hunter, M. G., & Stockdale, R. (2012). A framework for analyzing online communities. *International Journal of Sociotechnology and Knowledge Development*, 2(3), 11–25. 10.4018/jskd.2010070102

Hussain, S. (2019). Sensory marketing strategies and consumer behavior: Sensible selling using all five senses. *IUP Journal of Business Strategy, 16*(3).

Illes, J., & Bird, S. J. (2006). Neuroethics: A modern context for ethics in neuroscience. *Trends in Neurosciences*, 29(9), 511–517. 10.1016/j.tins.2006.07.00216859760

Imamovic, I., De Azevedo, A. J. A., & De Sousa, B. M. B. (2021). The Tourists' Sensory Experiences: Preliminary Insights of Urban Areas of Porto, Portugal. *Iberian Conference on Information Systems and Technologies, CISTI*. IEEE. 10.23919/CISTI52073.2021.9476371

Imschloss, M., & Kuehnl, C. (2019). Feel the Music! Exploring the Cross-modal Correspondence between Music and Haptic Perceptions of Softness. *Journal of Retailing*, 95(4), 158–169. 10.1016/j.jretai.2019.10.004

Isa, S. M., Mansor, A. A., & Razali, K. (2019). *Ethics in Neuromarketing and its Implications on Business to Stay Vigilant.* KnE Social Sciences., 10.18502/kss.v3i22.5082

Ismajli, A., Ziberi, B., & Metushi, A. (2022). The impact of neuromarketing on consumer behaviour. *Corporate Governance and Organizational Behavior Review*, 6(2), 95–103. 10.22495/cgobrv6i2p9

Jamal Abad, S. G., & Hossein, J. S. (2013). Conceptualization Of Customer Based Brand Equity In Financial Service Sector. *Studies in Business & Economics*, 8(1).

Jangid, J., & Bhardwaj, B. (2024). Relationship Between AI and Green Finance: Exploring the Changing Dynamics. In *Leveraging AI and Emotional Intelligence in Contemporary Business Organizations* (pp. 211-218). IGI Global. 10.4018/979-8-3693-1902-4.ch012

Jansen, R. A., Rafferty, A. N., & Griffiths, T. L. (2021). A rational model of the Dunning–Kruger effect supports insensitivity to evidence in low performers. *Nature Human Behaviour*, 5(6), 756–763. 10.1038/s41562-021-01057-033633375

Javor, A., Koller, M., Lee, N., & Breiter, H. C. (2022). Vulnerable consumers: Marketing research needs to pay more attention to the brain health of consumers. *Marketing Letters*, 34(2), 337–342. 10.1007/s11002-022-09654-336345295

Jayavardhan, G. V., & Rajan, N. (2023). Recent Trends in Neuro marketing–A Review. *Journal of Coastal Life Medicine*, 11, 139–148.

Jedidi, K., Mela, C. F., & Gupta, S. (1999). Managing advertising and promotion for long-run profitability. *Marketing Science*, 18(1), 1–22. 10.1287/mksc.18.1.1

Jiménez-Marín, G., Bellido-Pérez, E., & López-Cortés, Á. (2019). Sensory Marketing: The Concept, Its Techniques And Its Application At The Point Of Sale. *Revista de Comunicación'Vivat Academia*, (148).

Jindal, A., Jindal, P., & Chavan, L. (2023). Customer Engagement Through Emotional Branding. In *Promoting Consumer Engagement Through Emotional Branding and Sensory Marketing* (pp. 201–210). IGI Global.

Jonauskaite, D., Tremea, I., Bürki, L., Diouf, C. N., & Mohr, C. (2020). To see or not to see: Importance of color perception to color therapy. *Color Research and Application*, 45(3), 450–464. 10.1002/col.22490

Jongmans, E., Jeannot, F., Liang, L., & Dampérat, M. (2022). Impact of website visual design on user experience and website evaluation: The sequential mediating roles of usability and pleasure. *Journal of Marketing Management*, 38(17-18), 2078–2113. 10.1080/0267257X.2022.2085315

Joy, A., Wang, J. J., Orazi, D. C., Yoon, S., LaTour, K., & Peña, C. (2023). Co-creating affective atmospheres in retail experience. *Journal of Retailing*, 99(2), 297–317. 10.1016/j.jretai.2023.05.002

Juarez, D., Tur-Viñes, V., & Mengual, A. (2020). Neuromarketing Applied to Educational Toy Packaging. *Frontiers in Psychology*, 11, 2077. 10.3389/fpsyg.2020.0207732982857

Kacprzak, A., & Hensel, P. (2023). Exploring online customer experience: A systematic literature review and research agenda. *International Journal of Consumer Studies*, 47(6), 2583–2608. 10.1111/ijcs.12966

Kahneman, D., & Egan, P. (2011). *Thinking, Fast and Slow*. Farrar, Straus and Giroux.

Kajla, T., Raj, S., Kansra, P., Gupta, S. L., & Singh, N. (2024). Neuromarketing and consumer behavior: A bibliometric analysis. *Journal of Consumer Behaviour*, 23(2), 959–975. 10.1002/cb.2256

Kalaganis, F. P., Georgiadis, K., Oikonomou, V. P., Laskaris, N. A., Nikolopoulos, S., & Kompatsiaris, I. (2021). Unlocking the subconscious consumer bias: A survey on the past, present, and future of hybrid EEG schemes in neuromarketing. *Frontiers in Neuroergonomics*, 2, 672982. 10.3389/fnrgo.2021.67298238235255

Kamakura, W. A., & Russell, G. J. (1989). A probabilistic choice model for market segmentation and elasticity structure. *JMR, Journal of Marketing Research*, 26(4), 379–390. 10.1177/002224378902600401

Kamal, R. (2024). *Artificial Intelligence-Powered Political Advertising: Harnessing Data-Driven Insights for Campaign Strategies*. IGI Global. 10.4018/979-8-3693-2964-1.ch006

Kamal, R. (2024). Exploring the Synergy: Venture Capital's Impact on the Startup Ecosystem. In *Fostering Innovation in Venture Capital and Startup Ecosystems* (pp. 242-264). IGI Global.

Kamal, M., & Himel, A. S. (2023). Redefining Modern Marketing: An Analysis of AI and NLP's Influence on Consumer Engagement, Strategy, and Beyond. *Eigenpub Review of Science and Technology*, 7(1), 203–223.

Kant, S., & Yadete, F. D. (2023). Neuro-marketing in understanding consumer behavior: Systematic literature review. *RADINKA JOURNAL OF SCIENCE AND SYSTEMATIC LITERATURE REVIEW*, 1(1), 1–13. 10.56778/rjslr.v1i1.86

Kaplan, A. M., & Haenlein, M. (2010). Users of the world, unite! The challenges and opportunities of social media. *Business Horizons*, 53(1), 59–68. 10.1016/j.bushor.2009.09.003

Kapoor, A., Sahay, A., Singh, N. C., Pammi, V. C., & Banerjee, P. (2023). The neural correlates and the underlying processes of weak brand choices. *Journal of Business Research*, 154, 113230. 10.1016/j.jbusres.2022.07.056

Kardefelt-Winther, D., Rees, G., & Livingstone, S. (2020). Contextualising the link between adolescents' use of digital technology and their mental health: A multi-country study of time spent online and life satisfaction. *Journal of Child Psychology and Psychiatry, and Allied Disciplines*, 61(8), 875–889. 10.1111/jcpp.1328032634259

Karmarkar, U. R., & Plassmann, H. (2019). Consumer neuroscience: Past, present, and future. *Organizational Research Methods*, 22(1), 174–195. 10.1177/1094428117730598

Kaur, M., & Malhan, S. (2024). The Role of the Manufacturing Sector in Driving India's Long-Term Growth. Kumar, N., Sood, K., Özen, E. and Grima, S. (Ed.) *The Framework for Resilient Industry: A Holistic Approach for Developing Economies* (*Emerald Studies in Finance, Insurance, and Risk Management*). Emerald Publishing Limited, Leeds. 10.1108/978-1-83753-734-120241021

Kaur, M., Kaur, J., & Kaur, R. (2023). *Adapting to Technological Disruption: Challenges and Opportunities for Employment*. IEEE. .10.1109/ICCCIS60361.2023.10425266

Kaushal, V., & Yadav, R. (2023). Learning successful implementation of Chatbots in businesses from B2B customer experience perspective. *Concurrency and Computation*, 35(1), e7450. 10.1002/cpe.7450

Kayaman, R., & Arasli, H. (2007). Customer based brand equity: Evidence from the hotel industry. *Managing Service Quality*, 17(1), 92–109. 10.1108/09604520710720692

Keller, K. L., & Lehmann, D. R. (2003). How do brands create value? *Marketing management*, 12(3), 26-26.

Keller, K. L. (1993). Conceptualizing, measuring, and managing customer-based brand equity. *Journal of Marketing*, 57(1), 1–22. 10.1177/002224299305700101

Kelly, M. (2002). The Science of Shopping. Commercial Alert., Retrieved March 30, 2016, from.

Kessler, S. J., Jiang, F., & Hurley, R. A. (2020). The state of automated facial expression analysis (AFEA) in evaluating consumer packaged beverages. *Beverages*, 6(2), 27. 10.3390/beverages6020027

Khan, M. A., Vivek, , Minhaj, S. M., Saifi, M. A., Alam, S., & Hasan, A. (2022). Impact of Store Design and Atmosphere on Shoppers' Purchase Decisions: An Empirical Study with Special Reference to Delhi-NCR. *Sustainability (Basel)*, 15(1), 95. 10.3390/su15010095

Khondakar, M. F. K., Sarowar, M. H., Chowdhury, M. H., Majumder, S., Hossain, M. A., Dewan, M. A. A., & Hossain, Q. D. (2024). A systematic review on EEG-based neuromarketing: Recent trends and analyzing techniques. *Brain Informatics*, 11(1), 17. 10.1186/s40708-024-00229-838837089

Kim, J. H., Kim, M., Park, M., & Yoo, J. (2023). Immersive interactive technologies and virtual shopping experiences: Differences in consumer perceptions between augmented reality (AR) and virtual reality (VR). *Telematics and Informatics*, 77, 101936. 10.1016/j.tele.2022.101936

Compilation of References

Kim, J. Y., & Kim, M. J. (2024). Identifying customer preferences through the eye-tracking in travel websites focusing on neuromarketing. *Journal of Asian Architecture and Building Engineering*, 23(2), 515–527. 10.1080/13467581.2023.2244566

Kim, W. H., Lee, S. H., & Kim, K. S. (2020). Effects of sensory marketing on customer satisfaction and revisit intention in the hotel industry: The moderating roles of customers' prior experience and gender. *Anatolia*, 31(4), 523–535. 10.1080/13032917.2020.1783692

King, K. (2022). *AI Strategy for Sales and Marketing: Connecting Marketing, Sales and Customer Experience*. Kogan Page Publishers.

Klein, K., Melnyk, V., & Voelckner, F. (2021). Effects of background music on evaluations of visual images. *Psychology and Marketing*, 38(12), 2240–2246. 10.1002/mar.21588

Koszembar-Wiklik, M. (2019). Sensory marketing–sensory communication and its social perception. *Communication Today*, 10(2), 146–156.

Kotler, P., & Armstrong, G. (2001). *Principles of Marketing* (9th ed.).

Kottier, W. G. (2014). *The added value of neuromarketing tools in the area of marketing research* (Bachelor's thesis, University of Twente).

Krampe, C., Strelow, E., Haas, A., & Kenning, P. (2018). The application of mobile fNIRS to "shopper neuroscience" – first insights from a merchandising communication study. *European Journal of Marketing*, 52(1–2), 244–259. 10.1108/EJM-12-2016-0727

Krasnova, H., Spiekermann, S., Koroleva, K., & Hildebrand, T. (2010). Online social networks: Why we disclose. *Journal of Information Technology*, 25(2), 109–125. 10.1057/jit.2010.6

Krishna, A. (2012). An integrative review of sensory marketing: Engaging the senses to affect perception, judgment and behavior. *Journal of Consumer Psychology*, 22(3), 332–351. 10.1016/j.jcps.2011.08.003

Krishna, A. (2013). *Customer sense: How the 5 senses influence buying behavior*. Springer. 10.1057/9781137346056

Krishna, A., Cian, L., & Sokolova, T. (2016). The power of sensory marketing in advertising. *Current Opinion in Psychology*, 10, 142–147. 10.1016/j.copsyc.2016.01.007

Krishna, A., Elder, R. S., & Caldara, C. (2010). Feminine to smell but masculine to touch? Multisensory congruence and its effect on the aesthetic experience. *Journal of Consumer Psychology*, 20(4), 410–418. 10.1016/j.jcps.2010.06.010

Krishna, A., & Schwarz, N. (2014). ScienceDirect Sensory marketing, embodiment, and grounded cognition : A review and introduction. *Journal of Consumer Psychology*, 24(2), 159–168. Advance online publication. 10.1016/j.jcps.2013.12.006

Kulkarni, P., & Kolli, H. (2022). Sensory Marketing Theory: How Sensorial Stimuli Influence Consumer Behavior and Subconscious Decision-Making. *Journal of Student Research*, 11(3). Advance online publication. 10.47611/jsrhs.v11i3.3403

Kumar, H., Mathur, N., & Jauhari, S. (2017). A Study of Consumer Satisfaction Towards Neuromarketing in India With Special Reference To Kano Model. *GE-International Journal of Management Research (GE-IJMR), 5.*

Kumar, J., Arora, M., & Erkol Bayram, G. (2024). *Research, Innovation, and Industry Impacts of the Metaverse.* IGI Global.

Kumar, J., Arora, M., & Erkol Bayram, G. (Eds.). (2024) b. *Research, Innovation, and Industry Impacts of the Metaverse.* IGI Global.

Kumar, J., Arora, M., & Erkol Bayram, G. (Eds.). (2024). *Research, Innovation, and Industry Impacts of the Metaverse.* IGI Global.

Kumar, A., Gawande, A., & Brar, V. (2020). Neuro-Marketing: Opportunities and Challenges in India. *Vidyabharati International Interdisciplinary Research Journal*, 10(2), 214–217.

Kumar, J., Arora, M., & Erkol Bayram, G. (Eds.). (2024). *Exploring the Use of Metaverse in Business and Education.* IGI Global. 10.4018/979-8-3693-5868-9

Kumar, P., Chowdhury, S., & Madhavedi, S. (2024). Role of Neuromarketing and Artificial Intelligence in Futuristic Marketing Approach: An Empirical Study. *Journal of Informatics Education and Research.*, 4(2). 10.52783/jier.v4i2.809

Kumavat, R. (2023). Neuromarketing-current situation & available future trends in India with special reference to Jalgaon district. *International Journal of Contemporary Management.*

Kumra, R., & Arora, S. (2022). Digital sensory marketing factors affecting customers' intentions to continue organic online purchases during COVID in India. *FIIB Business Review, 23197145221105674.*

Kurtoğlu, A. L., & Ferman, A. M. (2020). An exploratory research among fashion business leaders and neuromarketing company executives on the perception of applied neuromarketing. [CrossRef]. *Pressacademia*, 11(1), 230–232. 10.17261/Pressacademia.2020.1274

Kushlev, K. (2018). Media technology and well-being: a complementarity-interference model. In Diener, E., Oishi, S., & Tay, L. (Eds.), *Handbook of Well-Being* (pp. 970–982). DEF Publishers.

Kuusinen, M. (2019). *Scenarios for digital marketing: a Delphi-based analysis for 2028.*

Lange, C. (2023). The Science of Color in Marketing: How to Use Color Psychology to Boost Your Brand. *Medium.* https://bootcamp.uxdesign.cc/the-science-of-color-in-marketing-how-to-use-color-psychology-to-boost-your-brand-299db0c8a3b2

Lauer-Schmaltz, M. W., Cash, P., Hansen, J. P., & Maier, A. (2024). Towards the Human Digital Twin: Definition and Design—A survey. *arXiv preprint arXiv:2402.07922.*

Compilation of References

Laukkanen, T., Xi, N., Hallikainen, H., Ruusunen, N., & Hamari, J. (2022). Virtual technologies supporting sustainable consumption: From a single-sensory stimulus to a multi-sensory experience. *International Journal of Information Management*, 63, 102455. 10.1016/j.ijinfomgt.2021.102455

Laureckis, E., & Miralpeix, À. M. (2016). Ethical and legal considerations in research subject and data protection. In *Springer eBooks* (pp. 89–100). 10.1007/978-3-319-45609-6_5

Lavoye, V. (2023). *Augmented reality in consumer retail: a presence theory approach.*

Lavoye, V., Tarkiainen, A., Sipilä, J., & Mero, J. (2023). More than skin-deep: The influence of presence dimensions on purchase intentions in augmented reality shopping. *Journal of Business Research*, 169, 114247. 10.1016/j.jbusres.2023.114247

Lavuri, R., & Akram, U. (2023). Role of virtual reality authentic experience on affective responses: Moderating role virtual reality attachment. *Journal of Ecotourism*, 1–19. 10.1080/14724049.2023.2237704

Lee, M., Lee, S., & Koh, Y. (2019). Multisensory experience for enhancing hotel guest experience: Empirical evidence from big data analytics. *International Journal of Contemporary Hospitality Management*, 31(11), 4313–4337. 10.1108/IJCHM-03-2018-0263

Lee, N., Brandes, L., Chamberlain, L., & Senior, C. (2017). This is Your Brain on Neuromarketing: Reflections on a Decade of Research. *Journal of Marketing Management*, 33(11-12), 878–892. 10.1080/0267257X.2017.1327249

Lee, N., Broderick, A. J., & Chamberlain, L. (2007). What is 'neuromarketing'? A discussion and agenda for future research. *International Journal of Psychophysiology*, 63(2), 199–204. 10.1016/j.ijpsycho.2006.03.00716769143

Leiva, F., Méndez, J., & Carmona, D. (2019). Measuring advertising effectiveness in Travel 2.0 websites through eye-tracking technology. *Physiology & Behavior*, 200, 83–95, 200. 10.1016/j.physbeh.2018.03.00229522796

Lelis, C., Leitao, S., Mealha, O., & Dunning, B. (2022). Typography: The constant vector of dynamic logos. *Visual Communication*, 21(1), 146–170. 10.1177/1470357220966775

Lhotáková, M., & Olšanová, K. (2013). The role of positioning in strategic brand management– case of home appliance market. *Global Journal of Commerce and Management Perspective*, 2(1), 71–81.

Lim, W. M. (2020). The sharing economy: A marketing perspective. *Australasian Marketing Journal*, 28(3), 4–13. 10.1016/j.ausmj.2020.06.007

Lindstrom, M. (2008). *Buy-ology: Truth and Lies About Why We Buy.*

Lindstrom, M. (2011). *Brand sense: Sensory secrets behind the stuff we buy.* Simon and Schuster.

Liu, Y. A., Shen, Y., Luo, C., & Chan, H. C. (2021). Reach out and touch: Eliciting the sense of touch through gesture-based interaction. *Journal of the Association for Information Systems*, 22(6), 1686–1714. 10.17705/1jais.00704

Liyin, J. I. N. (2009). Dimensions and determinants of website brand equity: From the perspective of website contents. *Frontiers of Business Research in China, 3*(4), 514-542.

Lluch, D. L., & Artiaga, L. N. (2017). 6. The sense of touch. In *Sensory and aroma marketing* (pp. 127–146). Academic. 10.3920/978-90-8686-841-4_6

Lombart, C., Millan, E., Normand, J. M., Verhulst, A., Labbé-Pinlon, B., & Moreau, G. (2020). Effects of physical, non-immersive virtual, and immersive virtual store environments on consumers' perceptions and purchase behavior. *Computers in Human Behavior*, 110, 106374. 10.1016/j.chb.2020.106374

Loureiro, S., Ruediger, K., & Demctris, V. (2012). Brand emotional connection and loyalty. *Journal of Brand Management*, 20(1), 13–27. 10.1057/bm.2012.3

Lycett, M., Meechao, K., & Reppel, A. (2024). *Materializing Design Fictions for Metaverse Services.*

Maes, P. (2018). *Disruptive Selling: A New Strategic Approach to Sales, Marketing and Customer Service*. Kogan Page Publishers.

Mahajan, V., Rao, V. R., & Srivastava, R. K. (1994). An approach to assess the importance of brand equity in acquisition decisions. *Journal of Product Innovation Management*, 11(3), 221–235. 10.1111/1540-5885.1130221

Maitlo, N., Noonari, N., Ghanghro, S. A., Duraisamy, S., & Ahmed, F. (2024). Color Recognition in Challenging Lighting Environments: CNN Approach. *arXiv preprint arXiv:2402.04762*. https://doi.org//arXiv.2402.0476210.1109/I2CT61223.2024.10543537

Makori, R. (2023). The Influence of Neuro-Marketing Techniques on Consumer Decision-Making in Strategic Marketing Campaigns. *Journal of Strategic Marketing Practice*, 1(1), 21–29.

Marcel, P., Lacramioara, R., Maniu, I., & Zaharie, M. (2009). Neuromarketing—Getting inside the customer's mind. *Ann. Univ. Oradea Econ. Sci.*, 4, 804–807.

Mariampolski, H. (2006). Ethnography for marketers: A guide to consumer immersion. *Sage (Atlanta, Ga.)*.

Marín, G., & Alvarado, M. (2022). Application of Sensory Marketing Techniques at Marengo, a Small Sustainable Men's Fashion Store in Spain: Based on the Hulten, Broweus and van Dijk Model. *Sustainability (Basel)*, 14(19), 12547. 10.3390/su141912547

Marr, B. (2021). *Extended reality in practice: 100+ amazing ways virtual, augmented and mixed reality are changing business and Society*. John Wiley & Sons.

Compilation of References

Martinez, L. M., Rando, B., Agante, L., & Abreu, A. M. (2021). True colors: Consumers' packaging choices depend on the color of retail environment. *Journal of Retailing and Consumer Services*, 59, 102372. 10.1016/j.jretconser.2020.102372

Martínez-López, F. J., Anaya-Sánchez, R., Aguilar-Illescas, R., & Molinillo, S. (2016). Types of virtual communities and virtual brand communities. In *Online Brand Communities* (pp. 125–140). Progress in IS. 10.1007/978-3-319-24826-4_8

Mashood, K., Kayani, H. U. R., Malik, A. A., & Tahir, A. (2023). ARTIFICIAL INTELLIGENCE RECENT TRENDS AND APPLICATIONS IN INDUSTRIES. *Pakistan Journal of Science*, 75(02). 10.57041/pjs.v75i02.855

Mashrur, F. R., Rahman, K. M., Miya, M. T. I., Vaidyanathan, R., Anwar, S. F., Sarker, F., & Mamun, K. A. (2022). An intelligent neuromarketing system for predicting consumers' future choice from electroencephalography signals. *Physiology & Behavior*, 253, 113847. 10.1016/j.physbeh.2022.11384735594931

Massa, E., & Ladhari, R. (2023). Augmented reality in marketing: Conceptualization and systematic review. *International Journal of Consumer Studies*, 47(6), 2335–2366. 10.1111/ijcs.12930

McKinsey & Co. (2022). *AI-powered marketing and sales reach new heights with generative AI*. McKinsey & Co. https://www.mckinsey.com/capabilities/growth-marketing-and-sales/our-insights/ai-powered-marketing-and-sales-reach-new-heights-with-generative-ai

Meijer, G. W., Lähteenmäki, L., Stadler, R. H., & Weiss, J. (2021). Issues surrounding consumer trust and acceptance of existing and emerging food processing technologies. *Critical Reviews in Food Science and Nutrition*, 61(1), 97–115. 10.1080/10408398.2020.171859732003225

Meißner, M., Pfeiffer, J., Peukert, C., Dietrich, H., & Pfeiffer, T. (2020). How virtual reality affects consumer choice. *Journal of Business Research*, 117, 219–231. 10.1016/j.jbusres.2020.06.004

Meyers-Levy, J., Bublitz, M. G., & Peracchio, L. A. (2011). The sounds of the marketplace: The role of audition in marketing. In *Sensory marketing*. Routledge.

Micu, A., Capatina, A., Micu, A. E., Geru, M., Aivaz, K. A., & Muntean, M. C. (2021). A NEW CHALLENGE IN DIGITAL ECONOMY: NEUROMARKETING APPLIED TO SOCIAL MEDIA. *Economic Computation and Economic Cybernetics Studies and Research*, 55(4).

Mishra, A., Shukla, A., Rana, N. P., & Dwivedi, Y. K. (2021). From "touch" to a "multisensory" experience: The impact of technology interface and product type on consumer responses. *Psychology and Marketing*, 38(3), 385–396. 10.1002/mar.21436

Misra, L. (2023). Neuromarketing insights into consumer behavior. *IUJ Journal of Management*, 11(1), 143–163.

Mittal, A., Mantri, A., Tandon, U., & Dwivedi, Y. K. (2022). A unified perspective on the adoption of online teaching in higher education during the COVID-19 pandemic. *Information Discovery and Delivery*, 50(2), 117–132. 10.1108/IDD-09-2020-0114

Mohamed, Ů. (2024). *Integrating Digital Techniques/Technologies in Developing Egyptian Museums (Case Study: Alexandria Library Museums-Alexandria City).* Sohag Engineering Journal.

Mood Media. (2018). *Quantifying the impact of sensory marketing.* Mood Media. https://us.moodmedia.com/sensory-marketing/

Moore, A. D. (2016). Privacy, Neuroscience, and Neuro-Surveillance. *Res Publica (Liverpool, England)*, 23(2), 159–177. 10.1007/s11158-016-9341-2

Mordor Intelligence Research & Advisory. (2023, September). *Neuromarketing Market Size & Share Analysis - Growth Trends & Forecasts (2024 - 2029).* Mordor Intelligence. https://www.mordorintelligence.com/industry-reports/neuromarketing-market

Morin, C. (2011b). Neuromarketing: The new science of consumer behavior. *Society*, 48(2), 131–135. 10.1007/s12115-010-9408-1

Morin, C., & Renvoisé, P. (2018). *The persuasion code: How neuromarketing can help you persuade anyone, anywhere, anytime.* John Wiley & Sons.

Morrin, M., & Tepper, B. J. (2021). Multisensory marketing: Effects of environmental aroma cues on perception, appetite, and consumption of foods and drinks. *Current Opinion in Food Science*, 40, 204–210. 10.1016/j.cofs.2021.04.008

Morton, J. (n.d.). *Substantial research shows why color matters and how color plays a pivotal role in all our visual experiences.* Colorcom. https://www.colorcom.com/research/why-color-matters#:~:text=Research%20reveals%20people%20make%20a,is%20based%20on%20color%20alone.&text=3.,are%20now%20made%20in%2Dstore

Mouammine, Y., & Azdimousa, H. (2023). An overview of ethical issues in neuromarketing: discussion and possible solutions. *Marketing Science & Inspirations, 18*(4).

Mouammine, Y., & Azdimousa, H. (2023). An overview of ethical issues in neuromarketing: Discussion and possible solutions. *Marketing Science and Inspirations*, 18(4), 29–47. 10.46286/msi.2023.18.4.3

Muniz, A. M.Jr, & O'Guinn, T. C. (2001). Brand Community. *The Journal of Consumer Research*, 27(4), 412–432. 10.1086/319618

Muñoz, J. M. (2023, October 5). neuroethics. Encyclopedia Britannica. https://www.britannica.com/topic/neuroethics

Murphy, E. R., Illes, J., & Reiner, P. B. (2008). Neuroethics of neuromarketing. *Journal of Consumer Behaviour*, 7(4-5), 293–302. 10.1002/cb.252

Nadanyiova, M., Kliestikova, J., & Kolencik, J. (2018). Sensory marketing from the perspective of a support tool for building brand value. *Economics and culture, 15*(1), 96-104.

Naji, K. K., Gunduz, M., Alhenzab, F., Al-Hababi, H., & Al-Qahtani, A. (2024). A Systematic Review of the Digital Transformation of the Building Construction Industry. *IEEE Access : Practical Innovations, Open Solutions*, 12, 31461–31487. 10.1109/ACCESS.2024.3365934

Nam, J., Ekinci, Y., & Whyatt, G. (2011). Brand equity, brand loyalty and consumer satisfaction. *Annals of Tourism Research*, 38(3), 1009–1030. 10.1016/j.annals.2011.01.015

Naslund, J. A., Aschbrenner, K. A., Marsch, L. A., & Bartels, S. J. (2016). The future of mental health care: Peer-to-peer support and social media. *Epidemiology and Psychiatric Sciences*, 25(2), 113–122. 10.1017/S2045796015001067 26744309

Nazma, Bhopal, R., & Devi, R. (2023). Sustainable Development Using Green Finance and Triple Bottom Line: A Bibliometric Review. *IMIB Journal of Innovation and Management*, 1-22. 10.1177/ijim.231184138

Nemati, H., Bakhshinezhad, E., Madadkhah, M., Kamyab, M., Taati, R., Faegh, S., & Jan, N. K. L. (2013). Brand Equity From The Perspective Of Customers. [Oman Chapter]. *Arabian Journal of Business and Management Review*, 2(10), 13–19. 10.12816/0002326

Nenkov, G. Y., Morrin, M., Maille, V., Rank-Christman, T., & Lwin, M. O. (2019). Sense and sensibility: The impact of visual and auditory sensory input on marketplace morality. *Journal of Business Research*, 95, 428–441. 10.1016/j.jbusres.2018.07.047

Neumeier, M. (2005). *The brand gap*. Peachpit Press.

Neurons Inc. (2024). *Why Brands Use Emotional Advertising & How to Effectively Measure Emotions*. Neurons Inc. https://www.neuronsinc.com/insights/emotional-advertising-effectively -measure-emotions

Neuwirth, R. J. (2023). Prohibited artificial intelligence practices in the proposed EU artificial intelligence act (AIA). *Computer Law & Security Report*, 48, 105798. 10.1016/j.clsr.2023.105798

Nielsen. (2022). *The need for consistent measurement in a digital-first landscape*. Nielsen. https://www.nielsen.com/insights/2023/need-for-consistent-measurement-2023-nielsen-annual -marketing-report/

Nilashi, M., & Abumalloh, R. A. (2023). Neuromarketing and Metaverse. *Journal of Soft Computing and Decision Support Systems*, 10(1), 1–3.

Nilashi, M., Yadegaridehkordi, E., Samad, S., Mardani, A., Ahani, A., Aljojo, N., Razali, N. S., & Tajuddin, T. (2020). Decision to adopt neuromarketing techniques for sustainable product marketing: A fuzzy decision-making approach. *Symmetry*, 12(2), 305. 10.3390/sym12020305

NMSBA Code of Ethics - NMSBA. (n.d.). *NMSBA Code of Ethics*. NMSBA. https://www.nmsba .com/neuromarketing-companies/code-of-ethics

North, A. C., Hargreaves, D. J., & McKendrick, J. (1999). The influence of in-store music on wine selections. *The Journal of Applied Psychology*, 84(2), 271–276. 10.1037/0021-9010.84.2.271

Nwachukwu, D. (2022, October 22). *Engaging skeptic customers through Sensory Marketing Strategies Part 2: Using the sense of touch (tactile marketing) to appeal to customers emotion.* LinkedIn. https://www.linkedin.com/pulse/engaging-skeptic-customers-through-sensory-marketing-nwachukwu-ph-d-1f/

Nwachukwu, D., Nwadighoha, E. E., Chukwu, E. N., & Udo, I. M. (2022). Gustative marketing strategy and customer patronage of restaurant businesses in Port Harcourt. *International Journal of Business & Entrepreneurship Research*, 13(6), 189–202.

O'connor, D. (2019). *Brand & Trademark Colours [Infographic].* Whiteriverdesign. https://www.whiteriverdesign.com/brand-and-trademark-colours/

Oduguwa, E. (2015). *How Taste and Sight Impact Brand Loyalty in Sensory Marketing.*

Oh, H. J., Ozkaya, E., & LaRose, R. (2014). How Does Online Social Networking Enhance Life Satisfaction? The Relationships Among Online Supportive Interaction, Affect, Perceived Social Support, Sense of Community, and Life Satisfaction. *Computers in Human Behavior*, 30, 69–78. 10.1016/j.chb.2013.07.053

Okorie, G. N., Udeh, C. A., & Adaga, E. M. (2024). Digital marketing in the age of IoT: A review of trends and impacts. *International Journal of Management & Entrepreneurship Research*, 6(1), 104–131. 10.51594/ijmer.v6i1.712

Olteanu, M. D. B. (2015). Neuroethics and responsibility in conducting neuromarketing research. *Neuroethics*, 8(2), 191–202. 10.1007/s12152-014-9227-y

Owano, N. (2012). *Consumer product giants' eye-trackers size up shoppers.* Physorg. https://phys.org/news/2012-07-consumer-product-giants-eye-trackers-size.html

Paivio, A. (1971). *Imagery and verbal processes.* Holt, Rinehart, and Winston.

Pamuru, V., Khern-am-nuai, W., & Kannan, K. (2021). The impact of an augmented-reality game on local businesses: A study of Pokémon go on restaurants. *Information Systems Research*, 32(3), 950–966. 10.1287/isre.2021.1004

Paquette, H. (2013). *Social media as a marketing tool: A literature review.*

Parchure, N. P., Parchure, S. N., & Bora, B. (2020, November). Role of neuromarketing in enhancing consumer behaviour. In *AIP Conference Proceedings* (Vol. 2273, No. 1). AIP Publishing. 10.1063/5.0024517

Parkinson, N. (2023). *The History of Color: A Universe of Chromatic Phenomena.* Frances Lincoln. https://www.google.co.in/books/edition/The_History_of_Color/FHu-EAAAQBAJ?hl=en&gbpv=1

Park, J., & Hadi, R. (2020). Shivering for status: When cold temperatures increase product evaluation. *Journal of Consumer Psychology*, 30(2), 314–328. 10.1002/jcpy.1133

Parks, K. M., & Steelman, L. A. (2008). Organizational wellness programs: A meta-analysis. *Journal of Occupational Health Psychology*, 13(1), 58–68. 10.1037/1076-8998.13.1.5818211169

Pereira, V., Fernández, V., & Freire, F. (2017). Neuroscience for Content Innovation on European Public Service Broadcasters. *Comunicar,25*(52), 09-18.

Perrachione, T. K., & Perrachione, J. R. (2008). Brains and brands: Developing mutually informative research in neuroscience and marketing. *Journal of Consumer Behaviour*, 7(4-5), 303–318. 10.1002/cb.253

Petit, O., Velasco, C., & Spence, C. (2019). Digital sensory marketing: Integrating new technologies into multisensory online experience. *Journal of Interactive Marketing*, 45(1), 42–61. 10.1016/j.intmar.2018.07.004

Peukert, C., Pfeiffer, J., Meißner, M., Pfeiffer, T., & Weinhardt, C. (2019). Shopping in virtual reality stores: The influence of immersion on system adoption. *Journal of Management Information Systems*, 36(3), 755–788. 10.1080/07421222.2019.1628889

Pham, P., & Wang, J. (2017, March). Understanding emotional responses to mobile video advertisements via physiological signal sensing and facial expression analysis. In *Proceedings of the 22nd International Conference on intelligent user interfaces* (pp. 67-78). ACM. 10.1145/3025171.3025186

Picmonkey. (n.d.). *Spice Up Your Branding with Secondary Color Palettes*. PicMonkey. https://www.picmonkey.com/blog/spice-up-your-branding-with-secondary-color-palettes

Pietronudo, M. C., & Leone, D. (2022). The Power of Augmented Reality for Smart Environments: An Explorative Analysis of the Business Process Management. In *Machine Learning for Smart Environments/Cities: An IoT Approach* (pp. 73–91). Springer International Publishing. 10.1007/978-3-030-97516-6_4

Pine, B. J., & Gilmore, J. H. (2011). *The experience economy*. Harvard Business Press.

Plotkina, D., Dinsmore, J., & Racat, M. (2022). Improving service brand personality with augmented reality marketing. *Journal of Services Marketing*, 36(6), 781–799. 10.1108/JSM-12-2020-0519

Pomirleanu, N., Gustafson, B. M., & Bi, S. (2020). Ooh, that's sour: An investigation of the role of sour taste and color saturation in consumer temptation avoidance. *Psychology and Marketing*, 37(8), 1068–1081. 10.1002/mar.21363

Ponnam, A. (2011). A case for customer based brand equity conceptualization within motivational perspective. *Academy of Marketing Studies Journal*, 15, 61–70.

Pop, N. A., Dabija, D., & Iorga, A. M. (2014). Ethical responsibility of neuromarketing companies in harnessing the market Research – a global exploratory approach. *DOAJ (DOAJ: Directory of Open Access Journals)*. https://doaj.org/article/7173bd2fbdaf4986982b6008a624633d

Pouromid, B., & Iranzadeh, S. (2012). The evaluation of the factors affects on the brand equity of Pars Khazar household appliances based on the vision of female consumer. *Middle East Journal of Scientific Research*, 12(8), 1050–1055.

Pulizzi, J. (2012). The Rise of Storytelling as the New Marketing. *Publishing Research Quarterly*, 28(2), 116–123. 10.1007/s12109-012-9264-5

Raghavan, S., & Pai, R. (2021). Changing Paradigm of Consumer Experience Through Martech–A Case Study on Indian Online Retail Industry. *International Journal of Case Studies in Business* [IJCSBE]. *IT and Education*, 5(1), 186–199.

Rajamannar, R. (2021). *Quantum marketing: mastering the new marketing mindset for tomorrow's consumers*. HarperCollins Leadership.

Raji, M. A., Olodo, H. B., Oke, T. T., Addy, W. A., Ofodile, O. C., & Oyewole, A. T. (2024). Business strategies in virtual reality: A review of market opportunities and consumer experience. *International Journal of Management & Entrepreneurship Research*, 6(3), 722–736. 10.51594/ijmer.v6i3.883

Raj, S., Sampat, B., Behl, A., & Jain, K. (2023). Understanding senior citizens' intentions to use virtual reality for religious tourism in India: A behavioural reasoning theory perspective. *Tourism Recreation Research*, 48(6), 983–999. 10.1080/02508281.2023.2246735

Ramsøy, T. Z. (2020). *An Introduction to Consumer Neuroscience & Neuromarketing [MOOC]*. Coursera. https://www.coursera.org/learn/neuromarketing?=&page=1

Ramsøy, T. Z. (2019). Building a foundation for neuromarketing and consumer neuroscience research: How researchers can apply academic rigor to the neuroscientific study of advertising effects. *Journal of Advertising Research*, 59(3), 281–294. 10.2501/JAR-2019-034

Ranaweera, A. T., Martin, B. A., & Jin, H. S. (2021). What you touch, touches you: The influence of haptic attributes on consumer product impressions. *Psychology and Marketing*, 38(1), 183–195. 10.1002/mar.21433

Randhir, R., Latasha, K., Tooraiven, P., & Monishan, B. (2016). Analysing the impact of sensory marketing on consumers: A case study of KFC. *Journal of US-China Public Administration*, 13(4), 278–292.

Rathee, R., & Rajain, P. (2017). Sensory marketing-investigating the use of five senses. *International Journal of Research in Finance and Marketing*, 7(5), 124–133.

Rathore, S., & Arora, M. (2024). Sustainability Reporting in the Metaverse: A Multi-Sectoral Analysis. In *Exploring the Use of Metaverse in Business and Education* (pp. 147-165). IGI Global. 10.4018/979-8-3693-5868-9.ch009

Rawnaque, F. S., Rahman, K. M., Anwar, S. F., Vaidyanathan, R., Chau, T., Sarker, F., & Mamun, K. A. (2020). Technological advancements and opportunities in Neuromarketing: A systematic review. *Brain Informatics*, 7(1), 10. Advance online publication. 10.1186/s40708-020-00109-x32955675

Compilation of References

Razbadauskaitė-Venskė, I. (2024). Neuromarketing: a tool to understand consumer behaviour. *Regional formation and development studies*, (1), 101-109.

Raz, C., Piper, D., Haller, R., Nicod, H., Dusart, N., & Giboreau, A. (2008). From sensory marketing to sensory design: How do consumers' input drive formulation? *Food Quality and Preference*, 19(8), 719–726. 10.1016/j.foodqual.2008.04.003

Renvoise, C., & Morin, P. (2007). *Neuromarketing: Understanding the "Buy Button" in Your Customer's Brain*. Thomas Nelson Publishers.

Reviglio della Venaria, U. (2020). Personalization in Social Media: Challenges and Opportunities for Democratic Societies.

Reyna, S. P. (2014). Free will, agency, and the cultural, reflexive brain. In *Springer eBooks* (pp. 323–342). 10.1007/978-94-007-4707-4_138

Ridings, C. M., & Gefen, D. (2004). Virtual community attraction: Why people hang out online. *Journal of Computer-Mediated Communication*, 10(1), JCMC1010. 10.1111/j.1083-6101.2004.tb00229.x

Robaina-Calderín, L., & Martín-Santana, J. D. (2021). A review of research on neuromarketing using content analysis: Key approaches and new avenues. *Cognitive Neurodynamics*, 15(6), 923–938. 10.1007/s11571-021-09693-y34790262

Rodgers, W., Yeung, F., Odindo, C., & Degbey, W. Y. (2021). Artificial intelligence-driven music biometrics influencing customers' retail buying behaviour. *Journal of Business Research*, 126, 401–414. 10.1016/j.jbusres.2020.12.039

Rodrigues, C., Skinner, H., Dennis, C., & Melewar, T. C. (2020). Towards a Theoretical Framework on Sensorial Place Brand Identity. *Journal of Place Management and Development.*, 13(3), 273–295. 10.1108/JPMD-11-2018-0087

Roggeveen, A. L., Grewal, D., & Schweiger, E. B. (2019). The DAST Framework for Retail Atmospherics : The Impact of In- and Out-of-Store Retail Journey Touchpoints on the Customer Experience. *Journal of Retailing.* 10.1016/j.jretai.2019.11.002

Romanchuk, J. (2023). *Brand Colors — Everything You Need to Know*. Hubspot. https://blog.hubspot.com/marketing/brand-colors#:~:text=Primary%20color%3A%20The%20main%20color,the%20primary%20and%20secondary%20colors

Rottigni, F., & Spence, C. (2024). Crying over food: An extraordinary response to a multisensory eating experience. *International Journal of Gastronomy and Food Science*, 36, 100943. 10.1016/j.ijgfs.2024.100943

Roy, A., & Chattopadhyay, S. P. (2010). Stealth marketing as a strategy. *Business Horizons*, 53(1), 69–79. 10.1016/j.bushor.2009.09.004

Royo-Vela, M., & Varga, Á. (2022). Unveiling neuromarketing and its research methodology. *Encyclopedia*, 2(2), 51. 10.3390/encyclopedia2020051

Roy, S., & Singh, P. (2023). The olfactory experience (in retail) scale: Construction, validation and generalisation. *Journal of Service Management*, 34(3), 403–432. 10.1108/JOSM-05-2021-0173

Ruanguttamanun, C. (2014). Neuromarketing: I put myself into a fMRI scanner and realized that I love Louis Vuitton ads. *Procedia: Social and Behavioral Sciences*, 148, 211–218. 10.1016/j.sbspro.2014.07.036

Rupini, R. V., & Nandagopal, R. (2015). A Study on the Influence of Senses and the Effectiveness of Sensory Branding. *Journal of Psychiatry*, 18(2), 236.

Russo, V., Bilucaglia, M., & Zito, M. (2022). From virtual reality to augmented reality: A neuromarketing perspective. *Frontiers in Psychology*, 13, 965499. 10.3389/fpsyg.2022.96549936160557

Ruzeviciute, R., Kamleitner, B., & Biswas, D. (2020). Designed to s (m) ell: When scented advertising induces proximity and enhances appeal. *JMR, Journal of Marketing Research*, 57(2), 315–331. 10.1177/0022243719888474

Sadowski, J. (2023). Total life insurance: Logics of anticipatory control and actuarial governance in insurance technology. *Social Studies of Science*, 03063127231186437.37427796

Saffronavenue. (n.d.). *How to Use Accent Colors in Your Brand*. Saffronavenue. https://saffronavenue.com/blog/logo-branding/how-to-use-accent-colors-within-your-brand/#:~:text=Accent%20Colors%20in%20Print%20Marketing&text=Be%20it%20business%20cards%2C%20stationery,tangible%20touchpoint%20a%20memorable%20interaction

Salluca, M. Y., Valeriano, D. Y. A., Gutierrez, R. A., & Valeriano, H. A. (2022). Marketing sensorial y su incidencia en la toma de decisiones de los consumidores. *Revista Venezolana de Gerencia*, 27(8), 1263–1279. 10.52080/rvgluz.27.8.34

Samuels, M. (2019). *The Power of Live Streaming in Social Media*. Social Media Today.

Sangeeta, & Tandon, U. (2021). Factors influencing adoption of online teaching by school teachers: A study during COVID-19 pandemic. *Journal of Public Affairs, 21*(4), e2503.

Sangeeta, & Tandon, U. (2021). Factors influencing adoption of online teaching by school teachers: A study during COVID-19 pandemic. *Journal of Public Affairs, 21*(4).

Santulli, M. (2019). *The influence of augmented reality on consumers' online purchase intention: the Sephora Virtual Artist case* [Doctoral dissertation].

Savickaite, S. (2024). *Using Virtual Reality to explore individual differences in perception due to neurodiversity* [Doctoral dissertation, University of Glasgow].

Schaeffer, E. (2017). *Industry X. 0: Realizing digital value in industrial sectors*. Kogan Page Publishers.

Schmitt, B. (1999). Experiential marketing. *Journal of Marketing Management*, 15(1-3), 53–67. 10.1362/026725799784870496

Schwarz, M. (2022). *Augmented Reality in Online Retail: Generational Differences Between Millennials and Generation Z Using Virtual Try-On's.*

Sebastian, V. (2014). Neuromarketing and Neuroethics. *Procedia: Social and Behavioral Sciences*, 127, 763–768. 10.1016/j.sbspro.2014.03.351

Sedkaoui, S. (Ed.). (2018). *Big data analytics for entrepreneurial success.* IGI Global.

Semerádová, T., & Weinlich, P. (2022). The place of virtual reality in e-retail: Viable shopping environment or just a game. In *Moving businesses online and embracing e-commerce: Impact and opportunities caused by COVID-19* (pp. 92–117). IGI Global. 10.4018/978-1-7998-8294-7.ch005

Sengupta, A., & Cao, L. (2022). Augmented reality's perceived immersion effect on the customer shopping process: Decision-making quality and privacy concerns. *International Journal of Retail & Distribution Management*, 50(8/9), 1039–1061. 10.1108/IJRDM-10-2021-0522

Shabgou, M., & Daryani, S. M. (2014). Towards the sensory marketing: Stimulating the five senses (sight, hearing, smell, touch and taste) and its impact on consumer behavior. *Indian Journal of Fundamental and Applied Life Sciences*, 4(1), 573–581.

Shahid, S., Paul, J., Gilal, F. G., & Ansari, S. (2022). The role of sensory marketing and brand experience in building emotional attachment and brand loyalty in luxury retail stores. *Psychology and Marketing*, 39(7), 1398–1412. 10.1002/mar.21661

Shahriari, M., Feiz, D., Zarei, A., & Kashi, E. (2020). The meta-analysis of neuro-marketing studies: Past, present and future. *Neuroethics*, 13(3), 261–273. 10.1007/s12152-019-09400-z

Sharma, A., & Singh, B. (2022). Measuring Impact of E-commerce on Small Scale Business: A Systematic Review. *Journal of Corporate Governance and International Business Law*, 5(1).

Shaw, S. D., & Bagozzi, R. P. (2018). The neuropsychology of consumer behavior and marketing. *Consumer Psychology Review, 1*(1), 22–40. 10.1002/arcp.1006

Shemesh, A., Leisman, G., Bar, M., & Grobman, Y. J. (2022). The emotional influence of different geometries in virtual spaces: A neurocognitive examination. *Journal of Environmental Psychology*, 81, 101802. 10.1016/j.jenvp.2022.101802

Sheth, J. N., Sinha, M., & Shah, R. (2016). *Breakout strategies for emerging markets: Business and marketing tactics for achieving growth.* FT Press.

Shocker, A. D., & Weitz, B. (1988). A perspective on brand equity principles and issues. *Report*, 88(104), 2–4.

Shukla, P., Awasthi, A., Kumari, S., Sahil, S., Gandh, N. K., Agustin, F. E., & Nneoma, N. R. (2024). The Role of Emotions in Consumer Brand Loyalty: A Neuromarketing Approach. [IJTHAP]. *International Journal of Tourism and Hospitality in Asia Pasific*, 7(1), 104–116. 10.32535/ijthap.v7i1.2901

Siddique, J., Shamim, A., Nawaz, M., & Abid, M. F. (2023). The hope and hype of neuromarketing: A bibliometric analysis. *Journal of Contemporary Marketing Science*, 6(1), 1–21. 10.1108/JCMARS-07-2022-0018

Simmonds, L., Bogomolova, S., Kennedy, R., Nenycz-Thiel, M., & Bellman, S. (2020). A dual-process model of how incorporating audio-visual sensory cues in video advertising promotes active attention. *Psychology and Marketing*, 37(8), 1057–1067. 10.1002/mar.21357

Simon, C. J., & Sullivan, M. W. (1993). The measurement and determinants of brand equity: A financial approach. *Marketing Science*, 12(1), 28–52. 10.1287/mksc.12.1.28

Sindhuja, S. (2023). A Review on the Potential Growth of Neuromarketing and Consumer Behaviour Research in India. *International Journal of Indian Psychology*, 11(4).

Singh, B. (2023). Blockchain Technology in Renovating Healthcare: Legal and Future Perspectives. In *Revolutionizing Healthcare Through Artificial Intelligence and Internet of Things Applications* (pp. 177-186). IGI Global.

Singha, R., & Singha, S. (2024). Building Capabilities and Workforce for Metaverse-Driven Retail Formats. In *Creator's Economy in Metaverse Platforms: Empowering Stakeholders Through Omnichannel Approach* (pp. 111-131). IGI Global. 10.4018/979-8-3693-3358-7.ch007

Singhal, S., & Khare, K. (2015). Does sense react for marketing–Sensory marketing. *International Journal of Management, IT and Engineering (IJMIE)*, 2249-0558.

Singh, B. (2019). Profiling Public Healthcare: A Comparative Analysis Based on the Multidimensional Healthcare Management and Legal Approach. *Indian Journal of Health and Medical Law*, 2(2), 1–5.

Singh, B. (2022). COVID-19 Pandemic and Public Healthcare: Endless Downward Spiral or Solution via Rapid Legal and Health Services Implementation with Patient Monitoring Program. *Justice and Law Bulletin*, 1(1), 1–7.

Singh, B. (2022). Relevance of Agriculture-Nutrition Linkage for Human Healthcare: A Conceptual Legal Framework of Implication and Pathways. *Justice and Law Bulletin*, 1(1), 44–49.

Singh, B. (2022). Understanding Legal Frameworks Concerning Transgender Healthcare in the Age of Dynamism. *ELECTRONIC JOURNAL OF SOCIAL AND STRATEGIC STUDIES*, 3(1), 56–65. 10.47362/EJSSS.2022.3104

Singh, B. (2023). Federated Learning for Envision Future Trajectory Smart Transport System for Climate Preservation and Smart Green Planet: Insights into Global Governance and SDG-9 (Industry, Innovation and Infrastructure). *National Journal of Environmental Law*, 6(2), 6–17.

Singh, B. (2024). Legal Dynamics Lensing Metaverse Crafted for Videogame Industry and E-Sports: Phenomenological Exploration Catalyst Complexity and Future. *Journal of Intellectual Property Rights Law*, 7(1), 8–14.

Singh, K. S. D., & Islam, M. A. (2017). Validating an instrument for measuring brand equity of CSR driven organizations in Malaysia. *Management & Marketing*, 12(2), 237–251. 10.1515/mmcks-2017-0015

Singh, P., Alhassan, I., & Khoshaim, L. (2023). What Do You Need to Know? A Systematic Review and Research Agenda on Neuromarketing Discipline. *Journal of Theoretical and Applied Electronic Commerce Research*, 18(4), 2007–2032. 10.3390/jtaer18040101

Singh, S. (2020). Impact of neuromarketing applications on consumers. *Journal of Business and Management*, 26(2), 33–52. 10.6347/JBM.202009_26(2).0002

Singh, S., Chandrakar, P., Jamsandekar, S., Ranjan, A., & Wanjari, S. (2020). A Review on The Impact of Sensory Marketing on Consumer Buying Behaviour. *Global Scientific Journals*, 8(6), 1308–1318.

Singh, V., Nanavati, B., Kar, A. K., & Gupta, A. (2023). How to maximize clicks for display advertisement in digital marketing? A reinforcement learning approach. *Information Systems Frontiers*, 25(4), 1621–1638. 10.1007/s10796-022-10314-0

Sinha, M., & Sheth, J. (2018). Growing the pie in emerging markets: Marketing strategies for increasing the ratio of non-users to users. *Journal of Business Research*, 86, 217–224. 10.1016/j.jbusres.2017.05.007

Smith, A. N. (2012). Shifting landscapes: The implications of social media for social marketing. *Journal of Marketing Theory and Practice*, 20(3), 239–253.

Smith, K., & Hanover, D. (2016). *Experiential marketing: Secrets, strategies, and success stories from the World's greatest brands*. John Wiley & Sons. 10.1002/9781119176688

Sohal, A., & Sharma, D. (2024). *Work-Family Conflict*. International Encyclopedia of Business Management., 10.1016/B978-0-443-13701-3.00061-X

Soliman, M., & Al Balushi, M. K. (2023). Unveiling destination evangelism through generative AI tools. *ROBONOMICS: The Journal of the Automated Economy*, 4(54), 1.

Solnais, C., Andreu-Perez, J., Sánchez-Fernández, J., & Andréu-Abela, J. (2013). The contribution of neuroscience to consumer research: A conceptual framework and empirical review. *Journal of Economic Psychology*, 36, 68–81. 10.1016/j.joep.2013.02.011

Song, J., Xu, F., & Jiang, Y. (2022). The colorful company: Effects of brand logo colorfulness on consumer judgments. *Psychology and Marketing*, 39(8), 1610–1620. 10.1002/mar.21674

Sood, K., Kaur, B., & Grima, S. (2022). Revamping Indian non-life insurance industry with a trusted network: Blockchain technology. In *Big Data: A game changer for insurance industry* (pp. 213-228). Emerald Publishing Limited.

Sood, K., Kaur, B., & Grima, S. (2022). Revamping Indian non-life insurance industry with a trusted network: Blockchain technology. In *Big Data: A game changer for insurance industry* (pp. 213–228). Emerald Publishing Limited. 10.1108/978-1-80262-605-620221014

Spangenberg, E. R., Crowley, A. E., & Henderson, P. W. (1996). Improving the store environment: Do olfactory cues affect evaluations and behaviors? *Journal of Marketing*, 60(2), 67–80. 10.1177/002224299606000205

Spence, C. (2020). On the ethics of neuromarketing and sensory marketing. *Organizational Neuroethics: Reflections on the Contributions of Neuroscience to Management Theories and Business Practices*, 9-29.

Spence, C. (2021). Musical scents: On the surprising absence of scented musical/auditory events, entertainments, and experiences. *i-Perception, 12*(5), 20416695211038747.

Spence, C. (2022). *Experimental atmospherics : a multi-sensory perspective*. QMR. 10.1108/QMR-04-2022-0070

Spence, C. (2024). Multisensory sweetness enhancement: Comparing olfaction and vision. *Smell, Taste, Eat: The Role of the Chemical Senses in Eating Behaviour*, 17–28.

Spence, C., & Levitan, C. A. (2021). Explaining crossmodal correspondences between colours and tastes. *i-Perception, 12*(3), 20416695211018223.

Spence, C. (2011). Crossmodal correspondences: A tutorial review. *Attention, Perception & Psychophysics*, 73(4), 971–995. 10.3758/s13414-010-0073-721264748

Spence, C. (2022). Gastrophysics: Getting creative with pairing flavours. *International Journal of Gastronomy and Food Science*, 27, 100433. 10.1016/j.ijgfs.2021.100433

Spence, C. (2022). On the use of ambient odours to influence the multisensory experience of dining. *International Journal of Gastronomy and Food Science*, 27, 100444. 10.1016/j.ijgfs.2021.100444

Spence, C. (2022). Sensehacking the guest's multisensory hotel experience. *Frontiers in Psychology*, 13, 1014818. 10.3389/fpsyg.2022.101481836600704

Spence, C. (2023). Explaining visual shape–taste crossmodal correspondences. *Multisensory Research*, 36(4), 313–345. 10.1163/22134808-bja1009637080553

Spence, C., & Gallace, A. (2011). Multisensory design: Reaching out to touch the consumer. *Psychology and Marketing*, 28(3), 267–308. 10.1002/mar.20392

Spence, C., Puccinelli, N. M., Grewal, D., & Roggeveen, A. L. (2014). Store atmospherics: A multisensory perspective. *Psychology and Marketing*, 31(7), 472–488. 10.1002/mar.20709

Spence, C., & Van Doorn, G. (2022). Visual communication via the design of food and beverage packaging. *Cognitive Research: Principles and Implications*, 7(1), 42. 10.1186/s41235-022-00391-935551542

Spence, E. H. (2015). Ethics of neuromarketing: Introduction. In *Handbook of neuroethics* (pp. 1621–1625). Springer Netherlands. 10.1007/978-94-007-4707-4_101

Srinivasan, V. (1979). Network models for estimating brand-specific effects in multi-attribute marketing models. *Management Science*, 25(1), 11–21. 10.1287/mnsc.25.1.11

Srinivasan, V., Park, C. S., & Chang, D. R. (2005). An approach to the measurement, analysis, and prediction of brand equity and its sources. *Management Science*, 51(9), 1433–1448. 10.1287/mnsc.1050.0405

Srivastava, G., & Bag, S. (2024). Modern-day marketing concepts based on face recognition and neuro-marketing: A review and future research directions. *Benchmarking*, 31(2), 410–438. 10.1108/BIJ-09-2022-0588

Stanton, S. J., Sinnott-Armstrong, W., & Huettel, S. A. (2017). Neuromarketing: Ethical implications of its use and potential misuse. *Journal of Business Ethics*, 144(4), 799–811. 10.1007/s10551-016-3059-0

Stasi, A., Songa, G., Mauri, M., Ciceri, A., Diotallevi, F., Nardone, G., & Russo, V. (2018). Neuromarketing empirical approaches and food choice: A systematic review. *Food Research International*, 108, 650–664. 10.1016/j.foodres.2017.11.04929735101

Stein, B. E., & Meredith, M. A. (1993). *The merging of the senses*. MIT press.

Stoll, M., Baecke, S., & Kenning, P. (2008). What they see is what they get? An fMRI-study on neural correlates of attractive packaging. *Journal of Consumer Behaviour*, 7(4-5), 342–359. 10.1002/cb.256

Sublimeeventdesigns. (2023). *The Wow Factor: Use of Color in Event Design*. Sublimeeventsdesign. https://www.sublimeeventdesigns.com/the-wow-factor-use-of-color-in-event-design/

Sung, B., Wilson, N. J., Yun, J. H., & Lee, E. J. (2020). What can neuroscience offer marketing research? *Asia Pacific Journal of Marketing and Logistics*, 32(5), 1089–1111. 10.1108/APJML-04-2019-0227

Suomala, J., Palokangas, L., Leminen, S., Westerlund, M., Heinonen, J., & Numminen, J. (2012). *Neuromarketing: Understanding customers' subconscious responses to marketing*.

Suriadi, J., Mardiyana, M., & Reza, B. (2022). The concept of color psychology and logos to strengthen brand personality of local products. *Linguistics and Culture Review*, 6(S1), 839–856. 10.21744/lingcure.v6nS1.2168

Swait, J., Erdem, T., Louviere, J., & Dubelaar, C. (1993). The equalization price: A measure of consumer-perceived brand equity. *International Journal of Research in Marketing*, 10(1), 23–45. 10.1016/0167-8116(93)90031-S

Syed, A. A., Gaol, F. L., Pradipto, Y. D., & Matsuo, T. (2021). Augmented and virtual reality in e-commerce—A survey. *ICIC Express Letters*, 15, 1227–1233.

Tembrevilla, G., Phillion, A., & Zeadin, M. (2024). Experiential learning in engineering education: A systematic literature review. *Journal of Engineering Education*, 113(1), 195–218. 10.1002/jee.20575

Thangaleela, S., Sivamaruthi, B. S., Kesika, P., Bharathi, M., Kunaviktikul, W., Klunklin, A., Chanthapoon, C., & Chaiyasut, C. (2022). Essential oils, phytoncides, aromachology, and aromatherapy—A review. *Applied Sciences (Basel, Switzerland)*, 12(9), 4495. 10.3390/app12094495

Thiripurasundari, U., & Natarajan, P. (2011). Determinants of brand equity in Indian car manufacturing firms. *International Journal of Trade. Economics and Finance*, 2(4), 346.

Thomas, S. (2021). Investigating interactive marketing technologies-adoption of augmented/virtual reality in the Indian context. *International Journal of Business Competition and Growth*, 7(3), 214–230. 10.1504/IJBCG.2021.116266

Trepte, S., Reinecke, L., & Juechems, K. (2017). The Social Media Privacy Model: Privacy and Communication in the Light of Social Media Affordances. *Communication Theory*, 27(4), 239–258.

Trettel, A., Cherubino, P., Cartocci, G., Rossi, D., Modica, E., Maglione, A. G., Di Flumeri, G., & Babiloni, F. (2016). Transparency and reliability in neuromarketing research. In *Springer eBooks* (pp. 101–111). 10.1007/978-3-319-45609-6_6

Tyagi, P. K., & Tyagi, P. (2022). Customer perception and brand image through sensory marketing. In *Disruptive Innovation and Emerging Technologies for Business Excellence in the Service Sector* (pp. 41–68). IGI Global. 10.4018/978-1-7998-9194-9.ch003

Tzampazaki, M., Zografos, C., Vrochidou, E., & Papakostas, G. A. (2024). Machine Vision—Moving from Industry 4.0 to Industry 5.0. *Applied Sciences (Basel, Switzerland)*, 14(4), 1471. 10.3390/app14041471

Ülman, Y. I., Çakar, T., & Yıldız, G. D. (2014). Ethical Issues in Neuromarketing: "I Consume, Therefore I am!". *Science and Engineering Ethics*, 21(5), 1271–1284. 10.1007/s11948-014-9581-525150848

Valdez, P., & Mehrabian, A. (1994). Effects of color on emotions. *Journal of Experimental Psychology. General*, 123(4), 394–409. 10.1037/0096-3445.123.4.3947996122

van Deursen, A. J., & van Dijk, J. A. (2014). The digital divide shifts to differences in usage. *New Media & Society*, 16(3), 507–526. 10.1177/1461444813487959

van Herpen, E., Pieters, R., & Zeelenberg, M. (2009). When demand accelerates demand: Trailing the bandwagon☆. *Journal of Consumer Psychology, 19*(3), 302–312. 10.1016/j.jcps.2009.01.001

van Kerrebroeck, H., Brengman, M., & Willems, K. (2017). When brands come to life: experimental research on the vividness effect of Virtual Reality in transformational marketing communications. *Virtual Reality, 21*(4), 177–191. 10.1007/s10055-017-0306-3

Varela, L., Putnik, G., & Romero, F. (2024). Collaborative manufacturing and management contextualization in the Industry 4.0 based on a systematic literature review. *International Journal of Management Science and Engineering Management*, 19(1), 78–95. 10.1080/17509653.2023.2174200

Vargas-Hernandez, J. G., & Christiansen, B. (2014). Neuromarketing as a business strategy. In *Handbook of Research on Effective Marketing in Contemporary Globalism* (pp. 146–155). IGI Global. 10.4018/978-1-4666-6220-9.ch009

Velasco, C. (2020). Fundamentals of Multisensory Experiences. *Multisensory Experiences: Where the senses meet technology*. Oxford Online. ,10.1093/oso/9780198849629.003.0002

Velasco, C., & Spence, C. (2019). The multisensory analysis of product packaging framework. *Multisensory packaging: Designing new product experiences*, 191-223.

Velasco, C., & Obrist, M. (2020). *Multisensory experiences: Where the senses meet technology.* Oxford University Press. 10.1093/oso/9780198849629.001.0001

Velasco, C., & Obrist, M. (2021). Multisensory experiences: A primer. *Frontiers of Computer Science*, 3, 614524. 10.3389/fcomp.2021.614524

Vences, N. A., Díaz-Campo, J., & Rosales, D. F. G. (2020). Neuromarketing as an emotional connection tool between organizations and audiences in social networks. A theoretical review. *Frontiers in psychology, 11*.

Vences, N. A., Díaz-Campo, J., & Rosales, D. F. G. (2020). Neuromarketing as an Emotional Connection Tool Between Organizations and Audiences in Social Networks. A Theoretical Review. *Frontiers in Psychology*, 11, 1787. 10.3389/fpsyg.2020.0178732849055

Venkatesh, D. N. (2021). *Winning with employees: Leveraging employee experience for a competitive edge.* SAGE Publishing India.

Vidal-Raméntol, S. (2020). Neuromarketing and Sustainability. [CrossRef]. *Advances in Social Sciences Research Journal*, 7(12), 181–191. 10.14738/assrj.712.9360

Vinaykarthik, B. C. (2022, October). Design of Artificial Intelligence (AI) based User Experience Websites for E-commerce Application and Future of Digital Marketing. In *2022 3rd International Conference on Smart Electronics and Communication (ICOSEC)* (pp. 1023-1029). IEEE.

Vraga, E. K., & Bode, L. (2020). Defining Misinformation and Understanding its Bounded Nature: Using Expertise and Evidence for Describing Misinformation. *Political Communication*, 37(1), 136–144. 10.1080/10584609.2020.1716500

Vuong, N. A., & Mai, T. T. (2023). Unveiling the Synergy: Exploring the Intersection of AI and NLP in Redefining Modern Marketing for Enhanced Consumer Engagement and Strategy Optimization. *Quarterly Journal of Emerging Technologies and Innovations*, 8(3), 103–118.

Wala, A., Czyrka, K., & Frąś, J. (2019). Sensory branding and marketing stimulate the relationship between the buyer and the brand. *Organizacja i Zarządzanie: kwartalnik naukowy*, (1), 109-120.

Wang, J., Sun, Y., Zhang, L., Zhang, S., Feng, L., & Morrison, A. M. (2024). Effect of display methods on intentions to use virtual reality in museum tourism. *Journal of Travel Research*, 63(2), 314–334. 10.1177/00472875231164987

Wang, T., & Ji, P. (2010). Understanding customer needs through quantitative analysis of Kano's model. *International Journal of Quality & Reliability Management*, 27(2), 173–184. 10.1108/02656711011014294

Wang, Y., Pan, Y., & Li, H. (2020). What is brain health and why is it important? *BMJ (Clinical Research Ed.)*, m3683, m3683. 10.1136/bmj.m368333037002

Waterlander, W. E., Jiang, Y., Steenhuis, I. H. M., & Ni Mhurchu, C. (2015). Using a 3D virtual supermarket to measure food purchase behavior: A validation study. *Journal of Medical Internet Research, 17*(4), e107. 10.2196/jmir.3774

Wenting, F., Yuelong, Z., Xianyun, S., & Chenling, L. (2022). Green advertising is more environmentally friendly? The influence of advertising color on consumers' preferences for green products. *Frontiers in Psychology*, 13, 959746. 10.3389/fpsyg.2022.95974636389554

Wheeler, J. (2023). *The Digital-First Customer Experience: Seven Design Strategies from the World's Leading Brands*. Kogan Page Publishers.

Wiedmann, K. P., Labenz, F., Haase, J., & Hennigs, N. (2018). The power of experiential marketing: Exploring the causal relationships among multisensory marketing, brand experience, customer perceived value and brand strength. *Journal of Brand Management*, 25(2), 101–118. 10.1057/s41262-017-0061-5

Wiedmann, K.-P., Hennigs, N., Klarmann, C., & Behrens, S. (2013). Creating multi-sensory experiences in luxury marketing. *Marketing Review St. Gallen*, 30(6), 60–68. 10.1365/s11621-013-0300-4

Williams, J. (2010). *Campbell's Soup Neuromarketing Redux:● There's Chunks of Real Science in That Recipe*. FastCompany. https://www.fastcompany.com/article/rebuttal-pseudo-science-in-campbells-soup-not-so-fast

Wind, Y. J., & Hays, C. F. (2016). *Beyond advertising: Creating value through all customer touchpoints*. John Wiley & Sons.

Wistoft, K., & Qvortrup, L. (2021). Seven dimensions of taste—taste in a sociological and educational perspective. In *Gastronomy and food science* (pp. 227–251). Academic Press. 10.1016/B978-0-12-820057-5.00012-1

Wood, W., & Neal, D. T. (2009). The habitual consumer. *Journal of Consumer Psychology*, 19(4), 579–592. 10.1016/j.jcps.2009.08.003

Wörfel, P., Frentz, F., & Tautu, C. (2022). Marketing comes to its senses: A bibliometric review and integrated framework of sensory experience in marketing. *European Journal of Marketing*, 56(3), 704–737. 10.1108/EJM-07-2020-0510

Wright, K. B., Bell, S. B., Wright, K. B., & Bell, S. B. (2003). Health-related support groups on the Internet: Linking empirical findings to social support and computer-mediated communication theory. *Journal of Health Psychology*, 8(1), 39–54. 10.1177/1359105303008001429221113899

Compilation of References

Wu, L., King, C. A., Lu, L., & Guchait, P. (2020). Hospitality aesthetic labor management: Consumers' and prospective employees' perspectives of hospitality brands. *International Journal of Hospitality Management*, 87, 102373. 10.1016/j.ijhm.2019.102373

Xiao, C., Zhu, H., Wang, X., & Wu, L. (2021). Vividly warm: The color saturation of logos on brands' customer sensitivity judgment. *Color Research and Application*, 46(6), 1347–1359. 10.1002/col.22682

Xue, L. (2022). *Designing effective augmented reality platforms to enhance the consumer shopping experiences* [Doctoral dissertation, Loughborough University].

Yadava, M., Kumar, P., Saini, R., Roy, P. P., & Prosad Dogra, D. (2017). Analysis of EEG signals and its application to Neuromarketing. *Multimedia Tools and Applications*, 76(18), 19087–19111. 10.1007/s11042-017-4580-6

Yadete, F. D., & Kant, S. (2023). Neuro-Marketing in Understanding Consumer Behavior: Systematic Literature Review. *Partners Universal International Innovation Journal*, 1(2), 105–116.

Yang, L., Kumar, R., Kaur, R., Babbar, A., Makhanshahi, G. S., Singh, A., Kumar, R., Bhowmik, A., & Alawadi, A. H. (2024). Exploring the role of computer vision in product design and development: A comprehensive review. [IJIDeM]. *International Journal on Interactive Design and Manufacturing*, 1–48. 10.1007/s12008-024-01765-7

Ye, H., Bhatt, S., Jeong, H., Zhang, J., & Suri, R. (2020). Red price? Red flag! Eye-tracking reveals how one red price can hurt a retailer. *Psychology and Marketing*, 37(7), 928–941. 10.1002/mar.21331

Yim, M. Y. C., & Park, S. Y. (2019). "I am not satisfied with my body, so I like augmented reality (AR)": Consumer responses to AR-based product presentations. *Journal of Business Research*, 100, 581–589. 10.1016/j.jbusres.2018.10.041

Yoganathan, V., Osburg, V. S., & Akhtar, P. (2019). Sensory stimulation for sensible consumption: Multisensory marketing for e-tailing of ethical brands. *Journal of Business Research*, 96, 386–396. 10.1016/j.jbusres.2018.06.005

Yoo, B., Donthu, N., & Lee, S. (2000). An examination of selected marketing mix elements and brand equity. *Journal of the Academy of Marketing Science*, 28(2), 195–211. 10.1177/0092070300282002

Yüksel, D. (2023). Investigation of Web-Based Eye-Tracking System Performance under Different Lighting Conditions for Neuromarketing. *Journal of Theoretical and Applied Electronic Commerce Research*, 18(4), 2092–2106. 10.3390/jtaer18040105

Zaki, H. O. (2022). The Impact Of Artificial Intelligence On Content Marketing. *Journal of Strategic Digital Transformation In Society*, 2(3).

Zha, D. (2021). Gustative signatures as corporate brand identifiers: exploring the sensuality of taste as a marketing strategy. In *Corporate Brand Design* (pp. 251–263). Routledge. 10.4324/9781003054153-21

Zha, D., Foroudi, P., Melewar, T. C., & Jin, Z. (2022). Experiencing the sense of the brand: The mining, processing and application of brand data through sensory brand experiences. *Qualitative Market Research*, 25(2), 205–232. 10.1108/QMR-09-2021-0118

Zhang, M., & Park, J. (2023). A Study of "Five Senses" in Application of Packaging Design of Products. *Studies in Art and Architecture*, 2(4), 43–49. 10.56397/SAA.2023.12.07

Zhou, Y., & Tse, C. S. (2022). Sweet taste brings happiness, but happiness does not taste sweet: The unidirectionality of taste-emotion metaphoric association. *Journal of Cognitive Psychology*, 34(3), 339–361. 10.1080/20445911.2021.2020797

Zhu, W., Owen, C. B., Li, H., & Lee, J. H. (2024). Personalized in-store e-commerce with the promopad: An augmented reality shopping assistant. *Electronic Journal for E-commerce Tools and Applications*, 1(3), 1–19.

Zito, M., Fici, A., Bilucaglia, M., Ambrogetti, F. S., & Russo, V. (2021). Assessing the emotional response in social communication: The role of neuromarketing. *Frontiers in Psychology*, 12, 625570. 10.3389/fpsyg.2021.62557034149513

Zoëga Ramsøy, T., Michael, N., & Michael, I. (2019). A consumer neuroscience study of conscious and subconscious destination preference. *Scientific Reports*, 9(1), 15102. 10.1038/s41598-019-51567-131641234

Zurawicki, L. (2010). *Neuromarketing: Exploring the brain of the consumer*. Springer Science & Business Media. 10.1007/978-3-540-77829-5

About the Contributors

Reena Malik presently working as an Assistant Professor in Chitkara Business School, Chitkara University, Punjab, India. She is Ph.D in Management and Post graduate in Management and Commerce. She has qualified UGC/NTA NET in both Commerce and Management. She has published more than 20 papers in reputed national and international journals and presented papers in various government sponsored seminar and conferences. She has published various research papers and book chapters in Emerald Publication, IGI Global, CRC Taylor and Francis, Wiley and Sage Publications etc. Awarded Gold Medal in M.A (Mass communication), Kurukshetra University. Awarded by women Dedication Magazine. She has five books to her credit. Having a teaching experience of more than 12 years she is actively working in research areas like Consumer Behavior, Brand Management, Customer satisfaction etc. she has 9 patents and 5 copyrights to her credit and edited three books with reputed publishers like Wiley, Taylor and Francis and IGI Global.

Shivani Malhan is working as an Assistant Professor in Chitkara University. She has done her MBA from University Business School, Panjab University and PhD in Marketing Management in the area of Brand Loyalty. She has a corporate experience of two years in Tata Motors and an experience of nine years in teaching. Moreover, she has published many research papers in UGC Care listed journals and scopus indexed journals and has attended many national and international conferences and seminars. She has been awarded the "Best research paper presentation award" by IIT Roorkee. Furthermore, she was a member of the team which organised Carpe Diem in collaboration with IIM Ahmedabad and was given the award of honour for being an active member of NSS while she was working in DAV University.

Anupal Mongia is a working professional in Mody University of Science and Technology. She possesses twelve years of experience in the field of Marketing.

Manpreet Arora, a Senior Assistant Professor of Management at the Central University of Himachal Pradesh, Dharamshala, India, brings over twenty-two years of rich teaching experience. She holds academic accolades including a Ph.D. in International Trade, an M.Phil, a gold medalist and several other academic distinctions from Himachal Pradesh University, Shimla. Dr. Arora's diverse research interests encompass Accounting, Finance, Strategic Management, Entrepreneurship, Qualitative Research and Microfinance. She works on Mixed methods research. Noteworthy for guiding doctoral research and delving into Microfinance, Entrepreneurship, Behavioral Finance and corporate reporting, she has presented at numerous seminars, delivering talks on various academic subjects across multiple universities and colleges. An accomplished academic, she has an impressive publication record, having authored over 30 papers in esteemed national and international journals listed in Scopus, WOS and Category journals, alongside contributing to fifty-five book chapters in publications by reputed publishers like Emerald, Routledge, CABI, Springer Nature, AAP, Wiley and more. Her commitment to management research is evident through the editing of six books. She is presently working in the area of Metaverse. Her impactful contributions showcase a multifaceted professional excelling in academia, research, and social advocacy.

Surbhi Bhardwaj is currently working as PhD research scholar at Department of Business Administration, National Institute of Technology, Kurukshetra, India. She completed her post-graduation in Management from The Technological Institute of Textile and Sciences, Bhiwani in 2015. Her area of interest includes Artificial Intelligence and marketing.

Rachna Bhopal is an engineering graduate with post-graduation from NMIMS Mumbai. Currently she is a research scholar in HPKVBS, department of Management at Central University of Himachal Pradesh availing the ICSSR Doctoral Fellowship. Prior to joining as research scholar, she has worked as software engineer in Infosys.

Rita Devi currently working as Assistant Professor at HPKV Business School, Central University of Himachal Pradesh. Her area of Specialization is HRM and OB. She has 7 Years of teaching and research experience. She has been meritorious throughout her studies and was awarded JRF for pursuing her Ph.D. degree. She has published various research papers in peer reviewed/UGC listed journals. She has participated in different national and international conferences. She has also attended numerous faculty development programs along with workshops. Her research interest area is leadership, organization development, cross-cultural management and emotional intelligence and entrepreneurship.

Shivani Dixit, an Associate Professor at the Department of Management, IMS Ghaziabad (University Courses Campus), boasts over 16 years of teaching experience and a strong academic background in General Management, Economics, International Business, and Marketing, making her a respected authority in these areas.

Seema Garg is an Associate Professor at AIBS, Amity University, Noida, where she teaches Business Statistics, Operations Research, Business Research Methods, Decision Sciences, and Business Maths. She has also significantly enhanced scientific understanding by participating in several conferences and chairing technical sessions.

Prashant Gundawar is a versatile experienced person, currently he is the Chief Academic Officer for the Sasmira group of Institutes and also Director at Sasmira Institute of Management Studies and Research. He has more than two decades experience in management education, research, training and consultancy. He has been a Ph.D. Guide of the Savitribai Phule Pune University (SPPU), JJT University, Rajasthan. He has co-authored books on "Customer Relationship Management", "International Marketing" and "International Business Environment". To his credit are two patents and multiple research papers across UGC Care, ABDC and Scopus listed journals. His doctoral work was in the area of impact of cultural diversity on work performance in global business. His areas of interest include intercultural management, international economics, international marketing strategies, branding and consumer buying behavior. He has presented and published his research work across the National and International platforms. He has been conferred with prestigious awards like 'Best Teacher Award' by Lions Club, "India's Most Innovative Education Leader Award" by World Education Congress, Taj Lands End (Mumbai), "Excellence in Education Development Award" by Asia Africa Development Council (Mumbai). He has chaired many conferences as a keynote speaker across Pune and Mumbai. He is self-directed resourceful and enthusiastic, a thorough academician with genuine interest in holistic student development. He is associated with various professional and social organizations. His rich industrial and academic experience has helped shape the careers of hundreds of students due to his guidance and directions. Under his tutelage, the institute got A+ accreditation form NAAC. Dr.Prashant Gundawar has been a Viva-Voce Refree and PhD thesis examiner for many University scholars until now.

Aayushi Jain is a research scholar at SRM university. she is graduated BBA and post graduated M.com. She has published various papers in SCOPUS AMD UGC Care and attended various conferences. Her areas of interest include Marketing Management, Rural Marketing, Business research methods.

About the Contributors

Ansh Jindal is pursuing MBA (Finance) at Chitkara Business School, Chitkara University, Punjab, India. He has successfully obtained a Bachelor's degree in Business Administration with a specialization in Financial Technology. He has participated in various competitions and won cash prize. He has been granted more than 12 design and utility patents. He is mostly interested in the fields of banking, finance, and marketing. He has completed his summer internship program from 4th July to 19th July 2022 at Nottingham university, Malaysia while pursuing his BBA (Fintech) degree. During his MBA studies, he participated in a remarkable Global Immersion Program in the United Arab Emirates (Dubai & Abu Dhabi).

Priya Jindal is currently working as an Assistant Dean (Commerce) and Associate Professor at Chitkara Business School, Chitkara University, Punjab, India and holds a master degree in commerce and economics. She earned her doctorate in management. She has contributed more than 17 years in teaching. She supervised five Ph.D. research scholars and two M.Phil candidates. There are numerous research papers to her credit in leading journals. Her areas of research included Banking, Finance and insurance. She has filed more than 21 patents and two copyright. She is the editor of three books under IGI and Nova publications and the book got indexed in Scopus.

Shweta Kakhtan is a senior research fellow at the School of Management and Entrepreneurship, Indian Institute of Technology Jodhpur, Rajasthan, India. Her thesis work is sponsored by the UGC NET Research Fellowship. Her areas of interest are multisensory experiences, neuromarketing, sensory technologies AR/VR, consumer choices, and retailing. She completed her post-graduate studies (specializing in International Business and Marketing) and undergraduate studies in Commerce from the University of Delhi, New Delhi, India. As a part of her thesis work, she is inclined toward the application of neuroscientific tools such as electroencephalogram (EEG), eye-trackers, and galvanic skin response (GSR) system to understand consumer responses to multisensory stimuli.

Anuj Pal Kapoor holds a PhD from the Faculty of Management Studies (FMS), University of Delhi, and his research areas include consumer psychology towards web-based platforms, multisensory experiences, collaborative consumption, and digital transformation & maturity. During his Ph.D., he developed a framework for strategic partnerships between banks and e-commerce players based on the digital consumption patterns of consumers across India. Prior to joining the PhD program, he has worked in the industry for six years across marketing, innovation and consulting domains. He was responsible for setting up the innovations function at HDFC Life based out of Mumbai and spearheaded the analytics function at Michael Page India, Gurgaon. Anuj also holds an MBA from Symbiosis International University; Bremen University of Applied Sciences (Germany) and B.E in Electronics and Communications from Institute of Technology & Management, Gurgaon. He also holds a certificate in Innovation Management from Massachusetts Institute of Technology (MIT, USA). Anuj is the recipient of ICSSR doctoral fellowship and was awarded the UNESCO fellow (Paris) award.

Christian Kaunert is Professor of International Security at Dublin City University, Ireland. He is also Professor of Policing and Security, as well as Director of the International Centre for Policing and Security at the University of South Wales. In addition, he is Jean Monnet Chair, Director of the Jean Monnet Centre of Excellence and Director of the Jean Monnet Network on EU Counter-Terrorism (www.eucter.net).

Neeraj Kaushik, PhD, is currently working as an Associate Professor and Head in the Department of Business Administration, National Institute of Technology, Kurukshetra, India. His interest areas are services marketing and research methodology. He has to his credit 60 articles published in Indian and international journals and conferences.

Sharad Khattar is a professor at AIBS, Amity University, Noida, and is a seasoned academician with 15 + years of teaching experience of teaching International business and Operations management. He has also significantly enhanced scientific understanding by participating in several conferences and chairing technical sessions.

Pawan Kumar is a Marketing graduate with and Doctorate in Business Management from Haryana School of Business, GJUS&T, Hisar, Dr Pawan Kumar, has a strong inclination towards academics and research. He has about 4 years of teaching experience to his credit. He has published more than 15 research articles in various International and National journals of repute. He has participated in and presented research papers at more than 25 international and national conferences at IIM, IIT, and Internationally, etc. His areas of interest include Marketing Management, Rural Marketing, Computer Applications in Business, and Business Research Methods.

Anchal Luthra, an Assistant Professor at AIBS, Amity University Noida, brings a wealth of expertise in Data Analytics, HR administration, and consulting. With 12 years of experience in administration, research, academia, and consulting projects, she has published papers in Scopus and ABDC-listed journals, presented her research at national and international conferences, and chaired technical sessions.

Shivani Malhan is working as an Assistant Professor in Chitkara University. She completed her PhD in July,2020. Also, she has a corporate experience of two years in Tata Motors where she worked as a Territory Sales Manager and Regional Accessories manager. Moreover, she has worked as an Assistant Professor in DAV University in Marketing Management for five years. She has published many research papers in UGC Care listed journals and scopus indexed journals and has attended many national and international conferences and seminars. She has been awarded the "Best research paper presentation award" by IIT Roorkee.

Reena Malik presently working as an Assistant Professor in Chitkara Business School, Chitkara University, Punjab, India. She is Ph.D in Management and Post graduate in Management,Mass Communication (Gold Medal) and Commerce. She has qualified UGC/NTA NET in both Commerce and Management. She has published more than 30 papers in reputed national and international journals and presented papers in various government sponsored seminar and conferences. She has five books to her credit. Having a teaching experience of more than nine years, she is actively working in the research area of Marketing and Finance.

Namrata Prakash been associated with teaching as a profession for the last nineteen years and currently I am serving Graphic Era Hill University, as an Associate Professor. I did my graduation from Lady Shriram College, Delhi University and my M.Com from BHU Varanasi. I am a gold medalist in M.Com. I am an avid researcher and currently supervising four research scholars. Ph.d degree has been awarded to one scholar. In order to keep myself abreast with the latest trends and brush up my knowledge I have undergone various refresher courses . I feel learning never stops.

Kavita Sharma Working as Professor in University School of Business- MBA, Chandigarh University, Mohali. Having 22 years in Teaching and 3 years in Research.

Swati Sharma is working as assistant professor in university school of business, Chandigarh University. She has done master in philosophy in Human resource, master's in business management with dual specialization in human resource management and finance and pursuing PHD in human resource. She has published many research paper, articles and book chapters in renowned journals and books. She has 8 years of core experience as academician in renowned universities and institutes.

Priya Shukla is a dedicated scholar and seasoned professional with a diverse background in IT, operations, and research. Armed with an MBA in IT and Operations, she has embarked on a doctoral journey to delve deeper into her passion for research. Priya possesses a keen acumen for analytical technologies, particularly specializing in IBM and SAS platforms, which she has honed over more than 5 years of hands-on experience in the field. Her research areas span a wide spectrum, encompassing topics such as data analytics, business intelligence, machine learning, and operational efficiency optimization. With a blend of academic rigor and practical industry insight, Priya strives to contribute meaningfully to the advancement of knowledge and innovation in her field.

About the Contributors

Rishi P. Shukla is an accomplished professional with over 15 years of academic and industry experience, primarily specializing in Analytics and Marketing. Currently serving as the Associate Director at Chandigarh University's Centre of Excellence for Data Analytics and Digital Transformation, he plays a pivotal role in research guidance for Ph.D. candidates and manages projects related to predictive analytics using tools such as SAS Miner, IBM Watson, PLS SEM, and SPSS Modeler. With a strong foundation in statistical modeling, Dr. Shukla holds certifications in Cognitive Computing from IBM and Predictive Analytics using IBM SPSS Modeler. His innovative contributions extend to utility patents in logistics, production and marketing management, and cost management using digital technology. Engaged in ongoing doctoral research on the impact of webrooming experience on customer buying intention and a comparative study of product placement in Bollywood and Hollywood films, Dr. Shukla has previously supervised awarded doctoral studies in mutual fund investment selection criteria and customer preferences for fast food. His extensive teaching career spans various prestigious institutions, including Symbiosis International Universit, Balaji Institute of Telecom Management, and Symbiosis Institute of Business Management, covering domains such as economics, statistics, and marketing research methods. Dr. Shukla's academic journey includes a Ph.D. in Management from Symbiosis International University, Pune, and an MBA in Marketing. He has published numerous research papers, received awards for significant contributions in journalism, and actively participates in conferences and research projects. Proficient in English, Hindi, Marathi, and Sanskrit, Dr. Rishi P. Shukla is a versatile professional committed to advancing knowledge in the fields of Analytics and Marketing.

Anamica Singh currently serves Amity University, Noida, as an Assistant Professor in AIBS. She has more than ten years of industry experience and academic experience, and her areas of expertise include various domains of Information Technology and management.

Bhupinder Singh working as Professor at Sharda University, India. Also, Honorary Professor in University of South Wales UK and Santo Tomas University Tunja, Colombia. His areas of publications as Smart Healthcare, Medicines, fuzzy logics, artificial intelligence, robotics, machine learning, deep learning, federated learning, IoT, PV Glasses, metaverse and many more. He has 3 books, 139 paper publications, 163 paper presentations in international/national conferences and seminars, participated in more than 40 workshops/FDP's/QIP's, 25 courses from international universities of repute, organized more than 59 events with international and national academicians and industry people's, editor-in-chief and co-editor in journals, developed new courses. He has given talks at international universities, resource person in international conferences such as in Nanyang Technological University Singapore, Tashkent State University of Law Uzbekistan; KIMEP University Kazakhstan, All'ah meh Tabatabi University Iran, the Iranian Association of International Criminal law, Iran and Hague Center for International Law and Investment, The Netherlands, Northumbria University Newcastle UK, Taylor's University Malaysia, AFM Krakow University Poland, European Institute for Research and Development Georgia, Business and Technology University Georgia, Texas A & M University US name a few. His leadership, teaching, research and industry experience is of 16 years and 3 Months. His research interests are health law, criminal law, research methodology and emerging multidisciplinary areas as Blockchain Technology, IoT, Machine Learning, Artificial Intelligence, Genome-editing, Photovoltaic PV Glass, SDG's and many more.

Bhavna Taneja has a doctorate in Management and an MBA specializing in marketing and finance. She has over 18 years of teaching experience In premium institutes like Xiss, Xaviers College Ranchi, Birsa Agricultural University, etc. Presently she is associated with Amity University Jharkhand. She has several publications to her name. Dr. Taneja is an active Rotarian and is presently on the board of directors of the Rotary Club of Ranchi. She is a Pranic healer.

Sanjay Taneja is currently an Associate Professor in Research at Graphic Era University, Dehradun, India. His significant thrust areas are Banking Regulations, Banking and Finance (Fin Tech, Green Finance), Risks, Insurance Management, Green Economics and Management of Innovation in Insurance. He holds a double master's degree (MBA &M.Com.) in management with a specialization in Finance and Marketing. He received his PG degrees in Management (Gold Medalist) from Chaudhary Devi University, Sirsa, India in 2012. He earned his Doctor of Philosophy (Sponsored By ICSSR) in Banking and Finance entitled "An Appraisal of financial performance of Indian Banking Sector: A Comparative study of Public, Private and Foreign banks in 2016 from Chaudhary Devi University, Sirsa, India. He received his Post Doctoral Degree from faculty of Social Sciences, Department of Banking and Insurance, Usak University, Turkey entitled on "Impact of the European Green Deal on Carbon (CO_2) Emission in Turkey" in 2023. He has published research papers in reputed SCOPUS/Web of Science/SCI/ABDC/UGC Care Journals. Prof. Taneja has more than fifty publications in total (Scopus/ABDC/Web of Science- 27)

Index

Ensure Quality Research is Introduced to the Academic Community

Become a Reviewer for IGI Global Authored Book Projects

  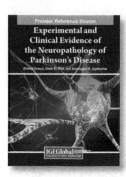 

The overall success of an authored book project is dependent on quality and timely manuscript evaluations.

Applications and Inquiries may be sent to:
development@igi-global.com

Applicants must have a doctorate (or equivalent degree) as well as publishing, research, and reviewing experience. Authored Book Evaluators are appointed for one-year terms and are expected to complete at least three evaluations per term. Upon successful completion of this term, evaluators can be considered for an additional term.

If you have a colleague that may be interested in this opportunity, we encourage you to share this information with them.

www.igi-global.com

Publishing Tomorrow's Research Today
IGI Global's Open Access Journal Program

Including Nearly 200 Peer-Reviewed, Gold (Full) Open Access Journals across IGI Global's Three Academic Subject Areas: Business & Management; Scientific, Technical, and Medical (STM); and Education

Consider Submitting Your Manuscript to One of These Nearly 200 Open Access Journals for to Increase Their Discoverability & Citation Impact

| Web of Science Impact Factor | 6.5 | Web of Science Impact Factor | 4.7 | Web of Science Impact Factor | 3.2 | Web of Science Impact Factor | 2.6 |

JOURNAL OF
Organizational and End User Computing

JOURNAL OF
Global Information Management

INTERNATIONAL JOURNAL ON
Semantic Web and Information Systems

JOURNAL OF
Database Management

Choosing IGI Global's Open Access Journal Program Can Greatly Increase the Reach of Your Research

Higher Usage
Open access papers are 2-3 times more likely to be read than non-open access papers.

Higher Download Rates
Open access papers benefit from 89% higher download rates than non-open access papers.

Higher Citation Rates
Open access papers are 47% more likely to be cited than non-open access papers.

Submitting an article to a journal offers an invaluable opportunity for you to share your work with the broader academic community, fostering knowledge dissemination and constructive feedback.

Submit an Article and Browse the IGI Global Call for Papers Pages

We can work with you to find the journal most well-suited for your next research manuscript.
For open access publishing support, contact: journaleditor@igi-global.com